HOMELAND
FASCISM

HOMELAND FASCISM:
CORPORATIST GOVERNMENT IN THE NEW AMERICAN CENTURY

Herman & Julia Schwendinger

Thought|Crimes
2016

HOMELAND FASCISM:
CORPORATIST GOVERNMENT IN THE NEW AMERICAN CENTURY

First published 2016 by

Thought|Crimes *an imprint of*

punctum books

spontaneous acts of scholarly combustion
earth, milky way * punctumbooks.com

ISBN-13: 978-0692715161
ISBN-10: 0692715169

please download & share the full book, various formats:

www.thoughtcrimespress.org

For Submissions: visit our
Open Monograph Press website
(a Public Knowledge Project) at:

press.radicalcriminology.org

a project of the Critical Criminology Working Group,
publishers of the #openaccess journal:

Radical Criminology:

JOURNAL.RADICALCRIMINOLOGY.ORG

Contact: Jeff Shantz (Editor),
Dept. of Criminology, KPU
12666 72 Ave. Surrey, BC V3W 2M8

[+ design & open format publishing: pj lilley]

*This book is dedicated to Leni and
Joseph Schwendinger.*

ACKNOWLEDGEMENT

Our thanks to Robert Schwendinger for proofing the original editions.

AUTHOR'S NOTE

An earlier version of this work was completed in 2002 and entitled *Big Brother Is Looking At You, Kid: InfoTech and Weapons of Mass Repression.*[1] It denounced the Bush wars of aggression and the creation of an information technology paralleling the technology adopted in Nazi Germany. Subsequently we realized that were chronicling the rise of an incipient fascist infrastructure.

Consequently, in 2008, we created a website, **homelandfascism101.com**, which offered successive eBook editions subtitled *Is Homeland Fascism Possible?* We offered our manuscript at no charge to anyone who wanted to download it. This book is the last edition. Although America is traveling down the highway to fascism, we have to stop tracking it and turn to other tasks. Fortunately, as the Bibliography demonstrates, many writers are offering interpretations of why America is descending into barbarism and what should be done about it.

NOW AVAILABLE FOR DOWNLOAD AT THOUGHTCRIMESPRESS.ORG

---

1 It was published a year later in *Nature, Society, and Thought*, Vol. 16, No.1

NOTES ON THE COVER

The main image is the floor of the US Congress, with the symbol of the fasces on each side of the center podium.

The earlier version of this work { ◄ see previous page } featured a comparison of these two illustrations on it's cover:

The Official Seal of the Pentagon's 'Total Information Awareness Project' (2002).

In the fine print here: DARPA is the acronym for "Defense Advanced Research Program" and "Scientia Est Potentia" is translatable as "Science is Power."

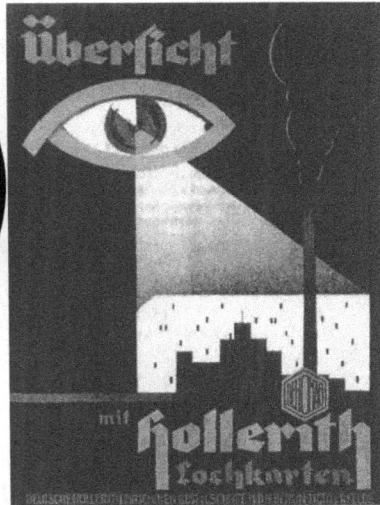

The IBM 1934 German subsidiary, Deutsche Hollerith Maschinen Gesellschaft (DEHOMAG). At the top, the word, "Übersicht," means "Oversight;" & "mit Hollerith Lochkarten" stands for "with Hollerith punch cards."

Contents

Editor's Preface   {Jeff Shantz}   **iii**
"Homeland Fascism Today: An Introduction"

PART ONE
CLASSICAL FASCISM   **45**

Introduction   47
1 | Weapons of Mass Repression   57
2 | Searching for Parallels   65
3 | Hitler's Terrorism   91

PART TWO
ROAD SIGNS & REST STOPS   **135**

4 | Highway to Fascism   137
5 | Friendly Fascism   177
6 | Consolidating Power   213

PART THREE
SETTING UP THE APPARAT   **239**

7 | Creating the Apparat   241
8 | PsyOp & Cyberwar   261
9 | Violence & Mass Protests   293
10 | Paramilitary "Training"   315

PART FOUR
UNCHECKS & IMBALANCES   **335**

11 | Decapitating the Judiciary   337
12 | Changing Drivers & Moving On   359
13 | Widening Terrorism   379

PART FIVE
RIGHT-WING CULTURE WARS   **401**
    14 | Culture Wars   403
    15 | Mainstream & Alternative Media   433

PART SIX
REVIVING THE INQUISITION   **453**
    16 | The New Inquisitors   455
    17 | The Counter Reformation   475
    18 | Behind the Scenes   499

PART SEVEN
FASCISM OR DEMOCRACY   **525**
    19 | Reassembling the *Fasces*   527
    20 | Turning Points   551
    21 | Fighting Customary Repression   583
    22 | Impeachment & Prosecution   607

PART EIGHT
THE STRUGGLE CONTINUES   **631**
    23 | Doing the Hokey-Pokey   633
    24 | For *Bread* And *Roses*   663
    25 | Inequality and Neo-Fascism   683

Bibliography   **705**
About the Authors   **725**

A great

democracy is coming,

perhaps helped by a flicker of

Reichstag fire, hint of Battleship Maine,

whiff of Lusitania, scent of

Gulf of Tonkin? Yes.

o yes a great democracy where

tongues will be

cut out,

fingernails pulled out,

and fingers chopped

and rapes in dank

barracks.

All who love democracy will be

treated equally. Like

the good old days, we

will have open doors.

Gene Grabiner, 2002

Editor's Preface

"Homeland Fascism Today: An Introduction"

Jeff Shantz

There is a certain complacency, perhaps arrogance, among commentators in the United States concerning the prospects for violent uprisings or mobilizations in the US. It is widely held that violent uprisings, coups, oppositional movements, will not, even *cannot*, emerge or take hold in the United States. America is viewed as a stable system with democratic checks and balances and a civil makeup mitigating against such dramatic eruptions in the body politic. Furthermore, truly oppositional movements are viewed as being too small, too marginal, or too trivial to pose a real challenge to the liberal democratic order of things in the United States.

There are some recurring factors that historically appear as what might be preconditions for dramatic social upheaval and change. These are: extreme economic inequality; significant, major economic or political crisis or shock, usually unexpected; a middle strata that feels threatened or is experiencing economic threats (Judson 2009, 174). Conflict can be triggered by a dramatic event such as a *coup d'état*, riots, a terrorist attack, etc. (Judson 2009, 174).

Responses to these issues are also important. Does the middle strata mobilize against specific scapegoats (migrants, minorities, unionists, etc.) or focus anger at a ruling elite? Does the government lose legitimacy or offer a believable remedy to the problems? Does it maintain legalistic means or resort to force and violence?

Conditions typically giving rise to upheaval are present throughout US society. Millions have lost jobs and others the prospect of finding jobs that pay a sustainable living wage and/or offer some financial security. Millions have seen savings vanish or pensions, deferred wages, decline or evaporate. Millions have lost their homes and more are facing foreclosure or eviction. Large sections of the population are desperately in debt.

Numerous writers and commentators have sensed that growing inequality in the United States raises an existential challenge to the future of America and its social and political systems. Inequality in the United States has reached levels that have historically preceded political upheaval and rupture.

America has long been a plutocracy ruled by those one percent in whom wealth and power are concentrated. The group sees its incomes rise regardless of which of the two parties of capital runs Washington at any given time. In 2005 the top one percent of Americans (those with incomes over $348,000) received their largest portion of national income since 1928 (Tritch 2006). From 2003 to 2004 the real average income for the top one percent of households (those with income over $315,000) grew by almost 17 percent. That top one percent enjoyed 36 percent of all income gains in that period (after enjoying 30 percent in 2003) (Tritch 2006).

The current context in the US is one of extreme economic inequality coupled with a middle strata (middle class) that is increasingly impoverished and increasingly feels imperiled. In 2008 the *Wall Street Journal* reported that upward mobility had remained stagnant for the past two decades (2008). Debts are equal to or more than annual income for the average family in the United States. In the *New York Times* David Brooks suggested that the economic decline was producing a new social layer—the formerly middle class. Brooks suggested that the alienation and political reaction associated with the development of this new strata would produce the next major social movement (Brooks 2008). This movement could be progressive or regressive and reactionary. The form moved depending on social circumstances.

Economic inequality is recognized as the greatest predictor or precedent of social rupture or revolution. Economic inequality and the social divisions that accompany it render societies vulnerable to the effects of disruptive social forces such as militant right wing movements. In the present day United States, economic inequality has reached disastrous levels.

The activities of organized extremists could render flammable tensions explosive. The social pressures could be further sparked by a flashpoint event such as terrorist attack or state action, such as a clampdown on a popular oppositional group or movement.

Some point, with amnesia, to a supposed lack of domestic terrorist violence and terrorist groups in the US enacting street level violence as a possible counter to the possible emergence of fascism. Yet, as the great US historian Richard Hofstadter wrote, this is a matter of repression in the national consciousness (quoted in Rappaport 2008, 167–168). Examples of domestic terrorism range from the Sons of Liberty, through the Klan, night riders, up through the Michigan Militia to the Minutemen and Patriots today. The examples in the US context have historically been rightist in character.

Increasing anger and misery in the present period can create a climate more sympathetic to terroristic reactionary violence—to fascism. As in some Republican campaign events in 2015 and 2016, groups may feel emboldened to act aggressively or violently toward representatives of scapegoated groups. If popular support for such aggression increases, the opportunity for larger expressions of fascist aggression may develop. For some time now, commentators have noted a "populist rage coursing through America" (Rich 2009).

The consumerist desire for immediate or instant gratification can further prepare a ground for receptivity to the appeals of a demagogue. A consumerist ethos is conditioned to look for short term, easy answers or satisfactions. These are the ready-made offerings of the demagogic leader. And this clarifies why pundits and political campaign opponents miss the point when they clamor for specific answers during debates or bemoan the lack of clear or consistent policy statements.

Thus one might reflect on the quickly mobilized support for a blustering opportunist claiming to "Make America Great Again" by getting tough on a spectrum of scapegoats while standing up to political elites (and erstwhile friends and golfing partners).

FACTORS FAVORING FASCISM

From a reading of the vast historical and social science literature on social change, Bruce Judson identifies five significant risk factors for dramatic social change. The first is the distribution of wealth and the gap between rich and poor in the society. The second is the impact of political or economic shocks. Third is the failure to meet rising expectations or hopes. Fourth is a broad perception of social unfairness. And finally the fifth factor involves the history and effectiveness of prominent social institutions.

Historians and philosophers from Plutarch and Aristotle have noted the part played by inequality in political rupture. Plutarch is said to have asserted, "An imbalance between rich and poor is the oldest and most fatal ailment of all republics." For Aristotle, as for sociologists like Durkheim and Tönnies, economic disparities or divisions break apart relations of cohesion and connection in society.

Even a conservative figure like former US Secretary of Labor Robert Reich concludes:

> After a point, as inequality widened, the bonds that kept our society together would snap. Every decision we tried to arrive at together—about trade, immigration, education, taxes and social insurance (health, welfare, retirement)—

> would be harder to make because it would have
> such different consequences for the relatively
> rich than for the relatively poor. We could no
> longer draw upon a common reservoir of trust
> and agreed-upon norms to deal with such differ-
> ences. We would begin to lose our capacity for
> democratic governance. (2002, 19–20)

This from someone who was part of a regime, that of Bill Clinton, that imposed neoliberal austerity policies, including massive cuts to social assistance programs, a dismantling of welfare really, and which brought in the anti-working class, pro-capital, North American Free Trade Agreement (NAFTA) as well as fundamentally deregulating Wall Street. All of these have played significant parts in the expansion of wealth inequality in the United States.

One outcome of income disparity is the active garrisoning of the elites in insulated and secured enclaves (social and geographical) separate from the rest of society. The wealthy seclude themselves in gated neighborhoods (not communities) with all of the amenities denied to the majority of the society's population. Private schools, top universities, excellent health care, clean and safe drinking water. Clean environments. These garrison spaces are physically sealed off from the rest of society by private (and often public) security and surveillance.

This positions them as less connected to others not like them and without regard for public services that they do not need but which others depend on (public health care, public schools, public transit, public post-secondary education, public parks, unemployment insurance, social assistance, social housing, etc.). This plays out in opposition to taxation for public services (apart from support for public money for police and military expenditures which they view as essential for their own security and thus as the main aspects of governance). Their wealth is put to fund neoliberal, tax-cutting, deregulating, social austerity pushing politicians who cut programs of the working class and poor and impose restrictions and controls on the poorest in society.

The result is a further redistribution of wealth upwards—taking supports from the working class and poor and investing in social spending that further benefits capital and the wealthy (tax cuts, corporate grants, deregulation, policing. This increases social inequality further and sharpens tensions in society. Typically it renders the deprived more deprived.

The rising expectations associated with the Obama elections have given way to a sustained period of disappointment and dashed hopes. This can play into a broadening of dissatisfactions and support for a demagogue claiming to help America "win again" or make America "great again."

The American Dream in the US is a myth that has successfully worked to secure middle strata loyalty and allegiance to an unequal system of broad maldistribution of wealth and resources. Yet upward mobility in the United States is much lower than it is in most European countries and Canada (Blanden, Gregg, and Machin 2005). If a larger proportion of middle strata believers comes to see this reality and the American Dream as a false myth, despair, frustration, and a sense of betrayal can contribute to aGothic desire for political change of a vengeful character.

Relative deprivation and status frustration theories in sociology and criminology have long pointed to the role of perceptions of economic injustice or status inequality combined with economic inequality or poverty in contributing to anger and resentment within stratified societies that claim to be democratic or meritocratic. These approaches suggest that it is not absolute poverty or misery that is key. Rather it is the level of dissatisfaction or frustration one feels relative to others in their social environment or relative to social expectations (or promised social rewards).

Perceptions and contexts can matter as much as or more than specific experiences. Someone in the middle strata may become frustrated and perceive themselves as being deprived even though they are materially better off than many in their society or globally. Their frame of comparison is members of their own strata or those doing better, not those doing worse. These feelings of frustration can be manipulated where political actors make unfair and opportunistic comparisons to members of specific groups (migrants, religious minorities, welfare recipients) who are portrayed as doing better as a group or as being unworthily or unfairly benefiting from perceived social privileges (through social programs, migratory "queue jumping," affirmative action policies etc.).

Political repression by ruling governments plays a regular role in periods of dramatic change. Recent attention to police violence, including the killings of civilians, shows that repression and use of armed force by the state is a regular feature readily available within liberal democracies. For the most part this violence is deployed against minorities and political opponents. Should such violence be deployed against more privileged sectors—white, middle strata, conservative males—it could contribute to the growth of armed defense movements such as militias or so-called patriot groups which could revive broader support than usual.

In this context, a US Army War College report in 2008 suggested that an economic crisis in the United States could lead to mass civil unrest which would require military intervention to restore order (Washington Valdez 2008). 2008 marked the first time in which the United States has come to deploy an active duty regular Army combat unit in full-time use to deal with civil unrest *inside* the country (National Terror Alert Response Center 2008). The use of state violence against unarmed minorities while restraint is shown by police facing armed right wing groups sends the message that such groups have legitimate grievances around which they are organizing in legitimate or at least tolerated ways.

Domestic regimes are frequently imperiled by unpopular foreign military adventures. This is particularly true when the domestic public become resentful over expenditures in such adventures at a time when they are experiencing economic insecurity or risk.

The question of government competence could be quickly raised in the event of a larger scale terrorist attack. One can point to the rise in racist anger in response to even smaller assaults. A dramatic shock, whether economic or political is often a precursor to dramatic social change. This could well be a terrorist attack in the context of a national government seen to be soft or conciliatory in the popular imagination. A shock in the context of a lack of trust in the existing government (entirely justifiable), and in the absence of effective progressive mobilization, can provide an opening for a demagogue promising security, vengeance, or setting things "right" (against a liberal democracy seen to be impotent, or passive, or gridlocked, or "politically correct.")

INEQUALITY

Based on the percent of income gained by the top ten percent of US families, the United States is now at the highest level of economic inequality in the nation's history. The United States has moved beyond the levels of economic inequality that a society can typically sustain. Earlier this century the United States reached a signal, infamous moment. In 2006, the top earning ten percent of US families received 49.3% of all US household income, including capital gains. This compared with the much lower 34.2% of the nation's total income received by the top ten percent in 1979 (Saez 2008). In 2006, economic inequality in the United States reached the highest levels since systematic accurate records became available in 1913 (Judson 2009, 51). These stark realities show the potent impacts of decades of neoliberal social and economic policies and capitalist restructuring.

Not surprisingly perhaps the great increases ratcheting up social inequality in the United States have developed over the last 35 years, in the period initiated with the election of Ronald Reagan as President and the imposition of Reaganomics, the voodoo economics of neoliberalism which has become something of an article of faith for politicians of various stripes. In 1979 the economic top one percent of Americans received ten percent of total income for the nation. By 2006 this number had jumped to more than 22.8 percent (Saez 2008). Even more the top one percent of families in the US take home one-quarter to one-fifth of all household income (Judson 2009, 52). Judson concludes that already the US has turned into an economic oligopoly (2009, 53).

In the United States economic inequality had peaked in the 1928–1929 period before the Crash then declined through the low points reached between the late 1950s and late 1970s. The decline in inequality reached the low point at which the top one percent received 8.9 percent of the nation's income in 1976 (down from 23.9 percent in 1928 and 11.3 in 1944). The upward thrust began, notably, under Reagan starting in 1980. It reached the point in 2006 at which the top one percent had risen to over 22.8 percent of all household income (Judson 2009, 53). That is a percentage only surpassed, again, in that precipice year of 1928 when the top one percent received about 24 percent.

Bruce Judson notes that the peaks of inequality in 1929 and 2008 preceded the stunning economic crashes that shook the system in the US. Broad economic inequality goes hand in hand with political instability and disruption. Conflict is a consistently appearing outcome in historical examples. Current conditions of economic inequality have resulted in a range of crises including the Crash of 2008. The effects of that crash are not yet played out.

Between 1952 and 1975, pre-Reagan, the top one percent received around nine to eleven percent of total household income in the United States (Judson 2009, 109). Incredibly, the figures show even more concentration if one looks at the top 0.1 percent of American households. In that case the top 0.1 percent gained 11.6 percent of total income for all US households in 2006. That compares with 2.7 percent in 1978, right before Reagan (Judson 2009, 110).

Numerous studies pinpoint 1979 as the fundamental turning point. Before Reagan, the United States was significantly more equal. Even more, there has emerged a strong rift between economic growth and productivity and workers' incomes. Productivity is the value in income produced by each worker (after adjustment for inflation).

Increases in productivity are not leading to growth in wages and living standards for workers. Between the 1940s and the late 1970s income shares among different groups in the United States increased at closer rates. With the 1980s income gains occurred mostly for the highest earning Americans (Judson 2009, 113). While productivity of the average worker in the United States has increased by almost 50 percent since 1973, it seems clear that workers have gained virtually nothing over this period (Krugman 2007, 24).

Wealth is the most significant means of inequality. It provides a bulwark against crisis. It also provides a basis for influencing political activity in liberal democracies. The distribution of wealth in the United States is even more divergent than the distribution of income. In 2004, Edward Wolff of New York University reported that the top 20 percent in the United States owned around 85 percent of the nation's wealth. The top ten percent held 70 percent of all of the nation's wealth. Even more the top one percent of all households held more total wealth than the bottom 90 percent of households (Wolff 2007, 2). A 2008 study by the OECD reported that of 24 countries examined, the United States had the highest income inequality outside of Mexico and Turkey (BBC News 2008). The 2007 Census Bureau report put the Gini coefficient for the US at .463, over the international warning line.

This put the US Gini scale in the neighborhood of Sri Lanka and Mali (DeNavas-Walt, Proctor, and Smith 2008, 7).

Between 1978 and 2006 the top 0.1 percent enjoyed real income gains of more than 235 percent. For the top one percent the gain was 90 percent. For the United States the median real income only increased by 13 percent.

The UN-Habitat *State of the World Cities Report 2008/2009* notes that US cities like Atlanta, Washington, Miami, and New York have levels of inequality similar to Abidjan, Nairobi, and Santiago (2008, 51). These levels of inequality lead to social separation and a disintegration of broader social bonds.

Economic inequality affects social trust. As inequality increases so too do levels of mistrust. This can contribute to scapegoating as social mistrust attaches to specific groups who are constructed as symbols of mistrust. All levels of trust seem to be reaching 30 to 40 year lows in the United States (Judson 2009, 185). One level is generalized trust within society. Generalized trust has consistently decreased through the period of growing social inequality in the US. The General Social Survey which provides a biannual report of American social values and an overview of social trends concludes that between 1972 and 1980, the year of Reagan again, the percentage of people who agreed with the sentiment that "most people can be trusted" (as opposed to the statement that "you can't be too careful in dealing with people") remained relatively constant (Judson 2009, 185–186). This despite the experience of Watergate and the opportunistic and cynical pardoning of Richard Nixon by Gerald Ford in the intervening period. Between 1980 and 2006, however, the percentage of people who generally trust others decreased from 44 percent to 32 percent. These were the lowest levels of trust recorded at any point in the history of the survey (Judson 2009, 186). According to commentator Eric Uslaner in *The Moral Foundations of Trust*, based on a study of a range of surveys done over several decades: "If you believe that things are going to get better—and that you have the capacity to control your life—trusting others isn't so risky" (2002, 33). Economic crises can spark further drops in trust.

MIDDLE STRATA FEAR AND LOATHING

In terms of a contemporary fascism it is likely, as in Germany in the 1930s, that the impetus will come, not from the industrial working class and poor, but from an increasingly disaffected, alienated, and imperiled middle strata. Uprisings emerge where these groups come to distrust the dominant system of governance.

The American Dream is a middle strata fiction. As more middle strata members feel that dream slipping away, the fiction crumbling, for their children, frustration can shift to resentment, a sense of having been lied to, anger, and violence. The middle strata anger can develop a dual sense of resentment. One is focused, rightly, on the ruling classes and economic and political elites who have accumulated increasing wealth, resources, and power while the middle strata has experienced a squeeze or decline. The other is focused, vengefully, on the poor and less fortunate who are viewed as unfairly benefiting from government largesse based on the labors (or taxes) of the middle strata rather than the fruits of their own labors.

Middle strata frustration can move to anger and aggression in a context of crises (financial, terrorist, etc.). This anger can be funneled toward cultural difference and scapegoats representing middle strata fears and, politically manipulated, social phobias—from undocumented migrants to religious difference (see Ramadan and Shantz 2016).

The period of Obama's two terms in office has perhaps further prepared the ground for a fascist turn. Obama has campaigned on and held out the promise of hope for the middle strata. Yet his administrations have failed to deliver on this hope. The mix of rising expectations met with unmet gains may have contributed to the sense of a lack of alternatives and faith in the system that has found expression in the rise of, say, a Donald Trump, or the growth of militias and paramilitaries set to do it for themselves and prepared to take things into their own hands through force.

Economic crisis further plays into brooding fears which can seek and find ready scapegoats. Economic crisis can create or exacerbate social phobias which can be manipulated by governments and hard populist figureheads alike. The rise of the Donald Trump campaign for Republican Party leadership is an example of how this can be played and spread rather quickly in a mass social media environment.

Relatedly, anger can grow and explode beyond the usual safety valves of protests or demonstrations. Established government can quickly become a target (legitimately and rightly so) as a cause or contributor to crisis or because of mishandling of crisis that openly favors specific groups (like investors, state allies, etc.).

Years of economic crisis have taken a toll on the

supposed middle class in the United States. Some commentators suggest that the immiseration of the proletariat and division of the US into the two class society predicted by Marx are now realities. Even mainstream figures like Elizabeth Warren, the government head of the Congressional Oversight Panel, suggest that America is moving to a two class economy—an upper class and a large underclass (Parker 2009). This is the economic reality named by Occupy Wall Street as the division of society between the "1% and the 99%."

While OWS has received much attention, the prospects for rightist extremism loom in relation to shifts in perceptions among the middle strata that large numbers of the middle strata feel they are losing ground or not realizing expectations (and see no resolution offered in the OWS manifestations).

Attempts by the middle strata to cling to the American Dream are underwritten today by record levels of debt. Economic inequality, job loss, declining wages have been matched by rising levels of debt to family income. In 1979 debt was 74 percent of household income. In the first quarter of 2008 total household debt was at 132 percent of personal disposable income (Weller 2008). In 1981 personal spending was at 88 percent of disposable income. By 2008, it was about 100 percent (Kedrosky 2009).

High levels of debt along with economic crisis, declining income, unemployment, growing costs, rising home payments, and rents create an explosive context. Job loss or medical emergency can mean instant disaster for families. A 2006 study concluded that 78 percent of middle strata families lacked net assets (all assets except home equity and minus debt) to sustain three months with spending at three-quarters of current expense levels if they lost their source of income (Wheary, Shapiro, and Draut 2007). They lack the financial security to sustain an economic crisis in other words.

Lack of assets leaves middle strata families vulnerable and feeling vulnerable. In April 2009 there were 5.4 employees seeking work for every available job opening (Shierholz 2009). Finding a job when unemployed is far from being a sure thing.

Social mobility is a myth for most Americans particularly the poorest. The myth of mobility has served to gain consent as well as an acceptance of inequality and lack of social programs. The middle class as an ideological support is quite potent. A study by the Pew Research Center in 2008 found that around 40 percent of people with incomes under $20,000 believed themselves to be middle class. The median household income in the United States is about $50,000 and in no city would an income under $20,000 be considered middle range (2008). But the perception of being, or having a decent chance at being middle class plays an important buffer role in maintaining American stratification systems.

UNEQUAL STRUCTURES AND FASCIST POSSIBILITIES

These are issues that cannot be easily resolved in the current social structure. But populists with easy answers and scapegoats at hand, particularly the less powerful, can find ready audiences for their messages. In this context liberal democracy is seen to distort or corrupt the better instincts of the people, especially the frustrated middle strata. They express a dissatisfaction with the false virtues of the institutional status quo.

As revolutionary syndicalist theorist Georges Sorel has pointed out:

> The masses who are led have a very vague and extremely simple idea of the means by which their lot can be improved; demagogues easily get them to believe that the best way is to utilize the power of the State to pester the rich. We pass thus from jealousy to vengeance, and it is well known that vengeance is a sentiment of extraordinary power, especially with the weak. (1950, 186)

It is not to be understated that the current context of fascist possibility did not spring up overnight. Like the case of fascism in Germany and Italy it emerges from decades of economic crisis and uncertainty, political economic change and social inequality. This is part of a process evolving over 30 years.

Underlying all of this have been the advance of political, economic, and cultural transformations associated with a market fundamentalism, the wholesale handing over of social relations to market logics and market supportive initiatives. The market fundamentalism asserts a morality of austerity and scarcity as public goods. The unequal distribution of wealth is viewed straightforwardly as a proper market outcome. There is no excess for the wealthy since the market only appropriately allocates resources according to the market fundamentalists. Inequality is posed as a natural and legitimate market outcome. Related to this is a sense of entitlement for the privileged and a sense that the poor are undeserving.

The current period of fascist possibility emerges from three decades of anti-labor, pro-capital policies instituted as part of mainstream social policy and mainstream cultural values promoted by the state since Reagan attacked the striking air traffic controllers in 1981. It is sometimes difficult to convey to younger people how much the social ethos of public policy and discourse has changed. All of this can prepare the ground for fascist poor bashing, union busting, and corporatism.

The great divide in social inequality has also sent a cultural message that some lives are worth more than others. In 2007, the average pay of CEO's for S and P 500 companies sat at $10.8 million. This was roughly 270 times the average pay of full-time non-management workers which was at $40,000 (Sahadi 2007). In 2015, CEO pay at the nation's largest companies was 303 times that of the average pay of their employees, according to analysis from the Economic Policy Institute (EPI). The average total compensation of CEOs at the 350 largest firms, including stock options and other bonuses, totaled $16.3 million in 2014, according to EPI. That compares with the relatively miniscule $50,000 in pay for their workers (Isidore 2015.)

This after downsizing and corporate restructuring and re-engineering have decimated blue collar and lower management positions. This has been accompanied by regressive taxation changes. Bruce Judson notes that when Dwight D. Eisenhower took office the top marginal tax for individuals was at 92 percent. Under Reagan these rates were cut from 69 percent when he first entered the presidency to 28 percent in 1988, his final year of his second term in office.

In 2006 the effective tax rate (the rate at which people actually pay taxes) for the 400 top earning Americans, those with reported incomes of $263 million or more, was at 17.2 percent (Drucker 2009). Capitalist Warren Buffet reported that he paid lower tax rates than his receptionist. He paid 17.7 percent of his taxable income while his receptionist paid around 30 percent (Murakami Tse 2007). According to Larry Bartels: "[T]he most significant domestic policy initiative of the past decade has been a massive government-engineered transfer of additional wealth from the lower and middle classes to the rich in the form of substantial reductions in federal income taxes" (2008, 161–162). This is further impelled by other social transformations of neoliberal capitalism.

A cornerstone of fascism is the assault on unions and other forms or autonomous workers organization. These provide the most potent and durable counter forces to corporatism and far right wing mobilization. In the mid-1950s, 35 percent of US workers were in unions. By 2009 only 7.5 percent of private sector workers and 12.1 percent of all workers in the United States are in unions (Judson 2009, 168). Since Ronald Reagan anti-union actions and ideas have become cornerstones of a certain type of US patriotism (Judson 2009, 168).

The current climate in the United States is one of dashed hopes (after the electoral high of Obama's 2008 election and the end of eight years of Bush) and unmet expectations. There is a lingering bitterness particularly raw among those who were not crazy for Obama in the first place. There is also a solid cynicism (rightly deserved) about status quo politics and the current practice of US democracy (if not the myth of democracy or American political selectness or uniqueness more broadly).

The contemporary middle strata in the United States certainly experiences a sense of threatened prosperity and security. Job losses and precarization, threats to pensions, actual losses and decreases in pensions, a perceived loss of social mobility and more.

The connection between economic inequality and economic disasters is borne out by the examples of the Great Depression and the Crash of 2008. Both crashes came following the two periods of most extreme inequalities over the last century (Judson 2009, 182). Rising inequality transfers money upwards from those who will spend it more consistently to those who will not. The economy becomes dependent on investment in new projects and on high levels of spending on luxuries which are less predictable. This further renders the economy more precarious.

Fascist Histories in America

Times of economic turmoil and depression have led to fascist mobilization in the United States previously. In the 1930s the hard populism of Huey Long and Father Coughlin stirred angry, often ugly, passions. At the same time the US offered its own version of a March on Rome when the Bonus Marchers of World War One veterans marched to Washington DC from across the country demanding compensation for their wartime service. Unlike the vacillating state troops in Italy who failed to disperse their marchers, the Bonus Marchers were routed by the army under direction of later war hero, and then discredited war monger, General Douglas MacArthur. Otherwise the outcome might have been quite different.

All of this occurred while corporate plotters were looking at an explicitly fascist coup to overthrow Franklin Delano Roosevelt. As the Schwendingers detail in *Homeland Fascism* the United States has come closer to a fascist takeover at the highest levels than may be known, remembered, or acknowledged. In March of 1934 the House Special Committee on Un-American Activities heard testimony from the legendary, highly decorated, retired Marine General Smedley Butler that William Doyle, the commander of the American Legion's Massachusetts branch and bond salesman Gerald MacGuire had attempted to recruit him to organize a military coup to topple the FDR administration. Butler's account of events was corroborated by a reporter from the *New York Evening Post* and the *Philadelphia Record*, Paul Comly French. French testified that he overheard MacGuire suggest that, "We need a Fascist government in this country to save the Nation from the Communists who want to tear it down and wreck all that we have built in America. The only men who have patriotism to do it are the soldiers and Smedley Butler is the ideal leader. He could organize one million overnight" (quoted in Stone and Kuznick 2012, 64).

Testimony in the hearings uncovered the fact that Doyle and MacGuire were fronts for the numerous bankers and industrialists who had formed the American Liberty League to oppose progressive New Deal policies and FDR. For its part the House Committee, chaired by John McCormack of Massachusetts, reported that it was successfully "able to verify all the pertinent statements made by General Butler" (quoted in Stone and Kuznick 2012, 64). It came to the dire conclusion that "attempts to establish a fascist organization in the United States...were discussed, were planned, and might have been placed in execution when and if the financial backers deemed it expedient" (quoted in Stone and Kuznick 2012, 64). MacGuire had gone so far as to travel to France to study fascist veterans' movements there. He saw these as a viable model for the type of fascist force that could be raised and mobilized in the United States.

These bankers and industrialists along with their political agents moved quickly to discredit the claims resulting from the Committee hearings. New York Mayor Fiorello LeGuardia derisively referred to the plans as the "cocktail putsch." Incredibly the committee chose not to call key figures implicated in the coup plot to testify. These included Colonel Grayson Murphy, Al Smith, John Davis, Hugh Johnson, Thomas Lamot, Hanford MacNider, former American Legion Commander, and General Douglas MacArthur. Butler always expressed disappointment that the names of those involved were left out of the final report—a stunning outcome indeed.

In addition to the actual failed coup there were other rumblings very near the president's office of possibilities for explicit dictatorship. Walter Lippman, a popular columnist and commentator, who was among the first to use the concept Cold War and who coined the term stereotype in its current meaning, wrote that, "A mild form of dictatorship will help us over the roughest spots on the road ahead (Alter 2006, 187). Lippman apparently met with FDR a month before his inauguration to press this idea directly with the incoming president that he might take on the powers of a dictator for an indeterminate period. Far from being a fringe crank with marginal ideas, according to an FDR biographer, Lippman "spoke for the American political establishment" (Alter 2006, 187).

In 1932, New York Congressman Hamilton Fish Jr. proclaimed, with regard to dictatorship, that, "If we don't give it under the existing system, the people will change the system" (Manchester 1974, 58). The very next year Fish Jr. wrote to FDR to assure him that Republicans were prepared to "give you any power you need" (Manchester 1974, 58).

FDR himself was aid to have contemplated using the word dictatorship in his first inaugural address when he asserted the possibility of seeking "broad executive power to wage war against the emergency" (Alter 2006, 219). And, as the Schwendingers point out in *Homeland Fascism*, the appeal to exceptional measures in states of emergency is now as much as ever available for politicians seeking to wield them.

FUNDAMENTAL FASCISM

Aggrieved members of the middle strata express outrage in terms of a loss of values, a change in the American values they knew. This is often posed as a threat to Western values or Christian values. In an earlier work on fascist tendencies in the United States, journalist Chris Hedges focuses exclusively on fundamentalist Christianity. Indeed the fundamentalist Christian strands of authoritarianism and hard populism stretch through various rightist movements from the Tea Party to Patriots.

A strange moment came during the 2016 presidential primary season when Dr. Ben Carson, then a candidate for Republican presidential nomination, took a break in campaigning but attended the National Prayer Breakfast. One might suggest that particularly deep, yet largely unexamined, fascist roots in fundamentalism are found in the elite network of The Family, the shadowy grouping behind the National Prayer Breakfast. The faith motivating the National Prayer Breakfast is an authoritarian mix of free market fundamentalism and imperial desire. The shadowy and secretive group has maintained a worship of capitalism and a fondness for dictators. And a strong admiration for the leadership approach of one Adolph Hitler. Sharlet identifies American fundamentalism as exemplified in the family as a movement that recreates theology in terms of empire. It is imperialist. Theirs is a "biblical capitalism" (Sharlet 2008, 3). The Family has strong ties with business people in strategic industries like aerospace and oil (Sharlet 2008, 19). The Family's headquarters, The Cedars, was purchased with money donated by a CEO of arms manufacturer Raytheon, several oil executives, and other corporate leaders and bankers (Sharlet 2008, 26). Membership in the Family was estimated at around 20,000 (from an insider) with around 350 in central positions (Sharlet 2008, 20).

A direct line can be drawn from the corporate opponents of the New Deal to the congressional legislators and fundamentalist Christians who gather each year right up through the 2016 presidential campaigns at the National Prayer Breakfast. Journalist Jeff Sharlet documents relationships of the Family with Nazi business people after World War Two and continued support for dictators through the twentieth and twenty-first centuries. Even more the fascist connections have been direct. In 1963, Family founder Abraham Vereide claimed that the Family had cells in and moved freely in Franco's Spain (Sharlet 2008, 396).

The men of the Family explicitly believe that they are preparing themselves (and the way) for a spiritual war in which they are weapons (Sharlet 2008, 1). The Family instituted an authoritarian faith of and for power alone. One member suggests, as reported by Sharlet, that they were there to "soften our hearts to authority" (2008, 40). Democracy was rebelliousness and the inner rebel must be crushed (Sharlet 2008, 40).

Their respect was paid often to Hitler as an organizing example. One member of the Family gives a fascist description of their bundled strength. In his description: "Look at it like this: take a bunch of sticks, light each one of 'em on fire. Separate they go out. Put 'em together, though, and light the bundle. *Now* you're ready to burn" (quoted in Sharlet 2008, 3).

The Family is little known publicly. Even Hedges gave them no attention in his detailed study. What is known to some of the public and much of the mass media is the National Prayer Breakfast, an event held every February at the Washington, DC Hilton. Starting with Eisenhower, every president has attended the National Prayer Breakfast founded by Vereide in 1953. The National Prayer Breakfast hosts some 3000 dignitaries who pay a fee (around $450) to attend. These figures are predominantly national political leaders and major corporate players. Most meet for a breakfast and prayer but many stay for days of seminars on Christ's message for their particular industries (Sharlet 2008, 22). Executives in oil, banking, defense, and insurance take part. Previous attendees include Benazir Bhutto and a Sudanese general linked to the genocide in Darfur (Sharlet 2008, 22–23). The Family's "key man" in Africa is Uganda's longtime president for life Yoveri Museveni (Sharlet 2008, 23). The National Prayer Breakfast offers access for these figures to the President of the United States that circumvents the State Department and regular administration vetting (Sharlet 2008, 24).

Over the years the Family has networked in Congress on behalf of Brazilian dictator General Costa e Silva, Indonesian dictator General Suharto, and South Korean dictator Park Chung Hee, among others. The Family was key in building friendships between the Reagan administration and Latin American dictators. It built links between the Reagan administration and Salvadorian General Carlos Eugenios Vides Casanova, responsible for torturing thousands, and Honduran General Gustavo Alvarez Martinez, linked to death squads and the CIA (Sharlet 2008, 25),

A fascist formation will likely come from within, or in close alliance with, the Republican Party, as the Trump campaign makes rather clear. The Family is composed largely of Republicans in its key circles. It was said to have suggested the pardoning of Nixon to Gerald Ford (Sharlet 2008, 19). President George HW Bush praised Family leader Doug Coe at a National Prayer Breakfast for what he termed "quiet diplomacy" in violation of the Logan Act, one of the oldest laws in the US, which prohibits private citizens from doing that very thing precisely because it raises the prospect of a foreign policy beyond even limited democratic access, accountability, or control (Sharlet 2008, 26).

Family founding figure Abraham Vereide had a trickle-down theory of compassion. In this trickle-down view, the powerful must hold large reserves that they can shower on the weak (Sharlet 2008, 89). This was a "big man" view of society and history. Only the "big man" can change the world. What they really seek is a Christian Adolph. Vereide's vision, which he worked to make real was a "ruling class of Christ-committed men bound in a fellowship of the anointed, the chosen, key men in a voluntary dictatorship of the divine" (Sharlet 2008, 91). For Abram, the will of god was order, the enemy were not even human (Sharlet 2008, 107).

And religion is viewed explicitly to soothe the angers of the poor, to put a cap on their aspirations for social change and economic redistribution to benefit the poor. The vision of Christianity rejected the social Gospel and good works for the poor in favor of a laissez faire Jesus, bare chested and muscular like Mussolini.

Vereide even coined a phrase for his view for the nation (one that George HW Bush would make part of the national lexicon): the "new world order" (Sharlet 2008, 90). The new world order for Vereide was an explicitly corporatist one. It would be based on cooperation between management and labor—in which labor cooperated by submitting and admitting its sins to capital (Sharlet 2008, 112).

Tellingly the Family started as a business anti-labor alliance in Seattle in 1935. Notably, the only person Vereide identifies in his early notes as an enemy is a union organizer, likely with the Industrial Workers of the World (IWW), a militant syndicalist union, Harry Bridges, a longshore worker, or Dave Beck, a Teamster organizer in Seattle—or an amalgam of the two

(Sharlet 2008, 99). The first task of the elite funda-mentalism of Vereide was the destruction of rank and file labor militance (Sharlet 2008, 109).

BROWNSHIRTS OF THEIR OWN: MILITIAS AND MORE

Some argue that despite the rightist anger of the current period and the concerns over the fascist tenor of the Trump campaign the prospects for fascism in the United States are unlikely due to the absence of street fighting brownshirt forces, an apparently crucial component of fascist movements. Yet, one does not need to look very far at present to see that the forces providing potential brownshirt cadres are present and mobilizing. Even more the present period poses the ominous threat that they are converging, the disparate forces of right wing anger and hate seeing and recognizing in each other kindred spirits ready and willing to act together. Klan, Patriots, militias, Minutemen, Oath Keepers, Tea Partiers.

Those who hold wealth and resources in unequal societies do not give up that wealth and those resources without a fight. A move to fascism may be an effort to head off attempts at social reform or wealth redistribution. This impetus has played a part in the right wing militia and Patriot movements which are in large part responses to civil rights movements and advances made by social minorities in the US since the 1970s.

On Saturday, January 2, less than 48 hours into the new year of 2016, several hundred armed right wing militia members, self-styled patriots, affiliated with the Bundy Ranch in Nevada marched on a federal building in Oregon, took it over, occupied it, and vowed to defend it with arms. The patriots, claiming to be defenders of the Constitution, called on others sympathetic to their cause to take up arms in a show of force and support. The reason for the occupation of the Malheur National Wildlife Refuge building was outrage at the conviction of their allies, Dwight Hammond and his son Steven Hammond, convictions that the Bundy militia view as unconstitutional.

This is but one of the recent, very public, mobilizations of right wing armed groups in the United States. Notably, like others before it, the Bundy militia was able to march openly en masse while armed with automatic assault weapons in full view of police who did nothing to discourage or halt their assembly or advance.

One might well contrast this with the extreme, usually lethal, violence deployed against African American civilians, including youth and children armed with nothing more than cell phones or toys, if that, by militarized and trigger-ready police force in various sub/urban contexts across the United States.

The police (non)response to organized, angry, armed right wing militia groupings is also a far cry from the extreme violence regularly deployed against non-violent protesters and progressive and left wing activists at social justice demonstrations, alternative globalization protests, and Occupy actions and encampments. In each of those cases people have been subjected to police assaults, use of munitions including tasers, rubber bullets, tear gas, pepper spray, kettling, mass arrests, and detentions. Student protesters doing nothing more than sitting down on their own campus grounds have been subjected to beatings and pepper spraying by police.

All of this sends a clear message to would be brownshirts that the state will target their enemies, anarchists, leftists, progressives, etc. for extreme, even lethal force, while offering minimal or no intervention in the face of armed and aggressive rightist mobilization, even large scale actions designed to show force and intimidate local populations. This is a key element in the rise of openly fascist movements.

At this point in time it is clear that brownshirts in waiting appear across the landscape of politics in the United States. These include, but are not limited to, militia groups, Tea Party supporters, the Klan, Oath Keepers, Patriots, and border patrols like the Minutemen, in addition to explicitly neo-Nazi groups. What is perhaps emerging in the present period is the convergence, and more open convergence, of these groupings under the "Make America Great" Trump banner. This may be a convergence that propels the would-be brownshirts into actual brownshirts on a broader, organized, basis. Though that point has not yet arrived.

BORDER MILITIAS

One of the formations that may most likely coalesce into a street fascist point of convergence are the border militias. Border militias are organized groups of armed citizens in the United States who mobilize to patrol the border between the US and Mexico and interfere with the movement of immigrants from Mexico into the US. Militia patrols have been most active in Arizona and Texas. It is estimated that there are as many as 500 militia troops currently patrolling the US-Mexico border in Arizona. Most militia patrols are made up of small groups, however, with patrols generally consisting of fewer than a dozen members. In addition to physical patrols of border areas, militias have engaged in political pressuring, especially through rallies and protests, of politicians to pass restrictive immigration laws, to deport migrants, and to toughen border security. Militias have also mobilized political campaigns to defeat politicians deemed to be "soft" on immigration reform. In addition, militias have waged publicity campaigns demonizing immigrants deemed to be "illegal" (or who have entered the US through unofficial channels).

Militias typically operate on their own with no oversight from state authorities at any level. They do not formally coordinate their efforts with the US Border Patrol and do not communicate their movements or actions. Most militia members have no formal firearms or tactical training, nor do they have training in conflict resolution or de-escalation or health issues. Indeed the border militias are strictly vigilante groups who operate according to their own sets of rules and responsibilities. At the same time there have been reported instances of Border Patrol agents cooperating with militia groups and providing logistical support (map readings). Militia members report receiving positive feedback and support from Border Patrol agents. Publicly, US Customs and Border Protection (CBP) disavows the militias and cautions against their activities.

Serious concerns have been raised about the nativist, and indeed explicitly racist expressions and practices of border militia groups. Even more there have been cases of physical violence inflicted by militia groups on migrants they claim to have intercepted crossing the border. Border militias have also been associated with racist extremists and white supremacists, either directly through militia membership or through appearance at militia events. Neo-Nazi groups have openly participated in border militia rallies. The Southern Poverty Law Center, a major civil rights group and human rights monitor in the US, has designated the Minutemen militia an "extreme nativist" group.

Due to the clandestine and secretive character of most of the border militia groups (including the widespread wearing of bandanas and camouflage to mask individual identities) little is known about the composition (class, culture, background) of militia group membership. Perhaps not surprisingly most attendees at open militia events are of Euro-American backgrounds (i.e. white). Militia members are believed to come from a range of socioeconomic strata and occupational backgrounds.

The formation of border militias speaks to the intersection of socio-political developments in the twenty-first century. These include economic crisis, deindustrialization, and increasing unemployment which give rise to and reinforce fears of job loss (conceived as being lost to lower cost migrant labor, for example). There is also the socio-political climate stoked by fears of terrorism and terrorists following 9/11. Along with this are growing phobias of the migrant "other" associated with fears of infiltration or invasion. These come together with demographic changes in the US, including growing visible minority populations, and shifts in political influence and policy (real and/or perceived) that reinforce anxieties among Euro-Americans over a loss in privilege or status. There is also a political distrust of government efficiency reflected in movements like the Tea Party. In these contexts the border militias, like the Tea Party, express a form of activist reactionary politics.

The border militia group that has gained the most notoriety, nationally and internationally, is the Minutemen, founded in 2005 to patrol the US-Mexico border in Arizona and with the stated aim to intercept and return migrants. Co-founded by Jim Gilchrist, the Minutemen take their name from the Minutemen militias that fought during the American Revolution. The nod to the American revolutionaries, and the hard nativist discourse espoused by Minutement leaders and general members mark the Minutemen among broader Rightwing populist movements, such as those associated with the Tea Party movement of the Republican Party.

The Minutemen have been lauded by well known conservative public figures including Arnold Schwarzenegger, who praised the Minutemen while governor of California, and media figure Sean Hannity. Schwarzenegger invited the Minutemen to patrol the border between California and Mexico.

During the summer of 2014, militias mobilized in mass numbers to patrol the Texas-Mexico border, after US Border Services and Texas Governor Rick Parry reported growing numbers of migrants from Central America. As a result the US Border Patrol was moved to warn off militias publicly, requesting that they not get involved. While more than ten militias are said to be active in Texas, most are made up of fewer than a dozen members, leaving roughly 100 members actively patrolling. Republican state Representative Doug Miller, a three-time representative, publicly praised the militia for their activities in Texas.

Groups operating along the border in Texas include Operation Secure Our Border: Texas (formerly Operation Secure Our Border: Laredo Sector), the Central Valley Citizen's Militia, the Independent Citizen's Militia, Bolinas Border Patrol, Alpha Team, Bravo Team, Camp Geronimo, Whiskey Bravo, and the Oathkeepers. Militias have recently taken to coordinating their efforts across groups and locales. They have established the Patriot Information Hotline, a 24-hour conference line maintained by militia groups to coordinate their efforts.

In response to the border militia movement there have been mobilizations opposing militia groups publicly. Opposition has particularly strong among anti-racist activists, Leftwing groups, immigrant defense movements, and African American and Latin American groups. In 2005 a mass demonstration of more than 300 people, including members of the League of United Latin American Citizens, attempted to stop a speech by Minutemen members, one of whom was founder Jim Gilchrist. Police intervened to end the protest by declaring it an unlawful assembly.

Students and community groups have confronted Minutemen representatives on various campuses across the US when the militia group has attempted to address college and university audiences. In 2006 several dozen students and community organizers disrupted a presentation by Minutemen members at Columbia University in New York City. Protesters took the stage to halt proceedings while chants decrying racism within the border militias were leveled from the audience. Again, security intervened to break up the protests and allow the Minutemen to continue.

The Southern Poverty Law Center suggests that the border militias have been most involved in heated rhetoric against immigrants and immigration, a concern in and of itself, but have actually undertaken few initiatives outside of some cases in Arizona and recent events in Texas. At the same time the border militia movement, and especially the Minutemen, have been of great interest to national and international media and played a part in public debates about immigration and immigration reform in the US. They have been particularly influential in promoting punitive and restrictive approaches to immigration.

CONCLUSION

Obviously the campaign of Donald Trump for Republican candidate for president has raised the prospect of a mass mobilization along fascist lines in the United States. Of perhaps greatest significance the Trump campaign shows the very real coming together of elements of high (elite, corporate, government) fascism and low or street fascism. In Trump's campaign the prospect of a rightist demagogue gaining control of the instruments of government, and the already high fascist mechanisms discussed in detail by Julia and Herman Schwendinger, comes together along with, and through, the mass mobilization of fighting forces in the streets (and campaign rallies). This is a significant shift in politics in the US (in scale certainly if not in character) and has brought developments that have been previously seen as fringe (individuals at Tea party rallies or Patriot meetings) or obscure into the mainstream and into day to day politics on an open basis. It shows too that fascist mobilization or development in the United States need not be, and will not only be, friendly.

Whatever the specific outcome of the Trump campaign for the Republican leadership or the presidency, the terms of analysis and action in the United States have shifted. The mechanisms of fascism within existing government structures, as outlined by the Schwendingers, are in place and available for expansion or further deployment by a rightist demagogue. The actors who favor and promote them are in place. Even more, the low or street fascist elements have become more organized, open, engaged, and confident. They have found a safe space for open mobilization, their ideas given daily broadcast in mainstream media. They have found their audience. They now feel secure in stepping forward right arm outstretched, reaching for their very own führer.

Jeff Shantz, April 2016,

Surrey, B.C. (unceded Coast Salish territories)

References

Akers Chacon, Justin and Mike Davis. 2006. No One Is Illegal: Fighting Racism and State Violence on the US-Mexico Border. Chicago: Haymarket.

Alter, Jonathan. 2006. *The Defining Moment: FDR's Hundred Days and the Triumph of Hope.* New York: Simon and Schuster

Bartels, Larry. 2008. *Unequal Democracy: The Political Economy of the New Gilded Age.*

Princeton: Princeton University Press

BBC News. 2008. "'More Inequality' in Rich Nations." BBC News. October 21. http://news.bbc.co.uk/2/hi/business/7681435.stm

Blanden, Jo, Paul Gregg, and Stephen Machin. 2005. *Intergenerational Mobility in Europe and North America*. Centre for Economic Performance, London School of Economics. http://cep.lse.ac.uk/about/news/IntergenerationalM obility.pdf

Brooks, David. 2008. "The Formerly Middle Class." *The New York Times*. November 17. http://www.nytimes.com/2008/11/18/opinion/18bro oks.html

DeNavas-Walt, Carmen, Bernadette D. Proctor, and Jessica D. Smith. 2008. *Income, Poverty, and Health Insurance Coverage in the United States: 2007*. US Census Bureau. https://www.census.gov/prod/2008pubs/p60-235.pdf

Doty, Roxanne Lynn. 2009. The Law Into Their Own Hands: Immigration and the Politics of Exceptionalism. Tucson: University of Arizona Press.

Drucker, Jesse. 2009. "For 'Fortune 400,' a Tumbling Tax Rate." *Wall Street Journal*. January 30. http://www.wsj.com/articles/SB12332818712473132 7

Isidore, Chris. 2015. "CEO Pay is 300 Times Greater than Their Employees." *CNN Money*. June 22. http://money.cnn.com/2015/06/22/news/companie s/ceo-pay/

Judson, Bruce. 2009. *It Could Happen Here: America on the Brink*. New York: HarperLuxe.

Kedrosky, Paul. 2009. "US Savings Over Time: The Interactive Edition." *Infectious Greed: Finance and the Money Culture*. March 2. http://paul.kedrosky.com/archives/2009/03/us_savings_over.html

Krugman, Paul. 2007. *The Conscience of a Liberal*. New York: Norton.

Manchester, William. 1974. *The Glory and the Dream: A Narrative History of America 1932–1972*. Boston: Little Brown.

Murakami Tse, Tomoeh. 2007. "Buffet Slams Tax System Disparities." *Washington Post*. http://www.washingtonpost.com/wp-dyn/content/article/2007/06/27/AR2007062700097.html

National Terror Alert Response Center. 2008. "US Army Brigade Deploys for Homeland Mission." nationalterroralert.com September 30. http://www.nationalterroralert.com/2008/09/30/us-army-brigade-deploys-for-homeland-mission/

Neiwert, David. 2013. *And Hell Followed With Her: Crossing the Dark Side of the American Border*. New York: Nation Books.

Parker, Kimberly. 2009. "Elizabeth Warren: Middle Class Lacks Security." *US News and World Report*. February 9. http://money.usnews.com/money/blogs/alpha-consumer/2009/02/09/elizabeth-warren-middle-class-lacks-security

Pew Research Center. 2008. *Inside the Middle Class: Bad Times Hit the Good Times*. Pew Social Trends. April 9. http://www.pewsocialtrends.org/2008/04/09/inside-the-middle-class-bad-times-hit-the-good-life/

Ramadan, Hisham and Jeff Shantz, eds. 2016. *Manufacturing Phobias: The Political Production of Fear in Theory and Practice*. Toronto: University of Toronto Press.

Rappaport, David C. 2008. "Before the Bombs There Were the Mobs: American Experience with Terror." *Terrorism and Political Violence* 20(2): 167–194

Reich, Robert. 2002. *I'll Be Short: Essentials for a Decent Working Society*. Boston: Beacon Press.

Rich, Frank. 2009. "Slumdogs Unite!" *The New York Times*. February 7. http://www.nytimes.com/2009/02/08/opinion/08rich.html?_r=0

Saez, Emmanuel. 2008. "Striking it Richer: The Evolution of Top Incomes in the United States." http://elsa.berkeley.edu/~saez/

Sahadi, Jeanne. 2007. "CEO Pay 364 Times More than Workers." CNN Money. August 29. http://money.cnn.com/2007/08/28/news/economy/ceo_pay_workers/index.htm?section=money_topstories

Shantz, Jeff (ed.). 2010a. Racial Profiling and Borders: International, Interdisciplinary Perspectives. Lake Mary: Vandeplas.

Shantz, Jeff (ed.). 2010b. Racism and Borders: Representation, Repression, Resistance. New York: Algora.

Sharlet, Jeff. 2008. *The Family: The Secret Fundamentalism at the Heart of American Power*. New York: Harper Perennial.

Shierholz, Heidi. 2009. "Less than One Job Opening for Every Five Job Seekers." Economic Policy Institute. June 9.

http://www.epi.org/publication/jolts_20090609/

Stone, Oliver and Peter Kuznick. 2012. *The Untold History of the United States*. New York: Gallery Books

Tritch, Teresa. 2006. "The Rise of the Super-Rich." *New York Times*. July 19. http://www.nytimes.com/2006/07/19/opinion/19t alkingpoints.html?pagewanted=all&_r=0

UN-Habitat. 2008. *State of the World's Cities 2008/2009: Harmonious Cities*. London: Earthscan.

Uslaner, Eric. 2002. *The Moral Foundations of Trust*. Cambridge: Cambridge University Press.

Wall Street Journal. 2008. "Report Shows Stagnant Upward Mobility in US." *The Wall Street Journal*. November 12. http://blogs.wsj.com/economics/2008/11/12/repor t-shows-stagnant-upward-mobility-in-us/

Weller, Christian. 2008. *Economic Snapshot: September 2008*. Center for American Progress. https://cdn.americanprogress.org/wp-content/uploads/issues/2008/09/pdf/sep08_econ _snapshot.pdf

Washington Valdez. 2008. "Unrest Caused by Bad Economy May Require Military Action, Report Says." *El Paso Times*. December 30. http://truth-out.org/archive/component/k2/item/81759:unrest-caused-by-bad-economy-may-require-military-action-report-says

Wheary, Jennifer, Thomas M. Shapiro, and Tamara Draut. 2007. *By a Thread: The New Experience of Americas Middle Class*. Dēmos and the Institute on Assets and Social Policy at Brandeis University.

https://iasp.brandeis.edu/pdfs/2007/By%20A
%20Thread%20New%20Experience.pdf

Wolff, Edward N. 2007. "Recent Trends in Household
Wealth in the United States: Rising Debt and the
Middle Class Squeeze." Working Paper 502. Levy
Economics Institute of Bard College.

PART ONE

CLASSICAL FASCISM

—◊—

Introduction

TERRORISM, NEIGHBORS, AND NUREMBERG

> *To initiate a war of aggression... is not only an international crime; it is the supreme international crime differing only from other war crimes in that it contains within itself the accumulated evil of the whole.*
>
> —Robert H. Jackson,
> Supreme Court Justice & Chief
> American Prosecutor, Nuremberg Tribunal

On September 11, 2001 two passenger jets smashed into the World Trade Center's twin towers. Wrapped in fire and smoke, the towers collapsed into an immense pile of toxic rubble. People were glued to the televised reruns of this catastrophe when President G. W. Bush returned to Washington from a safe haven in Nebraska and grimly declared: *This is War!*

Immediately, our Florida neighbors joined millions of other patriots and unfurled Old Glory. People in supermarkets walked proudly with red, white, and blue ribbons pinned to their lapels and sported T-shirts imprinted with patriotic sentiments such as *"You're Gonna Get Yours Bin Laden! Death to Terrorists!"* Wherever we went, we heard, "Bomb the shit out of the Taliban!" "Nuke 'em!" A red-blooded neighbor snapped, "Who gives a rat's ass about their civilians? *They* killed 6000 *American* civilians!"[2] (Later the media reduced the estimate to 2,830—still a lot of people.) In accord with the President's declaration of war, officials, journalists, and policy pundits confronted critics with the classic one-liner from the President's speech to Congress: "If you aren't with *us*, you're with *them*." How should an informed person deal with these gut reactions? Take the example of one of our neighbors who, although successful, never graduated from high school. He might nod off before the end of a post-911 newscast but he certainly knew that we had our heads screwed on right if we agreed that the terrorists should be hunted down and killed!

Still, it was not easy to summon credible "talking points" that would get people to back off and think about the whole picture. The President and mass

---

2 People were using the 6000 figure because it was aired during the week following 9/11 but when a more accurate count became available the estimate proved to be lower.

media had underplayed America's role in Afghanistan. Our government had originally helped the warlords, the Taliban and other fundamentalists to crush their secular opposition—and establish one of the most politically repressive and sexist regimes in the world. Our leadership and mainstream press had reported nothing about the financial support and military equipment given by the CIA to Osama bin Laden. And even those who knew about this support cynically wrote it off as just another stupid mistake by our unbelievably imperfect government. Nonetheless, the historical events leading to the atrocities in New York City and elsewhere on 9/11 might at least provide answers for a neighbor who complained, *"Why did these Muslims do it? We didn't hurt them."*

In fact, *why* they did it was a well-kept secret. There wasn't a single individual in our Florida community who knew about the US Middle East policies that supported the Israeli hardliners against the Palestinian Muslims—or about the CIA's overthrow of Mossadegh's democratic regime in Iran. No one had been told about the sanctions that had created shortages of food, medicine, etc., and killed half a million civilians in Iraq; or about the dictatorships propped up by the US in Saudi Arabia, Kuwait, and Pakistan, where immensely wealthy families oppressed millions of impoverished people. Familiarity with these policies *did* provide some idea of why the terrorists despised the US—and why they personalized it as The Great Satan, an angel who has defied God and fallen from grace. Yet our neighbors had never heard about these policies.

And then, to top it all, newspapers reported that everybody was fearful of an anthrax attack from terrorists. Panicked Americans bought rubber gloves to open their mail. Families agonized over whether to "risk" a commercial flight to Disneyland in Orlando, Florida. We live on Florida's gulf coast, in a Republican bastion called Bayonet Point. Here, very few people have heard about the global economic forces that have been slowly grinding Middle Eastern farmers and shopkeepers into the dirt. Anglo, Dutch, and American corporations have helped destroy the hopes and dreams of secular movements and democratic forces in these oil-rich countries. Their populaces were left with "utopian" images about a past where tribal elders and religion kept order. A past where one did not have to serve Satan by growing opium for American addicts, or to run desperately from drones trying to "shock and awe" insurgents and terrorists, in addition to women and children, into submission.

President Bush attributed the World Trade Center atrocity to forces of evil and religious fanatics. In a moment of candor, however, he voiced a fanatical call for a Christian jihad, exhorting Americans to resurrect the Crusades. But, before his "endless war against terrorism" continued to unleash America's arsenal against the modern Saracens and the 60 nations that house millions of Muslims, he was deaf to the international recoil from the huge number of civilian killings and the monstrous devastation of their communities.

Unfortunately, while the American blitzkrieg crushed the Iraqi Republican Guard, neither the

Nuremberg Tribunal nor the Geneva Conventions provided unequivocal standards condemning civilian deaths in war. As the chief prosecutor at Nuremberg, General Telford Taylor, noted, the Nuremberg (and Tokyo) judicial precedents would not have prohibited the aerial bombardment of North Vietnam, either.[3] Ignoring any distinction between civilians and combatants, American planes dropped thousands of antipersonnel bombs, each releasing several hundred pellets to kill or wound all living creatures within two-thirds of a square mile—even in the most densely populated parts of North Vietnam. In 1966, 25 provincial cities were bombed—six of which were completely razed. The 16,000 inhabitants of Dong Hoi were bombed 396 times, including 160 night attacks. Of the 110 district centers, 72 were bombed, 12 were left in ruins and 25 entirely destroyed.

The killing of civilians and the war against terrorism—are these the same thing? How can we trust the US government's promises of a better life for the countries it occupies by force? While at the same terrorizing or backing terrorists in Nicaragua, Brazil, Uruguay, Cuba, Guatemala, Indonesia, East Timor, Zaire, Angola and South Africa. With civilian deaths in warfare whitewashed as "collateral damage"? And providing sanctuary for the Miami Cuban "refugee" terror network? The U.S. has even provided sanctuary for terrorists fleeing Vietnam, El Salvador, Haiti, and Nazi Germany.

Unquestionably, the terrorists who targeted civilians on 9/11 committed a crime against humanity.

---

3 Taylor, General Telford. 1970. *Nuremberg and Vietnam: An American Tragedy*. New York: Times Books.

Nevertheless, given Nuremberg, Vietnam, and the thousands who died directly and indirectly from bombing the only pharmaceutical plant in Somalia, the legitimacy of a "war against terrorism" should never be taken for granted.

MANUFACTURING "WAR"

The justifications for President George W. Bush's declarations of war were bizarre. The invasion of Afghanistan and Iraq (as we will indicate in a coming chapter) had little or nothing to do with policies deliberately supported by their governments. In fact, 15 of the 19 terrorists who carried out the Twin Towers attack were Saudi Arabians, three were Egyptians or from the United Arab Emirates. Another was Lebanese.

Nevertheless, Bush declared war against Afghanistan after equating al-Qaeda's attack with the Japanese attack on Pearl Harbor. He also declared that invading Afghanistan would be a *preemptive* strike for peace. With regard to Iraq, he claimed that an invasion would terminate a diabolical dictator whose weapons of mass destruction endangered the world's greatest military power.[4] *But Hussein did not possess weapons of mass destruction.* In 2002, Count Hans von Sponeck (a former UN under-secretary general as well as a UN coordinator in Iraq) and

---

4 William Rivers Pitt with Scott Ritter, 2002. *War on Iraq: What Team Bush Doesn't Want You to Know.* New York: Context Books. Pitt (p. 9) notes Hussein is "a secular leader who has worked for years to crush fundamentalist Islam within Iraq, and if he were to give weapons of any kind to Al Qaeda, they would turn it on him."

Scott Ritter (the UN's chief weapons inspector) had said that the US was lying about Iraq's weapons program. Ritter insisted the previous inspection program destroyed most of Iraq's mass-destruction weapons and he doubted Saddam could have rebuilt his stocks this soon. Other notables, such as Ramsey Clark, a former US Attorney General, observed that the Gulf War, incessant air attacks and the 10-year embargo had weakened Iraq's military forces, battered its economy and killed a million people. Clark claimed that even though Iraq may not have been completely disarmed, Saddam Hussein could not pose a realistic threat to the US.

Nevertheless, the State Department justified the invasion. On February 5, 2003, Secretary of State Colin Powell addressed the Security Council. He tried to provide evidence that Iraq posed an immediate threat because it had violated the 1991 Security Council Resolutions. But, after scrutinizing these accusations, Dr. Glen Rangwala, a University of Cambridge analyst and lecturer, found reports by UN inspectors that sharply contradicted Powell.[5] In addition, a British government report citing "new intelligence material," praised by Powell, was a humiliation, plagiarized from academic articles, some several years old.

So, who was telling the truth? Bush and Powell? Or von Sponeck, Ritter, Clark and Rangwala? *Someone*

---

5 Dr. Glen Rangwala. February 2003. "Claims and Evaluations of Iraq's Proscribed Weapons." Posted on Traprock Peace Center (traprockpeace.org/weapons). The British report is entitled "Iraq - Its Infrastructure Of Concealment, Deception And Intimidation." See also: Michael White and Brian Whitaker. 2003 "British Intelligence lifted from academic articles." *The Guardian*. Feb.7

was lying. And, because of what it foreshadowed, it was a *Big* Lie—comparable to that uttered by Hermann Goering, the Prussian Minister of the Interior following the Reichstag fire. Hitler exploited a terroristic act of arson to justify the annihilation of its political opposition—the republican defenders of the Weimar Republic and the social democrats, communists and labor leaders.

In a similar spirit, Bush lied in order to carry out the biggest oil-and-power grab in recent history.[6] His ultimate goal was the expansion and supremacy of the American Empire. But his lies were not merely instigated by imperial aims. His cynical exploitation of popular fears over an "endless war against terrorism," "weapons of mass destruction," and an "axis of evil" led to the greatest plundering of public revenues in the history of our own country. This looting represented a class war for which ordinary Americans and their children will pay dearly for decades to come. And if we were right about the Bush government's goals, there were other "weapons" the American public should have been concerned about and these were *weapons of mass repression* in order to suppress Americans who spoke out and took to the streets to stop Bush's *putsch* to reorder the world.

Yet, despite our concerns, we never expected an unprecedented expansion and reorganization of the *domestic apparatus* for producing these weapons. The Democrats won the 2008 election and attempts to shrink the American *Apparat* and imperial aims— by September 2010—were largely unsuccessful. De-

---

6 Michael T. Klare. October 1 2002. "Oiling the Wheels of War." AlterNet.org. Consider, also, the administration's inability to find credible evidence of Iraq weapons of mass destruction.

spite campaign promises, President Barack Obama's administration continued the wars in Afghanistan and Iraq and expanded their scope. In addition, some of his decrees have activated the repressive policies introduced during the previous administration. Despite his rather limited success in revitalizing or introducing welfare-state policies, the gaps between Obama's demagogic rhetoric and actual practice suggested that it was being controlled by systemic forces that overrode the professed intentions of top officials.

These forces will be described in the following chapters.

1 I Weapons of Mass Repression

"The rightward shift of political power as a result of the 1980 presidential election has sharpened the prospects... for a revival of domestic intelligence structures and operations."

—Frank J. Donner,
The Age of Surveillance, 1981[7]

INFOTECH & WEAPONS OF MASS REPRESSION

Many Americans know that the Bush administration lied about Iraq's weapons of mass destruction. But they were not aware until recently of its unshakable efforts to convert information technology into weapons of *mass repression.* To show

---

7 Frank J. Donner. 1981. *The Age of Surveillance: The Aims and Methods of America's Political Intelligence System.* New York: Vintage Books Edition, p. ix.

how harmful this technology can be, we should recall how it helped the German fascists identify, imprison, and slaughter millions of Jews, Gypsies, social democrats, communists, labor leaders, homosexuals, Jehovah Witnesses, and other pacifists as well as physically and mentally handicapped individuals.[8]

Instrumental in this genocidal agenda was information technology originally dependent upon primitive but powerful data-processing equipment. Data was keypunched onto Hollerith cards, then sorted and collated with machines first developed by IBM for census tabulations and corporate purposes. In 1927, IBM used its Hollerith procedures to assist a racist, eugenic American research project that espoused sterilization of "inferior races" and "eugenically impaired" individuals. To confirm its theories "scientifically," the project wanted to estimate what were considered racially determined characteristics (*e.g.*, cranial size and IQ scores) and "eugenic" attributes (*e.g.*, alcoholism and epilepsy) of thousands of individuals.[9]

Then, during the Thirties and Forties, the German IBM subsidiary, Deutsche Hollerith Maschinen Gesellschaft (DEHOMAG) used this technology to serve the Nazi regime's census bureau, armed forces, factories, railroads, concentration camps, and other agencies.[10] According to Edwin Black, the author of

---

8 Missaglia's lithograph "Fascismo Assassino" (i.e., "Fascism is the Assassin") was purchased in Milano in 1974.

9 For a description of this Eugenics project, see Edwin Black. 2003. The War Against the Weak. New York: Four Walls Eight Windows, pp. 289-91.

10 European subsidiaries located in conquered or so-called "neutral"

IBM and the Holocaust: The Strategic Alliance Between Nazi Germany and America's Most Powerful Corporation, IBM maintained DEHOMAG during the Thirties.[11] Throughout the war, it provided covert support for DEHOMAG through subsidiaries in neutral countries.

Following the trail of IBM memos and FBI, State Department, and American military and German government files, Black discovered that IBM data processing equipment made a dramatic difference in the numbers of Jews whose property the Gestapo seized and either killed outright or sent east to be starved, gassed, enslaved, and worked to death in factories and concentration camps. In Holland, for example, IBM equipment helped the Germans create a diabolically efficient killing machine. Jewish quotas were established with the aid of the data-processing equipment and the overwhelming majority of Jews in that country were rapidly identified, rounded up, and sent to death camps.[12]

In France, however, this technology was sabotaged. The Germans had appointed Rene Carmille administrator of the French statistical service. Carmille—unbeknownst to the German authorities—was a leader in the underground resistance movement. He sabotaged the German attempt to develop

---

countries, including France, Holland, Norway, Belgium, Austria, Poland, Italy, Bulgaria, Yugoslavia, Czechoslovakia, Sweden, Switzerland, and Spain also provided support.

11 Edwin Black. 2001. *IBM and the Holocaust: The Strategic Alliance Between Nazi Germany and America's Most Powerful Corporation.* New York: Crown Publishers.

12 All occupied countries (and their concentration camps) had this equipment.

a database comparable to Holland's and instead used its files for the resistance, generating databases identifying men whose occupational skills and military backgrounds enhanced the struggle against the German forces. His work, for instance, enabled the Free French to mobilize the resistance against the Germans in Algeria virtually overnight.

At the cost of his own life, Carmille saved the lives of tens of thousands of Jews in France. When the Gestapo finally discovered that his department had defied their directives, Carmille was arrested, tortured by Klaus Barbie, the infamous *Butcher of Lyon*, and sent to Dachau, where he perished.

Black reports:

> Of an estimated 140,000 Dutch Jews, more than 107,000 were deported [to concentration camps], and of those 102,000 were murdered – a death ratio of approximately 73 percent.

> Of an estimated 300,000 to 350,000 Jews living in France, both zones, about 85,000 were deported – of these barely 3,000 survived. The death ratio [of the French Jews] was approximately 25 percent.[13]

It is important to note that the German fascists' deadly policies and tactics were nearly matched by events in the US government's history, dating back to the people who settled our country. In the 19th century, the US military launched genocidal attacks against Native Americans. Such attacks were also repeatedly conducted by civilian formations, in hunts

---

13 See Black, op. cit., p. 332.

organized and financed by groups of white settlers. In pogrom-like attacks, Native Americans were killed and scalped regardless of their age or gender.[14]

But there were, of course, historical differences that distinguish Nazi Germany from the settling of North America. Native Americans fought back against the plunderers, resisting the exploitation of their lands and natural resources. The settler's attacks did not attempt to rid the world of a 'race' that spawned *worldwide* conspiracies. In Nazi dogma, killing Jews meant an end to Bolshevism, democratic egalitarianism and the corruption of the Aryan race.[15]

Significantly, the genocidal slaughter of Native Americans primarily took place most violently in the 18th and 19th centuries. Thus, in regard to employment of information technology for political repression and genocide, the Nazi regime represents the most important if not sole historical precursor.

THE UNITED STATES

Although Hitler's crimes were perpetrated more than a half-century ago, the files held by the FBI, believe it or not, still contained Nazi allegations about German immigrants. Take, for instance, the FBI file

---

14 See, for instance, the chapter, Episodes in Extermination (pp. 56-78) in Theodora Kroeber's (1969) *Ishi in Two Worlds: A Biography of the Last Wild Indian in North America*. Berkeley: University of California Press.

15 Adolph Hitler. 1939. *Mein Kampf*. New York: Hurst and Blackett Ltd. For examples, see Chapter XI, Race and People and Chapter VII, The Conflict with the Red Forces.

on Albert Einstein. The FBI hounded Einstein because he was a socialist and anti-fascist who had publicly urged individuals subpoenaed by the House Un-American Activities Committee (HUAC) to invoke their First Amendment rights and refuse to testify. Angered by Einstein's anti-fascism, J. Edgar Hoover and his agents tapped Einstein's phone and read his mail. They shadowed him at public events. They filled his file with stories about his connections with communist conspirators that were supplied by raving anti-Semites, con-men, and lunatics. They even stuffed his file with false allegations taken from the Gestapo's infamous "Jewish Desk" and the Thirties pro-Nazi German press.[16]

The FBI had also hounded Paul Robeson and Martin Luther King—stuffing their files with rumors, gossip, and lies. And who knows how much bullshit can be found in the FBI files of 10 million other Americans? Of course, the government did not use the FBI files to round up millions of people and gas them. But the files were still employed as weapons of mass repression. During the so-called "McCarthy period," initiated by Truman's administration, these files influenced job loss, blacklisting, family hardship, forced isolation, humiliation, and suicide.

The files helped the FBI undermine democracy. They provided a database for another weapon—the undercover war against the American people—officially designated as the Counter Intelligence Program (COINTELPRO). Frank Donner's classic, *The Age of*

---

16 Fred Jerome. 2002. *The Einstein File: J. Edgar Hoover's Secret War Against the World's Most Famous Scientist*. New York: St. Martin's Press, p. xvi. Einstein's opposition to Hitler and Franco's fascist regime especially angered Hoover.

Surveillance, was based upon his long experience as a Director of the ACLU's Project on Political Surveillance and describes the endless number of "dirty tricks" and "black bag" operations conducted throughout the Fifties, Sixties, and Seventies by government agencies. Affiliation with the FBI, CIA, IRS, and military-intelligence agencies enabled agents to get away with slandering political dissenters, the forging of their signatures, the breaking-up and harassing of their families. The list of black ops against law-abiding but dissenting Americans involved burglarizing their homes and offices, tapping their phones, instigating loss of their employment, disrupting political demonstrations, and encouraging unlawful arrests and unwarranted IRS audits.

In the cases of Fred Hampton, Mark Clark, and other African-Americans, 28 people were killed in an 18-month period during an assault against the Black Panther Party.[17] In addition to socialists, communists, civil rights workers, Native American organizations, and the Black Panther Party, COINTELPRO aimed at repressing anyone who was actively opposed to the unjust war in Vietnam in which more than 58,000 American troops were killed, 153,000 wounded and over *two million* Vietnamese slaughtered.

Of course despite their enormity, even these egre-

---

17 Regarding FBI and police complicity in murders of Black Panther leaders, see Donner, op cit, pp. 221-232. (The estimate of deaths can be found on p. 231.) Also, see Donner. 1990. *Protectors of Privilege: Red Squads and Political Repression in Urban America.* Berkeley: University of California. Also, Noam Chomsky. 1976. *COINTELPRO: The FBI's Secret War on Political Freedom.* New York: Monad Press; and Brian Glick. 1989. *War at Home.* Boston: South End Press.

gious abuses of power do not place the US' use of weapons of mass repression in the same league as Nazi Germany's 12-year Gotterdammerung. But they *do* justify a comparison that makes these weapons a paradoxical facet of American political reality.

To explain, the US government is not the entity idealized in public school civics classes. Like Janus, the Roman God of gateways and exits, the Statue of Liberty, the gateway to the US signals a vista of democratic spirits and American dreams. But this seascape enters upon shores flooded by tides of political repression. The US government is a Janus-faced institution, concurrently incorporating the highly touted *Democratic* and incipient *Neofascist* States.

There was a temple to Janus in ancient Rome. When its doors were closed, it signified that Rome was at peace. When open, Rome was at war!

Two-faced head of Janus, Vatican museum, Rome.
Photo: Loudon Dodd, Wikipedia (CC-BY-SA 3.0)

2 | Searching for Parallels

'Fascism is on the march today in America. Millionaires are marching to the tune. It will come in this country unless a strong defense is set up by all liberal and progressive forces. . . A clique of US industrialists is hell-bent to bring a fascist state to supplant our democratic government, and is working closely with the fascist regime in Germany and Italy. Aboard ship a prominent executive of one of America's largest financial corporations told me point blank that if the progressive trend of the Roosevelt administration continued, he would be ready to take definite action to bring fascism to America.' —William Dodd, US Ambassador to Germany, 1938

CONTEMPLATING PARALLELS

What forces shore up the dark side of our Janus-faced government at the expense of the democratic side? How do modern politicians get their power to oppress millions of American citizens? For answers, writers understandably use German, Italian, or Japanese fascism as benchmarks.[18] They search for "parallels" (or similarities) with classical fascism to reckon whether the US is headed in the same direction.

In 2003, for instance, Bernard Weiner, co-editor of the thoughtful website, *The Crisis Papers*, wrote, "If my email is any indication, a goodly number of folks wonder if they're living in America in 2003 or Germany in 1933." To show that his email respondents have their feet on the ground, Weiner listed the following parallels between current conditions and the conditions supporting Hitler's appointment as Reich Chancellor:

> All this emphasis on nationalism, the militarization of society, identifying 'The Leader' as the nation, a constant state of fear and anxiety heightened by the authorities, repressive laws that shred constitutional guarantees of due process, wars of aggression launched on weaker nations, the desire to assume global domination, the merging of corporate and governmental interests, vast mass-media propaganda campaigns, a populace that tends to believe the slogans and lies it's fed without asking too many questions, a timid opposition that barely contests the administration's reckless adventurism abroad and police-state policies at home, etc. etc.[19]

18 Bertram Gross. 1980. *Friendly Fascism: The New Face of Power in America*. New York: Boston. (pp. xiff.)

19 Bernard Weiner. June 9 2003. "Germany in 1933: The Easy Slide

Weiner admits,

> The parallels are not exact, of course; America in 2003 and Germany seventy years earlier are not the same, and Bush certainly is not Adolph Hitler. But there are enough disquieting similarities in the two periods at least to see what we can learn—cautionary tales, as it were—and then figure out what to do with our knowledge.

Therefore, before figuring out what to do, we should recognize that numerous parallels can be found and that some have significant strategic importance when estimating the factors that jump-start a fascist regime. Also, the parallels themselves may have similar causes. For example, leaders of imperialist nations have always employed lies, slogans, and propaganda campaigns to get support for their policies. Nationalism, militarization, wars of aggression, and desires for global domination characterize imperialist nations as well. Millions of ordinary Germans were harnessed by Orwellian "Newspeak"—by patriotic calls to duty and the promise of rich rewards from the conquest of European, Russian, and African nations. But their role in the chain of events leading to fascism also begs the question of *causal priority*. For instance, how and under what conditions did so many Germans acquire their devotion to fascist leaders? Did the Great Depression make millions of unemployed men and women vote for Hitler because he promised to get them jobs that would put ham, sauerkraut, and bread on their families' tables?

Into Fascism." *The Crisis Papers*. (https://crisispapers.org/Editorials/germany-1933.htm.) The original paragraph was in italics.

Imperialism itself may be a necessary condition for the development of fascism in industrialized nations but it is certainly not sufficient. Great Britain, France, and the US have upheld imperialist policies and fascism abroad without capitulating to fascism at home. What strategies made the difference in Germany or Italy?[20]

Since full-blown fascism may be preceded by *incipient* fascism, *proto*-fascism or even *creeping* fascism, the search for parallels is further complicated by distinct phases in fascism's rise. Identifying a formative phase is especially difficult because it may evolve gradually and exhibit *transitional* characteristics. It may include influential democratic institutions inherited from the past as well as fascistic changes heralding the future. Germany exhibited these paradoxical characteristics for more than a decade before Hitler became Reich Chancellor and forcibly consolidated his fascist regime virtually overnight.

Yet, despite its bewildering conditions, identifying a formative period is doable because surveillance programs, paramilitary agencies, supportive class alliances, and other prerequisites of fully developed fascism surface during a formative period. Furthermore, incipient fascist developments during this period can be stopped cold if, among other things, antifascist movements and officials are unified and strong enough to prevent the exploitation of condi-

---

20 Our historical account concentrates on Germany although the rise of fascism in Italy provided a blueprint for German fascists. Mussolini's storm troopers did not at first view Jews as an enemy, but they suppressed the left and employed terror to seize power.

tions comparable to those that triggered fascism in Germany.

For instance, let us describe the conditions that blocked a fascist attempt to overthrow the US government yet succeeded in jump-starting fascism in Germany.

Plot to Overthrow FDR

In the same year Hitler seized power in Germany, representatives of a group of wealthy American fascists approached the most decorated Marine in US history, Major General Smedley Darlington Butler, and asked him to stage an American *coup d'état*. But he refused to cooperate and exposed their attempt to overthrow the U.S. government. Richard Sanders, editor of a Canadian journal published by the Coalition to Oppose the Arms Trade, recalls that a group of industrialists and bankers approached Gen. Butler because

> [T]hey hated US President Franklin D. Roosevelt with a passion, and saw his "New Deal" policies as the start of a communist takeover that threatened their interests. FDR even had the temerity to announce that the US would stop using its military to interfere in Latin American affairs! Wall Street's plutocrats were aghast! They had long been accustomed to wielding tremendous control over the government's economic policies, including the use of US forces to protect their precious foreign investments. Because of Butler's steadfast military role in upholding US business interests

abroad, the plotters mistakenly thought they
could recruit him to muster a "super-army" of
veterans to use as pawns in their plan to subjugate or, if necessary, eliminate FDR.[21]

Butler identified the conspirators while testifying
in 1934 before the McCormack-Dickstein subcommittee of the House Committee on Un-American
Activities (HUAC). Among the plotters was Grayson
Murphy, a director of Goodyear, Bethlehem Steel,
and J.P. Morgan banks. He had financed the formation of the American Legion after World War I in order to repress organized labor and left-wing
Americans. John W. Davis, a former Democratic
candidate for president of the United States and a senior attorney for J.P. Morgan and Company, was
also included. Yet another member was Al Smith, a
former New York governor who hated FDR. In addition to being a Democratic Party leader, Smith was a
Co-Director of the American Liberty League, a fascist
organization, financed by right-wing industrialist
Irenee Du Pont.

Butler also told the HUAC subcommittee that the
conspirators' planned to use American Legionnaires

---

21 Richard Sanders. 2004. "John Spivak." March (#53) *Press for
Conversion!* Online publication from The Coalition to Oppose the
Arms Trade (COAT).
http://coat.ncf.ca/our_magazine/links/53/newmasses.html
Sanders' source is found in his reprinting of:
(1) Spivak, John. 1935. "Wall Street's Fascist Conspiracy:
Testimony that the Dickstein MacCormack Committee
Suppressed." *New Masses*. January 29.
[https://archive.org/details/WallStreetsFascistConspiracyTestimony
ThatTheDicksteinMaccormack | Accessed March 12, 2016.]
(2) Spivak, John. 1935. "Wall Street's Fascist Conspiracy: Morgan
Pulls the Strings." *New Masses*. February 5, 1935.

and the American Liberty League to both provide a fascist veterans' army and coordinate popular support. This plan was based on recommendations from one of the plotters—who had traveled to Europe to study the role of veterans in German, Italian and French fascist movements. The plotter found that veterans formed the backbone of all of these movements but the organization that seemed to fit the American requirements best was a right-wing cadre of French "super-soldiers." This cadre was known as the Croix de Feu, which in 1934 assisted a failed attempt to overthrow the French government.

Predictably, the infamous House Committee tried to cover up the conspiracy by editing the proceedings and suppressing most of Butler's testimony under the guise of protecting national security. The Committee never questioned, arrested, or charged the fascist conspirators with treason. It even deleted the names of the bankers and corporate executives identified by Butler's testimony in its report!

Information supplied by Gen. Butler had indicated that the conspirators included Irenee DuPont, E. Roland Harriman, William Randolph Hearst, Samuel Pryor, Max Warburg, and various directors of J.P. Morgan banking interests. The conspirators also included Prescott S. Bush, G.W. Bush's paternal grandfather, and George Herbert Walker, Bush's maternal grandfather.

The plotters opposed anti-fascist movements in America and provided political support, easy credit, and investment capital for Nazi industrialists. Citing the *Trading with the Enemy Act*, the U.S. government, for instance, seized the Union Banking Corporation's stock ten months after the Second World War began because it fronted for the *Vereinigte Stahlwerke* (German Steel Trust) led by Fritz Thyssen and his two brothers. (All of this stock was owned by Prescott Bush, E. R. Harriman, three Nazi executives, and two other associates of Bush.) In addition, Samuel Pryor who had helped Bush found Union Banking was chairman of Remington Arms. Senate arms-traffic investigators probed Remington after it negotiated a cartel agreement on explosives with the Nazi firm I.G. Farben. They found that Pryor had supplied a great number of Thompson submachine guns and revolvers to Hitler's *Brownshirts*.

Outraged by the subcommittee's refusal to include the members of the conspiracy in its report, Butler went on national radio to expose the committee. A sympathetic reporter from the *Philadelphia Herald*, Paul Comly French, was one of the few mainstream journalists to help Butler.[22] French told the subcommittee that he had interviewed one of the conspirators who said, "We might go along with Roosevelt and then do with him what Mussolini did with the King of Italy."

In addition, John Spivak, a reporter from the so-

---

22 Butler turned to the editor of the *Philadelphia Herald* who had given supportive coverage to his efforts to smash illegal drinking and to expose political corruption. Paul Comly French was a reporter enlisted to interview Butler and to write an article exposing Butler's testimony to the McCormick-Dickstein House Committee on Un-American Activities. Public Statement on Preliminary findings of HUAC, November 24, 1934, released by the McCormick-Dickstein Subcommittee. (WIKISOURCE has posted a copy of this statement online.)

cialist magazine *New Masses*, interviewed Butler and helped him put the coup plotters' names on the public record.[23] But the corporate media generally ignored the story or ridiculed him. (George Seldes, a famous anti-fascist journalist, foreign correspondent and media critic, described the media's cover-up of the Wall Street plot in his book *1000 Americans*.)[24]

FDR was a progressive but he was not a saint. He supported racist Nativists. He uprooted and interned in detention camps more than one hundred thousand Japanese immigrants and Japanese Americans. He refused to allow thousands of Jews who were escaping the Nazis from emigrating to the US. He also backed Dixiecrats and was devoted to safeguarding America's imperial designs in order to save capitalism. Yet FDR recognized that the government had to accommodate itself to the explosive rise of organized labor and to working-class demands for welfare-state policies, such as social security and full-employment programs, during the greatest economic crisis America had ever experienced.

Furthermore, to curb harmful and corrupt corporate practices, FDR reinforced the Food and Drug Administration and created a number of regulatory agencies such as the Securities and Exchange Commission. Although Butler informed Roosevelt to pre-

23 Spivak wrote two important articles that exposed the 1930's plot against President Roosevelt. (See footnote 21.) These articles are available as PDF files on the Coalition to Oppose the Arms Trade website: http://coat.ncf.ca/our_magazine/links/53/newmasses.html | To expose Nazi and anti-Semitic movements in America, he wrote other articles for the *New Masses*. See, for instance, Spivak's summary of the fascist plot in "The Plot and the Main Players."

24 George Seldes. 1947. *1000 Americans*. New York: Boni & Gaer.

vent the coup, the Wall Street conspirators continued their collusion to get rid of FDR and smash his "New Deal."

A 1936 letter to Roosevelt by William Dodd, the US Ambassador to Germany, refers to additional efforts to regain control of the White House. Dodd wrote,

> A clique of US industrialists is hell-bent to bring a fascist state to supplant our democratic government and is working closely with the fascist regime in Germany and Italy. I have had plenty of opportunity in my post in Berlin to witness how close some of our American ruling families are to the Nazi regime...A prominent executive of one of the largest corporations told me point blank that he would be ready to take definite action to bring fascism into America if President Roosevelt continued his progressive policies. Certain American industrialists had a great deal to do with bringing fascist regimes into being in both Germany and Italy. They extended aid to help fascism occupy the seat of power, and they are helping to keep it there. Propagandists for fascist groups try to dismiss the fascist scare. We should be aware of the symptoms. When industrialists ignore laws designed for social and economic progress they will seek recourse to a fascist state when the institutions of our government compel them to comply with the provisions.[25]

---

25 Higham, Charles. 1983. *Trading with the Enemy*, New York: Barnes & Noble, p.162.

STATE WITHIN A STATE

The search for parallels has traditionally focused on factors contributing to the rise of fascism in Italy or Germany. As a result, "classical" fascism has been repeatedly linked to dozens of causal factors and defining characteristics. Some experts justifiably associate it with Big Lies and the annihilation of socialist movements.

Hitler's party, for instance, called itself the National Socialist Workers Party and it criticized capitalism—even though its members battled the Social Democrat *paramilitary force* (the *Reichsbanner*) and the Communist Red Front Fighter's League (the *Rote Front*) in the streets of Berlin. Mussolini, too, at first gave lip service to socialist aims and speechified in favor of the great 1919 strike in Milan. But then, flipping from revolution to counterrevolution, he imprisoned trade-union leaders and abolished all socialist parties. Mussolini and Hitler, despite their anti-capitalist rhetoric, discredited social democrats and communists and cynically accepted money and support from capitalists who controlled heavy industries, munitions firms and financial institutions.

Jacque Delarue, a member of the French *Sûreté Nationale* who had been in the resistance during the Second World War,[26] emphasizes the role of anti-Semitism in Germany. Hitler declared that Jewish liberals and leftists had betrayed Germany during

---

26 Jacques Delarue. 1964. *The Gestapo: A History of Horror*. New York: Dell Publishing, pp. 14-15. Delarue was a member of the Direction de la Sûreté National in Paris and in charge of the liquidation of Occupation records in France.

the First World War and stabbed its "indomitable" armed forces in the back. His party blamed Jewish bankers for hyperinflation and "Jewish Woolworths" for massive numbers of bankrupt shopkeepers, self-employed artisans, impoverished farmers, and unemployed workers. Fascist movements throughout Europe also used anti-Semitism to justify their criminal policies.

But anti-Semitism was not adopted as the only justification for fascism. During the Great Depression, right-wing populism also attracted millions of Germans to the Nazi Party. And throughout the world, fascist movements exploited indigenous storehouses of racial and ethnic stereotypes to justify attempts to overcome their governments.[27]

In addition, most Americans are not fully aware of the degree to which paramilitary terrorism ensured popular support and Hitler's seizure of power—even though it is hard to believe that the German Officer Corps allowed Hitler's storm troopers to terrorize and kill people merely because they had swallowed his propaganda or submitted to civilian rule. But why did the *Reichswehr*—the German army—refrain from crushing the Brownshirts when they terrorized people in order to influence the outcome of the Weimar Republic's final election? Why did they tolerate the dissolution of the German parliament and Hitler's ascension to power?

---

27 Kurt Patzold. 1989. "Terror and Demagoguery in the Consolidation of the Fascist Dictatorship in Germany, 1933-34." In Michael Dobkowski and Isidor Wallimann. 1989. *Radical Perspectives on the Rise of Fascism in Germany, 1919-1945*. New York: Monthly Review Press, pp. 231-246.

The answer is simple: The army was told to stand down by a class coalition that included semi-feudal agribusinesses, largely owned by Prussian *Junkers* who were aristocratic landowners with great political power. Feudal serfs no longer produced the crops possessed by these aristocrats; instead, their wealth was largely based on paid labor, tenant farmers, and the sale of agrarian commodities. Also, the industrial revolution had occurred in Germany much later than Western Europe and, although the monarchy had been overthrown in 1918 and replaced by the Republic, the *Junkers* remained a distinct hereditary "status group."

These aristocrats controlled the German Officer Corps and had privileged access to the highest positions in government. A critical mass within the Corps itself represented a state within a state. Every crucial step toward fascism required its imprimatur. In fact, the Officer Corps had existed to fulfill imperial dreams and it contained a tight network whose monarchist leanings and loyalties favored the rebirth of a German imperial state. This network never accepted the Weimar Republic and it turned to the right-wing enemies of the Republic to regain its power and status.

Unlike American officers such as Butler—whose actions stopped the plotters in their tracks—leading members of the German Officer Corps played a very different role.

Corporate Capital

During the years leading up to the decisive 1933–1934 period—when Hitler was given the power to dissolve the Weimar Republic's parliament—President Paul von Hindenburg, Chancellor Franz von Papen, Chancellor Kurt von Schleicher, and other aristocrats who had been members of the Officer Corps enacted a tragedy that helped lower the Republic's coffin into the grave. Yet, as the coffin descended, the aristocracy, the captains of basic industries, and their associates—including munitions makers and financiers—stood solemnly beside the grave and winked conspiratorially.

Evidence presented at Nuremberg identified some of the industrialists and financiers. On January 30, 1933, Hindenburg appointed Hitler as Chancellor and secret documents captured by the Allies revealed that Hitler spoke to these powerful men a month later. On this occasion, Dr. Hjalmar Schacht, former president of the *Reichsbank*, acted as host—while Goering and Hitler informed Gustav Krupp von Bohlen und Halbach, the munitions king, Albert Voegler, head of Germany's United Steel Works, Carl Bosch and George von Schnitzler of I. G. Farben, and others—that a dictatorship would provide a way out of the Great Depression. At the meeting, Hitler chillingly declared:

> Private enterprise cannot be maintained in the age of democracy; it is conceivable only if the people have a sound idea of authority and personality . . . All the worldly goods we possess we owe to the struggle of the chosen . . . We

must not forget that all the benefits of culture must be introduced more or less with an iron fist.

Hitler vowed to annihilate "the Marxists"—the archenemies of capitalism. He promised to revitalize the armed forces as well. He threatened to stay in power *by force* if his Party did not win enough votes in a coming election.

He kept his word.

Schacht, testifying in the dock at Nuremberg, recalled that Goering had collected millions after he asked for contributions to the Nazi Party. Also, after examining the minutes of the meeting, William L. Shirer, the celebrated American foreign correspondent, found that the guests responded enthusiastically to Hitler's promise to end democracy, disarmament, and the "infernal [parliamentary] elections."[28] Fritz Thyssen, a foremost iron-and-steel magnate, wrote later in *I Paid Hitler* that even the munitions baron Krupp von Bohlen und Halbach, who had previously opposed Hitler, turned into a "super-Nazi" when Hitler became Chancellor.[29]

Germany was the second-largest industrial power in the world, but its political landscape during the Great Depression was packed with bomb craters and minefields. Millions had lost their jobs. Agricultural prices had plummeted. Farmers, shopkeepers and self-employed craftsmen went bankrupt—and major industrialists and financiers found their profits van-

28 Shirer, William L. . 1959. *The Rise and Fall of the Third Reich: A History of Nazi Germany*. New York: Simon and Shuster.

29 Thyssen, Fritz. 1941. *I Paid Hitler*. New York: Farrar & Reinhardt, pp. 107–108.

ishing. Hitler promised policies that would ensure profits, provide jobs, and end the Depression.

Granted, the industrial magnates and financiers risked some of their independence by backing Hitler. However, at the end of World War II, most of them walked away from the Depression and over 50-million graves with their corporations intact and money in their pockets.

In later chapters parallels will be drawn between the economic interests underlying Hitler's wars of aggression and the American "war on terrorism."

WELFARE STATE

Toward the end of the 19th century, Chancellor Otto von Bismarck after failing to suppress the Social Democratic Workers Party adopted unprecedented domestic policies. To regain working class support and political stability, he co-opted the part of its socialist platform that advocated the creation of an officially supported safety net for working class citizens. Eventually, governments assuming similar responsibilities for citizens' welfare, for their employment, social security, health care, and education, among others, became known as "Welfare States."

German welfare-state policies were maintained to the present day. In addition, the German labor movement during the Twenties was possibly the largest in the world and, from 1924 to 1928, it supported welfare-state policies advanced by coalitions of Center parties and Social Democrats. But the price that it had requested for its support was a

Sozialpolitik aimed at favorable wage settlements, workers' compensation, and other costly welfare-state policies that improved working-class living standards.[30]

According to the brilliant historian David Abraham, the class coalitions supporting the Weimar Republic's welfare-state policies prior to the Great Depression included organized labor on one hand, and the dynamic export and manufacturing industries on the other.[31] However, during the Great Depression, the coalitions unraveled. Simultaneously, taxes, protectionism, and economic concessions achieved by trade unions became particularly divisive issues. For example, manipulated by large landowners and Nazi demagogues, small farmers and small business owners raged at having to pay taxes for programs that appeared to benefit urban workers only. Also, while urban workers supported the import of inexpensive food from surrounding countries like Poland, farmers wanted tariffs and subsidies because the imports were driving them into bankruptcy.

Basic industry—especially iron, steel, and coal industries in the Ruhr Valley—opposed the Weimar Republic for additional reasons. First, the industrialists and financiers controlling these industries believed that reducing costly welfare-state programs and cutting wages would lower their taxes and pro-

---

30 Abraham, David. 1986. *The Collapse of the Weimar Republic: Political Economy and Crisis.* (Second Edition) New York: Holmes & Mercer.

31 See David Abraham, op. cit., Chapter Six, "In Search of a Viable Bloc."

duction costs, thereby increasing industry's revenues. (In fact, these German firms engaged in a feeding frenzy for state contracts after Hitler seized power.) Second, eliminating the parliamentary system and free elections that supported the welfare state and organized labor promised to end the political leverage exerted by socialists as well as centrists on national policies.

Parliaments are vehicles through which ruling classes legitimate their exploitative relationships; but they also provide an avenue by which working classes can defend their particular interests. The industrialists and landowners were determined to close this avenue off. As a result, the historical adversaries of fascism were by no means limited to social democrats and communists. They also included liberals and conservatives who epitomized the intellectual and republican principles of the Enlightenment.

TRAITOR BAITING

Eradicating the German parliament blocked legislative opposition from the parties that would have resisted preparations for the Second World War. Centrists, Social Democrats, and Communists in 1934 opposed Hitler's plan to subjugate the "inferior races" of Europe and to appropriate *lebensraum* (living space) in the East. And, despite his demagogic call for cooperation with the West against "Judeo-Bolshevism," Germans sharing Hitler's standpoint knew that he would eventually attack France—Germany's traditional enemy.[32]

Millions of Germans were also opposed to another imperial war. The First World War had closed shortly after the German Naval Command in Kiel, realizing that surrender was inevitable, secretly planned a suicide attack against the British Royal Navy. When German sailors at Kiel (and Wilmershaven) discovered the plan, they mutinied and forced the warships to return to their bases. Subsequently, Worker's, Soldiers and Sailor's Councils appeared in Kiel. Within weeks, Councils throughout Germany adopted demands for peace and political reforms and encouraged insurrections in Hamburg, Bremen, Lubeck, and Munich. The Councils finally secured the war's closure. They forced the Kaiser to flee and gave rise to the Weimar Republic.

Of course, the war would have come to a close regardless. The entrance of US armed forces had made German defeat a certainty. Furthermore, the German army's 1918 spring offensive—its final attempt to forestall this defeat—had failed.

Nevertheless, the Officer Corps in 1918 refused to share the blame for losing "their" war. Officers in 1918 politicized the legend of the *Dolchstoss*—the "stab in the back" that brought down the hero Siegfried in Wagner's *Ring*. When the war ended,

---

32 Hitler believed that the French would never abandon the effort to destroy Germany. In *Mein Kampf*, he declared, there must be a "final active reckoning with France...only then will we be able to end the eternal and essentially fruitless struggle between ourselves and France." He added: "Germany actually regards the destruction of France as only a means which will afterward enable her to finally give our people the expansion made possible elsewhere."

they created "educational officers" (*Bildungsof-fiziere*) to inculcate the legend of the *Dolchstoss* within their military units. In their version of the Great War, the Jews, Socialists and Communists were traitors. *They* had betrayed Germany! Among those who became one of these officers was a heroic lance corporal named Adolph Hitler. During the war, Hitler had been awarded five medals, including an Iron Cross for bravery, and had recovered from blindness caused by British chlorine gas.

In later chapters, we will draw parallels between the legend of the *Dolchstoss* and the traitor-baiting perpetrated by the Bush administration and its political supporters in defense of its occupation of Iraq.

THE FREIKORPS

At the beginning of the war, Friedrich Ebert and other leading social democrats had persuaded most of their party delegates to back the monarchy and vote in favor of war appropriations. Demanding continual support for the war, however, eventually split the Social Democratic Party and led to the expulsion in 1915 of left-wing delegates who opposed the war. The delegates at first organized the Independent Social Democratic Party of Germany (USPD). Shortly afterward, they formed the Spartacus League (*Spartakusbund*) with other leftists and left the USPD.

In December 1918, the League was renamed the Communist Party of Germany (KPD). One month later, KPD networks sparked huge demonstrations aimed at destabilizing the Weimar government. The

KPD was accused of attempting to forcibly overthrow the government and its "uprising" was quickly crushed by units of the German army (*Reichswehr*) and free-lance paramilitary units called *Freikorps*.

The use of the army was sanctioned by Ebert, who had become the first Chancellor of the newly formed Weimar Republic.[33] He had had secret conversations with General Wilhelm Groener, who had remained the army's supreme commander, culminating in an agreement to use armed forces against communist insurgents. The agreement included recruiting jobless decommissioned army officers and soldiers who were forming *Freikorps* units to crush left-wing uprisings. Thousands of insurrectionists were murdered or imprisoned. KPD leaders, Karl Liebknecht and Rosa Luxemburg, were arrested. They were assassinated after being released from prison. Liebknecht was shot. A *Freikorps* officer used the butt of his rifle to crush Luxemburg's skull.[34]

Before they smashed the Spartacus uprising, the *Freikorps* had fulfilled similar aims by attacking demonstrations led by organized labor in Berlin. Later, they suppressed communist uprisings in Hamburg, the Ruhr and elsewhere. The *Reichswehr* and Bavarian *Freikorps* abolished the short-lived 'Bavarian Soviet Republic' in Munich. The socialist prime minister of Bavaria was assassinated. (Right-wing terrorists perpetrated more than 83% of almost 400 assassinations of public officials and political leaders taking place between 1919 and 1922.) The

---

33 Ebert was elected President of the Weimar Republic afterward and served until 1925.

34 To finish the job, the SA officer then shot her.

leftist assassins were the only ones given lengthy prison terms and death sentences.

The German army had been drastically downgraded by the terms of surrender and, later, by the Versailles Treaty. Nevertheless, SPD leaders and the Officer Corps (i.e., the "state within a state") secretly sidestepped these terms by arming and supporting the *Freikorps* and urging these privatized units to reinforce the Allies invasion of Russia. They aided the Allied forces in the creation of the *Cordon Sanitaire* in Poland that forcibly quarantined the spread of "Bolshevism."

The Freikorps were supported by the Weimar government for suppressing the left but it regarded the government with contempt. The Freikorps largely consisted of elite units called "storm troopers" because of their ability to break through enemy lines at the head of attacking forces. After the war, these units were dominated by right-wing fanatics who believed that they had put their lives on the line in defense of the fatherland but they had been "stabbed in the back" by the social democrats as well as the communists.

Nigel Jones, an historian, indicates how the Freikorps by militarizing German politics blazed a trail for Hitler and his political coalitions. As Franz Seldte, a Freikorps leader who founded the Stalhelm (Steel-Helmet) fighting league of front-line veterans, declared: "We must fight to get the men into power who will depend on us front soldiers for support—men who will call upon us to smash once and for all these damned revolutionary rats and choke them by sticking their heads into their own shit!"[35]

RIGHT-WING INSURRECTIONS

The Weimar Republic held its first nationwide election for the German parliament (*Reichstag*) in 1919. Although the Communists boycotted the election, the Social Democratic and Independent Socialist Parties got 45% of the vote. The Social Democratic Party, German Democratic Party and the (Catholic) Center Party formed the first coalition government.

But, unlike the peaceful outcomes of American elections, German elections and parliamentary politics did not stop right-wing insurrections. In 1920, *Freikorps* units marched into Berlin to establish a rightwing military dictatorship headed by a politician, Wolfgang Kapp, and a former naval commander, Herman Ehrhardt.

The Kapp Putsch shocked the nation but socialist organizations and labor unions responded immediately. Germany had the largest independent labor movement in Europe, which called for a general strike that paralyzed Berlin. Strikes and massive demonstrations drove the *Freikorp* units sympathizing with Kapp from the nation's municipalities. Fifty-thousand men seized guns and artillery from the armories and formed a "Red Army" in the Ruhr. Armed workers across the country took possession of

---

35 Nigel Jones. 2004. *A History of the Birth of The Nazis: How the Freikorps Blazed a Trail for Hitler*. Revised Paperback Edition. New York: Carol and Graf Publishers. p.120.

post offices, railway stations, and town halls. The monarchist *coup d'état* fell apart and Kapp and his cabinet fled Berlin.

Despite the failed putsch, a second right-wing insurrection occurred in 1923—led this time by Hitler. After the Nazi party was established, *Freikorp* units helped form its paramilitary force, the *Sturmabteilung* (*SA*). (The English equivalent for the *SA* is "Storm Troops", known also via their brown uniforms as "Brownshirts.") In the Twenties and early Thirties, the *SA* was the principal Nazi propaganda agency. Moreover, as prosecutor Colonel Robert Storey observed during the Nuremberg Trials, it also functioned as the Nazi's principle paramilitary agency. "The *SA* was employed as a *terroristic group,*" wrote Storey, "in order to gain for the Nazis possession and control of the streets." Towards this objective, the *SA* beat, terrorized and assassinated political opponents of the Nazi party.[36]

The Hitler-led army of terrorists in 1923 attempted to overthrow the Bavarian provincial government in Munich, in hopes of instigating further insurrections in the Germany's north. But the Weimar government in Berlin ordered Munich police units to open fire against the Nazi paramilitary force when it attempted to take over a military base. After the gunfire ceased, 14 Brownshirts were killed and 100 wounded. Seriously wounded, Hermann Goering—a celebrated fighter pilot and last commander of the famed Richthofen Squadron—fled abroad

---

36 See, for example. *Nuremberg Trial Proceedings.* Volume 4. "Twenty-third Day—Morning Session Wednesday, 19 December 1945." The Avalon Project at Yale Law School p. 135.

until an amnesty was granted.

Captain Ernst Roehm, General Erich Ludendorff, Rudolph Hess, and Heinrich Himmler were also among Hitler's chief accomplices. Although captured, Roehm played a major role in the formation of the *SA* and his connections with the local army garrison enabled him to be freed immediately. Hitler and three accomplices underwent what Delarue calls a "parody of a trial." As they left the courtroom, their supporters cheered and sang the national hymn. In prison Hitler wrote *Mein Kampf* and was released after serving 13 months under very favorable conditions.[37]

Ludendorff—who had marched at Hitler's side in the column of Nazi troops—was acquitted. During the war, Ludendorff had been Chief of Staff under General Paul von Hindenburg, who had won decisive victories over the Russians. Ludendorff had supported the unrestricted submarine warfare that propelled America's entrance into the War and pressured the Kaiser to dismiss officers who favored a negotiated peace settlement. After Germany surrendered, he fled to Sweden where he published works about the *Dolchstoss* legend, claiming that the unbeaten German Army had been stabbed in the back by left-wing politicians. He said that the mutinous Sailors' and Soldiers' Councils had destroyed the army and handed the victorious German fleet over to the enemy.

He declared,

---

37 Delarue says Hitler was treated as a guest. Hitler wrote *Mein Kampf* while he was imprisoned with the help of his cell mate, Rudolph Hess.

> Such was the gratitude of the new homeland to the German soldiers who had bled and died for it in millions. The destruction of Germany's power to defend itself—the work of Germans— was the most tragic crime the world has witnessed![38]

Ludendorff eventually returned to Germany, and was a participant in both the 1920 Kapp Putsch and Hitler's 1923 Munich Putsch. He became one of the first Nazi representatives to the Reichstag.

After the Munich insurrection was crushed, Hitler's party participated in parliamentary and presidential elections. Nigel reports that the Freikorps movement itself divided into two streams. Some of its units were reluctantly absorbed by the *Reichswehr* while others went underground and continued their war "from the shadows against the republic with the methods of terror and murder."[39]

The Nazi's backed-up their electoral tactics with beatings, torture, and assassinations. The sheer magnitude of the terrorism unleashed by the *SA* during this formative period of German fascism has no parallel in current American developments. Does this mean that a fascist regime will never emerge in the US? Perhaps. Still, if American fascism ever moves beyond a formative stage, it will undoubtedly have to rely on American law enforcement, paramilitary, and military forces to suppress its opposition.

---

38 Eric Ludendorff- 1919. *My War Memories, 1914–1918.* London: Hutchinson.

39 Nigel, op.cit. p.202.

3 | Hitler's Terrorism

'I am not so senseless as to want war. We want peace and understanding, nothing else. We want to give our hand to our former enemies ... When has the German people ever broken its word?'

— Adolf Hitler, Berlin, 1933

MILITARY-INDUSTRIAL COMPLEX

In the early Twenties, Germany was plagued by unemployment, poverty, national debt, and hyperinflation. Since it was the second-largest industrial power in the world, the political instability caused by these conditions alarmed the Allied powers.

The plan imposed by the Allies for the repayment of reparations could not be sustained by Germany's deteriorating economy. In 1923, it finally defaulted and, in response, France and Belgium marched into the Ruhr Valley. Since the Ruhr was the heartland of Germany's coal and steel industries, their occupation caused massive inflation and unemployment.

In 1924 Germany was offered the US Dawes Plan, which hastened the withdrawal of French troops from the Ruhr, drastically reduced reparations payments, introduced a new currency, and provided colossal sums to rebuild industry. The stimulus funds were primarily provided by American banks and financiers in the form of investment loans that made Germany somewhat dependent on American finance capital. The Dawes Plan sparked a four-year economic revival accompanied by a huge increase in support for the Social Democratic Party (SPD), the largest in the Reichstag. The Social Democrats also governed Prussia, which included two-thirds of the country's population and the capital, Berlin. The revitalized economy reinvigorated politics-as-usual. In the Reichstag election, the Nazi Party won a mere 12 seats out of 474. Many voters regarded Adolph Hitler as a demented clown.

But the crisis-free years between 1924 and 1929 came to an abrupt end despite the surging profits based on concessions abolishing the eight-hour day, imposed by the Dawes Plan (i.e., American finance capital) and conceded by the SPD and the trade unions. Industrialists as early as 1927 began to complain bitterly about overcapacity, wage concessions, and *welfare-state* costs. Then, in 1929, the German economy collapsed. The inflow of investment capital sharply decreased and German capital as a whole began to experience a devastating squeeze in profits. Timetables required by reparation and foreign-loan payments could not be met. Following the crash on

Wall Street (USA) and the disintegration of world-wide markets, Germany was hit by bank failures, vanished savings, and currency devaluation. Once again, export markets were shattered, millions of workers lost their jobs, and agricultural prices plummeted. Farmers, shopkeepers, and self-employed craftsmen were ruined.

The Social Democratic leadership, ostensibly, had encouraged concessions to corporate interests and participated in parliamentary coalitions because they appeared to offer a peaceful transition to socialist policies and goals. But the economic base of the blocs headed by the aristocracy was hardly affected by SPD policies because the SPD leadership did not fight for agrarian reforms that would have weakened the great landowners (the *Junkers*) and their supporters.[40]

Furthermore, as indicated, the German economy prior to the onset of the Depression had recovered some of its vitality and members of the aristocracy were ready to fight openly for an imperial state. Parliament's decision to fund the construction of *Panzerschiffes*—fast heavily armed and armored dreadnoughts designed to prey on commercial vessels—indicated that the Officer Corps and aristocracy had maintained their ties with iron and steel magnates as well as other robber barons who for almost a decade kept the German military-industrial complex alive.[41]

---

40 An agrarian reform program was part of its platform but never implemented.

41 The government misrepresented their tonnage to slip them by Versailles prohibitions.

Some of these ties were above board and others were kept under wraps. Despite the restrictions imposed by the Versailles Treaty and despite opposition within the parliament, the Officer Corps had stealthily assembled military forces that required government complicity and support from arms producers at each stage of the operation. The Corps dominated, financed, trained, and armed the Freikorps, border patrols, home guards, the *Stalhelm*, the SA, and "patriotic" youth organizations. "Finally," as E. J. Gumbel points out, these military groups "included an array of fanatic terroristic organizations, small in size, but important for their work of political assassination in eliminating first the leaders of the Revolution, then prominent Republicans, and finally the enemies of the illegal rearmament."

Gumbel was a Professor of Statistics at the University of Heidelberg from 1923 to 1932. (After the Second World War he served on the industrial engineering faculty at Columbia University.) His article on clandestine rearmament under the Weimar Republic indicates:

> The League of Nations convention against arms shipments was not ratified by a sufficient number of countries. (The U.S.A. did not do so, for example.) This fate was typical of the fruitless and interminable disarmament negotiations of the 1920s. *By 1929, League of Nations statistics listed Germany as the major arms supplier of thirteen countries.* France and Belgium gave Germany as their chief foreign source. In addition to the discrepancies in the League of Nations statistics themselves— imports and exports reported never balanced—

so much trade was camouflaged under false customs declarations, etc., that estimates range up to five times the reported figure.[42] (Our emphasis)

The large German aircraft of 1925-1935 were actually intended as prototype bombers. In 1930 Germany exported war planes, especially to China for arming rival warlords and for use against the Japanese. During that year the first German tests of rockets and missiles including liquid fuels and solid propellants were made. The government used neutral banks to make loans that enabled German magnates to initiate the construction of the German U-Boat fleet in Holland. After the Nazis took power covert armament production was no longer kept under wraps because it became legal.

Krupp family enterprises were at the center of Germany's vast military industrial complex. In 1900 Krupp was the largest company in Europe. When the Weimar Republic was founded, Krupp's mammoth coal and iron mines, steel and iron works, steamships and barges supplied Krupp factories producing sophisticated cannons, diesel powered armored vehicles, rapid-firing Maxim machine-guns, and smokeless gunpowder (based on Nobel's formula) that kept artillery positions from being detected. Prior to the First World War, Krupp facilities in Kiel, Essen, Annen, Rheinhausen, and Magdeburg produced an entire fleet of naval vessels arranged

---

42 E. J. Gumbel. 1958. "Disarmament and Clandestine Rearmament under the Weimar Republic." In *Inspection for Disarmament* (ed. Seymour Melman. 1958). New York: Columbia University Press, pp.203 -219. For the quote, see pp.213–214.

under cost-plus contracts. In the 1920s, in fact, Krupp employed dummy corporations to hide its production of submarines in Holland. It also owned a part of Bofors, in Sweden, and produced arms there.

Krupp labor policies were oppressive. Tens of thousands of Krupp workers lived in "company towns" where undercover police spied on union activists. Instant dismissal and nationwide blacklists were employed to keep workers in line. Company rules banned membership in the social democratic labor party and other left wing parties.

Krupp enterprises employed a vast army of workers and, during the Second World War, estimates indicate that this army included over a hundred thousand slave laborers drawn from prisoners of war, Jewish concentration camp inmates (including children), and forcibly conscripted workers from occupied territories. These slaves were regimented by whips, torture, starvation and executions.

At Nuremburg, Gustav, the owner, CEO and eldest male member of the Krupp family escaped trial because he was considered medically unfit. Alfred, his son—along with other Krupp administrators—was found guilty of crimes against humanity. The Krupp enterprises were confiscated by the Allies.

Nevertheless, a general amnesty was declared for the criminals convicted at Nuremberg when the Cold War heated up. In 1951—only two years after their sentences—Alfred and almost all of his imprisoned administrators were set free. (In an aside, William Manchester, the author of a comprehensive work on the Krupp dynasty, wryly observed that Senator

Joseph McCarthy nodded in approval in Washington and remarked that the amnesty was an "extremely wise" decree.) Alfred was allowed to resume control and ownership of his firm in 1953 despite worldwide protests. The hearths, mines, ore fields, and seventy-odd enterprises worth a half billion dollars once more belonged to the Krupp family.[43]

THE FASCIST MOVEMENT

After World War I, in 1919, members of the Officer Corps—acutely conscious of the uprisings that overthrew the Kaiser and suppressed the Kapp insurrection—began to emphasize the need for ideological and political strategies ensuring popular support for the restoration of Imperial Germany.

In addition, during the 1920s, Krupp, Thyssen, Sachs, and other industrial and financial giants collaborated with prominent *Junkers* and members of the Officer Corps in the effort to destroy the Weimar Republic. Eventually, the Great Depression increased the number of these counter-revolutionaries. Industrialists and financiers from all segments of the economy shifted to the right—forming coalitions with the aristocracy.

The counter-revolutionaries eventually homed-in on the National Socialist Party (led by Hitler, Goering and other war heroes) as their key agent of change.[44] Still, one can reasonably ask whether the

43 William Manchester. 1968. *The Arms of Krupp: 1587-1968*. New York: Little Brown and Co.

44 The photo of Hitler (and Goering) at a Nazi rally was obtained

Hitler at a 1928 Nazi party rally, Nuremberg, Germany

creation of a fascist state was absolutely dependent on Hitler's presence. *If Hitler did not exist would fascism have remained an option?* In answering, we must recall that the forces instigating Germany's rearmament were in motion more than a decade before Hitler assured the "masters of the [German] universe" that he would advance their interests. As early as 1923, these forces were being backed by terrorists. The Weimar Minister of Justice in 1923, for instance, had officially confirmed the existence of a terrorist campaign conducted by members of the former Imperial Army against the opponents of rear-

from Wikipedia's *Sturmabteilung* entry.

mament, including the fact that the murderers, with few exceptions, were not brought to justice. According to Gumbel, "Altogether there were about four hundred political assassinations of the nationalists' foes."

Even though the public was strongly opposed to the secret rearmament, the courts—following the German Supreme Court—labeled press reports exposing the illegal rearmament "high treason." To assure convictions, army officers engaging in the armament were used as witnesses for the prosecution. And to intimidate the public, many more indictments and trials were initiated than could ever be completed. "As a rule," Gumbel observes, "no proof of the illegal activities was admitted in court. By this procedure, the Supreme Court could affirm at the same time that secret armaments did not exist and that any publication of such a fact was a crime."

Gumbel contends that the production of poison gas for the army caused a Hamburg chemical factory explosion in 1928, killing eleven persons. In addition, Germany maintained large powder factories for "sporting arms." (Germany, by 1924, was DuPont's greatest competitor in Europe.) Estimates also show that in 1924 Germany could within a year produce arms at First World War rates!

Furthermore, the army (*Reichswehr*) exploited every loophole in the Versailles disarmament regulations and constructed a "shadow army" modeled after the Imperial Army. Gumbel observes, "The legal army maintained close liaison with various groups which trained men in arms, and had a variety of 'cover' identities to shield them from view as military groups." For example, The *Stahlhelm, Bund der Frontsoldaten* (Steel Helmet, League of Frontline Soldiers) was a nationalistic, middle-class organization. It advocated the merit of military life and agitated publicly for restoration of the armed forces.

Founded at the end of World War I, the *Stahlhelm* attracted veterans who wanted to reinstate the monarchy and its imperial regime.[45] As a right-wing counter-revolutionary organization, it opposed the Weimar Republic and eventually enabled the German armed forces (*Reichswehr*) to expand its numbers beyond the 100,000 limit imposed by the Versailles Treaty. The *Stahlhelm* became one of the largest paramilitary organizations in Germany. It had 500,000 members by 1930. The *Stalhelm* had originally claimed it was not a political entity; however, it finally dropped this pretext and openly supported the formation of a dictatorship, the recreation of an imperial Germany, and the termination of social democracy and "Jewish mercantilism."

The German National People's Party (NSDAP) also favored counter-revolutionary aims. It was a creation of landowners and wealthy industrialists and, along with the *Stalhelm*, eventually formed a "national opposition" with the Nazi Party. The coalition was influential even though it was unstable because Hitler insisted on being the uncontested leader. But Hitler's insistence on being *The Fuehrer* did not necessarily mean that the rise of fascism would never have occurred without him. An emerging fascist movement supported the build-up of the

---

45 Jewish veterans were denied admission and formed their own organization.

A Demonstration Conducted by the Red Front Fighter's League in Berlin, May 1928

German war machine and the militarization of German politics during the 1920s. If Hitler had vanished from the political scene, the members of that movement would probably have converged on another charismatic demagogue to replace him.

Right-wing paramilitary forces were confronted by left wing forces.[46] German communists, as indicated, had attempted to stage a coup right after the war but it failed. However, responding to the terrorism unleashed by the SA, a paramilitary organization, *Der Rote Frontkämpferbund* (Red Front Fighters' League), was formed in July 1924 by the Communist Party and it fought the SA in the streets.[47]

---

46 The photo of the Red Front Fighter's League Demonstration was obtained from Wikipedia.

47 Like other paramilitary formations (e.g., the Nazi Jugenbund), it

But the largest paramilitary organization in Germany was composed of social democrats. It was called *The Reichsbanner Schwarz-Rot-Gold* (Black, Red, Gold Banner of the Realm). It was founded in 1924 to safeguard the Weimar Republic. Although it

Reichsbanner Demonstration in Magdeburg. February 1926.

claimed to be a multiparty organization, estimates indicate that almost 90% of its members supported the SPD. Accordingly, it opposed internal subversion and celebrated the Weimar Republic, its flag and constitution.

The *Reichsbanner* was enormous. No other paramilitary force could muster a comparable force. The *Reichsbanner* in 1932 contained almost three million men!

The *Wehrmacht*—the armed forces—appeared to be caught in the middle. Although it was originally

---

included a youth section, the Rote Jungfront (Young Red Front).

led by officers who wanted to revive the monarchy, they had concluded that the survival of imperial Germany depended on their adoption of a long-range plan that coped pragmatically with centrists, social democrats and communists. One solution, as the military historian, Keith W. Bird, points out, was adoption of the "cover of neutrality." (In American, we could call this cover "bipartisanship"). Although the officers commanding the naval squadrons in Kiel, for example, were monarchists, they manipulated circumstances in order to appear as *apolitical* "servants of the state." Simultaneously, they tacitly discriminated against sailors who were suspected of socialist—and especially communist—sympathies. They even complained that the local police forces weren't giving their intelligence agents enough support by providing the names of sailors who frequented bars attended by communists.[48]

WELFARE STATE AND VOTE SWITCHING

After Hitler emerged from prison, the Nazi Party attempted to become a credible contender for parliamentary offices. Adopting a variety of demagogic tactics, it cultivated racial and religious stereotypes among the electorate and raised alarms about the 'Red Menace'. It said liberals were socialists, socialists were communists, and communists were traitors. It claimed that bureaucrats were lazy, intellectuals were crackpots, businessmen put profits

---

48 Bird, Keith W. 1977. *Weimar, The German Naval Officer Corps and the Rise of National Socialism*. Amsterdam: B.R. Gruner Publishing Co. See pgs.138–141.

above patriotism, and the aristocracy had become arrogant and decadent.

Hitler cajoled the electorate by proclaiming over the radio and in the press that he opposed the separation of church and state.[49] The pro-Nazi media informed the nation that Jesus Christ himself sanctioned a Third Reich. The front page of the Party publication *Der Sturmer* featured a depiction of a *Hitler Jugend* (Hitler Youth) brigade marching forward in a Crusade to "drive evil from their land."

Hitler declared that he was trying to re-establish "the unity of the spirit and will" of the German people and announced his determination of defend family values because the family was "the constituent cell of the body of the people and the State."[50] He also appealed to material interests.[51] He promised to employ federal policies to recover and expand the economy and this promise became particularly influential when the Great Depression occurred.

As indicated, Abraham points out that the dispute

---

49 Moreover, after Hitler seized power, the leading Protestant and Catholic bishops pledged their allegiance and extolled his regime.

50 Delarue, op cit. p.28.

51 Appeals to material interests had also been important in Italy. A study conducted by a sociologist, William Brustein, for instance, found that after World War I, numerous Italian farm tenants who became owners wanted to acquire more land. Although socialist land reforms in 1919 and 1920 had helped them, the socialists were abandoned in 1921 because they advocated nationalizing land and introducing collective farms. Tenant farmers who were interested in independent farming and had prospered switched votes because they were attracted to the Fascist agrarian program. See William Brustein. "The 'Red Menace' and the Rise of Italian Fascism." *American Sociological Review*, Vol. 56, No. 5 (Oct., 1991) pp.652–664.

about welfare state policies (e.g. increasing support for the unemployed or education) despite a soaring deficit played a key role in determining what kind of German state would survive the Depression. (He uses the word, *Sozialpolitik,* to denote welfare state policies especially those brought into question by centrist and conservative parties.) "It was not by chance," Abraham writes, "that the last parliamentary government collapsed over a central issue of *Sozialpolitik,* and that the political influence of the dominant classes... grew steadily thereafter."[52]

Conservative attacks on welfare state policies were driven by the desire to bail out corporate and financial organizations. The Social Democratic and Communist Parties tried to maintain support for working-class families and refused to roll back gains made by trade unions. However, conservative parties objected to the soaring deficits created by the economic crisis. They predictably blamed these deficits on welfare state expenditures and fought to slash unemployment benefits and deny benefits to seasonal workers. Some, citing the government's 730 million (Reich marks) deficit and the rising unemployment, proposed to abandon the unemployment insurance program altogether.

The parliamentary deadlocks over whose material interests would be favored did not cease. Tariffs that would protect large and small farmers but raise prices paid by urban workers were at issue. Other demands by representatives of the industrialists, great landowners, financial corporations, small and middle-size businesses, trade unions, etc., seemed ir-

_____
52 Abraham, op. cit., p.270.

reconcilable.

During this period, many Germans became increasingly cynical about the possibility of finding a parliamentary resolution to the effects of the crisis. The rapid turnover of parliamentary coalitions testified to the hardening and uncompromising stances taken by oppositional parties. Apparently, the Nazi Party's strength among the electorate increased because the conservative, center and social democratic parties were unable to agree on how to deal with the crisis.

A 1989 study employing time-series data in six countries since the Second World War suggests that voters may lose confidence in a government because of its poor performance. Yet voters will still legitimize *democratic* institutions regardless of the government's performance. Their unwillingness to go along with a poor government depends on the degree to which they believe their parliamentary system itself has become unworkable. [53]

On the other hand, being faced with an unstable parliament may not have made voters change their traditional affiliations and switch to a party that could bend the parliament (*Reichstag*) to its will— even if this switch ushered in a dictatorship. A sociologist, Rudolf Heberle, in 1944 conducted an "ecological study" of the changes in voting patterns in a Protestant North German region of Schleswig-Hol-

---

53 Frederick D Weil. 1989. "The Sources and Structure of Legitimation in Western Democracies: A Consolidated Model Tested with Time-Series Data in Six Countries Since World War II." *American Sociological Review*, Vol. 54, No. 5 (October) pp.682-706.

stein, a large electoral district in Prussia. This region from 1918 to 1932 was predominantly rural; but it was divided into three distinct sub regions that were characteristic of North Germany in general. The regions contained large estates, small farms, industrial and commercial wage earners, etc.

Heberle found,

> [The] vote of the farmers shifted from the Liberals to the Conservatives and finally in 1932 to the Nazis. The shift of the vote of the proprietor class in industry and commerce and in all industrial divisions together is also strikingly expressed in the strong positive correlations, first in 1921 with the Liberals, then in 1924 and 1930 with the Conservatives, and finally in 1932 with the Nazis. On the other hand, the steadiness of the correlations between the percentages of wage earners and the parties is also very impressive. It indicates that on the whole labor must have adhered to the Socialist parties.[54]

It is important to note that Heberle employed ecological data to identify working class districts because they contained large-scale enterprises and, therefore, a large ratio of employees (wage and salary earners) to employers. In these districts, the socialist parties were stronger. Other parties, including the Nazis, were weaker. "We may then say that the Nazis did not gain much ground among the workers, especially not where large scale enterprises

---

54 Rudolf Heberle. 1944. "The Ecology of Political Parties: A Study of Elections in Rural Communities in Schleswig-Holstein, 1918–1932." *American Sociological Review*, Aug 1944, pp.401–414. See p. 414.

prevailed, be it in agriculture and forestry or in industry, commerce and transportation."[55]

The rural voters switching to Nazism especially included the "the middle strata (of small farmers and small entrepreneurs), and to some extent also the agricultural workers in family farm areas." According to Heberle, the most radical switches occurred "just in those middle layers of rural society, which, in the period before 1918 had been strong adherents of progressive Liberalism."

Heberle concludes,

> It may seem strange that the supposedly ideal back-bone of democracy—the family farmer—swayed from left to right like the reeds in the wind and finally supported a political movement which on the surface was diametrically opposed to their own political tradition.

But the changes in their voting patterns were due to a loss of faith in democratic institutions and the development of a political opportunism driven by materialistic aims.

Another study of voting patterns provides more information about the social base underlying the meteoric rise in support for the Nazi Party. Richard F. Hamilton in 1982 noted that religion affected voting patterns among small farmers. (Protestant farmers favored the Nazi Party but Catholics did not.) Nevertheless, Hamilton also found that socioeconomic fac-

---

55 However, ecological controls used by Heberle may have discounted Nazis votes provided by young unemployed workers who did not live in communities dominated by large scale industries.

tors were more important in urban areas.[56] Hitler enjoyed the greatest support in the upper-middle class and upper class residential areas. To back up this finding, Hamilton examined voting patterns among vacationers who cast their ballots at train stations and on German seafaring vessels. Most of these people were affluent and they voted disproportionately for Nazi Party candidates.

Andrei S. Markovits reviewed Hamilton's data and recognized that the Nazis received strong support from the Protestant evangelicals in rural areas and the privileged in the cities. But he is particularly taken with the theoretical implications of the socioeconomic findings. He concludes that Hamilton's data provide strong evidence for the validity of a structural Marxist evaluation of Hitler's rise to power.[57] In addition, the conversion of village notables and town judges to the Nazi cause, especially in the Protestant countryside, suggests that the dominant powers on all societal levels had never accepted the legitimacy of the Weimar Republic.

Markovits further observes that the Nazis would never have achieved prominence "had it not been for the tolerance-indeed active support-of their brutality . . . on the part of the courts, much of the political system, and ultimately the power elite. The Nazis gained such strength in such a short period because they shamelessly broke the rules that the powerful in

---

56 Hamilton, Richard F. 1982. *New Light on Hitler Voters: Who Voted for Hitler?* Princeton: Princeton University Press.

57 Markovits, Andrei S. . 1984. "Review of 'Who Voted for Hitler?'" by Richard Hamilton. *Contemporary Sociology*, January 1984, pp.19–21. See especially p. 21.

that society never accepted as legitimate.

Kurt Gossweiler's remarks about official tolerance of Nazi brutality should also be considered. He contends that the Social Democratic Party's (SPD's) compromises with the conservative parties unwittingly supported the rise of Nazism.[58] The SPD's capitulation reached a peak during the Great Depression when it refused to deal *militantly* with both the conservative and Nazi parties. These accommodations included von Papen's banning (on July 20, 1932) of the communist paramilitary force, the Red Front, when the *SA* and *SS* terrorist campaign was allowed to continue. [59] They also included the SPD's reluctance to advocate truly socialist proposals for ending the crisis because it would destabilize their attempts to obtain support from the centrist parties.

Crackpot realism was not limited to social democrats. The trade unions by 1931 had largely abandoned political aims that did not affect a worker's immediate interests. (As a contemporary American would say, they had become "business

---

58 Kurt Gossweiler. "Economy and Politics in the Destruction of the Weimar Republic." In Radical Perspectives on the Rise of Fascism in Germany, 1919–1945, edited by Michael N. Dobkowski and Isidor Wallimann. New York: Monthly Review Press, pp.150–171. These compromises, according to Gossweiler, occurred from the middle of the twenties when SPD leaders satisfied American financiers by going along with the abolition of the 8-hour day, The parliament's decision to build the pocket battleships is another example cited by Gossweiler that indicated the "shameful capitalization" of the SPD.

59 The official name of the Red Front was Roter Frontkämpferbund, i.e., "League of Red War Veterans."

unions" and avoided general strikes or paramilitary confrontations with the fascists.) When the Nazi terror campaign surged during the spring of 1931, the leaders of the General Federation of Unions even rejected progressive economic proposals recommended by the leader of the *Reichsbanner*. The Federation's leader felt that they were "too strongly political and agitational." A similar stance was taken by leading Social Democrats who mistakenly believed voters would only blame conservatives for parliament's inability to deal with the economic crisis.

Of course, leading social democrats could have been more aggressive in additional respects. They could have initiated land reforms during the 1920s that would have weakened the aristocracy. They could have certainly reacted more aggressively to Nazi appeals to disaffected and unemployed workers and given full employment and other welfare state polices topmost priority. But they did not want to alienate the centrists or powerful economic interests by taking a stand that would have radicalized the working class. By 1933, as Abraham points out, "All they did was appeal to the electorate to vote for the Social Democratic Party."[60]

Social Democrats and Trade Union leaders also failed to respond aggressively to the turn of events by preparing for civil war. Since the *Officer Corps* could not be relied upon to defend the Constitution, *Reichsbanner* commanders had previously offered to support the Republic by ordering their units to take arms against the Nazi terror. *However, the leaders*

---

60 *Ibid.*

of the Social Democratic Party and national labor organizations normalized and discounted the terror. Responding with *crackpot realism*, they interpreted an activation of the *Reichsbanner* as a warlike act and rejected the commanders' offer.[61] Their gutless response sealed the fate of the Weimar Republic.

Although the *Rote Front* continued to battle the *SA* in the streets, the Communist Party itself adopted political tactics that may have rigidified the Social Democrats' refusal to abandon their ineffectual centrist position and adamant stand against the Communists. Under the influence of Stalin's Comintern, the Communists called the Social Democrats "social fascists" and undermined the overriding importance of building a multi-party coalition to stop fascism— until it was too late.[62]

As a result, as Abraham indicated, the Social Democrats dealt with growing economic and political crises by doing nothing that mattered and appealing to the moderates in the Reichstag for support. This opportunistic tactic enabled Hitler and his storm troopers to goose-step through gaps created by their political opponents.

TAKING POWER

Eventually Hitler promised to serve the interests of the most powerful members of the economy even

---

61 See Abraham, op. cit., p.70.

62 Later, political blocs in France and other western European nations forestalled this possibility by developing "popular front" movements.

though one of the planks in the Nazi Party program had demanded the "total confiscation of all war profits." (Subsequently, this demagogic plank of the Party's program was quietly dropped.)[63] In addition, despite Hitler's scathing remarks, his stance toward capitalism *as a system* was by the thirties no longer in question. He assured the masters of the German universe that he would institute a dictatorship because "Private enterprise cannot be maintained in the age of democracy."

During the 1920s, the aristocracy and industrialists had, with a few exceptions, ignored Hitler's meager electoral impact; however, the *Reichstag's* bungling attempts to cope with the Depression encouraged unprecedented voting patterns that made them take notice. Unemployed workers and lower-middle class citizens broke with the ruling parties and shifted to the right. Hitler's party exceeded all expectations in the fall of 1930 after exploiting the initial effects of the Depression. It garnished an astonishing six-million votes—rising from 800,000 in the previous election. And it had finally appeared to be capable of actualizing a deceptive course of action (*sustained by a legalistic charade*) for transforming the Republic into a dictatorship—with or without monarchist trappings.

Furthermore, the Nazis consolidated their political and economic ties toward the end of 1931 by forging the "National Opposition." Collaborating with the German National People's Party and the anti-Weimar *Stahlhelm,* they staged a huge rally to commemorate this opposition. Gatherings accompanying

---

63 Manchester, op. cit. p.359.

this event included directors, lobbyists, and publicists of leading organizations of Ruhr industrialists. They also included political brokers who played an important role in linking the Nazi Party to the leaders of individual industrial firms.[64]

In 1932, Field Marshall Paul von Hindenburg won his second term as President. A national hero above and beyond his aristocratic status, von Hindenburg had commanded the German Eighth army during the war and vanquished the Russians at Tannenberg. Despite the fact that the Social Democratic Party supported him, von Hindenburg instantly selected Franz von Papen as his new Chancellor. Von Papen had been a General Staff Officer in the Imperial Army and his aristocratic loyalties leaned toward the Officer Corps, *Junkers*, and industrialists.

The previous Chancellor, Heinrich Bruening—a leader of the Catholic Center Party—had imposed a nation-wide ban on paramilitary rallies and parades. He even banned uniforms in order to quell paramilitary conflicts and the *SA* terror campaign. But von Papen immediately canceled the ban on *SA* units while maintaining the ban on the *Rote Front*. When the ban on the *SA* was lifted, they staged military parades and spectacular song-filled rallies with fluttering banners and never-ending columns of uniformed units. They continued to seek out, beat, wound, and assassinate political opponents and Jews. Simultane-

---

64 Because they are not the actual owners of the industrial firms, Turnbull considered the support extended to the Nazis by these kinds of individuals to be unimportant. But he appears to have little or no understanding of what kinds of social networks and political processes are required to achieve such support.

ously, the police and other law enforcement agencies suppressed the communist units.

However, von Papen's tenure as Chancellor was cut-short. The *SA* terror campaign provoked widespread outrage and when the Reichstag met, most of its deputies were furious. They censured von Papen and forced his resignation.

Outraged centrist and social democratic deputies then pressured von Hindenburg to make General Kurt von Schleicher the next Chancellor. Von Schleicher had served under von Hindenburg during the war. He helped organize the *Freikorps* and worked as von Hindenburg's political advisor during the Twenties.

But von Schleicher's tenure was similarly short-lived. He tried to revive the "Grand Coalition" that had existed during the 1920s and form a new alliance between the centrists and social democrats. To encourage this alliance, for instance, he "proposed [in a radio broadcast] to deal with the crisis with price controls, an end to wage cuts and the confiscation of Junker estates for peasants."[65] Von Hindenburg—who was an owner of one of these estates—immediately dismissed him. *The dismissal was roundly applauded by aristocrats and industrialists who were no longer willing to make concessions that adversely affected their immediate interests.*

Von Hindenburg was finally persuaded to offer Hitler the chancellorship. Scholars have debated whether changes in Hitler's electoral support during this period played a critical role or whether the aris-

---

65 Manchester, op. cit. p.362.

tocracy and industrialists were convinced that he would fulfill his pledges to restore German imperialism and annihilate their political enemies.[66] The Nazi Party had received 37.4 percent of the vote in the July 1932 election but their electoral support noticeably dropped to 33.1% in the November 1932 election, partly because of increases in support for Communist Party candidates. Even industrialists, financiers, and aristocrats who had been fence sitters during this period were alarmed at this development and poured money into the Nazi Party's coffers.

The money reversed Nazi fortunes. The November election had cost their Party dearly. It no longer had money "to pay Nazi functionaries, printers, and the SA thugs, who alone cost over two million marks a week," according to Manchester.[67] Two and a half million thugs had helped Hitler become chancellor and they had to be compensated to keep him in office.

Hindenburg may also have been persuaded that Hitler could now be easily controlled because his constituency had diminished. But whatever side is taken in this debate, it is widely agreed-upon that once Hitler seized control of the government, he boldly administered the final strokes that killed democracy and destroyed the opposition to fascism.

---

66 He did not control enough delegates to do as he pleased in parliament. Furthermore, he had to promise to abide by the Constitution in order to form a coalition (with Centrists) that provided a parliamentary majority.

67 Manchester, op.cit. p361.

Sᴛᴀᴛᴇ ᴏꜰ Eᴍᴇʀɢᴇɴᴄʏ

Nazi demagogic propaganda had an impact on voters especially when times got tough. Nevertheless, the transformation of the German government itself into a terrorist organization also ensured Hitler's coup d'état. When he became the *Reichschancellor* on January 30, 1933, he immediately placed Nazis in top levels of government. Goering was appointed the Prussian Minister of the Interior and Commander in Chief of the Prussian Police and the Gestapo. He rapidly purged hundreds of public officials and replaced them with Nazis. The police at every level were also purged and replaced. In addition, he created an auxiliary police force of 50,000 men, including 40,000 who were drawn from the Brownshirts (SA), and an elite unit called the *Schutzstaffel* (SS).[68]

The Weimar Constitution permitted a *Reichschancellor*, during a national emergency, to obtain dictatorial powers. But at least two thirds of the Reichstag delegates had to give their consent before these powers were handed over. Hitler could not at first get this consent. Nazi delegates had never amounted to a simple majority and the additional delegates provided by his coalition with the Nationalist Party merely enabled him to carry on the routine business of government. In fact, given that

---

68 The SS was formed from the ranks of the SA in 1925 to serve as Hitler's personal guard and to guard NSDAP meetings. On January 6, 1929 Hitler appointed Heinrich Himmler as its leader, which had only 280 people. By the end of 1932, however, it had grown to 52,000 members. A year later to more than 209,000 members.

coalition's slim majority, most people had expected it to be as short lived as the coalitions headed previously by von Papen and von Schleicher.

However, when Goering took command of law enforcement, he ordered his police to conduct a nationwide search of Communist headquarters and the homes of party leaders.[69] The *SA* collaborated with the police by kidnapping, torturing, and murdering adversaries whose identities, addresses, and political activities had been gathered previously by Nazi intelligence units. These units and their files were incorporated into the newly established *Geheimstadtpolizei* (Gestapo).

Hitler was determined to stay in power at all costs. Fifty-one anti-fascists were murdered during the previous electoral campaign. And, by the beginning of February 1933, his government had banned Communist meetings and shut down the Communist press. The SA and police also began to break-up or ban rallies conducted by the Social Democratic Party. The leading Socialist newspapers were repeatedly suspended. Even the Catholic Center Party and Catholic Trade Unions did not escape the Brownshirts who also attacked their leaders and members at political gatherings and union rallies.

---

69 The illustration on the opposite page reproduces John Heartfield's photomontage, *GOERING: Der Henker Des Dritten Reich* ▶ [*Goering: The Executioner of the Third Reich.*] Arbeiter-Illustrierte-Zeitung (AIZ, Prague), September 14, 1933, front page.

Even a master magician cannot cloak Hitler's moves at this juncture. Although revisionist historians (after the Second World War) contended that his electoral support legitimated his vicious seizure of power, two thirds of the German electorate did not actually vote for

Goering: The executioner of the Third Reich

him. He had refused von Hindenburg's first offer of the Chancellorship because he believed that another election would enable him to dissolve parliament straightaway. However, he still did not control enough delegates to do as he pleased after that election without "a state of emergency" that enabled him to decimate his parliamentary opposition and gut civil liberties and the Weimar Constitution.

Then, one month after Hitler became Chancellor, the Nazi Party initiated the first of two astounding pretexts for annihilating their opponents! After storming the Communist Party headquarters in Berlin on February 24, the police alleged that they had uncovered weapons, ammunition, and documents calling for a revolutionary uprising beginning with attacks on public buildings.

Finally, only three days later, on February 27, the building that housed the German parliament—one of the largest public buildings in the nation—was set on fire.[70]

Goering instantly declared that the Communists were preparing to overthrow the government and he ordered the police to attack anti-government demonstrations. The order was interpreted broadly. It was in practice applied to the entire spectrum of political organizations—whether they were Communist or not.[71]

70 The illustration on this page is obtained from Wikipedia's *Reichstag fire* site.

71 Heinrich Bruening, a former Chancellor representing the "Grand Coalition" forged by the Centre and Social Democratic Parties, for instance, had organized a protest meeting sponsored by Pfalz Wacht, a Catholic Association. The police killed and wounded people who attended the meeting; and although the Catholic newspaper, *Germania*, appealed to President Hindenburg, he did not reply.

Objections from provincial governments were swept aside. The Wurttemberg Minister of the Economy, for instance, protested the national government's attempts to deprive the Provinces of their rights. Since the Nazis didn't have the majority in any southern parliament, he called for a unified "defense of Republican legality, their rights and liberties." However, the Nazi Minister of the Interior, who had been appointed by Hitler, defied the Weimar Constitution and warned the Wurttemberg Minister that the federal government would impose its authority on the southern states *regardless* of its inability to command parliamentary majorities in the Provinces.[72]

WHO TORCHED THE REICHSTAG?

Jacques Delarue, a former resistance leader and a member of the French national police force (*Direction de la Sûreté Nationale*) was put in charge of the occupation records in France. After probing these records, he concluded that on February 27, 1933, ten Nazi storm troopers entered an underground tunnel connecting the Reichstag boiler room and the office building of the Reichstag's presidential palace located on the opposite side of Freidrich Ebertstrasse. Goering was the president of the Reichstag and he provided the keys enabling the Nazi squad to pass secretly through the tunnel and enter the building housing the Reichstag. [73]

---

72 Delarue, op. cit. p.30.

73 Delarue, op. cit. pp.68-71.

The squad members carried incendiary materials that were unloaded at preplanned locations throughout the building. But they did not ignite the materials until another part of their clandestine operation was completed. That part involved Marinus van der Lubbe who was reportedly a Dutch communist. Van der Lubbe was mentally disturbed and possibly drugged. He had climbed the Reichstag façade, smashed a window and entered it with a torch.

Soon after van der Lubbe entered the building, Karl Ernst, the Nazi squad leader, ordered his men to ignite their materials and flee back to Goering's palace through the underground passageway. When the police arrived, they only discovered an exultant van der Lubbe (shirtless with a blazing torch) exiting from the Reichstag. They arrested him.

Although many Germans believed Hitler's role as chancellor would soon be over, they did not entertain the possibility that the Nazis would actually torch the Reichstag so they could declare a "state of emergency" that "legalized" a fascist dictatorship. Nor did they expect the Nazis to destroy anyone in their way with such breathtaking speed. Before the Reichstag's flames had died down, Hitler, Goering and Goebbels shouted that the Communist revolution had finally begun. As the German media echoed this Big Lie, these men opened the curtain on the final act of their coup d'état. They ordered the police and paramilitary forces informed by Nazi intelligence files on thousands of antifascists—to race through German cities searching especially for communists. They closed down newspapers objecting to the repression. Social Democrats were also arrested and public protests were banned and suppressed.

The Reichstag fire occurred on February 27, 1933. The last democratic election held during Hitler's life took place a week later, on March 5, 1933. Social Democratic and Communist candidates were still on the ballots.

Despite the impact of the fire and massive effort to blame it on the Communists and to make the electorate believe that Hitler was the foremost defender of the nation, he had only received 44 per cent of the total vote. Despite all the terror and intimidation, the majority had once again rejected Hitler.

Nevertheless, Hitler's government continued to issue one repressive decree after another. The day after the fire, von Hindenburg and Hitler had extended the legalistic charade to justify the Nazi seizure of power. They issued a decree suspending civil liberties during a national emergency thus gutting constitutional rights to free speech, freedom of assembly and association, unlawful searches and seizures, the right to privacy when communicating through the post office, telegraph and radio, and so on.

While communists were being forced into hiding, arrested, assassinated, or sent to Dachau, Hitler staged a parliamentary charade. After excluding communist deputies, he barely obtained the two-thirds majority vote (among the *remaining* deputies) required by the Constitution for the passage of the Nazi Enabling Act, which dissolved the Reichstag and "ratified" his dictatorship. (The Social Democratic deputies who had not been arrested courageously voted against the Act.)

The Nazis systematically abolished all the other parties in Germany. In addition to creating a one-party state, they decreed that Jews and Communists could no longer practice law. Another Nazi decree forced them out of the civil service and medical professions. Still others denied their right to practice as educators, journalists, tax consultants, and other professions. Concurrently, the police seized the assets of individuals and organizations that had been opposed to Nazi policies.

Three months after his coup, Hitler proclaimed May 1, 1933 to be a national holiday and officially named it the "Day of National Labor."[74] To commemorate the new holiday, Hitler transported union leaders and huge delegations representing organized labor to Berlin from all parts of Germany. His speech before thousands at the Berlin airport denounced the Jews, social democrats, and communists who had discredited his sympathetic expression of solidarity with German workers. After his Orwellian speech, on the following morning, the Nazi police, the *SS* and *SA*, occupied trade union offices throughout the country. They dissolved the unions whose leaders were beaten, rounded up, and sent to concentration camps.[75] The government seized union funds including workers' savings and pension funds kept in cooperatives and credit unions, sponsored by organized

---

74 Although honoring the martyrs who died fighting for the eight-hour day on "May Day" had originated in America, it had been celebrated for half a century by trade unions and left-wing parties in every capital of the European continent.

75 Shirer, op. cit. pp.120-121. After the independent unions were dissolved, Hitler registered all workers and employers in a "National Labor Front" controlled by the Nazi Party.

labor.

Goebbels, who had been appointed Minister for Popular Enlightenment and Propaganda, commemorated the new holiday in an article published in every German newspaper on May 1, 1933. He declared that Marxism had to be destroyed so that a road to freedom could be opened up for German workers.

Finally, in November 1933, the government conducted its last election. Opposition parties were excluded. Voters were merely presented with Nazi candidates. The Nazi Party claimed that it received 92% of the vote although over three million voters submitted "invalid" ballots to protest against the dictatorship.

Professor Victor Klemperer's diary describes the fear and disgust instigated by the final Nazi campaign. Klemperer was Jewish and, until his dismissal and incarceration in a concentration camp, chaired the Department of Romance Languages and Literature at a Dresden university. Two days before the election, Klemperer asked, "What shall we do on November 12? No one believes that the secrecy of the ballot will be protected, no one believes in a *fair* counting of the votes; so why be a martyr?"[76]

The day before the election, he wrote,

> On every commercial vehicle, post office van, mailman's bicycle, on every house and shop window, on broad banners, which are stretched across the street-quotations from Hitler are everywhere and always "Yes" for

76 Victor Klemperer. 1999. I Will Bear Witness 1933–1941. New York: Random House. (The quotation can be found on pp.38–41.)

> peace! It is the most monstrous of
> hypocrisies. . . Demonstrations and chanting
> into the night, loudspeakers on streets,
> vehicles (with wireless apparatus playing mu-
> sic mounted on top), both cars and trams.

He added that a factory whistle announced the hour when Hitler addressed the nation over the radio.

Also, previously, between March 33 and August 31, the Nazis had conducted one of the most famous "show trials" of the decade. The German federal prosecutor, Rudolf Diels, who later became head of the Gestapo, accused five people of torching the Reichstag. He indicted Marinus van der Lubbe and three Bulgarian communists, Georgi Dimitrov, Vasil Tanev, and Blagoi Popov. The fifth "terrorist" was Ernst Torgler, the well-known leader of the communist delegates in the Reichstag.

The three Bulgarians had ironclad alibis and Torgler wasn't even in Berlin when the fire occurred. One hundred and twenty journalists from news agencies throughout the world (with the notable exception of the USSR who were not admitted) attended the trial and praised Dimitrov's astonishing ability to act as his own counsel and interrogate false witnesses.

An International Commission of Inquiry formed in London conducted an independent investigation and concluded that all the defendants with the exception of van der Lubbe were innocent. The Commission chairpersons included the American lawyer, Arthur Garfield Hays, who co-founded the ACLU and attended most of the trial; the celebrated British lawyer and Labor Party member, D. N. Pritt; the well-known French lawyer Vincent de Moro-Gia-ferri; a former Italian prime minister, Francesco Nitti; and a Swedish senator, Georg Branting.

Six judges presided at the Reichstag fire trial and even though they openly favored the Nazi prosecutors and witnesses, the international uproar forced them to acquit all defendants except van der Lubbe who could not defend himself because of his incoherence and unbalanced mental state. When the trial ended, van der Lubbe was beheaded.

Many years later, in March 2009, a professor of law, Michael E. Tigar, and a director of the Monthly Review Foundation, John Mage, published "The Reichstag Fire Trial, 1933-2008: the Production of Law and History." Their article reviewed the circumstances surrounding the Reichstag fire and it challenged the credibility of a notorious attempt to discredit the leaders of the London Commission.

Tigar and Mage wrote that West German courts during the Cold War were headed by judges who had supported Hitler. Some of them had even been convicted as war criminals. For instance,

> In one chamber of forty-nine judges, forty had been Nazis, some accused of murder. Some cases aroused intense international interest. One Dr. Hallbauer, a former Storm Trooper, had been a judge in Prague and had sentenced Czechs to death for listening to the BBC or trying to escape slave labor. When a Czech survivor of his "justice" discovered that Dr. Hallbauer was serving as a judge in Hamburg, he brought an action seeking compensation for

> his injuries. The West German courts ruled that Dr. Hallbauer's sentences had been "juristically correct." In 1962 the West German justice ministry prosecuted the Association of Victims of Nazis as "anticonstitutional"; the three judges assigned to the trial had all been Nazis, and one a Storm Trooper.

But "accusations that the new West German administration and armed forces were composed almost entirely of Nazi functionaries" during the Cold War were dismissed as communist propaganda. Furthermore, fraudulent efforts were made to counteract the scandalous reputation of the West German judiciary. The belated conservative opposition to the Nazis by a handful of officers toward the end of the war was exaggerated.[77] In addition, an absurd attempt to hide the bias shown by the pro-Nazi jurists at the trial claimed that their acquittal of the four communists verified the impartiality of the judiciary under Hitler. By implication, most of the judges in West Germany had administered justice without prejudice even though they had collaborated with Nazis.

Another attempt to whitewash the Reichstag fire trial and the West German legal system involved the claim that van der Lubbe was the sole arsonist. Tigar and Mage differ:

> [During the Cold War], Rudolf Augstein's weekly Der Spiegel—modeled on Time Magazine—largely filled the function of the primary anticommunist right-wing press (par-

---

77 This exaggeration included the belated and unsuccessful conspiracy "Operation Valkyrie," which was dramatized in 2008 by a Hollywood film.

allel to today's Murdoch media) in West Germany. In 1960 a series of articles by an unknown Fritz Tobias appeared in Der Spiegel, and in 1963 were collected in a book swiftly translated into English entitled *The Reichstag Fire*, and much publicized in the United States. Tobias attempted to disprove the conclusions of the London commission by alleging that van der Lubbe acted alone, that the Nazis [accused of committing the crime] were innocent, and that the defendants had received a fair trial.[78]

Tobias' attempts to 'prove' his case were based on shameless lies and misrepresentations. Nevertheless, Tigar and Mage declared,

> Despite its harsh ideological bias and many failings, under Cold War circumstances the Tobias version became authoritative, at least in West German and U.S. establishment accounts. Certainly no graduate student aspiring to a career in the West German or U.S. academy would have dared challenge the Tobias account for an entire generation.[79]

The legacy of this Cold War effort endured long after Tobias' account. In 2004, for example, Robert O. Paxton's noted book, *The Anatomy of Fascism*, claimed that Hitler was taken by surprise when the Reichstag's fire illuminated the sky. According to Paxton, the fire, provided Hitler with a "lucky break"

---

78 Michael E. Tigar. and John Mage. 2009. "The Reichstag Fire Trial 1933–2008." *Monthly Review*. Vol. 60. No. 10, March. (See pp. 44-46.)

79 *Ibid*. p.45. David Abraham might have been the graduate student they had in mind. Despite his admirers, unprincipled attacks on his work forced him to become a lawyer instead of an historian.

and "an excuse to carry out a virtual coup d'état from within, without a breath of opposition from right or center." In addition, Paxton seductively added,

> It was long believed that the Nazis themselves set the fire and then framed a dim-witted Dutch Communist youth found on the premises, Marinus van der Lubbe, in order to persuade the public to accept extreme anti-communist measures. Today most historians believe that van der Lubbe really lit the fire, and that Hitler and his associates, taken by surprise, really believed a communist coup had begun.[80]

In January 2008, however, the Federal Court of Justice of Germany finally overturned the verdict imposed on van der Lubbe. The court decided that he was incapable in his "damaged state" of defending himself at the trial, and that his sentence was politically motivated and unjust.

Furthermore, forensic evidence unequivocally contradicts Paxton's claim that van der Lubbe was the *sole person* responsible for the fires that had erupted at multiple locations before they merged throughout the immense building. As the Reichstag's fire died down, on February 27, Goering and his press chief, Martin Sommerfeldt, issued a press release reporting that the recovered incendiary materials were so heavy that more than seven and perhaps ten persons would have been necessary to carry them. (Goering obviously wanted the public to believe that a *communist* squad had committed the

---

80 Robert O. Paxton. 2004. *The Anatomy of Fascism*. New York: Alfred A. Knopf, pp. 107–107.

crime.) But, as recent as 2001, a study—published by historian Alexander Bahar and a physicist and psychologist Wilfried Kugel—reviewed previously unavailable files that had been the subject of earlier inquiries.[81] These experts concentrated on the forensic evidence and concluded that van der Lubbe could never have started the fires at most of the places where the fires were set. (He couldn't have even carried the amount of accelerant used to set the fires at these places.) As Tigar and Mage sarcastically remark, "Henceforward anyone defending the Tobias thesis needs either reject the entire forensic testimony at trial or the laws of nature, or both."[82]

Despite his impact on American fairy tales about the Reichstag fire, it turned out that Tobias did not have a degree in law or history. In fact, he had never completed secondary education. Furthermore, during the Second World War he was a member of the Geheime Feldpolizei, the Wehrmacht Gestapo.[83]

Evidence linking the Reichstag fire to higher Nazi officials was provided by proceedings at the Nuremberg tribunal at the close of the Second World War. An official in the Prussian Ministry of the Interior, Hans Gisevius, testified at the Tribunal that he had been told by one of the Nazi arsonists that his squad took direct orders from Karl Ernst, the commander of the Berlin SA.[84] As a member of the newly formed

---

81 The study, "Der Reichstagbrand—Wie Geschichte gemacht wird" ("The Reichstag Fire—How History is Created") is cited by Tigar and Mage, op. cit. p. 46.

82 *Ibid.*

83 *Ibid.*

84 Gisevius also testified that the squad used the underground tunnel

Gestapo in 1933, Gisevius had been assigned to the Reichstag Fire trial as an "observer."[85]

Diels, the chief of the Gestapo in 1933, also testified at the Nuremberg trial. He said, "It was Goebbels who first thought of setting the Reichstag on fire." He also stated that "Goering knew exactly how the fire was to be started." Finally, he testified that he had been ordered, "to prepare, prior to the fire, a list of people who were to be arrested immediately after it."

Goering denied that he had any part in setting the fire but General Franz Halder, Chief of the German General Staff during the early part of World War II, recalled at the trial, how Goering had on one occasion openly bragged about his deed.

The tribunal could not interrogate the men who actually torched the Reichstag because the SS and the Gestapo assassinated them. (As Delarue wryly observed, "The Gestapo did not like witnesses.")[86] One of them was murdered after he foolishly provided information about the fire in order to get a reduced sentence from a criminal court judge for another crime. Others were killed during "the night of the long knives" on June 30 1934, when Hitler assured the German Officer Corps that his Brownshirts would either be absorbed into the *Reichswehr* or merely utilized for propaganda purposes. To back his

---

connecting the Reichstag with Goering's palace and that van der Lubbe had been under the squad's control for several days before he was used as a dupe.

85 Tigar and Mage, op. cit. p. 44.

86 Delarue, op. cit. p.71.

pledge, eliminate a potential rival and SA leftists, he ordered the SS and the Gestapo to take the SA Chief of Staff, Ernst Roehm, and his close associates by surprise at a health resort and cut their throats.[87] (Because he had favored centrists rather than Nazis, and opposed von Papen, the assassins also went to von Schleicher's home and assassinated him and his wife.)

We do not have the space to review other accounts of who was responsible for the Reichstag fire but we would like to conclude by dispelling some illusions having to do with the makeup of the German and Italian regimes after their fascist parties had seized control. Most certainly, Mussolini and Hitler increased their power by consolidating their authority. Hitler, for instance, destroyed the federalism embodied in the Weimar constitution by suppressing and subordinating the powers of 17 provinces. His central government made provincial governors servile representatives. Fascist policies also perfected the organization and methods of police repression. The Gestapo (in Germany) and *Ovra* (in Italy) acquired nearly limitless power and material resources. These intelligence agencies were transformed into nationwide organizations with the ability to arrest, imprison and execute almost anyone without a trial. The German and Italian regimes also created educational curricula and militaristic youth organizations

---

87 It is also possible that Roehm could have also been eliminated because his support of the SA's independence strengthened his position as a party leader. In addition, a number of his supporters were radical Nazi's who had bought Hitler's demagogic socialist rhetoric. They were eliminated to assuage the aristocrats and industrialists who finally backed Hitler.

fascist textbooks. They educated you
phere of exaltation and fanaticism
students to spy on their parents, p
bors. Nevertheless, these regimes
compared to seamless blocks of gra
composed of corrupt officials who
terrorized underlings and heads of
tions. The authority of these officia
on patronage systems where loyalty
equated with subservience and bri
large capitalists were not exempt f
cesses.

A handful of capitalists and banke
ported Hitler actually fled Germany
ized that he was an egomaniac an
Party's attempt to control the world
failure. Members of the officer corp
with his policies also grew in numb
was being decimated on the eastern
these officers attempted to assassinat

Millions of Germans and Italians
governments as long as they seemed
When the Second World War had de
ing standards that had been propped
occupied territories, most of these
that their support had been a dead
imperial dreams of their fascist leade
be suicidal.

PART TWO

ROAD SIGNS & REST STOPS

—◇—

4 | Highway to Fascism

"... if and when a form of fascism appears in America, it will appear in a less openly aggressive guise. For if America has not the same vast territorial overseas possessions as Britain, yet her world power is so great that she can acquire whole sub-continents— such as South America—as fields of an increasingly exclusive American exploitation."

—John Strachey, 1933

If computer animations symbolized America's 2004 political climate, they might well depict armed convoys of motorized storm troopers speeding down a virtual superhighway to the wild world of *Friendly Fascism*. The first stretch of that electronic autobahn would be decorated with scintillating billboards hyping Patriot Acts I and II—or displaying brilliant green, blue, yellow, orange, and red terror-threat alerts. Partially obscured by trees along the roadside would be a sign promoting a law passed, in the dead of night, giving the President sweeping powers to use federal forces to enforce martial law. Another sign would highlight a decree authorizing the President to seize the assets of Americans who speak out against the wars in Afghanistan and Iraq.

Some billboards would point to off-highway "information stops" where patriotic Americans could be comforted by free coffee and flashy brochures touting warrantless surveillance of anti-war activists by Joint Terrorism Task Forces and the Pentagon. Still others would feature luminescent logos of that Kafkaesque constabulary—The Department of Homeland Security—depicting ever-vigilant federal and local law enforcement in huge bunkers glaring through night-vision goggles out of gun ports.

On this political landscape, instead of internet cafes, the highway rest stops might even contain stylish "internet outhouses"—comfortably referred to as Microsoft "Internet Loos."[88] To advertise Big Brother's services, some iLoo flat-screen monitors would flash scenes of American protesters being efficiently rounded up, clubbed, cuffed, herded, and jailed. Others would display court scenes in which defiant protesters are subjected to huge bails, fines, multiple counts, and months, even years, in prison for civil disobedience.

---

88 They are called "Loos" because they were originally intended for concerts and festivals in Britain where bathrooms are dubbed "Loos."

RESURRECTION OF THE SS

Still other screens could take a cue from ancient Rome's *Circus Maximus*: Travelers and spectators entertained with animated round-ups of swarthy aliens and cinematic images of "unlawful enemy combatants" being hog-tied, gagged, blindfolded, raped, and tortured in Abu Ghraib and Guantanamo. And, after May 2004, video screens at the "rest stops" would offer updates with genuine photos that shocked the world—American MPs in the Abu Ghraib prison torturing their prisoners, beating them with clubs, assaulting them with guard dogs, urinating on their food, dousing them with toxic chemicals and forcing them into degrading sexual acts.

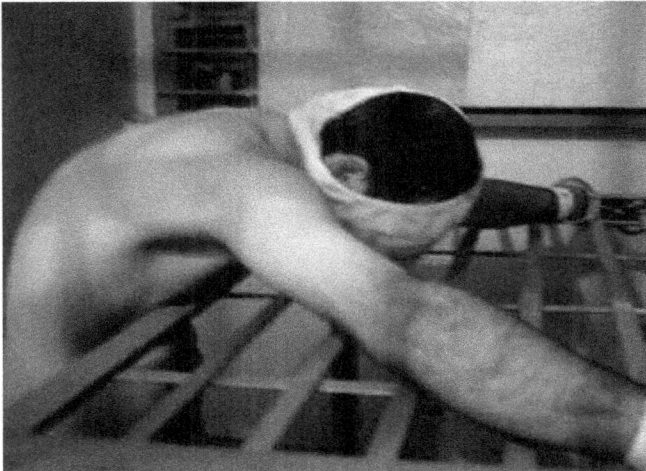

Photo: Wikipedia: Abu Ghraib

The MPs had "crucified" prisoners (by chaining their outstretched arms and legs to prison bars) and

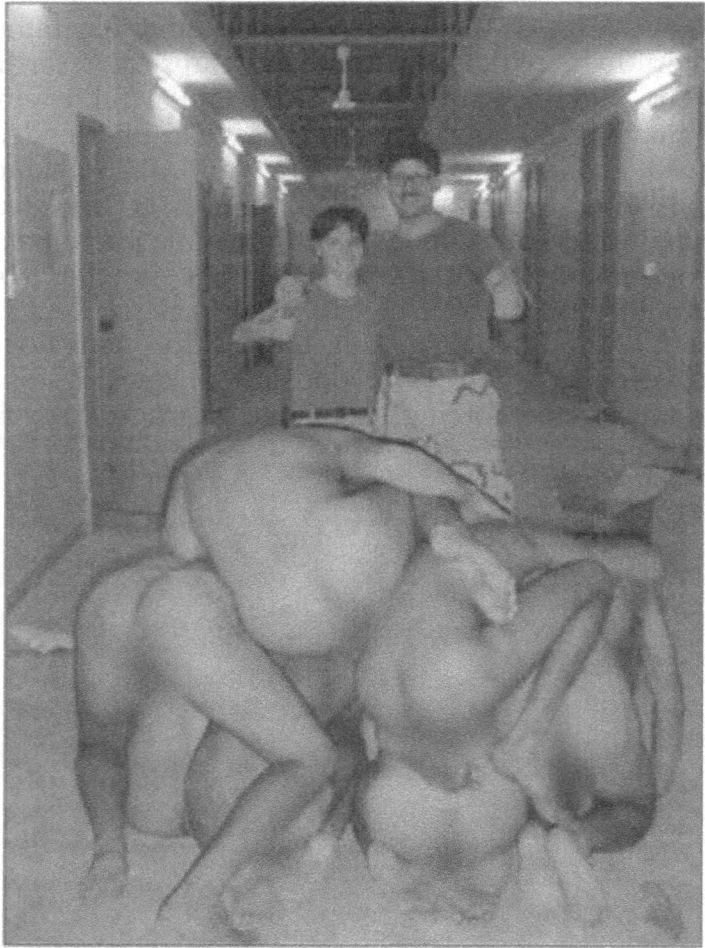

Photo of a pyramid of human bodies, taken by a soldier at Abu Ghraib. More info: https://commons.wikimedia.org/wiki/File:Abu _Ghraib_53.jpg

replicated sensory deprivation by covering their heads with black hoods.Then—like the Great White Hunters of a bygone age—these prison guards photographed one another alongside their naked "kills."

Faced with a public-relations catastrophe after Americans saw the photos, the Bush administration cynically condemned the cruelties. Defense Secretary Donald Rumsfeld, in an effort to diminish public outrage, pled down to the admission that a handful of "bad apples" had committed torture. Thousands of American troops, he said, conducted themselves honorably; therefore, torture was not encouraged by Pentagon policies nor was it the way the war was being run.[89]

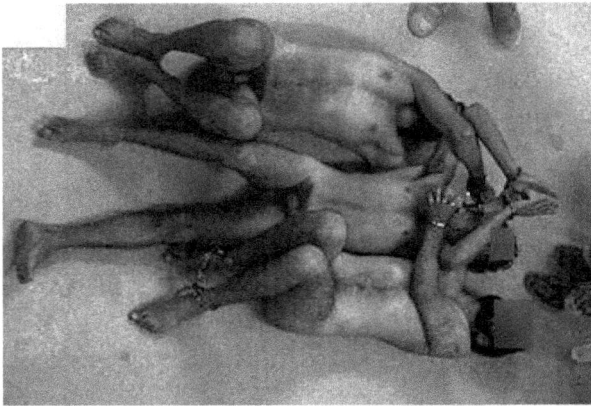

Photo: Wikipedia: Abu Ghraib

89 The Abu Ghraib photographs on the following pages were taken by US soldiers, and are sourced in Wikipedia's article on Abu Ghraib.

But not all critics bought Rumsfeld's plea of innocence. They recalled that a memorandum to the administration was written by Attorney General Alberto Gonzales, who had evaded the US Constitution and Geneva Conventions by authorizing indefinite detention in Guantanamo for prisoners seized in Afghanistan. And for the same extra-Constitutional reasons, the Pentagon and CIA was sending other Middle Easterners to be tortured on foreign soil—in nations such as Egypt, Syria, Jordan, Morocco, Uzbekistan, and parts of Eastern Europe—all places where human rights are nearly non-existent.

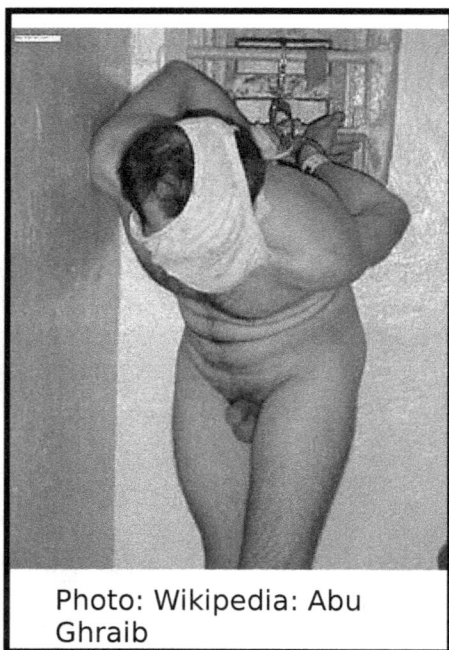

Photo: Wikipedia: Abu Ghraib

Critics also noted similarities between the torturers at Abu Ghraib and the torturers in Auschwitz.
Since the SS administered the concentration camps,
a Reuters' May 5, 2004 report about the Abu Ghraib
torture was entitled, "The Resurrection of the Nazi
SS in Iraq"—a reference to the SS-administered concentration camps implementing "The Final Solution."

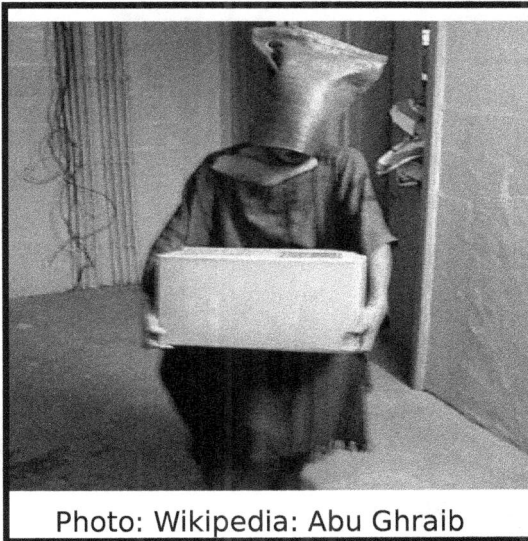

Photo: Wikipedia: Abu Ghraib

In 2004, the late Texas journalist Molly Ivins—
whose courageous observations sparkled with home-
spun humor—blamed America's leaders for the torture. When the torture was exposed, Ivins revealed
that the Pentagon claimed that only six low-level soldiers were responsible. Ivins responded: "Damned if
I think these six low-level soldiers should be hung
out there to take the blame for a set of explicitly written and signed policies made by people wearing ex-

pensive suits, getting paid big bucks and bearing some of the highest titles in the land."[90] Ivins urged Americans to read the memos and documents backing up the culpability of the Bush administration— because, she concluded, "It's important to know how fascism starts."

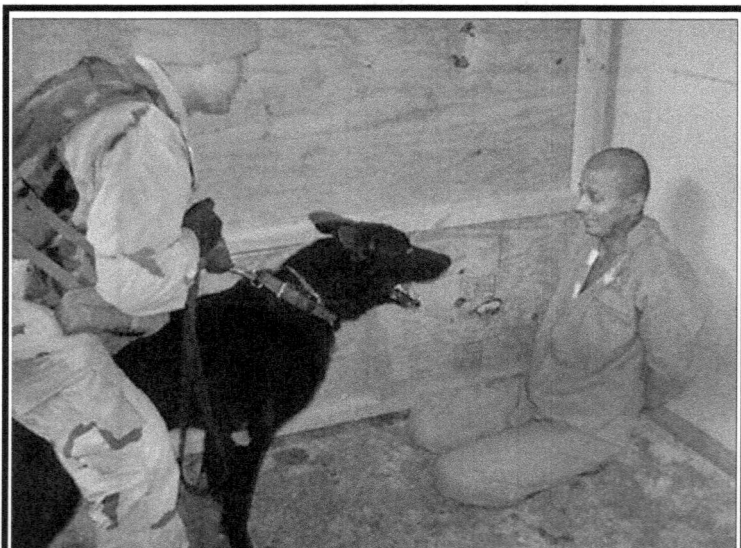

A prisoner in an orange jumpsuit is threatened with physical harm by a K-9 Military Personnel (MP, dog).
[Photo was made public in May 2004 by the *Washington Post*]

But the Bush administration responded with lies and more lies to criticism by human-rights organiza-

---

90 Molly Ivins. 5/20/04. "How Fascism Starts" (Creators Syndicate) Information Clearing House: News You Won't Find on CNN.

tions. It did not, for instance stop its policy of torture. As a result, Nat Hentoff and other civil libertarians were still condemning the torture more than three-and-a-half years later. At that point, Hentoff and others were noting the parallels between fascist policies in Germany and the policies introduced by the Bush administration. In an October, 2007 article entitled "The Gestapo Inheritance," Hentoff points out that torture was being conducted by the CIA in secret prisons. Bush repeatedly told Americans, "This government does not torture people." Nevertheless, he condoned "enhanced" interrogation techniques. "You know, we *stick to the US law and our international obligations," he reasoned. "Trained* personnel do the questioning—and we'll keep on." The Republican controlled Congress, on the other hand, had trouble swallowing Bush's feeble explanation. So it explicitly gave the torturers immunity from prosecution in the 2006 Military Commissions Act.[91]

Hentoff mocked the crude attempts being made to dodge the legal implications of the administration's culpability by comparing its use of torture to war-crimes tribunals judgments made after World War II. Wrote Hentoff: "What has recently—and star-tlingly—been revealed are the eerie parallels between these CIA "enhanced interrogation techniques" and the *verschärfte vernehmung* (German for "enhanced interrogation" methods of persuasion used by the Gestapo.)" Hentoff called for "penetrating investiga-

91 Hentoff, Nat. 2007. "The Gestapo Inheritance: 'We do not torture': Groans from the CIA's black sites beg to differ." *Village Voice*, October 23rd.

tions of these war crimes" in light of which Democrats could consider the possibility of Bush's complicity. To justify this demand, he pointed out that Nazi records actually showed that the Gestapo used hypothermia, waterboarding, cold baths, blows and kicks to the face and all over the body, and other methods similar or identical to those authorized by Bush and Rumsfeld. The Gestapo—like the CIA— even instructed its torturers in certain cases to leave no marks on their victims.[92]

CLIENT FASCISM

In addition to rest stops, Janus' highway to fascism is dotted with off-ramps that lead to a variety of semi-fascist and fascist regimes. And some of them— despite contrary opinions—are used more frequently than others.

For instance, writers cited the use of torture to subvert democracy in scathing criticisms of US policies at Abu Ghraib. The criticisms recalled the ignominious Pentagon "School for Torturers" at Fort Benning, Georgia, which has trained thousands of foreign-intelligence officers and operatives from US client states. These Fort Benning trainees, upon completing the curriculum, returned home to wantonly terrorize, rape, mutilate, and murder trade-union leaders, liberal democrats, social democrats, communists, and human rights activists.[93] The

---

92 Ibid.

93 See, for instance, Cockburn, Alexander and Jeffrey St. Clair. 2004. "Torture: as American as Apple Pie." *CounterPunch* 11(April 16-

Beating Prisoners at Abu Ghraib

butchers employed by the military juntas in Guatemala to massacre and torture thousands of indigenous people were graduates of the "School for Torturers." According to Canadian journalist Pat Kerans, "[One] graduate was El Salvador's Colonel Francisco Fuentes, who supervised the training of death squads, who planned and covered up the massacre of six Jesuits and who was described by the US Ambassador as 'among the worst in terms of human rights.'"[94]

Where else was torture administered in aiding and abetting fascism? A Uruguayan Senate investigation of the assassination in 1970 of Dan Mitrione

---

31)1-2. The School had been previously called School for Americas but the Pentagon took George Orwell's advice and changed its name to Western Hemisphere Institute for Security Cooperation.

94 Pat Kerans. 13/5/04. "Don't Be Surprised By US Torture," CBC Radio Commentary.

discovered that he was chief American advisor to Uruguayan police who systematically tortured the Tupamaros and their sympathizers. Torturing—for females as well as males—included lacing their food with urine, placing electric needles under the finger-nails, administering electric shocks to the body, par-ticularly on the captive's sexual organs.

Upon arriving in Uruguay in 1969, Mitrione im-ported from the US larger quantities of tear gas, po-lice batons, and other equipment for suppressing demonstrations. Benitez (a Uruguayan police official who worked with Mitrione) understood that smaller equipment came to Mitrione inside the US embassy's diplomatic pouch."[95] According to Benitez, Mitrione arranged for the police to get newer electric needles of varying thickness. "Some needles were so thin they could be slipped between the teeth."

In the face of these proven atrocities, it would scarcely be possible to deny US policies have been responsible for a worldwide network of client fascist regimes. Nevertheless, historian Robert O. Paxton denies that US interventions have produced fascist regimes in Latin America and Africa. He concedes that the regimes may be odious, but claims "they are best considered traditional dictatorships or tyrannies supported from outside."[96] Paxton reiterates they are simply not fascist.

A multiplicity of facts refute Paxton—facts that echo the fascist overthrows of democratic govern-ments throughout the world. Generalissimo Franco,

95 The Tupamaros assassinated him in return. See A. J. Langguth. 1978. *Hidden Terrors*. New York: Pantheon p.251.

96 Robert O. Paxton, op cit. p.201.

for example, overthrew a freely elected Social Democratic government in Spain. This dyed-in-the-wool fascist copied the Nazi seizure of power by imprisoning and killing liberals, socialists, and communists.

Likewise, the CIA helped Mobutu Sese-Seko to establish a long-lasting fascist regime in the Congo and Zaire after Congo's Prime Minister Patrice Lumumba was assassinated in 1961.[97] It also ensured the fascist overthrow in Brazil of another popularly elected official in 1964, President Joao Goulart. And the CIA was surely responsible for General Suharto's 1968 coup d'état in Indonesia, which deposed a democratically elected government and then killed-off a half-million leftists and their families.

But none of these examples can equal the killings that occurred when the US armed a group of Vietnamese officers who had served in the French colonial forces. These officers murdered the Prime Minister, Ngo Dinh Diem, as well as members of his family and cabinet. They then installed a fascist government in South Vietnam that reneged on an international accord calling for a nation-wide election.[98] Yet, after a decade and a half of armed conflict, neither the American forces nor their fascist puppets were victorious. In the end, over two million Vietnamese were killed in what the people of Vietnam call the "American War"—not the "Vietnam War."

Still, Paxton doesn't consider any of the governments mentioned above as fascist regimes. He con-

---

97 Belgium played an even more despicable role in supporting Mobutu.

98 The accord was reached between the French government and the Vietminh after the French were defeated.

tends that Franco didn't command a fascist dictatorship because he swept aside the small fascist Spanish Falangist Party and kept power to himself. Apparently, the fact that Franco would have hardly succeeded without the aid of Hitler and Mussolini's well-trained troops and Stuka Dive-Bombers is also ignored.

Paxton's objections in these cases only make sense because his candidates for fascism exclude political parties that do not *publicly* identify themselves as fascist parties. Also, in Paxton's writings, no seizure of power is smeared by the "*F*" word if the fascists are not supported by "popular acclaim."

Paxton grants that fascism succeeded in Germany because the "elites" fronted by von Hindenburg wanted to use it to destroy the Communists. But here Paxton conveniently ignores significant similarities between Germany, Italy, and other fascist regimes. Franco, for example, was responsible for overthrowing a social-democratic government. Moreover, Franco suppressed the same kinds of socialists, communists, liberal democrats, anarchists, and other anti-fascists that had been suppressed in Germany and Italy. Shouldn't this suppression count when the "*F*" word is considered? Given Paxton's criteria, even the Quisling government installed by the Germans in Norway cannot be legitimately called "client fascism"—to use Noam Chomsky and Edward S. Herman's term.[99]

The US aided and abetted one fascist regime after

---

99 Noam Chomsky and Edward S. Herman. 1979. *The Washington Connection and Third World Fascism*. Boston: South End Press.

another in the last half of the 20th century. Yet Paxton merely calls these regimes "traditional dictatorships" stating:

> Dictatorial regimes in Africa and Latin America that aided American or European interests (resource extraction, investment privileges, strategic support in the cold war) and were, in turn, propped up by Western protectors have been called "client fascism," "proxy fascism," or "colonial fascism." One thinks here of Chile under General Pinochet (1974-90) or Western protectorates in Africa like Mobutu's Congo (1965-97). These client states, however odious, cannot legitimately be called fascist, because they neither rested on popular acclaim nor were free to pursue expansionism. If they permitted the mobilization of popular opinion, they risked seeing it turn against their foreign masters and themselves. They are best-considered traditional dictatorships or tyrannies supported from outside.[100]

History does not confirm Paxton's defining criteria for fascism. The cynical exploitation of the votes for Hitler and the fraudulent invocation of emergency powers veiled the impact of Nazi terror and German ruling class interests. Nor should fascism be awarded a prize for making Germany "free to pursue expansionism." The conditions creating this "freedom" emerged years before the Nazis came to power when Germany began to rearm.

Historical events also contradict these criteria for Italy. Mussolini was made Prime Minister after his

---

100 Paxton, op cit, p. 201.

paramilitary forces had with impunity terrorized communities throughout northern Italy. In 1920, Italian officers, upon being demobilized, received four-fifths of their former pay from the government if they became officers in the *Fasci di Combattimento*. Thousands of ex-servicemen also joined fascist squads and—like the Freikorps in Germany—terrorized communities notable for their support of socialists, communists and trade unions.

The Italian government supported the fascist terror campaigns. It told the police not to interfere when fascist squads drove their lorries into a town, set fire to socialist, communist, and union headquarters and newspapers, looted and burned down municipal buildings, torched houses, and executed townspeople. "During the first six months of 1921 alone," the historian F.L. Carsten reports," the Fascists destroyed eighty-five agrarian cooperatives, fifty-nine chambers of labour, forty- three unions of agricultural workers, twenty-five people's centres, and many left-wing printing presses and newspapers."[101]

Fascist organizations advocated populist policies that appealed to lower and upper-middle class communities as well as to veterans who felt they had not been rewarded for risking their lives in war. But these organizations also appealed to the big industrialists and landowners who feared that the Socialists and Communists would seize their factories and estates. In fact, as Carsten noted, after Mussolini announced that his fascist army was about to begin the

---

101 F. L. Carsten. 1980. *The Rise of Fascism* (2nd Edition). Berkeley: The University of California Press. p. 58.

Infamous "March on Rome":

> The heads of the General Confederation of In-
> dustry, the Confederation of Agriculture and
> the Bankers' Association telegraphed to Rome
> asking that Mussolini should be appointed
> prime minister. Two Senators, the electrical
> magnate Conti, and the editor of the influen-
> tial newspaper Corriere della Sera, Albertini,
> sent a telegram to the prime minister, Facta,
> with the same request.[102]

The government's armed forces could have defeated the fascists, but King Victor Emmanuel III
made him prime minister without firing a shot!

IDEOLOGICAL ARTIFACTS

In addition to his lack of historical precision,
there are theoretical reasons why Paxton's refusal to
use the term 'client fascism' should be rejected. The
regimes led by Pinochet and other dictators arose after the Second World War when the word fascism
was utterly discredited. As a result, their characteristics should be subject to an analysis that does not depend solely on ideological categories adopted at that
time by Mussolini and others to justify their own
movements and dictatorial regimes. The word "fascism" in that context is an *ideological artifact*. It
provided a badge of honor, symbolizing strength
through discipline, unity, and solidarity. At the end
of the Second World War, however, the categories
that fascists used to justify their power and program-

---

102 Ibid. p.63.

matic aims were discredited throughout the world. The word "fascism" was generally adopted as a pejorative metaphor. As a result, powerful interests that achieved power through the use of terror were not interested in compounding their legitimacy problems by calling themselves "fascists."

How, then, can we identify a contemporary fascist (or neo-fascist) regime? *Fascist regimes aren't merely dictatorial regimes. They use terror to enrich or further enrich owners of industrial and finance capital and their power elites. This use requires the repression of political dissidents and the destruction of democratic institutions.* That destruction is short-listed by torture, mass arrests, warrantless surveillance, press censorship, assassination squads, denial of due process in legal proceedings, limitless reach of intelligence agencies, and intrusion of military forces in domestic policing.

Of course, contemporary spinmeisters can exploit the usage of "fascism" to avoid the possibilities that they, themselves, are fascists. When she was the US National Security Advisor, Condoleezza Rice, in an interview with Cox Newspapers on June 3, 2004, insisted that Bush will someday rank alongside such towering leaders in the war against fascism as Franklin Delano Roosevelt and Winston Churchill. Rumsfeld also recalled fascist Germany when he implored Asian defense ministers on June 4, 2004 to refrain from making deals with terrorists that would duplicate the mistakes made by nations trying to appease Hitler in the Thirties.

These laughable "revelations" are not the only ones invented by officials who at times could not tell the difference between their party line and the real world. After World War II, US officials used the "national security" rationale to subvert Third World governments opposing American investments abroad. The "Cold War" was grounded in superpower rivalry, but it was also used as a pretext for cultivating fascism abroad. The CIA and agencies such as the Agency for International Development (AID) bribed Third World officials. And for those who could not be bought, fascism provided an alternative.

Chile was the oldest democracy in Latin America. Nonetheless, in 1970 Richard Nixon ordered CIA Director Richard Helms to begin preparations for a military coup when social democrat Salvador Allende was popularly elected president. Henry Kissinger, National Security Adviser to Nixon, agreed, saying, "I don't see why we need to stand by and watch a country go communist because of the irresponsibility of its own people."

The US increased arms shipments to the Chilean military and stepped-up training for Chilean officers at The U.S. School of the Americas (also known as the "School of Torturers"). Both Latin America and North America were saturated with propaganda. While an economic crisis was being instigated by a US corporate boycott, Allende was demonized and his welfare state policies condemned.[103] And since the plans for the coup needed a pretext to justify turning Chile into a slaughterhouse, the US govern-

---

103 The CIA and American corporations poured millions into Chilean right-wing movements and trucking firms that demonstrated against government policies and disrupted the economy.

ment spread the Big Lie that a coup would be justified because it would save Chile from communism. Sound familiar?

The CIA financed nationwide strikes by transport workers and shopkeepers, engineered the sabotage of the public infrastructure and infiltrated all of the parties in Allende's coalition. (Ultimately, almost a third of the US embassy staff were on the CIA payroll.) Then, General Rene Schneider, commander-in-chief of the Chilean army, was assassinated because he refused to stage a coup. Allende—wrongly believing General Augusto Pinochet's promise to stay neutral—made Pinochet commander-in-chief. Pinochet immediately purged the officers who felt obligated to protect the Chilean Constitution.

Are these brute facts not reminiscent of Germany in 1933?

In 1979, Noam Chomsky and Edward S. Herman published *The Washington Connection and Third World Fascism*.[104] The first page graphically positioned the US in the Seventies as a "Sun" at the center of a "solar system" containing 26 "Planets," identified as client states. The graph showed the millions in US military appropriations and the thousands of troops stationed in these fascist states. It also revealed that 22 of these US clients practiced torture "on an administrative basis."

Words like "fascism" or "neofascism" in Chomsky and Herman's trenchant study referred to US policies backing the suppression of human rights and democracy in client states. The word "subfascism",

---

104 Chomsky and Herman, op.cit.

on the other hand, classified the oppressive policies adopted by these client states themselves. So the word "fascism" in their work has been reinterpreted for modern audiences to include imperial networks in which the terror, oppression, and obliteration of democracy associated with classical fascism reappeared after World War II.

MULTINATIONAL TERRORISTS

At the close of World War II, war crimes tribunals held officials at the highest levels of government accountable for crimes committed by their subordinates. But no one in the top echelons of the U.S. government was ever indicted for war crimes committed in Vietnam, Laos, Cambodia, Afghanistan, or Iraq. These horrific crimes included the assassination of South Vietnamese officials and their families, wars of aggression, indiscriminate bombings of villages and cities, and the use of 11 million gallons of Agent Orange. This lethal chemical poisoned food for humans and farm animals and it devastated more than a seventh of the country's land.

Nixon was impeached and forced to resign in 1974 but the felonies justifying his punishment (and Ford's pardon) began with an attempt to break into the Democratic National headquarters at the Watergate complex in Washington, D.C. The felonies did not refer to war crimes or crimes against humanity.

Nor has any highly placed American official been indicted for supporting the fascist coup d'état that killed and tortured thousands of Chileans in 1973, or the decades of terror and political repression imposed by *Operation Condor*, a collaborative effort involving military dictatorships in Argentina, Chile, Uruguay, Paraguay, Bolivia, and Brazil. (Ecuador and Peru were added later). The terror, abductions, disappearances, assassinations, and torture conducted by these fascist regimes were supported by the U.S. State Department, Pentagon, and CIA.

Operation Condor emerged during the 1960s and 1970s when liberal, nationalist, and socialist movements challenged South American dictatorships. The U.S. government actively supported *Condor* supposedly in order to forestall "communist" and "subversive activities" that had led to the 1959 overthrow of Batista's dictatorship in Cuba. Yet these so-called subversive activities were being carried out by officials, political parties, and movements that were fighting for democracy and national independence. They desperately needed economic and social reforms while the real targets of the death squads employed by *Condor* turned out to be dissident nationalists, liberals, leftists, leaders of union organizations and peasant movements, priests and nuns, journalists, students and their relatives (including children) as well as guerrillas.

Refugees fleeing the savage repression in Chile and the other military dictatorships had re-settled in adjoining nations where they felt safe from attacks by military and paramilitary squads. However, the intelligence agencies of the *Condor* nations evolved a three-part strategy beginning with surveillance operations and domestic repression, ending with a worldwide operation based on abductions and assassinations of noted legislators, ambassadors, labor leaders, and progressives. The officers who believed that military forces should be subordinated to constitutional authorities were also tracked down by these agencies and killed.

J. Patrice McSherry, a political scientist at Long Island University in Brooklyn, spent well over a decade researching *Condor*. She notes that *Condor* emerged in 1973 although it was not code named and formally instituted until 1975. "As *Condor* coalesced, a terrifying new wave of disappearances and murders took place across a vast region of South America. Hundreds of exiles who opposed the military dictatorships in their countries were pursued across borders and eliminated with pitiless effectiveness."[105] In Buenos Aires, Argentina, for example, *Condor* assassins killed the exiled Uruguayan legislators Zelmar Michelini and Héctor Gutiérrez Ruiz, the Bolivian ex-president Juan José Torres, and the constitutionalist Chilean General Carlos Prats and his wife, Sofía Cuthbert. In Washington, DC, *Condor* assassins used a car bomb to kill the former Chilean Minister Orlando Letelier and his American assistant, Ronni Moffitt.

Operation Condor officially ended in 1983 with the downfall of the Argentine dictatorship. But previously, in August 1974, the corpses of the first victims of *Condor*, Bolivian refugees, were found in Buenos

---

105 J. Patrice McSherry. 2005. *Predatory States: Operation Condor and Covert War in Latin America*. Boulder: Rowman & Littlefield. Also, J. Patrice McSherry. 2005. "The Undead Ghost of Operation Condor." *Logos*. (http://www.logosjournal.com/issue_4.2/mcsherry.htm)

Aires garbage dumps. Some estimates indicate that *around 30,000 victims were assassinated in Argentina alone.*

The U.S. provided *Condor* operations with organizational, intelligence, financial and technological assistance. The CIA laid the groundwork for *Condor* in the early 1970s. It encouraged collaboration between right-wing Latin American military and police officers. The U.S. School of the Americas trained *Condor* assassins and torturers. Using coded messages, *Condor* agents contacted and coordinated their efforts through a Pentagon communications installation in the Panama Canal Zone that covered Latin America.

Despite the mothers who mourned *los Desaparecidos* ("the disappeared ones") in silent vigils conducted in government plazas and despite the *Condor* car bombings and the broken, immolated or tortured bodies dropped off on city streets or in garbage dumps, the general public was never aware that these terrifying events had been produced by a secret *multinational* conspiracy until recently. On December 22, 1992, information about *Operation Condor* came to light when José Fernández, a Paraguayan judge, uncovered "terror archives" revealing that *Condor* had imprisoned 400,000 individuals, carried out 30,000 *"Desaparecidos"* and assassinated 50,000 persons.[106]

As a result, a number of Latin American countries have used the archives and eyewitness accounts in

---

106 Undoubtedly, the uncovered records were incomplete. The true magnitude of the terror committed by Condor agents will never be known.

recent years to prosecute former military officers. Furthermore, since the *victims* of *Condor* included European citizens, the disclosures sparked European investigations that provided further information. When a Spanish judge pressed charges against Pinochet in 1998 during the Clinton administration, for instance, the United States surprisingly agreed to Spain's request for 60,000 pages of secret files on Chile, including CIA operational files.

Former National Public Radio managing news editor and reporter, John Dinges, who had lived in Chile and was interrogated in a secret torture camp, examined archival documents and eyewitness accounts. And he published the terrifying story of *Operation Condor* in 2004.[107]

In 1998, Pinochet was arrested in London while undergoing medical treatment when British authorities responded to Spanish warrants charging him with illegal detention, torture, forced disappearances, and murder in Chile of Spanish citizens. (The case was unprecedented because it was in part based on the principle of universal jurisdiction, which assumes that crimes against humanity are so atrocious that they can be prosecuted in any court in the world.)

After a court battle, Pinochet was sent back to Chile. (He died before he could be tried.) Chile also indicted around 30 torturers including the commander of a major *Condor* intelligence agency for the disappearance of 20 victims.

---

107 John Dinges. 2004. *The Condor Years: How Pinochet and His Allies Brought Terrorism to Three Continents*. New York: The New Press.

Another Chilean was convicted in Argentina for the assassination of Carlos Prats and his wife. In addition, a top Uruguayan official, an ex-minister of foreign affairs and six officers, responsible for the disappearance of opponents to the Uruguayan dictatorship, were arrested in 2006.

General Raúl Iturriaga, former head of the Chilean secret police agency, was wanted in Argentina for the assassination of General Prats. He had escaped from Chilean authorities after being sentenced to prison for kidnapping and "disappearing" an opponent of Pinochet. He was recaptured in August 2007 in a Pacific coast town.

Although attempts are still being made to identify and punish the persons responsible for *Condor*, most of these people were not prosecuted because of amnesty laws passed by legislators after the collapse of the dictatorships. The legislators had insisted on "national reconciliation" rather than justice; consequently, continued attempts to find and prosecute *Condor* agents primarily depend on 'holes' in the amnesty laws or their repeal.

An Argentinean commission, for instance, investigated human rights abuses associated with *Condor*. After trying government leaders, it found upper echelon officers guilty of engaging in state terrorism. However, amnesty agreements that helped bring the Argentine dictatorship down stalled the trial until the agreements themselves were repealed by the Argentine Supreme Court in 2003. The repeal also ensured the current prosecution of another *Condor* agent, sentenced in absentia in France for the disappearance of two French nuns.

No American official or field agent who supported Condor has been punished. Henry Kissinger, for instance, was Secretary of State in the Nixon and Ford administrations. Consequently, he was held accountable for *Condor* even though he is a master of the CIA tactic called "plausible deniability." He would make a speech before a Latin American audience about the importance of human rights but inform people who were truly violating these rights not to take him seriously. He would prepare statements (at the instigation of State Department officials alarmed by *Condor)* that expressed his opposition to terror; but he never actually sent them to the governments that were sponsoring terror.

Since the disclosures suggested that Kissinger supported *Condor*, he was confronted in 2001 with one official investigation after another. A French judge in 2001 served Kissinger with a warrant while he was staying at the Hôtel Ritz in Paris. The judge wanted to question him about the "disappearances" of French nationals in Chile during the Pinochet dictatorship as well as U.S. involvement in *Condor*. Kissinger ignored the warrant and immediately left Paris.

During the same year, a Chilean judge wanted to question Kissinger about the 1973 killing of American reporter Charles Horman, whose execution was dramatized by the 1982 Costa-Gavras film, *Missing*. The Chilean Supreme Court had granted the judge the right to question Kissinger and the questions were sent to him via diplomatic routes. But they were not answered. Also, in 2001, the family of General René Schneider filed a civil suit in a Washington, D.C., federal court, asserting that Kissinger ordered General Schneider's assassination.

On 9/11, 2001, the 28th anniversary of the Pinochet coup, Chilean human rights lawyers filed a criminal case holding Kissinger, Pinochet, the former Bolivian general and president Hugo Banzer, the former Argentine dictator Jorge Rafael Videla, and the former Paraguayan president Alfredo Stroessner accountable for *Condor*. The case was brought on behalf of some fifteen victims, ten of whom were Chilean.

In late 2001, Brazil canceled an invitation for Kissinger to speak in Sao Paulo because it could no longer guarantee his immunity from judicial action. After viewing these incidents, Christopher Hitchens in 2002, wrote,

> Earlier this year, a London court agreed to hear an application for Kissinger's imprisonment on war crimes charges while he was briefly in the United Kingdom. It is known that there are many countries to which he cannot travel at all, and it is also known that he takes legal advice before traveling anywhere.[108]

Futile attempts to force Kissinger to testify about his role in Condor did not end in 2001. On February 16, 2007, a request for the extradition of Kissinger was filed at the Supreme Court of Uruguay on behalf of a political activist who was kidnapped, tortured, and disappeared by the dictatorial regime in 1976.

---

108 Christopher Hitchens, 2002. "The Latest Kissinger Outrage: Why is a proven liar and wanted man in charge of the 9/11 investigation?" *Slate*. (http://www.slate.com/?id=2074678)

Dinges and McSherry point to parallels between Condor and the Bush administration's use of torture, abduction, and extrajudicial transfer of a person from one state to another. (This transfer is spun as "extraordinary rendition" by contemporary State Department advisors.) But Kissinger has nothing to fear as long as he takes refuge in countries that will ignore requests for his extradition.

FOSTERING MIDDLE EASTERN TERRORISTS

Scanning the horizon through Janus' baleful eye requires a hidden government—a state within a state —whose covert operations are secured by tacit accommodations between officials in all branches of the American government. Even Congressional committees entrusted with monitoring criminal behavior by government officials normally keep the malevolent side of Janus under wraps.

For instance, government propaganda has deliberately underplayed the CIA's role in helping Islamic fundamentalists crush their secular opposition. The financial support given by the CIA to Osama bin Laden and his cronies hasn't been scrutinized deeply enough. Furthermore, as indicated, many journalists who know about this support cynically write it off as just another stupid mistake made by our incredibly imperfect government.

Actually, Ronald Reagan met in 1985 with a group of turbaned Afghanis who were leaders of the Mujaheedin. Reagan introduced them to the American media in these words: "These gentlemen are the moral equivalents of America's founding fathers."

"This was the moment," writes African Studies scholar Mahmood Mamdani, "when official America tried to harness one version of Islam in a struggle against the Soviet Union."[109]

Mamdani, the Herbert Lehman Professor of Government and Director of the Institute of African Studies at Columbia University, reports that the US-cultivated terrorism in order to undermine regimes it considered pro-Soviet. He adds, "In Southern Africa, the immediate result was a partnership between the US and apartheid South Africa, accused by the UN of perpetrating 'a crime against humanity.'" Reagan termed this new partnership "constructive engagement."

Such Cold War partnerships also supported other terrorist movements such as Renamo in Mozambique and UNITA in Angola. According to Mamdani,

> It was not simply that they were willing to tolerate a higher level of civilian casualties in military confrontations—what official America nowadays calls collateral damage. The new thing was that these terrorist movements specifically targeted civilians. It sought to kill and maim civilians, but not all of them. Always, the idea was to leave a few to go and tell the story, to spread fear. The object of spreading fear was to paralyze government.

The US employed this criminal tactic in Southeast

---

109 This and the following quotes are from Mahmood Mamdani. 2004. *Good Muslim, Bad Muslim: America, the Cold War, and the Roots of Terror*. New York: Pantheon Books.

Asia, Africa, Nicaragua, and El Salvador. The tactic was altered as the Cold War shifted from one arena to another. In Nicaragua, for example, the Contras employed this tactic when attacking rural communities and murdering village leaders and medical personnel.

The Middle East provided still another opportunity to employ terrorism. In 1978, a Communist coup overthrew a dictatorship in Afghanistan led by Mohammed Daoud Khan.[110] The Communist's regime lasted until 1992 but their heavy-handed attempts to impose rapid changes among traditional Muslims in the countryside—in landholding, education, marriage and family relations—led to insurrections and resentments that were rapidly exploited by the US.

President Carter in 1977 had cut aid to Pakistan because of its human-rights violations and intention to build nuclear weapons to counter India. But the Communist coup in Afghanistan changed everything: Carter now offered Pakistan hundreds of millions of dollars in exchange for aiding the rebels to overthrow the Communist regime in Afghanistan. Reagan upped the ante by making Pakistan the third- largest recipient of foreign aid after Israel and Egypt.

And when the Iranians rebelled, overthrew the Shah, and burst into the American embassy in Tehran, CIA and State Department documents seized at the embassy showed that the US had initi-

---

110 Khan was originally supported by leftist officers but he had purged them in 1975 and moved rightward.

ated its meetings with Afghan-rebel representatives in Pakistan eight months before the Soviet intervention. Zbigniew Brzezinski, President Carter's National Security Advisor, confirmed this information, admitting:

> According to the official version of history, CIA aid to the Mujaheedin began during the Eighties, that is to say, after the Soviet army invaded Afghanistan, 24 Dec. 1979. But the reality, secretly guarded until now, is completely otherwise: Indeed, it was 3 July 1979 that President Carter signed the first directive for secret aid to the opponents of the pro-Soviet regime in Kabul. And that very day, I wrote a note to the president in which I explained to him that in my opinion this aid was going to induce a Soviet military intervention.

The Reagan administration ensured the intervention. It attempted to turn the Afghan War into the Soviet Union's Vietnam. The CIA determined that "killing Russians" was the "real task" in Afghanistan: "Among the more influential 'bleeders' in Washington was Reagan's assistant secretary of defense, Richard Perle. He would later have a Second Coming as a prominent hawk on the George W. Bush team after 9/11. Mamdani reports:

> The Afghan War was originally underwritten by US funds. [In 1980, Saudi Arabia also pledged financial aid.] But, after President Reagan issued a National Security Directive in 1985, the intervention into Afghanistan became *the largest covert operation in the history of the CIA*. Congress ultimately provided almost 3 billion dollars in covert aid for the

Mujaheedin. This amount exceeded all other
CIA covert operations in the 1980s [sic] combined.

The CIA, at this point, tried to use tactics being
carried out by the Nicaraguan Contras in the early
Eighties—but a corresponding Afghani force that
could fulfill its aims could not be found. So the
agency recruited a new force composed of Islamist
recruits.

The CIA dispatched its recruiters into Algeria,
Saudi Arabia, Egypt, Indonesia, and Britain. Sheikh
Abdullah Azzam, dubbed "Gatekeeper of The Jihad"
in the mid-Eighties, for instance, was a recruiter.
Sheik Azzam was a Palestinian theologian with a
doctorate in Islamic law who had taught at King Ab-
dul Aziz University in Jidda. Here, one of his students was Osama bin Laden. Azzam toured the US in
the Eighties as a CIA asset recruiting for holy war,
presumably to be in Afghanistan only. But Azzam
also helped found Hamas, telling his recruits that
their jihad was both a political and religious duty to
be fulfilled through martyrdom. Mamdani indicates
that the Afghan jihad began as an *American* jihad.
This was fully realized during Reagan's second term
in office: In March 1985, Reagan's National Security
Decision Directive 166, authorizing "stepped-up
covert military aid to the Mujahedin" made clear
that the secret Afghan war's *new* goal was to defeat
Soviet troops there through covert action and ultimately encourage a Soviet withdrawal. In 1986, CIA
Director William Casey persuaded Congress to provide the Mujahedin with American advisers and
Stinger anti-aircraft missiles. The guerrilla war was

extended into the Soviet republics of Tajikistan and Uzbekistan but the guerrillas were pulled back when the USSR threatened to retaliate by attacking Pakistan. Finally, the recruitment of radical Islamists not from Afghanistan was stepped up. These steps deepened the belief that the war had broadened to oppose infidels *everywhere*.

Right-wing Islamism, Mamdani points out, was but a small and scattered movement before the Afghan War. The Afghan jihad gave it the organization, numbers, skills, and resources to become a global movement after 9/11. But these right-wingers primarily relied on isolated acts of urban terror. The Reagan administration claimed to create an "Islamic infrastructure of liberation but in reality [it] forged an 'infrastructure of terror' that used Islamic symbols to tap into Islamic networks and communities."

THE ISLAMIC FOREIGN LEGION

The *madrassahs*, Islamic religious schools in these countries, became political academies for recruiting and training jihadist cadres. "The Islamic world," Mamdani says, "had not seen an armed Jihad for centuries. But now the CIA was determined to create one. It was determined to put its [modern] version of tradition at the service of politics."

Among those recruited was the scion of a leading Saudi family: Osama Bin Laden. The Bin Ladens were cosmopolitans closely connected to the royal Saudi family and underwriters of endowment programs at universities such as Harvard and Yale.

Osama Bin Laden was selected as leader of Afghan jihad. He and others conducted a training program to create a corps of officers and fighters supporting the jihad. Madrassahs offered by General Zia were primarily used to train officers and fighters in Pakistan but some members of the officer corps and high-level Mujahedin recruits were trained in camps within the United States.[111]

Training in guerrilla tactics was combined with political indoctrination organized around politicized Islamic doctrines. This training, as Mamdani points out, created the "Islamic guerrillas." Dilip Hiro, an Indian journalist based in London, described the madrassah curriculum: "Predominant themes were that Islam was a complete sociopolitical ideology, that holy Islam was being violated by atheistic Soviet

111 The list of camps includes the High Rock Gun Club in Naugatuck, Connecticut; Fort Bragg, North Carolina; CIA's Camp Perry in Williamsburg, Virginia; a CIA-used Army Special Forces site, Harvey Point, North Carolina; Fort A. P. Hill, Virginia; and Camp Pickett, Virginia." Also, the mujahidin operated an Educational Center for Afghanistan during the 1980s. Pervez Hoodbhoy gives the following exam from children's textbooks designed for it by the University of Nebraska under a $50 million USAID grant that ran from September 1986 through June 1994. A third-grade mathematics textbook asks: "One group of mujahidin attack 50 Russian soldiers. In that attack 20 Russians are killed. How many Russians fled?" A fourth-grade textbook ups the ante: "The speed of a Kalashnikov [the ubiquitous Soviet-made semiautomatic machine gun] bullet is 800 meters per second. If a Russian is at a distance of 32.00 meters from a mujahid, and that mujahid aims at the Russian's head, calculate how many seconds it will take for the bullet to strike the Russian in the forehead." The program ended in 1994, but the books continued to circulate: "US-sponsored textbooks, which exhort Afghan children to pluck out the eyes of their enemies and cut off their legs, are still available in Afghanistan and Pakistan, some in their original form."

troops, and that the Islamic people of Afghanistan should reassert their independence by overthrowing the leftist Afghan regime propped up by Moscow."

Mamdani notes that the madrassahs also taught that the Islamic jihad in Afghanistan would fuel a revolution in countries with large Muslim populations, particularly in Soviet Central Asia. By the late Eighties, he writes, leading madrassahs in Pakistan "began to reserve places specifically for Central Asian radicals, who received a free education and a living allowance." Incubated in these schools were the Taliban [*talib* means 'student'] and other so-called "Islamic fundamentalists"—among the first students to be recruited for a wider war.

The CIA helped produce a foreign legion and Afghani Contras. The trainees were divided into Afghan Mujaheedin and non-Afghan jihadi volunteers. Brigadier Muhammad Yusuf, who commanded one of the Afghan units said, "During my four years, some 80,000 Mujaheedin were trained." Ahmed Rashid, a Pakistani journalist, estimates that Muslim radicals from 43 Islamic countries fought for the Mujaheedin between 1982 and 1992. Fighters from one "international brigade" received approximately $1,500 monthly—a fairly high salary at the time.

In addition to providing arms and money, the project created private volunteer militias—comparable to the German Freikorps—composed of fighters who doubled as terrorists. John K. Cooley, an American award-winning ABC news correspondent, reported about CIA training in the US camps:

> ... ranged from infiltration techniques to ways

of extracting prisoners or weapons from behind enemy lines to more than sixty assorted
"deadly skills." The skills passed on by trainers
to fighters included "the use of sophisticated
fuses, timers and explosives; automatic
weapons with armor-piercing ammunition, re-
mote-control devices for triggering mines and
bombs (used later in the volunteers' home
countries, and against the Israelis in occupied
Arab territory such as southern Lebanon)."
There were also local Afghan skills—such as
throat cutting and disemboweling—that the
CIA incorporated in its training.

A *Los Angeles Times* investigation into the worldwide after-effects of the Afghan War discovered that,
without exception, the principle leaders of every major terrorist attack—from 9/11 and before in New
York to France and Saudi Arabia—included veterans
of the Afghan War. Even Pakistan was included in
what the CIA call a "blowback."

AFGHANI CAPITALISM

After the Soviet Union withdrew from
Afghanistan, terror was unleashed in the name of
liberation. Different factions—the Northern Alliance
against the Taliban—fought each other and killed
thousands of civilians. Out of 15 million people, a
million had died, a million and a half had been
wounded and five million had become refugees. Today, as American troops try to ensure the Taliban
can't reinstate their theocratic despotism, mercantile
capitalists rule Afghanistan in the name of democracy.

The corporate media preferred to call these capitalists "warlords"—but their economic survival is largely dependent on the production and sale of such agrarian commodities as opium. Prior to the Afghan War, opium was largely produced for local markets; however, with the help of the CIA it quickly became Afghanistan's biggest cash crop. Furthermore, with the development of processing plants, high-grade heroin became one of its largest exports. And the primary market for this heroin is America. (The fact that this heroin is sold in American illegal markets makes no difference economically. An illegal market is a commodity market regardless.)

The mercantile capitalists created by the CIA included Gulbuddin Hikmatyar who had been a student in the American-sponsored Faculty of Engineering at Kabul University. He had led student protests against the Afghanistan king's secular reforms in Kabul during the late Sixties. In the Seventies, he ordered his followers to throw acid into the faces of women students who refused to wear veils. Hikmatyar served a prison sentence after being convicted of murdering a leftist student but he fled to Pakistan where he served as a member of a secret Afghan rebel group. He then joined the Pakistani army as a "contract revolutionary." When the CIA picked up the contract, Hikmatyar led an armed guerrilla force called Hizb-i-lslami. This force had meager support inside Afghanistan; nevertheless, it received more than half of all arms supplied by the CIA. With this support, it eventually became the Mujahedeen's largest guerrilla army as well as the force that enabled him to become Afghanistan's leading drug lord.

The CIA's support for the changes in the Afghanistan economy was buoyed by its interest in subverting Congressional legislation that had banned the further use of revenues to bring down South American governments. After public demonstrations against US policies, the Boland Amendment to the War Powers Act blocked CIA support to anyone "for the purpose of overthrowing the Government of Nicaragua."

But the CIA deliberately exploited the drug trade to sidestep the Boland Amendment. It secretly obtained funds to accomplish its criminal missions by using its undercover air services (and air forces of such other countries as El Salvador) to fly high-grade heroin into the US.

When Janus' gates in ancient Rome were opened, Roman legions paraded through the forum on the way to war. When Janus' gates were opened by Americans, the world was flooded with heroin.

5 | Friendly Fascism

"Sure, we'll have fascism, but it will come disguised as Americanism." This famous statement has been attributed in many forms to Senator Huey P. Long, the Louisiana populist with an affinity for the demagogues of classical European fascism. If he were alive today, I am positive he would add the words "and democracy." Indeed, to understand the difficulties facing the logic of true democracy, one must realize that the unfolding logic of friendly fascism leads directly to democratic disguises.

—Bertram M. Gross, 1980

B ecause of Bertram Gross's importance, we begin this chapter with a brief look at the closely related work of this distinguished scholar. In 1980, his work *Friendly Fascism: The New Face of Power in America* employed the phrase, "friendly fascism" as well as "classical fascism."[112] To introduce his prophetic book, Gross said, *"Friendly Fascism* portrays two conflicting trends in the United States and other countries of the so-called 'free world'."

The first trend was based on a "slow and powerful drift toward concentration of power and wealth in a repressive Big Business-Big Government partnership." Gross used the term "friendly fascism" to distinguish the new and subtly manipulative form of corporate serfdom being produced by this trend from the *"patently* vicious corporatism" created by the classical fascism of Germany, Italy and Japan.[113]

The second conflicting trend, on the other hand, was being produced by a "slower and less powerful drift toward a truer democracy, toward expanded human rights, civil rights and civil liberties." This trend was being bitterly fought because it encouraged egalitarian relations in the household, workplace, and other social spheres while opposing the dog-eat-dog competition and the commodification of social life.

---

112 Scott Galindez took the photo of "Coffin Bearers at the Los Angeles Pledge of Resistance Event." It was posted Thursday January 16, 2003 *on voice4change.org* and *la.indymedia.org.*

113 Bertram Gross, op cit., p. xi. We have emphasized the word "patently" because, despite critics, anyone familiar with Gross' work or who knew him personally would know that he never believed that "friendly fascism" would be achieved without force.

Gross recalled Sinclair Lewis' 1935 novel *It Can't Happen Here*, because its title deceptively and deliberately implied that classical fascism could actually arise in the US. In Lewis' story, a racist, anti-Semitic, flag-waving, army-backed American demagogue wins the 1936 presidential election and creates an Americanized version of Nazi Germany. But Gross disagreed with Lewis. He claimed that even in Germany, Italy, or Japan today, a fascist state would be different from the old regimes established by Hitler, Mussolini, and the Japanese oligarchs. He added:

> Anyone looking for black shirts, mass parties, or men on horseback will miss the telltale clues of creeping fascism. In any First World country of advanced capitalism, the new fascism will be colored by national and cultural heritage, ethnic and religious composition, formal political structure, and geopolitical environment. The Japanese or German versions would be quite different from the Italian variety—and still more different from the British, French, Belgian, Dutch, Australian, Canadian, or Israeli versions. In America, it would be super-modern and multi-ethnic—as American as Madison Avenue, executive luncheons, credit cards, and apple pie. It would be fascism with a smile. As a warning against its cosmetic facade, subtle manipulation, and velvet gloves, I call it friendly fascism. What scares me most is its subtle appeal.

Under "friendly fascism," the relations between Big Business and Big Government are tighter and supported by "new technocratic ideologies and more advanced arts of ruling." For example, multiparty systems would be "tolerated" with clandestine terror campaigns rather than the bare-knuckle, broad-day-light street thuggery that accompanied the rise of Hitler and Mussolini. Also characteristic of friendly fascism is subversion of democratic principles through the manipulation of federal and state legislatures. Supporting this process is the gradual drift towards greater concentration of power and wealth.

(Gross' prescient grasp of how fascism might arise in the United States was extraordinary! We will chronicle events in later chapters that have validated his prophetic allusions to incipient fascist developments.)

Third-world police states caught in the US imperial web are regarded by Gross as "subfascism" or "dependent fascism" whether or not they have 'democratic trappings'. The causal importance of Big Business is equally important in spotting dependent fascism. Third-world countries, Gross maintains, are often governed by brutal military dictatorships:

> Sheer brutality, however, does not qualify a regime as fascist; its regime must also be interlocked with concentrated capital. Yet big capital is growing in these countries—albeit in forms that are mainly dependent on First World support and initiatives. Hence these can be seen as countries of "dependent fascism." In some of the countries, as the domestic oligarchies become more closely linked with transnational capital, the regimes tend to become more sophisticated in drawing velvet gloves over iron fists and in assuming a "friendlier" visage.[114]

---

114 Gross, op. cit., p. 39.

The use of the phrase "velvet gloves" brings to mind the sociological "legitimacy problem," which is resolved by calling iron fists "necessary evils." Forcible repression in this context is legitimized in popular thinking because it appears to defend national security, traditional liberties, or individual well-being. At bottom, "friendly fascism" requires an array of tactics and manipulations that makes the rise of fascism acceptable to significant numbers of people and their representatives in the government.

DOES IT QUALIFY?

Still, in what ways would the United States' citizenry confront the presence of fascism in its midst? When fascism waits in the wings, how does it introduce itself? Gross' response to this dilemma appears to rely on splitting fascist trends into *ascending stages* of development. Friendly fascism, according to Gross, will emerge gradually rather than suddenly.

Gross's response makes sense especially if customary forms of repression are being used to advance a fascist agenda. Wouldn't they be employed during its formative stage? Or weren't they already in motion? Take, for instance, the long-standing policies for suppressing pro-labor and left-wing dissidents. Wouldn't these policies make it difficult to distinguish the fascist identity of any given oppressive policy today? Did Bush's uncompromising stance toward unions merely reflect the anti-union policies promulgated by the Taft-Hartley Bill and other measures during the 1950s?

Wasn't the incarceration of thousands of Middle Easterners under the Patriot Act another example? And wasn't that comparable to the Palmer Raids and the deportation of left-wing immigrants in 1920? Were we merely witnessing the *customary* use of unconstitutional measures to repress anti-war protests and civil rights rallies? Or do these measures also serve as road signs along the highway to fascism?

For example, after 9-11 Bush's administration had a number of options. It could have adopted law-enforcement tactics and counterintelligence procedures frequently employed against terrorism in industrialized countries. It could also have negotiated a multilateral enforcement strategy with the United Nations. Instead, Afghanistan was invaded and the Patriot Act was rushed through Congress. More than a thousand Middle Eastern immigrants were rounded-up and imprisoned. Attorney General John Ashcroft announced that suspected terrorists would be tried secretly before military tribunals. He also charged civil libertarians with disloyalty when they objected to his racist kangaroo courts.

Immediately, Bush, Ashcroft, and Congress initiated legislation and executive decrees restricting official information, freedom of assembly, and the right to a speedy and public trial. Monitoring religious and political institutions without lawful justifications became permissible. Officials were told to resist public-records requests. Librarians and other record keepers were threatened with prosecution if they revealed that the FBI had subpoenaed their records. Federal agencies could even monitor conversations between attorneys and federal prisoners and discriminate by denying legal aid (i.e., public defenders) for people accused of certain crimes. The legalization of repressive tactics enabled the FBI to search for and seize papers and effects of citizens without probable cause. Citizens could be jailed indefinitely without a trial or without being charged or being able to confront witnesses against them.

The facts speak for themselves here. Yet another development has been equally startling. The people truly targeted by these attacks were largely non-citizens, members of ethnic minorities, or small numbers of public officials and political dissidents.

The Patriot Act introduced centralization of control over government agencies, nation-wide surveillance programs, and other weapons of mass repression. In fact, Ashcroft even tightened *political* control over independent agencies such as the Bureau of Justice Statistics and the National Institute of Justice. Until passage of the Patriot Act, these agencies collected crime statistics and granted research awards reporting whether crime was increasing or decreasing, suggesting what causes it and what to do about it. According to a branch of the National Academy of Sciences, the National Resource Council, crime data must be released promptly in order to maintain credibility and freedom from political maneuvering. But authority was being taken from the directors of these agencies and given directly to the Justice Department. For example, statistical reports and decisions regarding research grants went to Attorney General Ashcroft's office for political vetting before release. In addition, Bureau of Justice Statistics employees were forbidden to speak directly to journalists. All media calls were rerouted to a public-affairs officer.

According to Professor Alfred Blumstein at Carnegie Mellon University, who helped found the Bureau of Justice Statistics in 1979, these changes represented "the most intrusive efforts by the political appointees in the Justice Department to control the shaping and dissemination of statistics since I have been involved."[115]

Ideological blinders and procedures were imposed on the National Institutes of Health, NASA, the Food and Drug Administration, and all the other federal agencies. Former Surgeon General Dr. Richard H. Carmona, who served from 2002 to 2006, informed a House Committee on Oversight and Government Reform that Bush's appointees censured his speeches on public-health issues. Dr. Carmona claims bureaucrats routinely pressured him to suppress information about stem cell research, abstinence-only sex education, emergency contraception, global warming and harmful effects of tobacco use, whenever the information contradicted political stands taken by the Bush Administration. "Anything that doesn't fit into the political appointees' ideological, theological or political agenda is often ignored, marginalized or simply buried," Carmona stated. "There is nothing worse than ignoring science or marginalizing the voice of science for reasons driven by changing political winds."

---

115 Fox Butterfield. 2002, Sept 22, "Some Experts Fear Political Influence on Crime Data Agencies," *New York Times*, p. 23.

CUSTOMARY REPRESSION

Quite possibly, the political climate in America for years to come will be fouled by a build-up of repressive policies at home. To underscore this point, there are numerous comparisons to be made with other historical periods of the rampant abuse of executive power. The economist and Nobel laureate, Paul Krugman, observed that the attack on civil liberties bore an eerie resemblance to the period just after World War I. "John Ashcroft," stated Krugman, "was re-enacting the Palmer raids, which swept up thousands of immigrants suspected of radicalism; the vast majority turned out to be innocent of any wrongdoing, and some turned out to be US citizens." The journalist Alexander Cockburn, in a similar vein, mentioned the McCarthy blacklists of the Fifties and the spying on anti-war protesters in the Sixties. Russ Feingold, the sole Senator to vote against the infamous Patriot Act, defended this vote by courageously speaking about the history of political repression in the US—from the Alien & Sedition Acts of 1798 to the FBI Counter Intelligence Program (COINTELPRO) of the Sixties. He called the Act "a breathtaking expansion of police power."

The Alien & Sedition Acts have been cited because they invoked national security to justify the repression of political dissent. The Acts prohibited people from criticizing the government and congressional legislation—including *criticizing the Acts themselves*!

The Acts also targeted immigrants. They tripled the time an immigrant had to live in the US before acquiring citizenship. They also gave the President power to summarily arrest and deport so-called 'dangerous' aliens who were stereotyped as violent French revolutionaries and Irish rebels.[116] Furthermore, the government was allowed to imprison "enemy aliens" during wartime without granting them legal representation or a trial.

The Federalist Party imposed the Alien & Sedition Acts because they wanted to curb political opponents and suppress critics objecting to their undeclared naval war with France. Fortunately, the Acts boomeranged. Many citizens found the new laws objectionable because they concentrated on immigrants who lived in the States long enough to become citizens and to vote for Jefferson's Republican Party rather than the Federalist Party. In addition, many people were outraged by the attacks on free speech. These attacks weren't limited to accusations of disloyalty of the sort expressed by Ashcroft two centuries later. Benjamin Franklin's grandson Benjamin Franklin Bache and other newspaper editors and writers supporting Jefferson were fined. Some received a two-year prison sentence because writing, uttering, or publishing anything that criticized the President or Congress represented treason.[117]

---

116 That authorization included French immigrants even though America's revolutionary army would not have defeated England without the French fleet, which had prevented the English navy from reinforcing Cornwallis at Yorktown.

117 Also, France reacted angrily when the Federalist Party got the Adams administration to sign a treaty with England. The United States had in 1778 entered into a formal alliance with France and promised to aid the French; but it broke its word. When the Federalist Party gained the upper hand in the government, it pressured the Adams administration to negotiate a treaty with England that weakened its treaties with France. France was furious.

(Later, we will note that a 2007 Presidential decree, issued but not activated, criminalizes anyone—including American journalists—who, according to the Justice Department, sabotaged government efforts to "stabilize Iraq.")

Jefferson, who was vice-president at the time, attacked the Federalists. Furthermore, his supporters defied the Alien and Sedition Acts and popular indignation helped him win the presidential election in 1800. He immediately pardoned the people imprisoned for sedition. Congress repaid their fines with interest while the changes to the immigration laws with one exception were tossed overboard. That exception involved the imprisonment of immigrants and other so-called "enemy aliens" without granting them legal representation or a trial during wartime.

Obviously, The Alien and Sedition Acts were precedent-setting landmarks. Nevertheless, as Frank Donner points out, political repression in the U.S as a *sustained mode of governance* arose much later.[118] Federal, state and local governments introduced this particular mode in the midst of class wars perpetrated by corporate interests.

On May 1, 1886, for instance, 80,000 people led by the Chicago Knights of Labor marched down Michigan Avenue in what became known as the first May Day parade. In the following days, 350,000 workers

---

As a result, French privateers seized American ships on the high seas. France and the US, like fighting cocks, adopted mutually hostile stands. The Adams government—dominated by the Federalists—stepped forward and alleged that a war with France was imminent. Jefferson, on the other hand, supported France.

118 This observation is made by Donner (1980), op. cit., who calls it the "Haymarket legacy."

struck 1,200 factories nationwide in support of the 8-hour day.) Two days later, on May 3, Chicago police brutally attacked strikers at the McCormick Reaper factory, killing four and wounding others. The public was outraged and an anarchist newspaper editor, August Spies, responded by writing a leaflet calling upon workers to arm themselves and to protest the killings by attending a rally in Haymarket Square. During the rally, Spies and others stood atop an open wagon and informed a large crowd that they did not want to incite violence.

The rally was so peaceful that the Mayor of Chicago, who was an observer, decided to leave and ordered the police not to intervene. But the police defied the order! After the mayor left, they marched in a threatening formation against the crowd and ordered it to disperse immediately. Suddenly, as the crowd

19th century newspaper engraving counterfeiting fires, smoke and terror at the "Haymarket Riot"

scattered, someone—whose identity was never discovered—threw a bomb at the formation. The police panicked and fired indiscriminately at the fleeing crowd. Dozens were wounded. Eleven people including eight officers were killed.

Newspapers—calling it "The Haymarket *Riot*" — misleadingly depicted the event as a gigantic terrorist attack on residential buildings and law enforcement officers. The original eight men who led the rally were indicted for conspiracy to commit murder. (Unsurprisingly, immigrants were an easy target: Five of the men were German immigrants while a sixth was a US citizen of German descent.) Five received death sentences even though the prosecution offered no evidence linking them to the bombing. The others received long prison sentences. Eventually, despite worldwide protest, four leaders were hung for a terrorist act they never committed. One committed suicide in his cell during the evening before his execution was to take place. He died in agony after blowing himself up with a smuggled dynamite cap held in his mouth.

The courts—including the US Supreme Court—turned down the appeals. However, the Illinois Governor Richard Oglesby commuted two of the men's sentences to life in prison after the appeals were exhausted. In addition, six years later, John Peter Altgeld became the first Democrat elected Illinois Governor in 40 years. Despite the grave cost to his political career, he concluded that all the men were innocent and pardoned the Haymarket martyrs who were still alive.

As indicated, the first *sustained* police-intelligence

operations aimed at labor organizations and political dissidents emerged toward the end of the 1880s. In addition, agencies on all levels of government around this time began to serve as components of a complex system devoted to domestic repression. Their political targets expanded significantly during the 20th century and the repression itself surged periodically. But the most violent phases in the initial phase of this repression were triggered when great corporations used armed guards, private security services, and state and federal troops to fight organized labor.

In 1913, for instance, Colorado mine workers put down their tools, striking for an eight-hour day, wage increases, union recognition, the removal of armed guards, effective enforcement of laws guaranteeing safe conditions in the mines, abolition of company scrip in company stores, election of checkweighmen who weighed the coal brought to the surfaced by miners, and the right of miners and their families to live in other than "company houses." At the beginning of this strike, 10,000 miners and their families left their company shacks in sleet and snow at the onset of a harsh fall and winter season. They set up tent colonies in the Colorado canyons and prepared for a long, drawn-out struggle. Violent encounters between strikers, armed guards, and sheriff deputies promptly erupted. In pitched battles and guerilla warfare, police armed with machine guns were confronted by miners wielding small arms.

Finally, the Colorado governor ordered the National Guard to "restore peace" in the minefields. However, under pressure from corporate executives, John D. Rockefeller and other mine owners, the Guard abandoned any pretense of neutrality. It began to protect scabs, rob and loot the miners, and attack their tent colonies. Its criminal activities in Ludlow reached a climax when, after a fierce battle, the Guard —and company thugs in Guard uniforms—routed the workers and burned the colony to the ground. Two women and 11 children were asphyxiated or burned alive under the flaming tents.

Colorado miners were enraged! State Federation of Labor officials sounded a call to arms, and thousands responded. According to historian Graham Adams:

> [The workers] seized possession of Ludlow and Trinidad. Then they pounced upon mine after mine in rampaging assaults which ranged 250 miles from their base. One [worker's] battalion stormed and captured Empire mine, killed three guards and left the property in ashes. A few days later some 300 besieged the Watsen and McNally mines. After a fifty-hour gun battle, wrathful laborers dynamited the property. At Forbes, hundreds swarmed into the hills and discharged terrific fusillades into the canyon below. They killed nine strikebreakers and policemen. Afterward these marauders set company buildings afire and laid waste to CFI [Rockefeller's Colorado and Fuel Iron] holdings 30 miles around. Similar armed bands burned, pillaged and desolated company resources at Delagua, Aguilar, Hastings and Black Hills. . . . for ten days a worker's army which controlled vast areas of territory clashed with state and company forces.[119]

On April 28, 1914, President Woodrow Wilson dispatched 3,000 federal troops to Colorado to

119 Graham, 1966. *The Age of Industrial Violence: 1910-1915*. New York: Columbia University Press, p.160

forcibly secure the mine owners' property rights.

In 1915, a federally established Industrial Relations Commission conducted hearings in Denver, Colorado, into the causes of the "Ludlow Massacre." The hearings exposed Rockefellers' control of the judiciary and state government. His Colorado Fuel and Iron Company was accused of owning "judges on the bench as they have owned their office boys." The company was also accused of controlling state attorneys and governors, of fashioning the law "to suit its own wishes" and preventing the enforcement of laws protecting miner's rights. The Commission Chair, Judge Ben B. Lindsey, announced that the "power of capital had become 'superior to that of the president of the United States." He astutely concluded that if nothing was going to be done about this, "the republican form of government would not be possible!"

The Industrial Relations Commission symbolized the paradoxical contrasts between progressive and repressive parts of America's Janus-style government. The Commission conducted its hearings during the First World War when President Wilson, suppressing freedom of speech, had shut down socialist newspapers and imprisoned anti-war activists. The socialist leader, Eugene V. Debs, for instance, was imprisoned in 1918 for making an anti-war speech. And while he was in prison, Debs received close to a million votes when he ran for the Presidency. His sentence was commuted in 1920 but he died in 1926, because his health had been severely undermined by his confinement.

What do the Palmer raids, mentioned by Krugman, also tell us about our history of political repression? Attorney General A. Mitchell Palmer and his

PEACE FRESNO MEMBERS PROTEST SHERIFF
DEPARTMENT "SPY JOB"

assistant, J. Edgar Hoover who directed the General
Intelligence Division of the Justice Department, conducted the infamous "Palmer raids" in 1920, climax-
ing a decades-old attempt by the government to
crush labor organizations and left-wing political parties. By 1920, thousands of socialists and communists—including Victor Berger, Nicola Sacco,
Bartolomeo Vanzetti, and Eugene V. Debs—had been
imprisoned, murdered or indicted on false charges
for their political beliefs.[120] Palmer responded to the

---

120 Adams Berger Jr. was elected to the state legislature yet he was
   prohibited from participation. He was subsequently imprisoned but
   the Supreme Court set him free. Sacco and Vanzetti were framed

post-war surge in union organizing and left-wing activities by exploiting the so-called "Red Scare," which had been fabricated by newspapers and corporations. The Red Scare alarmed many Americans because it alleged that anarchists and Bolsheviks were about to overthrow family, church, and government.

Palmer insisted that the government had to imprison or deport thousands of leftists in order to prevent a violent revolution.[121] He accused Congress of being criminally irresponsible because it ignored the menace of "vast organizations" conspiring to abolish the established order. He said Congress was not helping him to stamp out these seditious societies even though the fires of revolution "were licking the altars of the churches, leaping into the belfry of the school bell, crawling into the sacred corners of American homes, seeking to replace marriage vows with libertine laws, burning up the foundations of society." Fanatic Bolsheviks, who had formed The Communist Labor Party, were not genuine idealists, he declared. The Communists were aliens possessed with criminal minds and, although these Bolsheviks lived in the US rather than Moscow, they were taking orders from Lenin and Trotsky.

Palmer reported that his department had identified as many as 60,000 Bolshevik agents. Alarmingly, he said, "The whole purpose of communism appears to be a mass formation of the criminals of the world to overthrow the decencies of private life,

---

and electrocuted despite protests at home and around the world for allegedly shooting a guard and robbing a payroll.

121 A. Mitchell Palmer. 1920. "The Case Against the 'Reds,'" *Forum*. 63. pp. 173- 185.

to usurp property that they have not earned, to disrupt the present order of life regardless of health, sex or religious rights." Insisting, "first that the 'Reds' were criminal aliens and secondly that the American government must prevent crime," Palmer conducted a 'preemptive strike' by rounding up the usual suspects. People were beaten and arrested without warrants. Palmer's men smashed union offices and the headquarters of the socialist and communist parties. Over 5,000 individuals were arrested. Some were deported. Afterwards, another 6,000 were arrested, mostly members of the labor organization Industrial Workers of the World (IWW).

Palmer had insisted that the raids were absolutely necessary because a Communist revolution was to take place on May Day, 1920. When that day passed without a revolution, critics used the lack of evidence to accuse him of abusing civil rights and exploiting a Red Scare to secure the presidential nomination of the Democratic Party.

Subsequently, congressional committees accused Palmer of using government funds unlawfully. He was charged with violating constitutional amendments regarding free speech, searches and seizures, cruel and unusual punishment and due process. He had arrested people simply because they were members of political organizations listed by Hoover. He had planted covert FBI agents in socialist and communist organizations and dumped the Constitution by taking away citizenship from naturalized citizens.[122] And while Palmer's name may have been

---

122 For instance, Palmer deported more than 500 persons including Emma Goldman who was a naturalized citizen.

long forgotten the term "Palmer Raids" continues to be synonymous with political lawlessness and dirty tricks.

What can the attacks on civil liberties by the Federalists, Woodrow Wilson, and Palmer Raids tell us? First, mythical threats to national security have been used from the earliest years of the Republic to justify the repression of political dissent. Second, government officials have at least partly succeeded in their abuses of power especially when non-citizens, or citizens who are labeled "aliens," are being targeted. The men who instigated repression in these instances relied on stereotypes of aliens, reformers, and revolutionaries who allegedly threatened the nation with violence.

Yet the political context and outcomes of the repression conducted during the Wilson and Palmer years were also tied to the class war waged by great corporations from coast to coast.

"Corporate capitalism," as it was eventually called, introduced the seemingly endless use of repression to control organizations and movements composed primarily of small farmers and industrial workers. This repression, like the Alien and Sedition Acts, was not suddenly canceled and replaced by relatively freer conditions. It was continually restored and updated, targeting similar kinds of people. It created *customary forms* of repression—which Americans experience to this very day.

Examples of these forms of repression have been mentioned previously and the coming chapters will continue to describe the shape they took especially from the Thirties on.[123]

---

123 The customary nature is illustrated by the fact that corporations exploited the repression to sell their products. ▲ This 1930s poster, for instance, urged employers to stock bathrooms with Scot Tissue products to prevent turning their employees into communists because of unsanitary conditions.

WAVES OF REPRESSION

The scale of customary repression is not stable. Violent engagements between corporate wealth and labor organizations decreased enormously after the passage of the 1935 National Labor Relations Act, commonly called "The Wagner Act." The Act gave workers the right to organize and bargain collectively. It instituted peaceful procedures that forced corporations to engage in collective bargaining and protected labor from unfair practices aimed at suppressing union organizing. In addition to backing organized labor, Roosevelt's New Deal reforms prohibited corporations from stockpiling armaments (such as gas grenades, machine guns, and armored vehicles), and from employing company guards, private security agencies, and local police to crush strikes violently.

Still, the waves of customary repression continued to surge periodically throughout the second half of the 20th century. The last wave in that century crested with the lawless Counterintelligence Program (COINTELPRO), conducted secretly during the Vietnam War by the FBI, IRS, and local law enforcement agencies. Millions of people were targeted because they had participated in anti-war, civil-rights, organized labor, social justice, and environmental movements. This surge was also marked by assassinations perpetrated by police, collaborating with FBI agents, who were never punished for their crimes.

The infrastructure underlying customary repression in the US is considered "complex" because it exhibits properties that are analogous to the characteristics of fluids and gasses. For example, the motion of a molecule of air in a room is random at any given time but when the air is heated, the molecules on the average move in the same direction. The molecules move upward, across the room and then, forming "convection currents," descend as they are cooled.

Likewise, the operations conducted by a particular component in the system of customary repression, at any given time, are to some degree indeterminate. These components include among others civic organizations, corporate entities, law enforcement agencies, armed forces, legislative bodies, and private intelligence agencies. Also, the policies conducted by any component at any given time, for instance, may or may not target political dissidents. Nevertheless, the operations of the components *on the average move in the same direction*—especially when a repressive political climate heats up.

Why, then, is our concept of "customary repression" necessary? Because America is by no means an unadulterated democracy and a transition to fascism would probably, in its early stages, be heralded by a surge in customary repression. Without attention to the paradoxical combinations of early and later developments that characterize transitional states, one cannot fully appreciate the possibilities being unleashed today by the alarming expansion of police power in America.

This expansion is particularly frightening because it has in certain respects gone beyond repressive measures that most Americans take for granted. Usually, American citizens are apathetic and fearful in spite of their love of violent entertainment in which the "good guys" win. More than half the population rarely participates in local or national elections, and it is the corporate media that normally determines the way most people think. Unless they are hammered by economic crises or costly and unsuccessful wars, Americans usually believe that policies favoring the rich and imperial aims can't or shouldn't be changed.

Because of their cynical, racist, chauvinist, and bigoted attitudes, millions of Americans, despite calls for tolerance, provide easy marks for people in power. Law enforcement agencies, with critical exceptions, have especially targeted African Americans and immigrants identified by chauvinistic profiling. But the repression of political dissidents has also spiked. Law enforcements dragnets have produced thousands of false arrests and unjustified detentions, because millions remain silent about the growing assaults on civil liberties.

Astonishingly, virtually all the persons arrested and charged with terrorism, hyped during Bush's first term by Ashcroft and the media, involved investigations initiated before 9/11 or were based upon information known before that date. In fact, as indicated, Congressional investigation into the FBI's and CIA's failure to prevent the atrocities on 9/11 suggests that law-enforcement reforms, competent police and counterintelligence procedures, and adequate airport screening would have made the Patriot Act superfluous.

European nations have experienced hundreds of bombings, hostage-takings, bank robberies, kidnappings and passenger plane hijackings at the hands of terrorists from Basque, Corsican, French, German, Japanese, Middle Eastern, and Irish organizations.[125] Yet the US has never been invaded simply because some citizens supported one of these organizations. Great Britain, for example, never invaded the US even though Irish-Americans in New York City and Boston harbored and funded IRA terrorists for almost three-quarters of a century.

SUPPRESSING VOTING RIGHTS

The legacy of customary repression in the U.S. includes the suppression of voting rights. Until the Voting Rights Act of 1965, the old confederate states employed poll taxes, literacy tests and lynchings to keep the descendants of African slaves from voting.

The Voting Rights Act reduced this form of customary repression but it was not eliminated. Take the 2000 presidential election as an example. That election was a watershed in the development of "friendly fascism" because G. W. Bush was handed the most powerful position in the U.S. government. But his victory in that election was secured by suppressing voting rights.

The Republican culprits responsible for Bush's election exploited a unique characteristic of federal election procedures. Candidates for presidential offices in the U.S. are not selected directly by individual voters. Although ballots ask individuals to vote

125 Edgar O'balance. 1989. *Terrorism in the 1980s*. London: Arms and Armour.

for the President and Vice President, they actually vote for "electors" who in turn select the candidates. (In Florida, the electors based their selection on the Party that won the state's popular vote.) Presumably, this indirect procedure was originally mandated by the Constitution to protect the rights of smaller states even though it is archaic and inherently undemocratic.

Florida only had a bloc of 25 electoral candidates in the 2000 election but they proved to be crucially important. The sums for all the other states (and the District of Columbia) provided the Gore campaign with 260 electors. Bush's campaign won 246 electors. Only fourteen electors separated the two presidential candidates; therefore, Florida's 25 electors were enough to put whoever won in Florida over the top.

Yet, the electoral counts in Florida did not automatically decide the issue. Although Florida's voters elected slightly more Republican electors; the difference between them and the Democratic electors was so small that Florida law mandated a recount.

The recounts took place in a charged and confused atmosphere dominated by Republican officials. Jeb Bush, the Republican presidential candidate's brother, was Florida's *governor*. Furthermore, Katherine Harris, the Florida Secretary of State, was in charge of election procedures *even though she was the George W. Bush state campaign co-chair*.

When the recount took place, some counties refused to comply with the law and merely resubmitted previous tallies. But most counties began their recounts and Bush's margin of victory decreased as the counties began to submit their data. Florida's Division of Elections had originally declared that he had won by 1,784 votes. But his winning margin dropped to 327 votes. Six million votes were processed during the recount and Bush's winning margin was razor thin.

Immediately, investigative reporters and Democrats scrutinized the recount and uncovered irregularities. In one county, investigators found that a state employee had tampered with out-of-state Floridian ballots that had not been counted because they didn't have postmarks or other information required by election procedures. To increase Bush's count, this employee had spent days secretly inserting the missing information from on lists of registered Republicans.

In Dade County, the largest in Florida, thousands of registered Democrats—especially elderly Democrats—were so confused by badly formatted ballots that they voted for a third party candidate, Pat Buchanan, when they tried to vote for Gore. Still other obviously unreliable combinations of candidates were selected. After voting, voters complained about the ballots and, when the defective totals were reported, expressed their outrage in public protests.

Amazingly, some counties had difficulty conducting their recounts because their ballots had not been stored properly. The ballots were misplaced or lost. A bag stuffed with ballots that had never been brought to the storehouse was actually found in an automobile trunk.

Voting machines proved to be unreliable. Some were so erratic that reinserting the same ballots produced different results. Also, county employees found machines had not recorded the ballot when a voter's stylus had not fully penetrated the dot adjacent to a candidate's name. Visual inspection of these ballots found "dimples" or "dimpled chads" that hadn't been counted.

Elderly or disabled voters may not have had enough strength to push their stylus through the ballot. (These voters produced "dimples" or "dimpled chads.") But "hanging" or "pregnant" chads were produced when parts of a ballot were not cut cleanly or when a voter's stylus was blocked by chads that had accumulated (from previous use) in channels under the ballots. In fact, some counties had not cleared the accumulated chads from the channels after previous elections were held and thousands of ballots were not counted because the machines had not been maintained properly.

Gore noted the irregularities in four counties that had reported large numbers of uncounted ballots as well as little support for his candidacy in spite of the preponderance of registered Democrats. He asked the Florida Supreme Court to order recounts in these counties relying on a visual inspection of each ballot (i.e., "hand recounts"). Hand recounts, as Gore's legal team pointed out, were in accord with Florida's constitution and judicial precedents. Florida law considered a voter's *intentions* decisive when machine counts were in dispute and visual inspection spotted the dimples and chads not counted (or counted unreliably) by machines. The Florida Court granted Gore's request.

At this point, Harris stepped up and tried to nullify the hand counts by imposing an impossible deadline. Gore reacted by appealing to the Florida Supreme Court and it extended the deadline. Harris responded to Gore's move by appealing to the U.S. Supreme Court. Harris asked the Court to void the Florida recounts and the Florida Supreme Court's extension to her deadline. Although the Court was said to be "impartial" and "above politics," she banked on the fact that most of its justices had been appointed during Republican administrations.

Meanwhile, the hand counts commenced. Republican counters were paired with Democrats in the four counties and their agreement was required during the visual inspections. This requirement supposedly ensured an accurate and fair assessment, but the wily Republicans did everything possible to stall the recounts.

To top-off these developments, death threats were sent to the Miami Democrats who served as counters. In addition, out-of-state Republican Party "apparatchiks" got into the act. A screaming mob composed of Republican officials was flown at their Party's expense from other states,. The mob assaulted Miami's recount center and threatened the lives of the Democrat counters. After the mob was expelled from the building, the fearful Miami counters announced that they could not meet the deadline. The recount was shut down before it was completed.

Concurrently, the Supreme Court accepted Harris' appeal. First, however, the High Court unanimously remanded the case for clarification back to the Florida Supreme Court. Then a majority of one decided that the Florida Court had not protected the rights of Florida voters when it merely permitted hand counts in four counties. The decision was at odds with constitutional provisions and judicial precedents that had given states—not the federal government—the right to decide on how electors should be chosen.

The Supreme Court majority had so little faith in the soundness of their decision that they presented it as an unsigned or "Per Curiam" ruling; which was "limited to the present circumstances" and *could not be cited as a precedent by any other appeal.*

A famous civil rights lawyer and Harvard professor, Alan Dershowitz, called this decision an unprecedented *political* decision. He said that it completely contradicted the Court's constitutional role as an impartial judicial body. He declared that the Court had "hijacked" the 2000 election and added:

> The majority ruling in Bush vs. Gore marked a number of significant firsts. Never before in American history has a presidential election been decided by the Supreme Court. Never before in American history have so many law professors, historians, political scientists, Supreme Court litigators, journalists who cover the high court, and other experts—at all points along the political spectrum—been in agreement that the majority decision of the Court was not only "bad constitutional law" but "lawless," "illegitimate," "partisan," "fraudulent," "disingenuous," and motivated by improper considerations.[126]

126 Alan M Dershowitz. 2001. *Supreme Injustce: How the High Court Hijacked Election 2000*. Oxford University Press: New York

Dershowitz contended that the majority of the Court had actually committed fraud because their stands on "states' rights" in prior decisions sharply contradicted their support for Harris' appeal.

PURGE LISTS DISCOVERED

The U.S. Supreme Court shut down the hand recounts. Bush received Florida's electoral votes and won the election even though his nationwide popular vote was less than Gore's. (Even with the inclusion of the official Florida counts, Bush had only accumulated 47.9% (50,546,002) of the popular vote while Gore had 48.4% (50,999,897).

Unfortunately, Gore took the advice of his legal team and accepted the U.S. Supreme Court's ruling with exceeding civility. (See the award winning HBO docudrama starring Kevin Spacey that dramatizes the division between the "warriors" on Gore's team, and the "grey haired" Harvard lawyers who advised him to concede Bush's victory passively.)

Gore did not protest Bush's victory although Greg Palast, an American who worked as an investigative journalist for the British newspaper, the *Guardian*, and the British Broadcasting Corporation, had published an article during the election about the 40,000-plus voters Jeb Bush had barred from voting. Ninety percent of these voters were Democrats.[127]

---

p. 4.

127 Greg Palast. 2002. *The Best Democracy Money Can Buy: An Investigative Reporter Exposes the Truth About Globalization, Corporate Cons and High Finance Fraudsters*. Pluto Press: London, p.8. Although 90 per cent of these voters were Democrats, Palast could not get his original story reprinted in the U.S. But it

Florida is one of the old Confederate states where conservatives have repeatedly suppressed voting rights, especially when they were exercised by African Americans and citizens who favored democratic reforms. Consequently, the existence of voter purge lists that denied eligible voters the right to vote during the 2000 election was not surprising.

In 1998, the Florida legislature had enacted a law eliminating names from voting registration lists that represented people who had died, changed their residence (and not reregistered), or been convicted of a felony. Supposedly, this electoral "reform" was passed to prevent the voter fraud that had occurred in the 1997 Miami mayoral election. However, listing names of people who had committed a felony showed that huge numbers of African Americans and poor people who comprised the great majority of offenders were being denied the right to vote.

The Florida law also included an unprecedented requirement that had not been duplicated in other states. It specifically required the services of a private corporation for the task of identifying the names on purge lists. (As Palast observes, "No other state, either before or since, has privatized this key step in the elimination of citizens' civil rights.")

Database Technologies (DBT) received a $4,000,000 no-bid contract to create Florida's voter purge lists when Jeb Bush ran for governor in 1998. It continued to execute this contract for the 2000 election even though *The Nation* magazine had previously reported that DBT had carelessly removed

---

was available to the Gore team and its Harvard lawyers because it was published in England.

eligible voters in Jeb Bush's first election.

Before the 2000 election DBT had merged and become a division in ChoicePoint, Inc., which operated as a private intelligence service. ChoicePoint's database contained billions of records which it sold to public and private organizations, and Harris supplied ChoicePoint with a list of individuals who by law could be denied the right to vote in Florida because they had been convicted of a felony. ChoicePoint searched names in its massive database and, in turn, provided allegedly "comparable" or "matching" lists from its files. However, ChoicePoint declared that it did not verify the accuracy of its lists although it knew that they contained an enormous number of "false positives"—names similar to the names (or combinations of names) in Harris' list.

During the election, the *Guardian* financed an investigative team headed by Greg Palast. The team flew to Florida's capital, Tallahassee, and spent weeks interviewing politicians, officials, and employees. Some of the people contacted by the team provided candid reports about what went on during the election. In addition, some of them were whistleblowers who provided Palast's team with the computer discs containing Harris' felony list and her voter purge lists.

Palast's team discovered that Harris approved the lists provided by ChoicePoint even though she had not verified their accuracy. She purged voters whose names were close, but not exact matches, to individuals in her list of Florida felons. In addition, many names represented individuals who had moved to Florida but they were denied the right to vote in the

2000 election because they had committed a crime in another state. Palast reported, for instance that Johnny Jackson Jr. had lost his vote because John Fitzgerald Jackson committed a crime in Texas. The name, "Johnny Jackson Jr.," was similar but not the same as "John Fitzgerald Jackson" and it did not represent a person who had committed a felony in Florida.

Furthermore, Palast reported finding that "a list of 8,000 supposed Texas felons had committed nothing more serious than misdemeanors such as drunk driving (like their governor, George W. Bush)." Palast also observed:

> On the unlikely chance that Jackson of Florida is the same Jackson who served time in Texas, Florida now admits it had no right to take away his vote. In this small sample, Jackson of Texas, Butler of Illinois (#357) and Cooper of Ohio (#360) had the right to vote no matter their record. This error alone cost Gore six times as many votes as Bush's official victory margin.[128]

Later, Harris claimed that she had "corrected" the list of Floridians who had committed felonies in Texas. But Palast believed that her lists still contained enough names to swing the election in Bush's favor.

The purge of Texan ex-cons who were eligible to vote in Florida represented a fraction of the names purged by Jeb Bush's administration. After every list was scrutinized, Palast found that Floridians who had emigrated from as many as thirty five states

---

128 Op cit. p.19

were included in the felony purge lists. Although there were some exceptions, the use of the purge lists resulted in the unlawful inclusion of thousands of voters who were denied the right to vote. Palast concludes:

> In the months leading up to the November balloting, Florida Governor Jeb Bush and his Secretary of State Katherine Harris ordered local elections supervisors to purge 57,700 voters from registries on grounds they were felons not entitled to vote in Florida. As it turns out, these voters weren't felons, at most a handful. However, the voters on this "scrub list" were, notably, African-American (about 54 per cent) and most of the others wrongly barred from voting were white and Hispanic Democrats.

When media critics finally confronted Choice-Point-DBT with the inaccuracies, it tried to put the blame on the Jeb Bush administration. It claimed that the Florida administration was responsible because it did not verify the lists. This claim, of course, was arguable. After, all the data aggregation company had received millions to provide the lists. On the other hand, the ultimate responsibility for verifying accuracy cannot be denied. Florida's government was undoubtedly responsible and its refusal to correct the lists was obviously based on deliberate intentions to commit unlawful acts. The 2000 election was a fraud because it was committed by Florida officials with malice aforethought.

Malicious intent was demonstrated repeatedly by Harris' and Jeb Bush's refusal to grant the voting rights of Floridians who had out-of-state felony records. The Florida Court of Appeal, in *Schlenther vs. Florida Department of State* (1998) observed that Connecticut automatically restored civil rights after felons served their sentence. It ruled unanimously that a man "convicted in Connecticut 25 years earlier" could not be disenfranchised when he moved to Florida. Palast reports:

> The *Schlenther* decision was much of the talk at a summer 1998 meeting of county election officials in Orlando. So it was all the more surprising to Chuck Smith, systems administrator with Hillsborough County, that Harris's elections division chiefs exhorted local officials at the Orlando meeting to purge all out-of-state felons identified by DBT. Hillsborough was so concerned about this order, which appeared to fly in the face of the court edict, that the county's elections office demanded that the state put that position in writing – a request duly granted.

The Nation obtained the text of Harris' response to Hillsborough. Her letter arrived seven weeks before the presidential election, ordering the county to tell ex-felons trying to register that they would be forced to undergo months—if not years—of review before obtaining clemency from Jeb Bush. Harris' letter was deceitful because the Florida Appeals Court had barred this requirement when an ex-con entered Florida with civil rights restored by another state.

Electoral fraud handed G.W. Bush the most powerful position in the government. His coup d'état was a watershed in the development of friendly fascism because it undermined democratic rights and jump-started the unprecedented consolidation of government agencies that dominate American politics today.

6 I Consolidating Power

"Integration of government agencies and coordination of authority may be called the keystone principle of fascist administration."

—Bertram Gross, 1981

HOMELAND SECURITY

A truly shocking and unnecessary change by the Bush administration reflected attempts to create an integrated structure, commanded from the top—regardless of size, manifold functions or the competence of its staff. For instance, in accord with legislation passed on November 25, 2002, at least 22 long-established agencies, including the Coast Guard, Customs Service, Immigration Enforcement, Secret Service, and Federal Emergency Management Agency (FEMA) were incorporated into the Office of Homeland Security (OHS). In January 2003, the OHS was renamed the Department of Homeland Security (DHS) which had acquired the

White House Homeland Security Council—both of which were created in 2002. To enable the government to shadow everyone, the OHS quickly installed an intelligence division to receive information from the CIA and the FBI, ostensibly to investigate potential threats from terrorists.

Since the Homeland Security Act was never truly justifiable by Bush's "war on terrorism," critics had to shake the bushes to discover why it was approved. Instead of providing adequate emergency aid to the survivors of natural catastrophes, many Americans quickly discovered that the Act greatly increased the arbitrary powers of the executive branch to launch operations shielded from public scrutiny and freed of audits and official investigations.

That these shady operations predated the installation of OHS was hardly noticed. In 1997, for instance, Mitzi Waltz, an investigative reporter, psychologist, and anarchist, disclosed that, "Reporters covering the fall of Oliver North discovered that from FEMA's inception in 1979, the agency was handling domestic counterinsurgency planning as well. In 1984, it went so far as to hold national exercises for rounding up and detaining aliens and radicals in rural camps."[129]

In June, 2002, however, the threat to civil liberties posed by government agencies surged. The ACLU argued that the Homeland Security Act endangered access to the Freedom of Information Act, limited the OHS agencies' accountability to the public, prevented the Inspector General from auditing

---

129 Mitzi Waltz. 1997-Summer. "Policing Activists: Think Global Spy Local." *Covert Quarterly Times*.

and investigating agencies, denied OHS employees of safeguards provided by the federal Whistleblower Protection Act, enabled administrators to fire politically unreliable employees easily by forbidding them to form labor unions, and allowed files on individual Americans be shared without regard to privacy rights. [130]

These measures strengthened the executive branch's arbitrary powers and it enabled Republican power brokers to use OHS resources unlawfully to perpetuate a Republican majority in Congress. For example, House Majority leader Tom Delay—until he was tarred by scandals surrounding the corrupt lobbyist Jack Abramoff and money-laundering in Austin—forced the Texas legislature to adopt a Congressional redistricting plan. At his request, The Federal Aviation Administration—a department of the Office of Homeland Security—had in May, 2003 provided Texas authorities with the location of 51 Democrats in the Texas House who had fled to Oklahoma for four days to prevent a vote on a plan that had been unexpectedly initiated by the Republicans. After the Democrats brought the House to a standstill by failing to show up, state troopers, who are only authorized to enforce criminal laws, were given an illegal order to arrest them. The troopers went to their homes, to offices where members of their families worked, and even to the neonatal unit of a Galveston hospital, where one of the Democrat's newborn twins was under care. But the Democrats could not

---

130 The Republicans originally wanted to prevent an estimated 175,000 OHS employees from organizing unions. They also wanted to fire workers who believed they had a right to oppose the government.

be found until Homeland Security employees, after an eight-hour search, told DeLay that the Democrats were on a private plane that was about to land in an Oklahoma airport.

Although 36 Department employees helped track down a flight that had nothing to do with terrorism, official investigators subsequently found no wrongdoing by the Homeland Security agency. Later, an unofficial disclosure by the *Washington Post* of a Justice Department memo showed that Delay's redistricting plan violated the federal Voting Rights Act because it discriminated against minority voters. Nevertheless, senior Department of Justice officials endorsed the plan, and the redistricting was approved in 2003. In the 2004 elections, Texas Republicans gained five seats in the US House of Representatives, strengthening their party's control of Congress.

Ordinarily, redistricting is a traditional strategy employed by Democrats as well as Republicans to increase their hold on Congress. But the importance of this strategy during Bush's administration was heightened by a polarization in voting patterns. Republican successes in federal elections were being ensured by a narrow margin of votes; any tactic that secured that margin had enormous political consequences.

Furthermore, strengthening one-party rule in this case was supported by unlawful police practices. Neither the Texas criminal code nor the US Constitution justified the bundling of the state police with the assortment of organizational devices and strategies used to suppress the democratic side of our two-faced government.

THE "RED SQUADS"

Although the FBI is usually associated with suppression of political dissent, police departments in thousands of districts throughout the country also provided grunts on the ground to outflank the "enemy." These squads proliferated in the early Sixties when almost *300,000* men were assigned the mission of pursuing "subversive" Americans.[131] The squads were subsequently challenged by civil-liberties organizations, legislative committees and courts which, from the Seventies on, succeeded in making municipalities and their police forces leery of lawsuits and judicial restraints. Antiwar movements had also fought the repression; and their ongoing discoveries of police surveillance were duly and vigorously protested.

Nevertheless, even into the Eighties these groups were still engaged in running battles with repressive enforcement policies. In 1990, Frank Donner described the uncertain outcomes of these battles—and the right-wing backlash during the Reagan administration. In dismay he asked how far law enforcement would go if the nation were suddenly convulsed with protests and fears of economic downturn, racial disturbances, growth in nuclear weapons, and terrorism and military intervention abroad? He replied, "If the authorities were to misrepresent these threats, we might again . . . entrust the police [with] the very

---

131 Donner 1990, op cit. pp.1, 81-82.

[abusive] powers now denied them."[132] Donner's words were certainly prophetic. Once again mass hysteria had been exploited to justify unconstitutional powers!

In March 2002, the ACLU again demonstrated the need for vigilance. It sued the city of Denver to preserve its police files on political dissenters until questions about why they were kept were answered.[133] In this instance, the mayor of Denver, Wellington E. Webb, acknowledged that the police have "3,200 files on individuals and about 208 records on organizations." These files "have largely been collected in the last three years," he said.

The files include political groups the police believed have caused problems in other cities and countries. The police often classified political groups and activists as "criminal extremists." This label was applied to the American Friends Service Committee, a Quaker group that won the Nobel Peace Prize in 1947. An Amnesty International organizer's file listed his name, birth date, height, weight, eye color, hair color, driver's license number, and vehicle manufacturer and model. He was branded a "criminal extremist."

Still others were identified in the same manner because they belonged to groups opposed to police brutality. Finally, the members of The Chiapas Coalition were labeled "criminal extremists" because they opposed the "low-intensity war against the indige-

---

132 Ibid. p.364.

133 See Matthew Rothschild. 2002, March 14. "Red Squad Hits Denver." *The Progressive*.

nous peoples in Chiapas and other states in Mexico" and the harmful effects of the North American Free Trade Agreement (NAFTA).

Kerry Appel, the Chiapas Coalition founder, expressed anger and outrage: "I was incredulous at first," he said. "We're an open, public group. I think there's a political agenda here within the police department to impose their own labels on human-rights and peace and justice organizations to criminalize them and erode public confidence in the integrity of their work." Sister Antonia Anthony, a Franciscan nun who spent 25 years living among Indian groups of US and Mexico—and in Chiapas from 1991 to 1995—also objected: "I really don't like being on a police file, nor do I like the threat to our democracy of silencing protesters and stopping nonviolent actions." The Chiapas Coalition, she said, is devoted to consciousness-raising and nonviolent protest. "We are not violent; we are not terrorists," she said.

Subsequently, a panel of three former judges found that none of the 3,200 files met legal criteria of reasonable standards for criminal activities. *Not one out of 3,200 police files!* Mark Silverstein, ACLU executive director, expressed astonishment at the extent of the spying. Mayor Webb said:

> Perhaps I'm too naive. But I thought that after the revelations of COINTELPRO and the Red Squads, I guess I would have thought that police departments would have found far less need to do this kind of thing.

Since the files documented *police* misconduct, he stated: "We need to know why police regarded peaceful political protests as crime scenes." Similarly, Denver taxpayers ought to be told how much money the police spent to create these files.

THE HANDSCHU GUIDELINES

Similar questions were being asked in March 2002—a month later—when the New York Police Department (NYPD) petitioned a Federal District judge to lift restrictions that curtail police monitoring of political activity. These restrictions, the 'Handschu Guidelines,' stem from a 1971 suit filed by 16 plaintiffs, including one Barbara Handschu, who contended the department had violated their civil rights by unlawful surveillance. In 1985, the guidelines were approved because the court recognized that law-enforcement abuses had been committed for decades by the NYPD's notorious Red Squad. Nevertheless, while the guidelines only prohibited investigations of lawful political activity, the department wanted them *fully* lifted allegedly to fight terrorism.

Newsday reporter Leonard Levitt found this justification absurd. He reported that the New York police commissioner "could not cite one instance, real or hypothetical, in which the Handschu guidelines hindered police in fighting terrorism, the only thing to be said with certainty is that his attempt to abolish them is the Police Department's first power grab since the World Trade Center attack." The NYPD and FBI's failure to detect terrorists in the past—rather than having to do with the Handschu Guidelines—was in fact due to their stupidity and laziness, according to Levitt.[134]

Unfortunately, in February, 2003, US District Judge Charles S. Haight announced that he might expand New York's police powers in March [2003?] by "modifying" the guidelines. Although civil libertarians said his modifications would make the guidelines virtually unenforceable, Haight's announcement suggested that he had swallowed the claim that the guidelines were weakening NYPD's ability to fight terrorism.

NYPD officials promised Judge Haight that civil liberties would be respected, and the judge believed them but the NYPD a few months later showed what that promise was worth. During the protests against the war in Iraq, the NYPD interrogated demonstrators about their views on the war, whether they hated President Bush, if they had traveled to Africa or the Middle East, and what they thought might be different if Al Gore was president. When the New York Civil Liberties Union informed Haight about complaints from the protesters, Haight ruled that the interrogations merely reflected "operational ignorance" on the part of NYPD's highest officials. While he admitted that civil liberties lawyers could hold the city in contempt of court in the future if the police continued to violate people's rights, he did not impose new restrictions on the police.

As a result, the NYPD laughed up its collective sleeve and in 2004 revived its lawless policies. Records uncovered by civil liberties organizations revealed that undercover NYPD officers had flown to

---

134 Leonard Levitt. 2002, September 30. "No Connection to Intelligence." *Newsday*.

cities across the nation as well as Canada and Europe for more than a year before the 2004 Republican National Convention to engage in covert surveillance of progressives who planned to protest the Convention. The officers had traveled within the US to cities in California, Connecticut, Florida, Georgia, Illinois, Massachusetts, Michigan, Montreal, New Hampshire, New Mexico, Oregon, Tennessee, Texas, and Washington, D.C. as well as cities in Europe. They used any tactic imaginable to spy on progressives. They had attended meetings, posed as sympathizers, lied about their identities, made friends with antiwar activists, and shared meals with their families. And the officers had certainly hacked their email.

The records provided by this massive surveillance supposedly spotted a small handful of people who expressed interest in breaking the law when the Republican convention took place. Actually, some protesters engaging in civil disobedience proved to be the only unlawful acts conducted during the convention. Furthermore, the reports on these possible troublemakers were overwhelmingly outnumbered by reports about people who never expressed any intention of breaking the law.

The people being watched by undercover officers included members of street theater companies, music groups, church groups, and antiwar organizations, as well as environmentalists and people opposed to the death penalty, globalization, and other ill-conceived government policies. Three New York City elected officials were also watched, according to Jim Dwyer, a *New York Times* correspondent.

The delegates to the 2004 Republican National

Convention were greeted in Madison Square Garden by NYC Mayor Michael Bloomberg. The Americans who demonstrated against the Bush administration and the Republican Party were greeted instead by 10,000 New York police officers equipped with riot gear, body armor, rifles, and machine guns. The officers rounded-up and fingerprinted over 1,800 protesters and shoved them into Pier 57—a condemned, filthy, asbestos-poisoned bus depot, where they were imprisoned without charge for up to 24 hours or more![135]

Signs warned people not to enter the Pier without protective clothing and masks. Nevertheless, the protesters were forced without food or water to sleep on a cold concrete floor covered with oil and chemicals. Some were held for three days without being charged, arraigned, or allowed to contact a lawyer. All cell phones, bags, and purses were confiscated. Also, medications were confiscated.

Lawsuits filed by the NY ACLU reported that the fingerprint and detention practices employed by the NYPD violated the First, Fourth, and Fourteenth Amendments to the Constitution. (They also violated NY state law.) Documents obtained by the ACLU uncovered the millions spent on surveillance, arrests, and detention by the NYPD and the FBI and other Homeland Security agencies. The abusive treatment

---

135 "Pier 57" [Holding Cells for people who protested the 2004 Republican National Convention in New York.] The photo of prisoners awaiting detention at Pier 57 was obtained from *The Villager* (*thevillager.com/villager_237/convene.gif*) when the 2004 Republican National Convention took place. We do not know the photographer's identity.

of the people who protested the Convention indicates the far-reaching influence of neo-fascists who will do everything they can to shape the outcome of an election.

CHICAGO'S RED SQUAD

Chicago is a major city with a history of Red Squads. During the congressional debate over anti-terrorism provisions, some representatives mistrusted FBI agents who claimed their hands were tied before the Patriot Act was passed. For instance, Rep. Janice D. Schakowsky (D-Ill.) recalled, "In the Eighties, I was part of a housewife community organization that it turns out was spied upon secretly by a unit of the Chicago Police Department." This unit was Chicago's Red Squad and it spied on, infiltrated and harassed a wide variety of political groups.

Students at the University of Chicago also recalled the city's infamous Red Squad, officially called the Subversive Activities Unit, when these students rallied in February 2001 to defend freedom of speech against political police. They protested Judge Richard Posner's Appeals Court decision granting the police permission to collect political data on any community group or organization, and to label, at their discretion, certain groups to be "extreme." Police can then place these groups under surveillance and, in addition, routinely film all protest demonstrations supposedly "for training purposes."

Any probing inquiry will reveal that police across the nation had repeatedly claimed that repressive ac-

Pier 57 Holding Cells for people who protested the 2004 Republican National Convention in New York.

tivities ranging from unconstitutional surveillance to brutal "crowd management" tactics have been employed for "training purposes." This claim was a brazen lie. The impact of the tactics was certainly being evaluated by the feds. But the claim repeatedly justified lawlessness by pretending that the police were not criminals—because they never intended to *deliberately* harm anyone when these practices were planned and executed. Chicago's Red Squad had maintained "subversive dossiers" on more than 800 organizations, including the United Methodist Church, League of Women Voters, PTA, Catholic Interracial Council, NAACP, and Planned Parenthood Association. It collected information on 258,000 individuals and gave reports on their lawful political activity to the FBI and CIA. It gave 900 reports to the US Civil Service Commission, potentially to be used in denying job applicants federal employment. It perpetrated numerous crimes by burglarizing organizational files and membership lists, illegally wiretapping homes of political activists, infiltrating hundreds of organizations, and trying to sabotage such organizations as the National Lawyers Guild.

Judge Posner—in a departure from his nauseating act—granted that most of the groups previously harmed by Chicago's Red Squad, "including most of the politically extreme groups, were not only lawful, and engaged in expressive activities protected by the First Amendment, but also harmless." Nevertheless, he added, "The era in which the Red Squad flourished is history, along with the Red Squad itself." Reassuringly, he said, "The culture that created and nourished the Red Squad has evaporated." Referring to the Cold War era, he concluded that the "instabilities of that era have largely disappeared" and legal controls over police—and legal sanctions for the infringement of constitutional rights—have multiplied.

Was Posner sincere? He allowed police to decide what kind of "extreme behavior" merits surveillance even though the reasons city officials gave for being given this power were demonstrably false. Furthermore, in 1999, another federal judge, Ann Williams, had rejected the city's request. She presided over a trial demonstrating that the police could carry out their investigations without increasing their powers.

Especially egregious is Philadelphia, so-called "City of Brotherly Love," also boosted Red Squads. The Squads—comprised of intelligence units and heavily armed swat teams—were lawless. Their activities included illegal surveillance and infiltration, wrongful arrests and brutal assaults on African-American organizations. Yet even though its police department was barred from political spying without special permission in 1987, the Philadelphia Red Squads are still scanning the city for political prisoners.

What about Posner? Unbelievably, he was reputed to be a "liberal" even though his speech on how the US and Canada should respond to terrorism shocked the judges and barristers at an Australian Conference in 2007. Posner's speech supported secret trials for terrorists and putting an end to using the US or Canadian law to control surveillance. He adopted a defensive stance to reassure the members in his audience who may have thought that they were listening to a demagogue. He reportedly said that people *wrongly* proposed that national-security measures in the US could endanger liberty and undermine the political system. These measures, in his opinion, could not endanger Americans because our government could no longer conceal what it did: "We have a very aggressive media and a huge and complex government where many people in the government are quite willing to talk to the press." Therefore, he advised, "We should think of surveillance as preventative, not punitive. We should think of controls that have nothing to do with warrants or traditional criminal justice to prevent abuses."[136] Now *that's* blind justice!

---

136 David Nason. October 9, 2007. "Secret Trial for Terrorists, Says US Judge." *The Australian.*

Connecting The Dots

Not surprisingly, government-financed studies in recent decades have begun to evaluate and recommend changes in how to deal with dissidents. The impact of these studies was felt before Ashcroft's chilling exercise in Orwellian Newspeak, crooned off-tune about ♫ *The New Dawn in Law Enforcement* ♫. For instance, Dr. Mitzi Waltz, an anarchist who teaches journalism at the University of Sunderland, United Kingdom, recognized in 1997 that local political spying with help from the Feds was on the rise. (Like a vampire who has developed a tolerance for garlic, the Red Squads were back in business, Waltz affirmed.) Her article identified studies, conducted during the Nineties, by right-wing organizations such as RAND, the Heritage Foundation and private security companies that had called for the creation of an all-embracing law-enforcement system.[137] Astonishingly, the studies, *financed by federal grants*, explicitly proposed that Americans *could easily be scared by the specter of terrorism into supporting increased domestic spying*.[138]

Furthermore, after evaluating anti-terrorist measures in other countries, multi-jurisdictional taskforces were offered as the best way to sidestep civilian oversight. Waltz states, "[T]he RAND report explicitly touts taskforce participation as a way to get

---

137 See, for instance, Kevin Jack Riley and Bruce Hoffman. 1995. "Domestic Terrorism: A National Assessment of State and Local Preparedness." Rand (USA).

138 Attacks against US embassies and an unsuccessful attempt to bomb the World Trade Towers had occurred before 9/11.

around local laws restricting political intelligence work, and also promotes taskforces as a mechanism for putting such operations on the local and state agenda by providing funding, equipment, publicity, and other inducements." Four years later, when the FBI was setting up Joint Terrorist Task Forces (JT-TFs), it usually succeeded in getting local police to circumvent local restrictions on political surveillance.[139]

The Rand report suggested that multi-jurisdictional task forces would have other "benefits." Consider that police are responsive to demands from corporations and other organizations that influence political or budgetary matters. As a result, police interpret "terrorism" more broadly than the Feds, applying the label to environmentalists, animal rights, and union activists. For example, police working with private security officers harassed protesters attempting to close down the contaminated Hanford Nuclear Reservation in southern Washington. Also, during the Detroit newspaper strike, newspaper companies paid the police department over two million dollars for helping break the strike. Link this with legislation that redefines many types of lawful advocacy as "terrorism," for the purposes of federal prosecution, and the possibilities are frightening.

These possibilities include the collaboration between revitalized Red Squads in cities across the na-

---

139 Strategies for circumventing the law are not restricted to local police. National and international laws can be used in "information wars" involving computers, telecommunications and other advanced informational systems. Consequently, strategies for getting around these laws are being studied because the Internet has become a significant political medium.

tion. In 2002, Mara Verheyden-Hilliard of Partnership for Civil Justice, which has defended demonstrators in a suit against Washington DC police, believed that Philadelphia cops were helping DC police identify and arrest activists at a DC demonstration. Appearing at convention after convention was a Morristown, New Jersey, police sergeant. This officer—as well as members of DC and Philadelphia police forces—for instance, was spotted at a May Day protest in New York. (The Drug Enforcement Administration was also there.) In a discussion with environmental activist, Rob Fish, some of these police revealed that they knew all about his being beaten up in DC and having a police officer to confiscate his camera. They also revealed that they knew he'd been to Ruckus Society training in nonviolent forms of protest in Florida during spring break.[140] They were very open about who they were, some teasingly handing Fish their business cards.

Besides this interagency collaboration, the Joint Terrorist Task Forces (JTTF) in 2002 also set the stage for the national integration of present-day Red Squads.[141] In Portland, Oregon, municipal hearings

---

140 The Ruckus Society, in tune with Mahatma Gandhi and Martin Luther King, provides environmental, human rights, and social justice organizers with the tools, training and support.

141 Diane Lane. 2002. "Repression Goes Local: Joint Terrorism Task Forces could easily become the new 'Red Squads.'" *Toward Freedom Online Magazine.* Diane Lane is a writer, researcher, and member of Portland Copwatch. Paradoxically, the Portland police bureau got into the news by refusing a request by Ashcroft to question 200 locals of Arab descent. Portland officials cited a state law that prohibits police from collecting information on any group or individual without a "reasonable suspicion of criminal behavior."

showed that local officers recruited into the JTTF had been deputized as federal officers with security clearance; therefore, they could not disclose assignments to anyone outside their unit, including their police commanders. Independent oversight by Portland commissions was prohibited as well. Even the mayor and police chief could not review JTTF files. Incredibly, despite these appalling dictatorial restrictions, Portland officials renewed the JTTF contract.

As indicated, a variety of protesters will be burned on the JTTF altar. During the past decade, the Racketeer Influenced and Corrupt Organizations Act (RICO), originally installed in 1970 by the Feds to go after the mafia, has been applied to various activists engaged in civil disobedience. In Philadelphia, for example, a business owner filed a RICO lawsuit in 2002 against protesters demonstrating peacefully against animal cruelty outside his store, which showcases fur coats. Also, Diane Lane, a member of Portland Copwatch, a public-interest group, reported that the FBI's "domestic terrorism" chief had labeled vandalism against business property (including the release of minks) by environmentalists as "eco-terrorism," even though their actions haven't caused personal injury and could have been handled by criminal statutes. Labor unions were targets as well. In early 2001, Lane notes, "a labor union made plans to organize a rally at a construction site, unaware that a JTTF agent had informed the site manager about their intentions. On the day of the rally, union activists found the site shut down."

Surveillance of still other types of groups has been exposed. In October 2003, for instance, Peace

Fresno, an organization devoted to peace and social justice, discovered that Aaron Kilner, a Fresno County detective, had been engaging in undercover surveillance as a member for six months. He had used a false name, lied about his occupation and pretended to be sympathetic to Peace Fresno's aims. He died in a motorcycle accident on August 30, 2003 and his true identity, name, and affiliation with the sheriff's department, was discovered after a Fresno newspaper published this information and his picture. Peace Fresno members put the story together after they saw Kilner's picture and read about his connection to law enforcement. Peace Fresno was outraged when they found that Kilner was "assigned to the anti-terrorist team"—most likely the Fresno team that had been formed previously by Ashcroft.

Earlier, in May 2000, Fresno activists found that a police agent had infiltrated United Students Against Sweatshops. The agent attended meetings and monitored email messages. To justify her job, she filed grossly exaggerated reports about a planned demonstration against a Gap store that resulted in the deployment of a police helicopter and more than *100 heavily armed* officers in riot outfits to arrest 19 peaceful protesters at a local mall. (Several buses were in place before the demonstration began to haul away the protesters.) The presence of the agent was discovered during the initial phase of the criminal proceedings, but all charges against the anti-sweatshop activists were later dismissed.

Undercover surveillance of Peace Fresno also reenacted the operations conducted during the Eighties against the Fresno Latin American Support

Committee (LASC), which had been trying to end US intervention in Central America. The government agents in this case employed COINTELPRO-style tactics. They attempted to polarize LASC by proposing the use of violence and encouraging the group to raise money to buy weapons for Central American revolutionaries. Yet despite the criminal infiltration by *agents provocateur*, and despite years spent investigating and harassing LASC, the police and the FBI never uncovered illegal activities.

Following the discovery of Detective Kilner's identity and resulting complaints, the Fresno Police Department informed the community activists that they could not prevent the police or JTTF members from investigating and interrogating community members. Police Chief Jerry Dyer announced that Fresno is a hotbed of terrorist activity and that is why the JTTF had been established in this area. He added that Fresno could have "sleeper cells" (and maybe a clutch of Martians as well) involved directly or indirectly in illegal methamphetamine production to fund terrorist activities, and that all of this is somehow related to radical Muslim extremists. While this story without doubt seemed insane to Fresno activists, it enabled the police to receive millions of dollars in federal anti-terrorism funds.

The sheriff's office shamelessly confronted its critics. Despite the fact that Detective Kilner had been seen taking copious notes for six months at Peace Fresno meetings, the sheriff said that Peace Fresno was not and is not the subject of any investigation by its anti-terrorism unit, and his department did not have any reports, files, rosters, or notes on Peace Fresno or its meetings.

The anti-terrorist unit, the sheriff insisted, was dedicated to protecting the citizens of Fresno County. Consequently, to accomplish its mission, his office would continue to utilize "legal methods" for collecting, analyzing, and disseminating criminal in-

PEACE FRESNO MEMBERS PROTEST SHERIFF DEPARTMENT "SPY JOB"
[PHOTO: posted by Peace Fresno on *sf.indymedia.org*, Sunday October 05, 2003.

telligence on terrorists while respecting the constitutional rights of all persons. The sheriff argued that his office met stringent federal and state guidelines for intelligence gathering and civil-rights protections in order to prevent crime and protect the health and safety of residents of Fresno County and the State of California. Yet, despite these assurances, the Peace Fresno ingrates declined to raise a glass of champagne in the Sheriff's honor. Courageously, they held a protest instead of a cocktail party.

Prior to 9/11 the FBI installed the first six regional task forces (in addition to 34 major city operations) with plans to continually increase that number. After 9/11, the Justice Department mandated "anti-terrorist" task forces in every federal judicial district. On Dec. 1, 2001, the FBI also instructed all of its 56 field offices to establish JT-TFs. By consolidating its nationwide control of the local police, the FBI augmented the infrastructure for customary repression.

The "Sleeper Cell" Hoax

In January, 2008, the British Broadcasting Corporation broadcast an astonishing documentary entitled *The Power of Nightmares*. The hour-long program contended that before 9/11 Osama bin Laden was a member of a small, loose network that operated on the outermost fringe of the Islamic Egyptian, Algerian, Saudi Arabian, and other training camps in Afghanistan. The camps were composed of rebels interested in overthrowing their own governments. They refused to join a terrorist campaign directed at the United States.

Furthermore, bin Laden was important to this unorganized network because he provided funds for their operations. But he was not the formally designated leader because the network was not an "organization" in the sense that we understand this term. In addition, the label "Al Qaeda" wasn't even used by the network until Bush and his cabal created it. The BBC documentary also provided evidence demonstrating that the Bush administration fabricated the Al Qaeda myth to make it match the American criminal codes, which distinguished differences between (1) individual or unorganized networks of criminals and (2) organized networks like the mafia.

When 9/11 occurred and the Bush administration publicized its al Qaeda fabrication, bin Laden immediately exploited it to magnify the power of his network. Simultaneously, the administration succeeded in getting the American public to fear terrorists practically under their beds. It declared that bin Laden had implanted "sleeper cells" in every city and town in the nation.

Chief Dyer said that Fresno was a hotbed of terrorist activity and that was why the JTTF had been established in his area. But the chronicle of the attempts to find al Qaeda sleeper cells will go down in history as an example of how far corrupt, greedy, opportunistic and lying police chiefs and prosecutors would go to advance their careers by framing innocent Americans.

Jose Padilla a US citizen accused and convicted of being a terrorist is serving 17 years and four months. He was transformed into a zombie who cooperated with the prosecutors after being imprisoned *in solitary confinement* for more than three years without criminal charges. He had been accused originally of being a terrorist who transported a "dirty (radioactive) bomb" into the US. While imprisoned, he underwent sensory deprivation, sleep deprivation, enforced stress positions, and was given drugs. Yet his prosecutors never proved that he had actually transported a dirty bomb.

The Lackawanna Six provide another example of misguided justice. Six Yemeni-Americans from a Buffalo suburb attended an Al Qaeda training camp in the spring and summer of 2001 and some of them asserted that they fled the camp after they heard appeals for violence against America. Although the federal prosecutors never offered evidence that the defendants intended to commit an act of terrorism, they "persuaded" the defendants to plead guilty to "material support of terrorism." (This plea could mean simply that they had paid for their food at the training camp.) The feds obtained the guilty pleas by threatening to label the men "enemy combatants" and imprison them in Guantanamo where the charge of treason could result in their executions. Neal Sonnet, chairman of the American Bar Association's Task Force on Treatment of Enemy Combatants, stated: "The [Lackawanna] defendants believed that if they didn't plead guilty, they'd end up in a black hole forever. There's little difference between beating someone over the head and making a threat like that."

Additional cases in Miami, Tampa, and other cities demonstrated that the Justice Department—to fulfill its fanatical and opportunist desire to prove the existence of Al Qaeda sleeper cells—continued to violate the rule of law. The BBC documentary described the federal cases in Lackawanna, Miami, Tampa and elsewhere and concluded that every attempt to prove the existence of a sleeper cell was a failure. Yet the mass media blacked-out the documentary. Big Brother knew that the American public would (as one response to the video declared) "riot in the streets" after viewing it. As a result, *The Power of Nightmares* went largely unseen by the American public.

PART THREE

SETTING UP THE APPARAT

— ◊ —

7 | Creating the Apparat

"There's virtually no branch of the U.S. government that isn't in some way involved in monitoring or surveillance. We're operating in a brave new world."

—Matthew Aid,

Intelligence Historian

NATIONAL NETWORKS

Alberto Gonzales replaced John Ashcroft as Attorney General in 2004 and inherited his surveillance operations. Ashcroft left Gonzales a significant legacy. His unrelenting efforts had produced blueprints for a nationwide intelligence network in 2002 linking the Justice Department with every state and local law enforcement agency. This bureaucratic monstrosity was structurally evocative of a giant octopus—its tentacles linking 650,000 officers in local police departments to federal intelligence agencies. And it was nourished by hundreds of millions of dollars from taxes imposed on ordinary Americans—ensuring for the first time ever coordination between the feds and state, county, and local enforcement agents via electronic media.

"Helping the FBI and CIA [former competitors] work together" was the rationale used to justify this radical change. Allegedly, nationwide databases, on-line resources for local officers, and a law-enforcement network spanning every level of government would provide a solution to a traditional resistance to coordinate efforts. The word "overkill," however, only barely describes this projected plan for a 650,000-tentacled octopus.

The "war against terrorism" was also being used to justify these changes—but this didn't make it kosher, or even *halal*. The Supreme Court in 1997 said that even though the FBI could augment its power enormously by conscripting (without cost to itself) police officers within the 50 states, the separation of government power into distinct spheres, at the national, state and local levels, was important for maintaining constitutional checks and balances. "A healthy balance of power between the States and the Federal Government," the Court ruled, "will reduce the risk of tyranny and abuse from either front." Nevertheless, Ashcroft was determined to bring about exactly what the Court had warned against.

Furthermore, the plan for coordinating the FBI, CIA, and the local departments in all 50 states included the creation of nationwide databases. The names stored in these databases included, in addition to terrorists, people who were wanted for committing a felony or were previously convicted of a felony. It also included individuals or organizations where there was a "reasonable suspicion" of their engaging in criminal activities or where circumstances "reasonably indicate" they may commit a crime in the future. Since ordinary criminals are included and since the criterion of "reasonableness" is much looser than constitutional standards for judging criminal activities, Michelle J. Kinnucan, a scholar who served in the US armed forces, believes that the planned restructuring of intelligence gathering was unjustified, because it expanded the scope of intelligence far beyond requirements for the "war on terrorism." Kinnucan recalled:

> Another time that the federal government cooperated on an extensive basis with state and local police for intelligence purposes was in the era of the FBI's notorious Counterintelligence Programs (COINTELPRO) and COINTELPRO-style operations. These operations are mostly known for the activities—assassination, false imprisonment, forgery, perjury, infiltration, etc.—undertaken by the FBI and police to neutralize dissident religious and political activists and organizations.[142]

Kinnucan indicated that Ashcroft had also examined the prospects for intelligence gathering by Community Oriented Policing Services (or "COPS" model) and by doubling the proposed 10,000 Neighborhood Watch Groups (NWGs) operating through-

---

142 Kinnucan's article was first published in the July-August 2003 edition of *Agenda* (Ann Arbor, MI). See, Michelle J. Kinnucan, 2003. "Big Brother Gets Bigger: Domestic Spying & the Global Intelligence Working Group."

out the nation. Each of these entities could be linked to the increasingly pervasive domestic spy network being constructed by the federal government.

Spying on millions of Americans? But haven't eminent judges and criminologists said that times have changed and political repression is gone? Who's kidding who here? The FBI accumulated files on 10,000,000 Americans but Judge Posner—who allowed the Chicago police to collect political data on any community group or organization, and to label certain groups to be "extreme"—claimed that the period in which the Red Squad flourished is "history." Eminent criminologist James Q. Wilson, who has advised several presidents, also insisted that a return to systematic political repression by local police was unlikely. Like Posner, Wilson reassured Americans that the political passions behind the Red Scare of the Fifties and beyond no longer existed. "The country has responded to [Sept. 11] in a sober and adult way," he added.

It would take a breathalyzer test of the Attorney General's office to determine whether the Justice Department's Regional Information Sharing System (RISS) was one of these sober responses. RISS projects officially concentrated on drug and organized-crime activities. However, since criminal-intelligence units are being used in many jurisdictions to monitor political suspects as well, these units combined political activists' names with those of ordinary criminals. Importantly, to curb abuses of criminal intelligence data banks, the Justice Department, as early as 1993, passed guidelines restricting usage of RISS databanks for politically motivated crimes. Ironically, these rules provided the usual cover of "plausible deniability" for enforcement officials since the so-called "guidelines" publicly, if not actually, prohibited inclusion and sharing of data on dissidents.

PATRIOT ACT II

In early 2003, senior members of the Senate Judiciary Committee asked Justice Department representatives if they were drafting a "Patriot II" bill. The representatives denied such legislation was being planned. Fortunately, the Center for Public Integrity in Washington obtained a leaked copy of the draft legislation, written by the Justice's Office of Legal Policy. Although its official title in 2003 was "The Domestic Security Enhancement Act of 2003," the draft was commonly called "Patriot Act II."

After the seemingly endless instances of official attempts to repress political dissent, the following list of Patriot Act II provisions may seem redundant. But, please, tolerate our description of its frightening intent. The original draft of this bill aimed at further destruction of constitutional and due-process protections. The draft, Ashcroft said, authorized splitting up families if they threaten national security or if they commit a minor non-terrorist infraction. Their members—including legal permanent residents—can be rapidly deported, without criminal charges, evidence, or judicial review.[143]

---

143 A thorough analysis of Patriot Act II is provided by Timothy H. Edgar on Feb 14, 2003, Legislative Counsel, ACLU. It is entitled,

The original draft also called for a nationwide DNA database. Citizens and noncitizens would be included—allegedly in order to detect, investigate, prosecute, prevent, or respond to terrorist activities. Individuals could be forced to provide DNA samples without court orders—merely because a law-enforcement officer *suspects* them of wrongdoing. Refusal to provide a DNA cheek-swab could mean a $200,000 fine or imprisonment for a year.[144] (Given the 2005 disclosure that an employee at the federal forensic lab had favored prosecutors by falsifying DNA tests, it could even mean a conviction and a prison sentence.)

The use of warrantless wiretapping and Internet surveillance was to be further extended. Secret arrests would be permitted. People could suddenly "disappear" when detained on suspicion of terrorist activities until they were actually charged with a crime. The reason? Don't bother to ask. Law enforcement would be ordered not to release any information.

Chapter 6 pointed out that Patriot Act II was passed at the end of 2005. Because nationwide objections to the first and second versions of the Patriot Act had emerged, Congress voted to reconsider the most controversial provisions of Act II early in 2006. But this reconsideration left the most repres-

---

"Interested Persons Memo: Section-by-Section Analysis of DoJ Draft 'Domestic Security Enhancement Act of 2003. (Patriot Act II)." (aclu.org/SafeandFree/SafeandFree.cfm?ID=11835&c=206.)

144 Leaks and misuse of this database would be inevitable. *Wired News* on March 31 reported, "People with 'flawed' DNA have already suffered genetic discrimination at the hands of employers, insurance companies and the government."

sive segments of the Patriot Act intact.

SPYING ON NEIGHBORS

Among the other Kafkaesque attempts to cage American freedoms, the Justice Department had planned to ask people to help uncover terrorists by spying on their neighbors. The Office of Homeland Security intended to accomplish this goal by launching an experimental program entitled Terrorism Information and Prevention System (TIPS) in 10 cities during the winter of 2002. While waiting for legislative approval, TIPS had originally asked over a million American truckers, letter carriers, train conductors, ship captains, utility employees, and other "well positioned" private citizens to participate in "a formal way to report suspicious terrorist activity," according to the Homeland Security website. It was designated "a Citizen's Corps program" providing workers with the opportunity to report "unusual activities" they might observe to law enforcement agencies

Civil libertarians immediately denounced TIPS as a device for spying without a warrant on people's mail, homes, and conduct. Likewise, on July 24, 2002, in preparation for Ashcroft's appearance before the Senate Judiciary Committee, Senator Patrick Leahy's press secretary, David Carle, sent out a shocking news backgrounder that explained "the historical precedent for Operation TIPS." The backgrounder recalled that during the First World War the Department of Justice had established the American Protective League (APL), which enrolled a quarter of a million informants with considerable knowledge about their neighbors and others in their local communities to report suspicious conduct and investigate fellow citizens. The APL spied on workers and unions. It also organized raids on German-language newspapers. With the power to make arrests, "members of the League used such methods as tar and feathers, beatings, and forcing those who were suspected of disloyalty to kiss the flag." After the war, the New York Bar Association damned the APL with the statement, "No other one cause contributed so much to the oppression of innocent men as the systematic and indiscriminate agitation against what was claimed to be an all-pervasive system of German espionage."

Before the 2002 elections, a number of influential legislators had opposed the TIPS program, which had been besieged by criticism. Conservatives like Senator Joe Lieberman, who had originally supported TIPS, backed-off in the face of this criticism. Others agreed with Texas lawyer Paul Coggins, who said the House of Representatives had choked on TIPS because it would have transformed 2002 into the 'Year of the Rat' by getting Americans to spy on each other.[145] Patrick Leahy led the fight to exclude TIPS in the Senate Governmental Affairs Committee; Rep. Dick Armey led the same fight in the House.

Critics insisted that political prejudice, racial profiling, religious bigotry, and perhaps even a fellow citizen's taste in hairstyles, clothing, or loud music would motivate most of the information sent to the agencies managing TIPS. Leahy, then Chairman of

---

145 Paul Coggins. Sept 27 2002. "The Year of the Rats." *Law.com.*

the Senate Judiciary Committee, justifiably asked Ashcroft whether people applying for a government loan or a job might be told that a suspicious activity had been logged in a Homeland Security databank because somebody "didn't like their dog barking in the middle of the night" or the "political shirt" they were wearing. In reply to his critics, Ashcroft pledged that citizen spies wouldn't actually go inside homes to snoop and that the Justice Department would not maintain a central database for TIPS. In fact, he assured Leahy, that even though TIPS would not create a database that could be used against innocent citizens, millions of Americans would nevertheless be asked to report suspicious individuals.

But Leahy didn't buy Ashcroft's spin on TIPS. Neither did other legislators who recoiled from Ashcroft's "friendly neighborhood" spy program. As a result, the government during the summer of 2002 modified its sales pitch without abandoning the program. It softened the Department of Justice website text calling for volunteers among the citizenry at large as well as postal workers and teamsters; but it continued to ask for volunteers.

By September, Coggins noted that some people asked to volunteer had refused to become TIPSters. He sarcastically observed:

> Postal workers led a parade of occupations to opt out of the not-so-secret service. Congress is still skeptical of the attorney general's watered-down proposal, which has more holes than Swiss cheese – and it smells rotten to the public as well. That means you and I probably won't get our secret decoder rings in the mail

anytime soon. No secret handshake. No license to snoop. For now, a plumber is just a plumber, and an exterminator is there to get rid of bugs—not plant them. For now, it's still safe to chitchat with neighbors and officemates, read racy novels, watch steamy movies, cook foreign dishes and even speak a foreign language. We still live in "America, the Beautiful," not "America, the Bugged."[146]

Fortunately, opposition from liberals and conservatives alike forced the administration to delete the TIPS program from the Homeland Security Act before it was passed. TIPS appeared to be a four-letter flop.

Why then are we writing more about the TIPS program? Although it has been quietly put aside, the administration has, in the past, sent up trial balloons and dropped them if they generated enough opposition—only to revive them when the political climate allowed. But why was TIPS' mobilization of millions of citizens necessary? Besides overwhelming police with innumerable reports, what would be accomplished by TIPS? Would Homeland Security use TIPS to build needed resources to identify and corral thousands of political dissidents? Granted, even though identifying genuine terrorists among millions of tips would be as difficult as finding a needle in a haystack, ready cash appeared to solve the storage problem: The administration requested 772 million dollars in its 2003 budget for the OHS' information technology.[147]

---

146 Ibid.

147 These funds would also be spent on software that will integrate

Nonetheless, on the face of it, Ashcroft's program still lacked credibility. Supposedly, TIPS was to help uncover terrorists—but it intended to accomplish this goal by recruiting a million volunteers in just 10 cities. A million volunteers! How many more millions would Ashcroft have requested if TIPS had ever become a nation-wide program? Unless he had a hidden agenda, the numbers of volunteers simply did not make sense. But, they *could* make sense if TIPS were stood on its head and critics focused on the volunteers rather than their "suspects." Was TIPS originally an excuse to build a million-person database overnight—composed chiefly by chauvinistic, fearful, and self-righteous patriots? Given the existing political climate, who else would *actually* spy on their neighbors except people whose paranoiac reactions to panics—including those generated by repeated Homeland Security alerts—could be readily exploited by demagogues?[148] (During Hitler's reign, the Gestapo intimidated millions of Germans by encouraging "patriots" to denounce their friends, neighbors and family members who criticized the government or were reluctant to show respect for its authority.)

What could Ashcroft have accomplished with these eager volunteers? He could have used them to expand an aggressive right-wing movement targeting political dissidents. And a database identifying these people would have served as a valuable asset

---

data systems across OHS agencies.

148 Our characterization is not arbitrary. See Bob Altemeyer March/April 1988. "Marching in Step: A Psychological Explanation of State Terror." *The Sciences* pp. 30-38.

for collaborative efforts between the government and the vigilantes produced by this movement.

Consequently, TIPS—on a much grander scale—might have been designed to serve the aims adopted in the First World War by The American Protective League when it repressed labor unions and anti-war groups. This possibility would explain why Dubya Caesar and his General Ashcroft stubbornly tried to keep the TIPS proposal alive—until they were forced to trade it for a sizeable vote on the rest of the Homeland Security Act. Indeed, the information technology required by TIPS might have provided another weapon of mass repression, regardless of officially acknowledged aims.

Finally, since TIPS was only recruiting citizens, a separate program was planned to recruit noncitizens among Muslims. Toward this end, the Feds encouraged police departments to interview thousands of Middle Eastern immigrants.[149] The interviews, the Feds claimed, would be legal, voluntary, and necessary for uncovering terrorist "sleepers": "This is the least intrusive type of investigative technique that one can imagine," Assistant Attorney General Michael Chertoff told Congress. "This is not rousting people, this is not detaining people, this is not ar-

---

149 By 2002, the DOJ had created a database from several thousand interviews of Middle Eastern immigrants. Some FBI officials, however, felt the project would not produce domestic evidence against Al Qaeda and civil liberties groups were concerned that it would lead to racial profiling or entrapment. Others fear past abuses may be repeated. "It sounds to me like we are right back in the Thirties, the Forties and the Fifties," said Marquette University Professor Athan Theoharis, a leading historian dealing with the FBI and Justice Department.

resting people. This is approaching people and asking them if they will respond to questions." (After Bush won the 2004 election, he promoted Chertoff to head the Department of Homeland Security.) FBI Deputy Assistant Director Steve McCraw, as well, made everything sound very benign and user friendly, stating that the questioning was aimed at recruiting "individuals who may have information. They may not have information now, but they may come in contact with the information later."

Ostensibly, the feds were merely interested in possible witnesses, suspects, and covert informants in Muslim communities. But, in setting up the "voluntary" spy network, police officers, for instance, had been asked to obtain a detailed profile on every subject—movements, past residences, travel, education, and family members. Subjects were asked to reveal their views of terrorism and the 9/11 attack, and to give names of people who might support terrorism. Now how simple, straightforward, and benign does this sound? Yet, aside from obvious questions about how reliable or voluntary immigrant responses would be under these conditions—especially immigrants who are terrorists—using the interviews to prevent terrorism would inevitably converge on political, religious, and moral beliefs. Moreover, when Ashcroft's notions of terrorism are involved, abortion policies and homosexuality would be stigmatized. In other words, cast a net upon the waters and you will catch all sorts of strange creatures.

Didn't Succeed? Try Again

The Bush administration planned to install TIPS during the winter of 2002 but it was dropped like a hot potato after it was denounced nationwide as a device for spying without a warrant on people's mail, homes, and conduct. Nevertheless, in 2003, the FBI quietly dealt with this setback by expanding a preexisting program, called InfraGard. Since then, InfraGard, according to the ACLU, has become a corporate TIPS program. It has converted corporations into "surrogate eyes and ears for the FBI."

InfraGard has had little critical scrutiny; however, Matt Rothschild, an editor and reporter for *The Progressive* magazine, wrote an article in 2008 titled, "The FBI Deputizes Business." Rothschild claimed that over 23,000 business leaders were participating in the InfraGard and that some of their corporations were in a position to observe the activities of millions of individual customers. InfraGard participants can also observe millions of students because it includes academic institutions as well as state and local law-enforcement agencies. FBI Director Robert Mueller told an InfraGard convention, "Those of you in the private sector are the first line of defense." Mueller urged InfraGard members to report "suspicious activity or an unusual event." He also urged them to inform the FBI about "disgruntled employees who will use knowledge gained on the job against their employers." Who are these disgruntled employees? Union activists? Political dissidents? Whistleblowers?

Patriot Act II shields public officials and corporate

personnel who answer these questions. It grants police officers conducting illegal searches legal immunity if they are carrying out orders. To encourage spying, Patriot Act II also provides businesses that inform on their customers with immunity—even if their information was false or violated privacy agreements. Patriot Act II also permitted secret surveillance of American citizens by the US government, conducted on behalf of *foreign* countries, including dictatorships. Fifteen new proposed offenses were punishable by the death penalty. And then taking one step backward and two steps forward, a number of the "sunset provision"—concessions to congressional critics when Patriot I was passed—were rescinded. Some of the most egregious provisions in Patriot I were not canceled. US residents could be extradited at the request of tyrannical foreign governments—regardless of whether they were being persecuted for their race, nationality, creed, or political beliefs. Also, Patriot II's definitions of terrorism were so sweeping that political protests accompanied by violence could be labeled "terrorist" actions even though they may have been instigated by *agents provocateur*. Likewise, innocent contributions to nonprofit organizations could be considered "material support" for terrorism.

Under established law, "wartime exception" precedents allow the Attorney General to authorize wiretaps or break-ins without court authorization for a 15-day period following a "Declaration of War" by Congress. But, as stated, Patriot II eliminated the Declaration of War requirement. A mere congressional authorization for the use of force, or a presidential declaration of emergency caused by an attack on the US was sufficient. (Both of these looser conditions were met in the days after Sept. 11, 2001.) The new bill totally eviscerated the necessity, when obtaining a surveillance or break-in order, to show that the target is an agent of a "foreign power" or organization. The definition of "foreign power" can include individuals who are not acting on behalf of a foreign government or international organization.

Under Patriot II private credit reports and financial records can be seized without a court order or an individual's consent. The disclosure of such a non-court subpoena can be gagged by law enforcement. The Act also prohibits grand-jury witnesses from defending themselves by responding to false information or smears leaked to the press by prosecutors.

COINTEL-type programs were legalized by Patriot II. Restrictions on political surveillance, introduced during the Seventies to check local law enforcement, were officially swept aside. Restrictions on the use of "pen registers" were shredded. (Millions of Americans have seen Hollywood movies where a spy checks his telephones or rooms for electronic "bugs" that transmit private conversations to a recording device outside the room. A "pen register"—a very small pencil-shaped device—is also a "bug" but it is secretly plugged into a computer to obtain phone numbers, email addresses, and websites contacted by individuals.) A so-called "suspect" need not have any connection to terrorism. All that is necessary to justify planting this advanced wiretap device is that it will be used "to obtain foreign intelligence information."

The requirement that the individual's activities potentially violate federal law was effectively eradi-

cated. Purely *domestic* activity can be targeted by secret surveillance and investigation. A new category of
domestic security or domestic intelligence-gathering
was created. Besides "terrorist" activities, "conspira-
torial activities threatening the national security interest" can be interpreted so broadly that Justice
Department officials can readily consider any political activity opposing government policies or corporate interests to be terrorist.

Lawful immigrants can be readily deported without due process merely for engaging in activity
deemed a danger to the US's "economic interests",
such as walking in a union picket line. And, to punish
American citizens who oppose the government, the
bill resurrects McCarthyism by marking as traitors
those who support an organization the government
alleges to be terrorist. Moreover, these Americans
will be stripped of their citizenship and transformed
into "stateless" persons and deported. Even more unbelievably, if no foreign government will accept them,
they can be sent to be tortured in an "ungoverned
lawless territory," wherever that might be. Nat
Hentoff has written, "Until now, in our law, an American could only lose his or her citizenship by declaring a clear intent to abandon it. But—and read this
carefully from the new bill—the intent to relinquish
nationality need not be manifested in words, but can
be *inferred* from conduct."[150]

The Patriot Act II signified the fascistic leanings of
the junta that took power in the 2000 election. And,
no doubt, even though the most brazenly egregious

---

150 Hentoff. Feb. 28 2003. "Ashcroft Out of Control: Ominous
Sequel to USA Patriot Act." *Village Voice*. (Italics are Hentoff's.)

segments of this act were rejected at that time by Congress, the Department of Justice will reintroduce them after a terrorist attack, another "war against terrorism" or an unmanageable increase in the anti-war and anti-globalization movements.

On June 6, 2003, Ashcroft began the campaign to scare people into backing his "enhanced anti-terror law." Using terrorism as a pretext, he wanted to imprison more suspects indefinitely, extend the death penalty to more people accused of terrorism, and bring charges against anyone who helps or works with suspected terrorist groups as "material supporters"—among other things. Like Palmer and McCarthy before him, Ashcroft defended his policies at Congressional hearings by holding aloft what he said were copies of terrorist declarations of war against America. (One quoted a Muslim cleric who gave terrorists permission to bomb 10 million Americans.) Then, after reading names of people killed on 9/11, Ashcroft brazenly proclaimed that Patriot 1 has stopped more than 3,000 "foot soldiers of terror"— *even though* it "has several weaknesses which terrorists could exploit, undermining our defenses." He guaranteed that Patriot Act II would eliminate these "weaknesses."

"Toto, I have a feeling we're not in Kansas anymore!", opined Dorothy. But the *Wizard of Oz* was not resurrected by Ashcroft to make people believe they were in danger from a creepy magician who inhabited another world. Unfortunately, the chief architects of the Patriot Act and its proposed "enhancement" were very much of *this* world. One of their names is Viet Dinh, once Assistant Attorney

General for the [Ashcroft's] Office of Legal Policy. Dinh had also served as Special Counsel to the Senate Whitewater Committee and Senator Pete V. Domenici's impeachment trial of President Clinton.[151] In honor of his wretched contribution to democracy, at the Computers, Freedom, and Privacy Conference in 2003, Dinh was given the "Big Brother" award for Worst Public Official. (Privacy International's panel of lawyers, academics, consultants, journalists, and civil rights activists gives this annual award to those who have "done the most to invade personal privacy in the United States.") Dinh was especially singled out for enabling the FBI to engage in searches and monitoring of chat rooms, bulletin boards. and websites, without evidence of criminal wrongdoing.[152]

Was the history of political repression in the US merely repeating itself? Perhaps. Intelligence gathering on domestic dissent soared in the Sixties when innumerable files were produced on Americans who had committed no crimes. Then again, was history undergoing a qualitative change because the enormous expansion of political surveillance owed its existence to an Apparat required to do the job?

---

151 Dinh had also clerked for Supreme Court Justice Sandra Day O'Connor. He is a Vietnamese refugee whose father was imprisoned after the fall of the Saigon government.

152 Dinh was also "awarded" for spearheading the revision of the Attorney General's Guidelines, which relaxed the restrictions on federal law-enforcement activities and national security investigations. The revised guidelines permitted agents to visit public places and events in order to monitor individuals with no predicate of criminal suspicion. In addition, the guidelines were not limited to terrorism investigations—they could be used for any violation of federal law.

8 | PsyOp & Cyberwar

Now it will be easy to carry on the fight, for we can call on all the resources of the State. Radio and press are at our disposal. We shall stage a masterpiece of propaganda.
—Joseph Goebbels,
February 1933

PATRIOTIC SNAKE OIL

In July, 2003, the ACLU recalled that over a hundred communities and three state legislatures had passed resolutions condemning the destructive powers of the Patriot Act. Nevertheless, Ashcroft's office, blowing smoke in the public's eyes, misrepresented Patriot's powers. "[Justice] Department spokespersons," stated the ACLU, "have consistently made statements to the media and local officials that are either half-truths or are plainly and demonstrably false—and which are recognized as false by the Justice Department in its own documents." The ACLU backed its accusation with painstaking comparisons between sections of the Patriot Act and claims made by Ashcroft's subordinates. While smearing Americans opposed to Patriot, these subordinates had deceitfully argued that it could not harm American citizens because Patriot could only be employed against foreigners and terrorists.[153]

This deliberate misrepresentation posed a tactical problem for civil libertarians. Could they count on Congressional hearings that monitored Ashcroft's implementation of the Patriot Act II? Or should they chiefly devote themselves to its repeal? The National Coalition to Repeal the Patriot Act, for instance, called for immediate repeal and encouraged resolutions passed by cities, states, labor unions, and so forth. (Evanston, Illinois, among others, passed an unequivocal resolution that urged Congress to repeal Patriot and to refrain from passing any further legislation that violated the civil rights and liberties guaranteed by the US Constitution.) But the New York Civil Liberties Union (NYCLU) refused to call for an

---

153 These subordinates testified or were interviewed by state legislative committees. Examples include (1) the testimony of Timothy Burgess, US Attorney for Alaska, before the Alaska Senate State Affairs Committee; with (2) a speech by Viet Dinh, Assistant Attorney General, at the National Press Club in Washington D.C.; with (3) statements by Mark Corallo, a DoJ spokesman, printed in Florida, Maine and Massachusetts newspapers; with (4) a letter sent to an Albany New York, newspaper by Keith A. Devincentis, special Agent in Charge of the FBI's Albany office; and with (5) testimony provided for the House Judiciary Committee by Ashcroft himself.

outright repeal. Its resolution merely asked the New York City Council to get New York State Senators Schumer and Clinton and congressional representatives to support efforts to monitor the impact of the Patriot Act. The NYCLU explained that their refusal was based on "the *realpolitik* expectation that many of the terms of the Patriot Act are due to sunset in a few years."

In reply, the National Coalition to Repeal the Act angrily observed that the New York resolution did not enumerate which provisions infringed on civil rights and liberties. Most civil libertarians would want this stated outright, and it is curious that this requirement has been ignored. Added the Coalition, "Some argue that we must keep the resolution as general as possible—no specificity!—in order to win votes from those who might otherwise not support the resolution. This is either a rectifiable omission or a grievous opportunistic error." The Coalition believed "monitoring" implied that civil liberties must be abandoned in order to fight terrorism even though "the law itself is the abuse, not simply the tactics given license under it."[154]

To illustrate this abuse, the Justice Department admitted that the Patriot Act was being used more

---

154 The Coalition's objections were validated by the fact that the Act's provision giving the government access to telephone and Internet searches did not expire. Today, without probable cause, government agents can go to and request any Internet "server" (IPS) to monitor a person's email, record the websites they have visited, and monitor the server. "This aspect of ACLU policy, as reflected in the resolution before the NY City Council," the Coalition had noted, "would enable such non-sunsetting abuses of civil liberties to continue unchecked."

often to pursue ordinary criminals rather than terrorists. Patriot contained provisions that had been on prosecutors' wish lists for years. Civil-liberties and legal-defense groups said the government was routinely using harsh anti-terrorism laws to convict run-of-the-mill lawbreakers. Bureaucratic opportunists readily adopted these laws to sidestep the traditional restrictions imposed by the Bill of Rights that make everyone entitled to receive 'due process' in a court of law.

Furthermore, the deliberate misrepresentation of the Patriot Act had posed a tactical problem for civil libertarians. How could the ACLU expect mere monitoring to check Ashcroft effectively—given his demonstrated readiness to lie? He had already lied to the House Judiciary Committee about the Patriot's scope but, despite objections from a few brave members, nothing was done about it. Ashcroft defended his policies at congressional hearings by holding aloft what he said were copies of genuine terrorist declarations of war against America. Then, after intoning names of people killed on 9/11, he exclaimed that the Patriot Act has stopped more than 3,000 "foot soldiers of terror." Even if enough Senate Judiciary Committee members could have been found with the willingness and guts to control this demagogue, could they have coped successfully with his ranting before another terrorist act canceled the Patriot Act's sunset provisions? Was the vague call for "monitoring" the Patriot Act advised by *realpolitik* or crackpot realism?

It must have been crackpot realism. The Patriot Act was reauthorized in 2005 despite the fact that it did not offer congressional demagogues anything that would have safeguarded Americans without gutting civil liberties. Aside from a few changes, it remained as loathsome as ever.

Also, keep in mind that *government officials* interpret the provisions of Patriot and decide how to enforce them. The provisions violated constitutional liberties but the Act itself did not actually require any bureaucrat to specifically target antiwar protesters, environmentalists, striking workers, anti-globalization movements, and people opposed to government policies toward Latin America. It certainly did not force the Justice Department to indict three Dominican nuns—Sister Ardeth Platte, 66, Sister Jackie Hudson, 68, and Sister Carol Gilbert, 55—with obstructing national defense when they engaged in civil disobedience during a peaceful demonstration for nuclear disarmament. Consequently, simply monitoring the Act's provisions—or deleting them—would not have stopped Ashcroft. And monitoring the Act would not have prevented them or anyone else who stepped in their place from adopting other kinds of legislation to justify repression.

Furthermore, these efforts never stopped Ashcroft from using any excuse to trash constitutional liberties. For example, in April, 2002, the world-famous environmentalist organization Greenpeace led a movement opposed to Bush's environmental policies, including illegal trade in wood logged and exported from the Brazilian Amazon. To dramatize their campaign, Greenpeace used a well-known tactic—following a ship outside Miami that carried illegal mahogany and then boarding it. (The activists boarded the ship wearing Greenpeace jackets and carrying a sign reading, "President Bush: Stop Illegal Logging." This act of civil disobedience was effective. The Greenpeace activists unloaded the mahogany. They did not resist arrest. The opposition to Bush's policies and an illegal practice that encouraged environmental degradation was widely publicized. Eventually, the boarders pleaded guilty to a misdemeanor and were released.

Yet Ashcroft was not satisfied with this traditional penalty. Astonishingly, 15 months after the incident the Justice Department indicted the boarders by using an obscure and bizarre 1872 federal law that prohibited prostitutes from boarding vessels and luring sailors away from ships anchored in US harbors. The feds had only used the law twice during the century-and-a-half separating its enactment from the 2002 incident. Since the Greenpeace boarders were not prostitutes, only a right-wing fanatic or lunatic would consider the law appropriate in this case. Ashcroft deliberately threatened Greenpeace because it is a public-interest group that could have lost its tax-exempt status if its boarders had committed a felony.

Two months later, in October, 2003, the Port of Miami refused Greenpeace's ship, the Esperanza, from docking for supplies and bringing people on board to discuss the crew's efforts to protect the Amazon rainforest. Even though an indictment or formal charge against any person is not evidence of guilt, the politically corrupt administration of the Miami Port Authority decided that Greenpeace's constitutional rights were nullified when Ashcroft indicted Greenpeace for the protest action in 2002.

The constitution insists that the government has the burden of proving a person guilty beyond a reasonable doubt and, if it fails to do so, the person is not guilty in the eyes of the law. Since Greenpeace had not been tried in court when Miami prohibited it from docking, the port officials violated *the presumption of innocence*—a fundamental principle of criminal justice. They also got away with violating the constitution's *free speech* provision—by refusing to allow Greenpeace to dock for the purpose of educating people about the destruction of the rainforest. If allowed to dock, Greenpeace would have undoubtedly defended its right to oppose Ashcroft's suppression of their activities as well as his deliberate do-nothing policies about the illegal importation of Brazilian mahogany. Still, for its militant efforts, Greenpeace received praise from the European Union and the government of Brazil.

Misappropriating Funds

Ashcroft, on the other hand, had no qualms about launching propaganda campaigns to defend his policies. He began a national "speaking tour" of law-enforcement groups in order to conduct a preemptive strike against congressional critics. At the tour's start, toward the end of August 2003, he claimed that any attempt to strip law-enforcement agents of their expanded legal powers could open the way to terrorist attacks. He shamelessly declared, "To abandon these tools would senselessly imperil American lives and American liberty, and it would ignore the lessons of Sept. 11." Concurrently, Ashcroft's Justice Department posted a new web site on Patriot aimed at "dispelling some of the major myths perpetuated as part of the disinformation campaign" by critics of the Act. Ashcroft asked federal prosecutors around the country to sway public opinion by organizing so-called "town-hall meetings" on the Act in their municipalities.

Who should have paid for Ashcroft's public relations campaign? Justice Department spokesperson Barbara Comstock said Ashcroft's speaking tour had been thoroughly reviewed by department lawyers and was "entirely appropriate" under federal law. But the ACLU denounced the use of public funds to pay for the Ashcroft road show. Besides, Representative John Conyers Jr. of Michigan, the ranking Democrat on the House Judiciary Committee, reminded Ashcroft that he is accountable to Congress as well as the President. He demanded that Ashcroft should either "desist from further speaking engagements" or explain why and how they do not violate restrictions on political activities by government officials. Conyers stated that the public speeches in defense of the Act conflicted with congressional restrictions preventing the use of Justice Department money for "publicity or propaganda purposes not authorized by Congress." He claimed that Justice Department officials might also be violating the Anti-Lobbying Act and its restrictions on grassroots lobbying on legislative matters.

Take, for instance, the use of public funds to lobby for "sneak and peak" search warrants. The House of Representatives voted overwhelmingly to prohibit the use of federal funds for the execution of delayed-notice search warrants. ("Sneak and peek" warrants, which were authorized by Patriot, allowed law-enforcement officers to search a person's property, and delay notifying that person until *after* the search occurred.) But, a few weeks later, a Justice Department memorandum ordered all of its attorneys to contact congressional representatives and urge them to oppose any attempt to deny funding for delayed-notification warrants. In addition to a list of representatives, the memo identified those who had voted to prohibit these warrants. The memorandum was another example of how government employees were being ordered to become lobbyists despite grave questions about the legality of their efforts.[155]

Nevertheless, Ashcroft and his staff forged ahead —determined to convince Americans that terrorist attacks cannot be prevented unless civil liberties are crushed. Like Joseph Goebbels, who declared that Hitler would win an up-and-coming 1933 election because his party finally controlled government resources, Ashcroft's misappropriated funds converted his department into a propaganda agency.

---

155 *EPIC Alert*. October 17 2003 Vol. 10.21. Electronic Privacy Information Center (EPIC) Washington, D.C. EPIC had to file suit in federal district court because the DoJ refused to expedite the release (under the Freedom of Information Act) of DoJ records about the lobbying efforts of federal prosecutors that opposed legislative revisions to the PATRIOT Act.

TRAVEL? FORGET IT! YOU MIGHT BE A TERRORIST!

Incredibly, the obsession with political surveillance gave birth to still another all-embracing weapon. In September, 2003, Bush decreed the creation of a "Terrorist Screening Center" which produced the "Mother of All Lists" of "The Usual Suspects." The Center merged lists maintained by nine federal agencies into a single "terror watch list" composed of names, events, and attributes of

1. Over 100,000 "suspected terrorists"

2. International terror organizations

3. So-called "domestic terrorists" (e.g. antiabortionists suspected of bombing abortion clinics and environmentalists accused of torching gas-guzzling sport-utility vehicles)

4. People on "No Fly" lists composed of suspects barred from air travel

5. The National Crime Information Center's nationwide list of convicted felons, fugitives and other wanted people

6. Anti-war, civil-liberties, environmental, and other progressive groups opposing administration policies.

Segments of this so-called "terror watch list" were made available to law-enforcement agencies as well as airlines, power plants, and a variety of private-sector groups and corporate entities. (Security agencies were undoubtedly overjoyed when they acquired such lists—legitimately or not—and marketed them to corporate America.)

Since the massive database produced by the Terrorist Screening Center included people whose political activities had never violated the law, the plans for its "watch lists" sparked familiar constitutional issues. Would local police, without constitutionally backed legal authority (i.e., an arrest warrant) or even probable cause, detain people stopped for traffic violations on this "terror watch list"? Also, aside from problems due to incorrect or duplicate names that created endless trouble for innocent people, what redress do people have for correcting wrongful entries? Would this new list become a permanent blacklist? How broad was the list's definition of "terrorist"? Why wasn't the authority for creating the Terrorist Screening Center filtered through Congress —where answers to these questions could be openly debated?

Experience with surveillance lists for airline passengers shows how pathetic these omnibus lists can be for dealing with terrorists and how repressive they can be for dealing with political dissent. Since the airlines carry millions of people on international and domestic flights, monitoring the passenger lists is a colossal task. Nevertheless, despite the supposed urgency, the procedures for monitoring security threats have been beleaguered by mistaken identities, racial profiling, and unwillingness to rectify wrong information. And, unsurprisingly, passenger-monitoring procedures have been deliberately misused because of the lack of civil-liberties safeguards.

In 2002, democracy's defenders began to attack the "No Fly Lists" that were being used to harass and block dissidents. Originally, a Computer Assisted Passenger Pre-Screening System, known as CAPPS, identified suspect passengers before they boarded a commercial aircraft. This system was limited to PNR data (Passenger, Name, Record) provided by airline reservation and departure data. By 2003, however, a new government program, CAPPS II, was generating the suspect passenger list. According to the ACLU, this program encouraged a permanent blacklist even though it did not make airline passengers any safer. The most dangerous aspects of CAPPS II depended on procedures and databases that were not subjected to genuine public oversight.

While terrorists could dodge the system with false driver's licenses and passports, these "secret" databases were freeing the government to abuse the use of background checks. An ACLU suit pointed out:

> Innocent people have already been stopped and banned from flying because their name appeared on government "no fly" lists—and have been unable to clear their names in the federal bureaucracy. Since it is based on notoriously inaccurate government databases, this national system would only increase the delays and make it inevitable that innocent Americans—regular people traveling for work or vacations—would be delayed, hassled and even prevented from flying.[156]

The events behind ACLU public requests for examples of "no fly" harassment represented another

---

156 ACLU, "Oppose the New Airline Passenger Profiling System 'CAPPS II'" https://www.aclu.org/oppose-new-airline-passenger-profiling-system-capps-ii

skirmish in the war against repression. For instance, barely two months after 9/11, CAPPS II identified Green Party USA co-coordinator Nancy Oden as a "suspected terrorist."

Oden recalled that she left her farm (she is an organic grower) and drove 100 miles to the Bangor International Airport in Bangor, Maine. She had never been arrested; nevertheless, she was taken to a room where her baggage was x-rayed and she was searched. She was allowed to go to the waiting room designated for her flight, but after a short while, a National Guard team ordered her to submit to another search with a wand and all. Even though no weapon or other incriminating evidence was found, she was grabbed roughly by a corpsman with an automatic rifle who loudly accused her of being a terrorist. She twisted away from his brutal treatment and told him to stop. The corpsman then summoned a squad that humiliated her by marching through passenger-filled corridors to the front of the airport where he continued his abuse of Oden until a superior stopped him. Oden was then told that she could not fly out of the airport that day. She recalled:

> I was headed for Chicago for a Green Party USA National Coordinating Committee meeting, where I was to speak the next night on biochemical warfare and pesticides as weapons of war. I was also scheduled to interview job applicants, present several proposals and financial reports, and so on. I am a lead person on the National Coordinating Committee of the Green Party USA.[157]

---

157 This Party was the original Green Party, although there was...

The corpsman covered his ass by saying that Oden was uncooperative and had refused to be searched. (His lie implied that the rough treatment had nothing to do with a computer search for suspected terrorists or his political fanaticism. The airline repeated this fiction when the Green Party reported the story.) In point of fact, Oden was already flagged when she picked up her ticket. She was told at that time that she had not been selected randomly. CAPPS II had identified her as a suspected terrorist or a person who supported terrorism.

Doug Stuber, chairman of the North Carolina Green Party, is another example. Stuber was trying to go from Raleigh, North Carolina, to Prague when an officer accosted him in the airport and said he could not fly because of the DC sniper attacks. He was further informed that no Greens were allowed to fly that day. The next day, he was forced to buy a $2,600 "same day" round trip airfare even though he had originally purchased a $650 ticket for the previous day's flight. Just before boarding, the officer appeared again and prevented Stuber from boarding. Stuber was then confronted with two federal agents who took photographs, asked about his family, where he lived, who he knew, what the Greens were up to, and so forth. Stuber was finally allowed to ask the agents if they believed the Greens were equal to Al-Qaeda and they showed him a document from the Justice Department that actually identified the Greens as likely terrorists. Stuber missed his morning flight that second day but the two agents helped him get a ticket for a later flight. Considering the

---

...another Party that adopted a very similar name.

agents to be no different from the Nazi secret police, he said, "I was relieved that the SS hadn't stopped me from flying." But he was wrong. When he tried to board that plane, he was stopped a third time and advised to go to Greensboro for still another flight.

The feds also stopped peace activists. Alia Kate, 16, a high school student in Milwaukee, wanted to go to Washington, DC, on April 19, 2002, to protest The School of Americas (i.e., the "School for Torturers") run by the US military. Police pulled her from the line and held her back. Twenty members of the Peace Action Milwaukee group were also forced to miss the same flight. Milwaukee County deputies informed them that their names were on the "No Fly Watch List" supplied by the feds. On August 7, two more peace activists found themselves on the list and detained by police at the San Francisco airport.[158]

Two months later, the editors of *CounterPunch* reported seeing stories two or three times a week on the web about people detained from flying.[159] The police especially targeted racially profiled travelers. (In fact, Canada, in November, 2002, issued a travel advisory to Canadians with Middle Eastern backgrounds to avoid traveling by air in the US.)[160]

In 2003, Congress recommended putting CAPPS

---

158 Both incidents were reported in April 27 and October 16 1001 editions of *The Progressive*.

159 Editorial Introduction to Doug Stuber. October 1-15 2002. "Green and Grounded." *CounterPunch* p 6.

160 This advisory was issued after Canada discovered that the US had jailed Maher Arar, a Canadian citizen born in Syria and secretly deported him to Syria. In addition, this Canadian was merely in transit—he did not actually try to enter the U.S.

II on hold because of the overwhelming number of errors including misidentified people who were not political dissenters. Take, for example, Michael Robert's account concerning his 15-year-old son, Nick. Roberts said,

> Granted, he's a pretty big guy—just over six feet tall—and he's taken karate classes since elementary school. But he's also soft-spoken and studious. And while he's recently developed an interest in politics, reading Molly Ivins books and "Doonesbury" compilations is about as controversial as he gets.
>
> So why in hell did security concerns nearly prevent Nick, and the rest of our family, from flying on two different commercial airliners over an eight-day span? The reasons are complicated and confusing, like so much of post-9/11 life, but ultimately, the fault lies with his mother and me. Turns out we gave him the wrong name.

En route to a summer vacation, which would be spent near Fredericksburg, Virginia, Robert's family found themselves at Delta's Airlines Denver International Airport hub, trying to convince security agents that Nick was not a terrorist.[161]

Roberts repeated inquiries about why his family on two occasions was being delayed at the hub failed to get cooperation from airline officials, who wouldn't even speculate as to why Nick was being targeted. Roberts then searched online and found

---

161 Michael Roberts. 2004. "I Fathered a Terror Suspect: Losing the Name Game at our Country's Airports." *New Times, Inc.*

that his son's name was identical with a 50-year old unemployed Welshman named Nicholas Roberts, who was charged with sending packages in 2001 containing a suspicious white powder to a travel writer and the First Minister of Wales. The suspicious powder turned out to be flour. As a result, Michael's father sarcastically remarked:

> Roberts, [the Welshman] who'd previously appeared on the cops' radar after hurling eggs at the Queen of England's motorcade in Cardiff, was sentenced to two and a half years in stir back in July 2002. The length of the sentence probably means that this "crank," as one British tabloid dubbed him, can't jet to the US, but his influence lingers. Call it flour power.

The magnitude of mistaken identities listed by CAPPS II proved unacceptable. As a result, the ACLU in September, 2003 urged the Transportation Safety Administration (TSA) to abandon its plans for building the passenger screening system altogether. "CAPPS II contains fundamental flaws that cannot be fixed," said LaShawn Warren, an ACLU Legislative Counsel. "This system, which has not been shown to be an effective tool in blocking terrorists, would cast a cloud of suspicion over every traveler by subjecting their personal information to government scrutiny." The ACLU also accused the TSA for not including a safeguard mechanism to ensure that CAPPS II is not used to unfairly target racial, religious, and ethnic minorities.[162]

---

162 ACLU, September 30, 2003. "As Congress Puts Controversial CAPPS II Program on Hold, ACLU Urges TSA to Abandon Super Snoop Profiling System." See also, ACLU April 14, 2004. "Tell →

Campaigns against US profiling and CAPPS II had also been kicked off by European as well as American civil-liberties organizations. The European Digital Rights coalition (EDR) had questioned how many people are on the American ("No Fly") lists and who was responsible for the validity of the data. Members of the European Parliament wanted to know how many US agencies and corporations would have access to this data and whether the data being mandated by Homeland Security violated EU legislation protecting privacy.

By November 2008—as Bush was preparing to leave the White House—the ACLU accused the Department of Homeland Security's attempts to upgrade the no-fly database "wholly inadequate." In addition to the huge number of false positives produced by the database, the department still did not provide for individual access to or correction of the erroneous data. Instead of being tightly focused, it did not stop adding names that wasted screeners' time and diverted their energies from looking for true terrorists. The ACLU estimated that the list had over *one million* names by July 14, 2008!

POLITICAL DATA MINING

In 2003, American travelers were confronted by another hazard associated with CAPPS II when Jet-Blue Airline admitted that it had agreed to a Department of Defense request to provide files on over a

---

the Airlines to Protect your Data" and ACLU May 30, 2003. "ACLU Criticizes CAPPS II."

million passengers. The information was given to Torch Concepts Inc. (of Huntsville, Alabama), a Defense subcontractor, for a project said to involve military base security. Alarmed by widespread criticism, the airline implausibly claimed that the study had nothing to do with CAPPS II, even though it had violated its own public privacy policy. (Just to set things in perspective, this JetBlue incident occurred while the Federal Aviation Administration was weakening airport security by laying-off thousands of security guards.)

While responding to criticism, JetBlue flip-flopped. Immediately after its action was exposed, a company representative claimed that no customer information had been shared with the government to test CAPPS II. However, JetBlue then confessed that it had provided only limited data to Torch Concepts, a software company. (This data did not include personal financial information, credit-card information or Social Security numbers.) Even so, Torch Concepts, in a presentation for a Department of Homeland Security symposium, had shown how this information could be secured by linking the JetBlue files with another massive database containing Social Security numbers, occupations, family size, and credit history. (That presentation included the personal information that JetBlue said it did not provide.) JetBlue then claimed that it had no knowledge of the presentation and added, "This was a mistake on our part and I know you and many of our customers feel betrayed by it. We deeply regret that this happened and have taken steps to fix the situation and make sure that it never happens again." *Mea culpa.*

The disclosure of JetBlue betrayal of privacy rights had been preceded by the Electronic Privacy Information Center's (EPIC) exhausting two-year effort to obtain information about the government's post-9/11 air-travel security measures. In July, 2002, EPIC found that the National Aeronautics and Space Administration (NASA) had received three months of 2001 Northwest Airlines passenger data for use in a data-mining and passenger-profiling study. EPIC informed the Department of Transportation that Northwest's disclosure of this information without passengers' consent violated Northwest's public-privacy policy and constituted an unfair and deceptive trade practice. (It also had to sue NASA to obtain additional documents that the agency withheld.)[163]

The JetBlue scandal added fuel to the scorching criticism aimed at the Pentagon's Defense Advanced Research Projects Agency (DARPA). This agency had previously initiated the "data-mining" program—originally dubbed "the Total Information Awareness Project" (TIA)—that promised to promote an invasion of privacy on a mind-boggling scale. TIA would have broken new ground by networking computers to "mine" all electronically recorded information available anywhere including your and our credit

---

163 At that time, the reoccurrence of the massive invasion of privacy at JetBlue or another airline depended on the outcome of a Homeland Security investigation into possible links between the Torch Concepts study and still another study, conducted by SRS Technologies for Pentagon's infamous Total Information Awareness Project. Since SRS had subcontracted the Torch study, a government official may have violated federal privacy laws by linking the study with the Pentagon project.

card purchases, credit history, email messages, academic grades, magazine subscriptions, bank deposits, personal investments, Websites, Internet searches, travel, telephone, Social Security, income tax, library, and medical records.

Ironically, although better known for erasing thousands of email messages to cover-up his crimes, retired Rear Admiral John Poindexter, headed this program.[164] Poindexter, as Ronald Reagan's national security adviser, helped plan the sale of arms to Iran and illegally divert the proceeds to the contra terrorists in Nicaragua. He was indicted for defrauding the US Government in the Iran-Contra affair and was convicted of five felonies, including lying to Congress, obstruction of justice and destroying official documents.[165] (A *New York Times* editorial entitled, "A Snooper's Dream," noted that Poindexter never expressed remorse even though he was convicted. *He asserted it was his duty to withhold information from the American people.*)[166]

However, while alternative news sites and internet-privacy organizations were thrashing the TIA, the House-Senate Conference panel voted to block funding for DARPA itself until the Pentagon fully explained the project and assessed its impact on civil

164 A central computer had backed-up the messages. To provide a conduit for illegal sales, one message, for instance, authorized Oliver North to meet secretly with the General Noriega.

165 Subsequently, Poindexter's conviction was dismissed on a technicality. He had been granted immunity in exchange for his testimony before Congress even though that testimony turned out to be false. In the end, George H.W. Bush in 1992 pardoned the principals in the affair.

166 Editorial. Nov. 18 2002. "A Snooper's Dream." *New York Times*.

liberties. In addition, a group led by Senators Ron Wyden, a Democrat, and Charles Grassley, a Republican, introduced limits that would prevent TIA from targeting US citizens without prior congressional approval. Senator Russell Feingold, a foremost defender of American civil liberties, called for a suspension of the project until Congress had conducted a thorough review. Finally, Wyden and Grassley sponsored a budget amendment requesting "detailed information" from Ashcroft about his interagency plans for developing a working relationship between the TIA, the FBI, and the Justice Department.

An assortment of strange bedfellows made additional demands to end TIA and other mass-surveillance programs. The TIA project was forcefully criticized by the ACLU, American Conservative Union, Americans for Tax Reform, Center for Democracy and Technology, Center for National Security Studies, Eagle Forum, Electronic Frontier Foundation, Electronic Privacy Information Center, and Free Congress Foundation. This bloc of liberal and conservative organizations threatened the project's future even though the Pentagon was doing all it could to ensure its completion.

In response, Bush's Orwellian advisors rushed to the Pentagon. They got DARPA to quietly drop the TIA logo and change "Total Awareness" into "Terrorist Awareness." (The TIA logo with an "all-seeing eye" on top of a pyramid appears on the cover page of this book.) But public outcry continued until Poindexter was forced to resign after journalists disclosed DARPA's next move. It created an online "futures market" for people interested in gambling on where and when terrorist attacks would occur. *Can you imagine Joe Smith, an ordinary American, luckily winning a million dollars because New York, Chicago, or San Francisco was obliterated and he had bet that the Al Qaeda would succeed in detonating a nuclear bomb at these locations?*

Upon resigning, Poindexter declared that media misrepresentations and a highly charged political environment had distorted his aims. The TIA project, he insisted, was not a threat to civil liberties even though it would store every possible scrap of personal information on every American in a humongous database. "We never contemplated spying and saving data on Americans," said Poindexter disingenuously. "We only wanted to find specific patterns of activities that would lead us to foreign terrorists."

Really? Would other kinds of databases do the job more effectively without tapping every imaginable type of information identifying Americans and their everyday activities? And would a Total Awareness database actually mean that identifying genuine terrorists wouldn't be drowned in a sea of false positives?

Happily, in July 2003, Senator Wyden tried to outflank the Pentagon. He introduced the Citizens' Protection in Federal Databases Act of 2003—to hold government agencies accountable for the use of private and personal information. The legislation was a response to the TIA surveillance program, and other federal initiatives that proposed to collect private information on law-abiding Americans from numerous public and private databases.

However, the Bush administration subsequently spotted a break in its opponents' line and counterattacked. While Poindexter's resignation and severely curtailed funding had left the future of TIA in doubt, the administration funded a new system in Florida to serve much the same function. EPIC reported that Florida police agencies were developing a centralized-database surveillance system similar in structure to TIA (with funding assistance from both the Justice Department and the Department of Homeland Security). The system, dubbed Matrix, would also enable investigators to find patterns and links among people and events using a combination of police records and commercially available personal data. At least 135 police agencies signed up for the service, which was poised to expand to other states across the country. In 2004, a massive campaign led by the ACLU got 11 states to reject the Matrix project. Eventually, more than two-thirds of the states that had initially adopted it pulled out.

By May, 2005, attempts to expose unlawful data mining revealed still another TIA clone. The National Security Agency had secretly collected phone call records of tens of millions of Americans, using data provided by AT&T, Verizon, and BellSouth. *USA Today* reported that the NSA had gathered information about the calls of millions of Americans not suspected of any crime. The NSA claimed that it was merely using the data to analyze "calling patterns" composed of links between phone numbers in an effort to detect terrorist activity. However, in light of the government's attempts to sidestep the law and hide its data-mining projects from public scrutiny, this claim was not believable.

The White House repeatedly insisted that its eavesdropping program was lawful and that none of its domestic surveillance programs have been conducted without court approval. "The intelligence activities undertaken by the United States government are lawful, necessary and required to protect Americans from terrorist attacks," said Dana Perino, the deputy White House press secretary, who added that appropriate members of Congress have been briefed on intelligence activities.

Yet one of the persons interviewed by a *USA Today* reporter said that the surveillance project had produced "the largest database ever assembled in the world." (This person, like others who were acquainted with the database, declined to be identified.) Referring to NSA as "the agency," the informant added that the agency's goal is "to create a database of every call ever made" within the nation's borders. Ironically, data mining conducted by *private* corporations in 2005 surpassed the datasets compiled by the NSA. About half of the 40 billion dollars given that year to 15 United States intelligence agencies was spent on private contractors like ChoicePoint. Apparently some of these agencies outsourced their work in order to get around constitutional restrictions. (Corporations could compile and use information in ways that government could not. Government agencies were prohibited legally from violating privacy rights, for instance, but these restrictions did not apply to corporations.)

Greg Palast reported that ChoicePoint, the "Big

Banana" in the private-surveillance market, kept over *16-billion records* on Americans in 2005. These records included, among many other things, Social Security numbers, educational data, felony convictions, claims-history data, motor-vehicle records, police records, credit information, employment background screenings, medical and drug-testing services, public-record searches, shareholder information, and information about neighbors and relatives. In addition to marketing data to other firms, ChoicePoint sold its records to the FBI, Homeland Security, and other government agencies. In 2006, moreover, the feds fined ChoicePoint $10 million because it did not prevent identify thieves from stealing personal data linked to more than 163,000 Americans.

Information unearthed during the final days of the Bush administration indicated that police surveillance activities had spiraled out of control. Take the Maryland State troopers, for instance. The troopers had monitored advocacy groups devoted to such causes as promoting human rights, animal rights, establishing bike lanes, and opposing an increase in electricity rates. The DC Anti-War Network had been classified as a white supremacist group without justification. The world-renowned Amnesty International was found among the hundreds of pages in the file because of its opposition to the scheduled executions of two men.

An undercover trooper spent more than a year infiltrating peaceful advocacy groups and 53 individuals were labeled terrorists in a database that was shared with the FBI. Moreover, even though a new police superintendent and governor called the operation a "waste of resources" and "undemocratic," no official had been reprimanded or fired for authorizing the illegitimate surveillance program or the misuse of public funds. The undercover officer received two promotions.

BUNGLING AGENCIES & POLITICAL TARGETS

Ironically, while Ashcroft was rallying supporters, federal judge Alvin Hellerstein refused to dismiss lawsuits against American and United Airlines, the Boeing Company, and the Port Authority of New York and New Jersey, which were involved in the 9/11 attacks. Judge Hellerstein said the evidence he had seen indicated that adequate airport security screening procedures and onboard safeguards against hijackers could have prevented the World Center attacks and the crash of a hijacked plane in Pennsylvania.

Furthermore, increasing numbers of people realized that 9/11 represented the worst intelligence failure since Pearl Harbor. Senator Bob Graham, chairman of the Senate Intelligence Committee, announced that there were "systemic problems [that] might have prevented our government from detecting and disrupting al Qaeda's plot." He informed CNN that the intelligence agencies did not need a lot of luck: They needed "someone who could have asked and gotten answers to the right follow-up questions and then put it together."

Clearly, the government required competent

agencies—not the Patriot Act—to connect the dots and combat terrorism effectively. Why, then, were Ashcroft and his subordinates touring the nation justifying legislation that had gutted our civil liberties? The answer: because the Bush administration needed this legislation to shield its incompetence and plunder public revenues.[167]

In the meantime, the administration did little to protect Americans. While touring the country, Ashcroft unabashedly assured everyone that Bush was making every effort to protect our safety. But evaluations of critical sectors of the homeland's security—ports, chemical plants, and biodefense—indicated that he was not telling the truth.[168] Homeland Security was still trying to coordinate 22 agencies and 17,000 employees. It suffered from funding shortages, staff defections, confusion about its mission, and demoralizing interdepartmental turf battles. Homeland Security Secretary Tom Ridge faced a grilling on *Meet the Press* for attempting to trim the air marshals program as intelligence services were warning that al Qaeda was planning new attacks on US passenger planes.[169]

---

167 Even now as Nicholas Kristof pointed out, "Across the nation, state and local leaders have been forced to slash more than $100 billion in spending, laying off thousands of employees, cutting off health insurance for roughly one million people, and lowering America's standard of living. Washington is not just aloof from the pain out here in real America, but is making matters worse." Nicholas Kristof. July 19 2003. "Going Home, to Red Ink and Blues." *New York Times.*

168 David Corn. 9/22/2003. "Homeland Insecurity." *The Nation.*

169 Mary Jacoby. 9/12/03. "Homeland Security Sputters into reality." *St. Petersburg Times.*

The day after Ashcroft finished his tour, Bush submitted the first segments of Patriot Act II to Congress. Ashcroft and his Justice Department subordinates had just assured the public that Patriot did not threaten law-abiding Americans because its most invasive measures require a judge's sign-off. But Bush's new initiative in this regard was more candid: It wanted to enable federal agents to issue subpoenas, demand private records (business, medical, etc.), and compel testimony without the approval of a judge, grand jury, or even a federal prosecutor. It also wanted to deny bail without a judge's approval to defendants charged with financing terrorism. Finally, it even requested expansion of the death penalty for what it considered "terrorist financing" and a number of other activities, including "sabotage" of a defense installation or a nuclear facility. But no proposals were offered that would safeguard American civil liberties from being snowed under by these requests.

In September, 2003—two years after 9/11—these alarming possibilities sharpened the complaints about the Bush Administration. Ashcroft had rapidly expanded his department's ability to investigate and prosecute hundreds of criminal cases that had nothing to do with terrorism. Traditional conservatives as well as liberals were continuing to protest that he was using Patriot to circumvent the greater burden of proof required by the criminal law.

Prominent Norwegian criminologist Thomas Mathiesen notes that terrorist acts involve "violent and arbitrary actions consciously directed towards civilians, with a political or ideological goal in mind."[170] But the search for terrorists has produced databases composed of other crimes such as theft, robbery, or interference with information systems that have nothing to do with terrorism. More important is that acts of civil disobedience—Gandhi's long-established approach—were being included. Such non-violent actions as unlawful occupation of public facilities, "sit-down strikes" and "demonstrations" (used by unions in the Thirties, and by civil-liberties, environmentalist, and antiwar activists especially in the Sixties) in factories, nuclear facilities and public buildings were being called "terrorism." The same is true for anti-globalization demonstrations (despite the fact that their participants, however rowdy, overwhelmingly condemned violence—unless they were faced with violent police provocation and brutality). Furthermore, legislatures have coupled these repressive definitions of "terrorism" with an escalation of penalties—though excessive fines, long-term prison sentences, and death penalties, in these cases, aren't likely to deter genuine terrorists.

Ashcroft and his wily subordinates assured the public that Patriot II targeted terrorists. But, again, who would define words such as "terrorism" and "sabotage"? And, hypothetically, if this act had been ratified before December, 1999, what would have happened to the late Philip Berrigan, a former Josephite priest? Berrigan served a 30-month sentence for "malicious destruction of property" when

---

170 Thomas Mathiesen. 2002. "Expanding the Concept of Terrorism." In Phil Scraton (Ed), *Beyond September 11: An Anthology of Dissent*. London: Pluto Press.

he—and Susan Crane, Elizabeth Walz and Father Steve Kelly from *Plowshares v. Depleted Uranium*—hammered and poured blood on two USA-10 "Warthog" fighter planes. They believed these planes fired most of the depleted uranium in the war against Iraq and that they were used extensively against the people of former Yugoslavia, resulting in radioactive poisoning.[171] If the Patriot initiatives had been ratified, these heroic anti-war activists and environmentalists could have been sentenced to death.

---

171 See Philip Berrigan's autobiography, *Fighting the Lamb's War: Skirmishes with the American Empire*, published September 1996 by Common Courage Press.

9 | Violence & Mass Protests

I just want you to know that, when we talk about war, we're really talking about peace.

—George W. Bush,

June 18, 2002

RESPONDING TO PROTESTS

It doesn't take a UN inspection team to unearth Attorney General John Ashcroft's political views. But questions still remain. For instance, does 9/11 explain his ruthless devotion to domestic repression? Or do other events account for this frightening commitment?

Some of the answers reside in the violent repression of mass protest from 1999 on. At the start, 50,000 protesters rambunctiously denounced the Seattle World Trade Organization's (WTO) negotiations—forcing the negotiations to end in failure despite mass arrests, tear gas, and battering by police. In Philadelphia, Los Angeles, and Washington DC, additional demonstrations, protested the policies and terms of trade set by the North America Free Trade Agreement (NAFTA), the International Monetary Fund (IMF), and the World Bank. These global agencies were accused of ignoring the cruel repression of independent labor organizations while encouraging substandard wages, child labor, brutal sweatshops, and massive pollution in less developed countries.[172]

Countering the 1999 explosions of popular anger, government and business leaders (of 34 North, Central and South American nations) hastily staged a Summit "Free-Trade of the Americas Act" Conference in Quebec City, Canada. This time, while secret negotiations were taking place, columns of police in full riot gear were lined up along a two-mile chain-link fence erected to keep protesters from the conference. For two days and nights, the police lobbed tear gas and shot rubber bullets at the protesters, keeping them outside the fence and far from the meetings.

While the protests were taking place in Quebec City, the US Secret Service and FBI presented a court order to the Seattle Independent Media Center (IMC) to hand over logs and other records pertaining to the IMC's coverage of the protests. The FBI also imposed a gag order on the IMC, forbidding individuals at the Center to discuss the court order or even acknowledge the gag order's very existence.

---

172 Alexander Cockburn, Jeffrey St. Clair and Allan Sekula. 2000. *5 Days that Shook the World: Seattle and Beyond.* New York: Verso.

The Seattle IMC pulled a legal-defense team together with the aid of free speech advocates on the internet—the Electronic Frontier Foundation, the Electronic Privacy Information Center and the Center for Constitutional Rights. Six days after the first visit by the feds, when a legal challenge to the gag order was imminent, the order was vacated. Ashcroft's Justice Department was aware that their gag order at that time would never have stood up in court.[173]

But the FBI did not withdraw the court order for IMC's logs. To obtain this order while the Quebec conference was underway, the feds claimed they required the IMC's "server logs" in order to discover the identity of an anonymous correspondent who had stolen sensitive documents from Canadian police and then posted them to the IMC website. The Secret Service was involved because agents claimed falsely that the posted documents contained details of George W. Bush's travel itinerary. (Bush was, at the time, attending the Summit of the Americas in Quebec City.)

The FBI court order was based on additional misinformation. First, it defined the IMC as an Internet Service Provider (ISP) although an ISP is a commercial entity rather than a news organization. On the contrary, since journalists posting stories or photographs to IMC websites are part of a news organization, they are entitled to the same constitutional protections as any other members of the news media. In addition, on the internet, anonymity is partic-

---

173 It would not have been vacated after the Homeland Security Bill was passed but it could not be defended in court on April 21, 2001 —almost five months before Sept. 11th.

ularly important because it enables individuals to disguise identifying information that might lead to their persecution. In fact, although qualified, the constitution has recognized a journalist's right to resist court orders aimed at disclosing this information because they threaten a free press. As a result, historically, one finds many examples of anonymity in public discourse; even the Federalist Papers were published under a fictitious name.[174]

Upon inquiring into the validity of the feds' claims, Seattle IMC volunteers discovered that police in Quebec had already identified and arrested three suspects in the stolen documents case, without any information from the IMC. The people at the IMC felt justified in resisting the order because compliance would have meant handing over the individual internet addresses of over 1.25 million journalists, readers, and technical volunteers who accessed the IMC website during the protests.[175] Since the feds could have simply requested the identity of the anonymous person rather than try to net all the fish in the sea, IMC counsel Lee Tien, of the Electronic Frontier Foundation, declared:

> This kind of fishing expedition is another in a long line of overbroad and onerous attempts to chill political speech and activism. Back in 1956, Alabama tried to force the NAACP to give up its membership lists – but the Supreme

---

174 Alexander Hamilton, James Madison, and John Jay published the papers under the pen name of *Publius*.

175 Even if this figure included repeated communications from the same persons, the number of unduplicated addresses would still have been massive.

> Court stopped them. This order to IMC, even
> without the 'gag,' is a threat to free speech, free
> association, and privacy.

The confidence trick justifying the court order was
chump change compared to what happened next.
Despite knowing about the Canadian arrests of the
people who stole the information, the feds maintained the impression that they still needed the IMC
logs to catch the thieves. They neither amended nor
withdrew the order against the IMC for weeks. Instead, they harassed the volunteer organization,
sidetracking the attention of the IMC personnel and
its legal resources. IMC believed that the timing of
the original order, issued while mass protests were
still underway in Quebec City, suggested that the
government intended to intimidate IMC journalists
covering the protests—a suggestion strengthened by
the failure to withdraw its order after the Canadian
arrests.

Suddenly, six whole weeks after IMC had received
the order—and on the eve of the IMC's planned court
filing—the government *withdrew* the order for the
log. IMC speculated that government lawyers knew
the order would be struck down on constitutional
grounds, and decided to retreat rather than lose face
in court. But, as IMC counsel Nancy Chang of the
Center for Constitutional Rights significantly
pointed out, "Although the court order has been
withdrawn, the IMC's concerns over the government's ability to use internet technology for surveillance of political activists continue to linger."

Chang's concerns were certainly justified because
the underlying reasons for the court order may have

had nothing to do with Bush's security. After all, the so-called "server logs" contained a vast number of internet addresses of anti-globalization activists the world over. For the FBI and CIA, this database would have been "manna from heaven." (Can any sensible person *really* believe that the feds were merely interested in finding a solitary communication from an anonymous person?)

You don't have to be Sherlock Holmes to discover the Fed's real motives. First, the court order was served almost five months before 9/11. If it had been served afterwards, the order would have been for finding an Islamic terrorist. But it still would be used to plunder the database to create a weapon of mass repression. Second, there should be no illusions about the neofascist propensities of the Bush administration. This administration's concerns about the nation's security were not the sparks that fired its attempts to update its weapons. *It began to update them to forestall the new phase in American protest movements heralded by the Seattle demonstrations.*

Throughout the Bush administration, federal attorneys repeatedly attempted to force journalists to identify sources exposing government irregularities or to relinquish videos of demonstrations. Although these attempts had nothing to do with protecting America from terrorism, federal attorneys successfully imprisoned Judith Miller and Joshua Wolf, because they refused to cooperate with the government. A *New York Times* correspondent, Judy Miller, served 85 days in prison for refusing to relinquish her notes and sources on the investigation of Scooter Libby who had endangered Valerie Plame

—by revealing her status as a CIA agent. Joshua Wolf, a blogger, freelance journalist and filmmaker, served 226 days in prison for refusing to turn his videos—recording a 2005 San Francisco anti-war demonstration—over to the Department of Justice (DoJ).

To further intimidate the press, the DoJ also prosecuted Eric Lichtblau and James Risen of the *New York Times* for their Pulitzer prize-winning article revealing that the NSA was secretly wiretapping phone conversations without warrants. (The *Times* had submitted to pressure from the White House and delayed publication of their article for more than a year.) Dana Priest of the *Washington Post* was also prosecuted because she had exposed the existence of covert and illegal "black site" CIA prisons in Europe.[176]

MASS ARRESTS & DATABASES

As Yogi Berra declared: "It's déjà vu all over again." Like Orwell's animal farm and its cackling chickenhawks taking up arms in the name of freedom, the President and his cronies had astonished everybody because of their demagogic opposition to all domestic policies that would undercut their imperial aims. These "compassionate conservatives," "friends of the environment," "guardians of peace," and "true patriots" had refused to provide medical

---

176 For an excellent review of some of the cases, see Chapter Three in Molly Ivins and Lou Dubose. 2007. *Bill of Wrongs: The Executive Branch's Assault on America's Fundamenal Rights.* New York: Random House.

care or prescription drugs for people without Medicare or private insurance. They had made it harder for poor and middle-class Americans who faced overwhelming medical bills to file for bankruptcy. They had ignored the problem of unemployment, denied funds for strengthening workplace safety, training programs for dislocated workers, and advanced training for pediatricians. They had slashed budgets for public-housing repairs, new libraries, and research into alternative energy sources. They had cut massively into the Environmental Protection Agency budget and pulled out of the 1997 Kyoto Protocol agreement on global warming. They had rejected an accord enforcing the 1972 treaty banning germ warfare and had jettisoned the ABM treaty, which for half a century had restricted the proliferation of intercontinental ballistic missiles.[177]

On the international front, the perfidious dealings of this administration have kept the faith with the CIA's refusal to confront its own crimes. Examples of these crimes? As indicated, the CIA backed the violent overthrow of the democratically elected governments in Chile, Guatemala, Indonesia, and Iran. It supported terrorists in Nicaragua, Brazil, Uruguay, Cuba, Zaire, East Timor, Angola, and South Africa. In fact, one year after Sept. 11, 2001—while Americans mourned the thousands killed by Islamic terrorists—Chileans angrily protested the overthrow of President Salvador Allende's democratic government and the mass slaughter after a US backed coup

---

177 This list is partly derived from Michael Moore. 2001. *Stupid White Men...And Other Sorry Excuses for the State of the Nation!* New York: Regan Books.

launched 17 years of the military dictatorship on Sept. 11, 1973. *In fact, a Chilean bomber attacked Allende's presidential palace 31 years to the very day before the Al Qaeda terrorists piloted their planes into the World Trade Center and the Pentagon.*

Not surprisingly, in 2002, Bush refused to allow the world's first permanent International Criminal Court (ICC) to try US forces for war crimes, genocide, and other crimes against humanity.[178] In 2003, after concluding agreements with over 50 countries, Bush suspended military aid to 35 countries that have not backed his demand for immunity. But he did not let everyone know that their compliance would also dissuade the ICC from charging *him* with violations of the Geneva and Nuremberg Conventions—regarding the abusive treatment of prisoners of war and the responsibility for waging a war of aggression.

Official responses to anti-globalization demonstrators raising these issues have been brutal. Between the Quebec City demonstration and 9/11, for instance, over 100,000 protesters from all over Europe filled the streets of Genoa, Italy, in continued protest against the G-8 Summit Meeting's international policies and their effect on poverty, inequality, violent repression, and environmental degradation. (The Genoa demonstration was backed by simultaneous protests in 200 other cities worldwide.) Tak-

---

178 The ICC treaty has been signed by almost 140 countries, ratified by 66 and took effect July 1, 2002. Bush finally supported the treaty after extorting agreement to place US military forces beyond the reach of the court.

ing place in July, 2001, hundreds of demonstrators were arrested in Genoa with over 500 protesters left injured and one dead after violent clashes with the police. Even foreign journalists were beaten. For example, United Kingdom's *Sunday Times* correspondent John Elliot reported on July 22: "I was taking in the infernal scene of a water cannon truck cleaving through clouds of tear gas when I felt a massive blow to the back of my head." Two policemen had hit him with a club and then dragged him along the ground toward a signal box where he was ordered to put his head on a steel train track. The policemen kicked his head and legs until a senior officer commanded them to charge him with "resisting arrest with violence" and he was taken to the police station.

During the Genoa protest, a police squad reportedly composed of present-day Italian fascists ruthlessly vandalized and clubbed students sleeping at the Armando Diaz school complex, where protesters committed to nonviolence had been staying. Witnesses described students, Americans among them, crouching as they were kicked, pummeled with clubs and thrown downstairs. According to emergency room doctors on the scene, some of the injured would have died without treatment.[179] Television crews later filmed pools of blood and teeth knocked out during the raid. Despite this fascist brutality and the students' non-violent standpoint, Italy's TV mogul and prime minister Silvio Berlusconi called the students "terrorists."

During the prosecution of 29 officers in 2005, six

---

179 Ninety-two young people were dragged from their beds. Sixty were injured and over two dozen were hospitalized.

years after the contemporary fascists had forced their way into the Armando Diaz school complex and attacked the protesters, it was revealed that the victims were conned into signing a form that waived their right to contact their families and embassies.[180] The forms were in Italian and a police interpreter lied about its content. As a result, a British protester, Nicola Doherty, was imprisoned for five days despite suffering a broken wrist from the beating received at the school. "Nicola was forced to sign this form and did not know she had waived her right to contact the outside world while, outside, UK diplomats and her family were denied access," said British lawyer Matt Foot, who represented her in the trial of the police officers.

British journalist Mark Covell, who went into a coma from the beating he received outside the school, told BBC that photos supplied by the Italian police were doctored to put distance between his inert body and Francesco Gratteri, Italy's so-called "anti-terrorism" chief.[181]

Covell claims alternative photos show Gratteri was actually standing beside him as police broke 10 front teeth, ribs and fingers, and damaged his spine and lungs. Italian police were also accused of planting Molotov cocktails in the school to justify the raid, while Michelangelo Fournier, former deputy chief of

---

180 Tom Kington. July 10 2007. "Update: Italian Police Accused of Tricking G8 Protesters." *Guardian (UK)*. Also, Philip Willan. April 7, 2005. G8 Summit Officers on Trial. *Guardian/UK*.

181 "The photos purportedly show the bearded Gratteri 50 meters away from me," Covell said. "But it looks like the image of someone else who has had a beard electronically painted on him... In other frames you see the same man with no beard."

Rome's SWAT team, admitted that "harmless people" were beaten, according to Tom Kington, a staff writer for the *Guardian*.

Since 9/11, the American police have also responded to demonstrations with measures not seen since the Vietnam War. Two weeks after the anniversary of 9/11, demonstrations took place in Washington, DC. On the day before the main march, about 200 demonstrators led by members of a group called the "Anti-capitalist Convergence," followed behind the banner reading "Globalization, Not Devastation!" until they encountered a line of DC Metro Police. The marchers turned south, only to encounter more police. The protesters were blocked—unable to move forward or backward. Suddenly, according to observers, a "black-clad" individual broke a window of the Citibank at the corner. It was unclear where this individual came from. (The blocked-in demonstrators had been marching peacefully.) Comically, the police had more than enough men to surround 200 demonstrators, but not enough to capture and arrest one man (an *agent provocateur*?) who broke the window. Over 100 demonstrators, some of whom seemed to have been "targeted," were immediately arrested, hauled off on transit buses conveniently parked close to the bank, and driven to the Police Training Academy for processing.

Reportedly, at approximately 8:25AM, while these arrests were being processed, police in front of the Marriott Metro Hotel attacked John McGill and a woman friend. McGill, a development consultant for the Agency for International Development, and his friend were bicycling to work. By chance, Police

Chief Ramsey and motorcycle officers were nearby after converging upon a small group of activists. McGill and friend told Chief Ramsey that they were going to work. Ramsey replied, "You didn't have lights on your bike." But the bikers objected and pointed out that it was daylight. Ramsey then said, "You didn't have horns." Suddenly his police moved in. Reportedly, Officer W. C. Harris beat McGill's friend to the ground and McGill, after talking to reporters from the District of Columbia Indy Media (IMC), looked for a legal observer to help him get his friend out of jail.

Elsewhere, a larger crowd of demonstrators had gathered in Pershing Park. Thousands of police pulled from outlying regions and city precincts soon surrounded them. Since the demonstrators were outnumbered, reporters asked why so many police were present, and were told the gathering provided an opportunity for a "training exercise." A first-hand account by a 69-year-old father relates how the police conducted themselves at Pershing Park.[182] The father and his daughter Alexis, approaching Freedom Plaza found it surrounded by police who refused to allow any demonstrators to enter. When they moved to Pershing Park, it was also surrounded although the police were allowing demonstrators to enter. After ten minutes, the police ordered the father and his daughter to move into the park. They obeyed, as did every demonstrator around them. Soon, folding their

---

182 See "Joe." 2002. "A Day in the Park Amid Rumors of War." Washington DC-IMC. Also, Shawna Bader (2002, October 4) "Disgrace at Freedom Plaza." DC-IMC and Chuck D'Adamo (2002, Sept 28) "Denied The Right To Dance! Day One of the Protests against The IMF/World Bank." Baltimore Maryland IMC.

banner, they made two attempts to leave the park from adjacent streets. They were blocked from leaving both times, and forced back. Demonstrators arriving during this time, however, were still being permitted to enter the park. (Some later said they were also ordered or encouraged to enter the park.)

Without warning, riot-equipped police—with long black coats and helmets reminiscent of Darth Vader —gripped their batons with two hands and began a shoulder-to-shoulder advance into the area, forcing the demonstrators back. No demonstrator offered resistance. Packed together and confined to a small area where they were hardly visible from the streets, the police seized demonstrators and pinned their arms behind their backs with plastic cuffs. During this time, paperwork recording the demonstrators' names, addresses, telephone numbers, color of their hair and eyes, etc., was also completed.

Buses transported the demonstrators to the Police Academy. Despite the short distance between the park and the Academy, the bus trips were deliberately prolonged.[183] The demonstrators were forced into seats with their hands tightly bound behind their backs. Their pleas for loosening the painful handcuffs were ignored. Children were handcuffed and taken away from their parents. And even though they were only accused of failing to "obey a police command," the demonstrators had all their personal belongings, including belts and shoelaces, confiscated. Each person was fingerprinted, photographed and locked-up for over 24 hours in a gymnasium for an offense that had been compared to a traffic viola-

---

183 Some demonstrators reported their trips lasted 14 hours.

tion.

Every demonstrator was assigned to a specific gym mat on the floor, and was shackled at all times. One wrist was shackled to the opposite ankle, making it impossible to stand erect. Kneeling or moving from their assigned spot was forbidden. The police refused the prisoners access to legal assistance. They said that agreeing to pay a fine of $50 would result in speedy processing and early release. Anyone refusing to pay and insisting upon a court hearing was threatened with imprisonment for three more days until Monday. The prisoners were not told that local residents were released without payment for a traffic citation if they agreed to appear later in court. Obviously, the police were violating the Constitution's Fifth Amendment by extorting admissions of guilt and collecting fines from their political prisoners.

According to Alexis' father, the Washington, DC, Police Chief Charles Ramsey, brazenly stated his department had executed *a preemptive strike* against innocent American citizens. He said that the demonstrators would have broken the law—were they not arrested in advance. But no crimes were identified nor was evidence provided to support Ramsey's claim. In addition, he did not apologize for the police brutality. Some demonstrators were beaten for attempting the mildest form of civil disobedience—the time-honored Ghandian tactic of going limp rather than submitting compliantly to arrest.

Shamefully, the police "training exercise" included a mass arrest. Over 650 protesters were arrested that day and abused. Their identities were added to the police database even though they had broken no law.[184] Also arrested were bystanders, including pedestrians on the way to work. Significantly, reporters from online news service DC Independent Media were targeted and detained so they could not report the police action. Although a *US & World News* photographer was also arrested and a *Washington Times* photographer was pushed back from the police line, the corporate press and TV stations merely reported that hundreds of arrests were made. They did not expose the police brutality or the fact that some "Jane Does"—who refused to pay a fine and demanded that the charges be dropped were kept in jail for almost a week.

Police brutality has led to what is believed to be the largest settlements of class action suits brought by demonstrators. In July 2009, nearly seven years after they were arrested, some 400 Pershing Park demonstrators brought a class-action suit against Washington DC and were awarded 8.25 million dollars. (This settlement had followed another historic suit brought by almost 700 people who were arrested in April 2000 at another demonstration in Washington DC.)

There is more. Police Chief Ramsey apologized for his conduct and a federal judge called for the investigation and prosecution of officials responsible for the government's handling of evidence. A key report, radio transmissions, and a police log had vanished. Also, thousands of pages of police records and videotapes were not handed over to protesters' lawyers

---

184 Shawna Bader, (op cit.) who was also arrested, complained, "Sitting in a park watching people drum and dance is now a crime."

until years after the start of the suit.

In addition to the costs of the settlement, the government also lost more than a million in legal fees for private attorneys representing Ramsey and another top police official, Peter J. Newsham, who had ordered the arrests. A handful of protesters settled suits over the mass arrests, costing the city more money.

PREEMPTIVE ARRESTS

There are striking parallels between this event and one that occurred in Berkeley California three decades earlier. Hundreds of people, including high school students during lunch period, marched down University Avenue with signs protesting the Vietnam War—until a police cordon blocked their way. On being ordered to disperse, they found that police had blocked the streets in front, behind, and to either side. Perplexed and terrified because they were not being allowed to disperse, the teenagers and adults were informed by police bullhorns that they were being arrested for refusing to disperse. The marchers were herded into a large empty lot where—in addition to obtaining names and addresses—police fingerprinted and photographed hundreds of people one at a time. Buses for the detainees and trucks for the unloaded camera and fingerprinting equipment had been parked *prior* to the demonstration on the side of the lot. The arrest was unquestionably an attempt to terrorize Berkeley demonstrators. But it was *also* designed to obtain their names, mug shots, fingerprints, etc., for government files.

The illegal surveillance operation and taking of political prisoners years later in Washington DC was aimed at providing a new generation of police with experience in crowd control, extortion, and terror. Also, these tactics were designed to harvest information identifying large numbers of political dissidents. Furthermore, since the arrests took place in the nation's capital, police officials undoubtedly cleared their tactics with Attorney General Ashcroft and the DC's mayor.

After the "preemptive arrests" conducted by DC police under Chief Ramsey, attorneys for student protesters filed a class-action suit on October 15, 2002 against Ashcroft, the US Parks Department, the municipality of Washington, DC and its police department. This suit indicted the practice of "trap and arrest"—in which police surround persons engaged in lawful activity and prevent them from leaving the area. It also indicted the policy of arresting the journalists, bystanders, and observers caught within "trap-and-arrest" zones. The use of excessive force, abusive confinement, threats to secure no-contest pleas, the practice of denying access to counsel, and other Miranda rights were also cited. The suit charged that arrested individuals were kept in handcuffs for up to 24 hours or more; some arrestees were forced into a fetal position by handcuffing one wrist to the individual's opposing ankle. Compensatory relief was sought for denying the plaintiffs' rights under the First, Fourth, Fifth, Sixth, and Fourteenth Amendments of the United States Constitution.[185]

---

185 "George Washington U Students Sue After Preemptive Arrests on

In 2002, *justdissent.org*, a website devoted to nonviolent civil disobedience, listed 23 types of official actions aimed at shutting down legitimate dissent.[186] Court decisions had created shockingly excessive sanctions for what are essentially minor violations of law. The most outrageous example of this escalation involved people who had protested the "School for Torturers" maintained by American armed forces. Dorothy Pagosa reported that 71 people had served a combined total of over 40 years in prison for engaging in nonviolent resistance in a broad-based campaign to close the school."[187]

In May, 2003, *Freedom under Fire*, an ACLU report, surveyed the assaults upon civil liberties conducted throughout the nation.[188] The report observed that government officials and talk-show hosts have defamed protesters by denouncing them as "unpatriotic," "anti-American," "traitors," and "enemies of the state." Officials in Tampa, Pittsburgh and Phoenix have tried to stop demonstrations and forcibly removed protestors and their signs from rallies featuring Bush while people with signs favoring

S27 – Full text of the Lawsuit Against US Attorney General, US Parks Dept, DC Gov't, Metro Police Dept" (2002). The United States District Court For The District of Columbia, October 15, 2002. ACLU also filed a class-action suit on March 2003.

186 Editorial (2002) "Civil Disobedience under Attack." justdissent.org. Also, Patricia Nell Warren (2001, June) "14 Dollars." *A&U Magazine* (reprinted on justdissent.org)

187 See Dorothy Pagosa's (2002, July 13) "School of the Americas Protesters Lock Gate to Fort Benning After 37 Activists Sentenced." *School of the Americas Watch*, commondreams.org.

188 ACLU Report. 2003 May. *Freedom under Fire: Dissent in Post-9/11 America.*

Bush were not disturbed. City governments had used a shocking array of sleazy tricks to disrupt antiwar demonstrations. Police had without provocation searched, barricaded, tear-gassed, maced, punched, kicked, clubbed, or jailed protesters in Albuquerque, New York, Oakland, Chicago, Columbus, Los Angeles, Seattle, Baltimore, Westminster, Washington, Forest Park, and Evansville. They had smashed signs, banners, and floats. They had attacked correspondents and photographers who had caught them in the act of brutalizing demonstrators. They had shot protesters with rubber bullets, inflicting painful bruises, concussions, and bone fractures.

Political repression occurs in many forms. Some people have lost their jobs because of their political beliefs. Campus police have helped FBI agents to spy on professors and students. High-school students expressing anti-war views in such forms as political T-shirts and posters, writing assignments, artwork, or speaking out in class have received reprimands or suspensions. Libraries have posted warnings that federal agents may seize their records while some were actually shredding records to preserve their patrons' privacy.

Ominously, independent media correspondents have reported seeing Army, Navy, and Air Force observers at demonstrations.[189] (A Special Forces photographer was seen and photographed at the Sept.

---

189 The Posse Comitatus Act was breached in the infamous assault on the Waco Branch Davidian Compound. Military personnel and equipment were used at Waco to train domestic agents, fly choppers, supervise the use of equipment, and review the plans for the assault. Special Forces trained ATF agents were at Waco during the siege.

29, 2002 anti-IMF demonstration.[190]) While many believed the Posse Comitatus Act, (which prohibits the military from engaging in domestic police functions) is still in force, Gore Vidal pointed out that Act had been nullified by "anti-terrorism" legislation passed under the Clinton administration.[191] Unsurprisingly, Homeland Security department's core staff planned to work in an office building at the US Naval Security Station in Washington DC. In addition, the Department of Defense had begun creating military command centers in the US for the domestic deployment of armed units.

---

190 Carol Bass and Greg Burns. "Photos of US Military Sightseeing at Anti-IMF Demo." Atlanta IMC (8:45am Sun Sep 29 '02)

191 Gore Vidal declares, "Six years ago, in response to the Oklahoma City bombing (which, if indeed perpetrated by a lone nut armed only with a rental van and fertilizer, begs the question of why sweeping new legislation was necessary), Congress passed the Anti-Terrorism and Effective Death Penalty Act, and this 'antiterrorism' legislation gives the attorney general the power to use the armed services against the civilian population." Vidal adds that the legislation selectively suspended habeas corpus, "the heart of Anglo-American liberty." Gore Vidal. July 18 2002. "The New War on Freedom." Reprinted by *AlterNet*.

10 | Paramilitary "Training"

In the times in which we live, this is what democracy looks like. Thousands of soldiers, calling themselves police, deployed in US cities to protect the power brokers from the masses. Posse Comitatus is just a Latin phrase. Vigilantes like John Timoney roam from city to city, organizing militias to hunt the dangerous radicals who threaten the good order. And damned be the journalist who dares to say it – or film it – like it is.

— Jeremy Scahill, 2004

A s indicated, the repression of political dissent in the US is a culmination of historical trends beginning with the Haymarket bombing in 1886

315

and its aftermath. Haymarket is especially important because it underscores the official condemnation of left-wing dissent. A survey published by The International Association of Chiefs of Police states:

> The Haymarket bomb was responsible for the first major red scare in American history, and led to the immediate popular condemnation of Socialism, Communism and Anarchism by the national press and opinion leaders. In addition, the bomb resulted in the establishment of the first sustained American police intelligence operation aimed at leftist groups. Two years after the Haymarket riot the Chicago police declared that they had learned an invaluable lesson in 1886, that "the revolutionary movement must be carefully observed and crushed if it showed signs of growth."[192]

After Haymarket, the determination to crush left-wing dissent broadened. In addition to activists in the eight-hour day movement, government agencies targeted the millions who protested the sentences imposed on the speakers at the Haymarket gathering. Large numbers of people regardless of their political bias began to associate political repression with the denial of constitutionally protected freedoms.

Frank Donner observes that police responses to outdoor meetings and protests rapidly evolved after Haymarket. They included dragnet and pretext arrests, force or the threat of force to disperse gatherings, indiscriminate clubbing, physical dispersal and mounted charges, along with vigilante offensives

---

192 Frank Donner. op. cit. p.5.

conducted with police support. Furthermore, as the forms of political dissent changed, police intervention intensified:

> Indoor meetings and activities were also targeted, as were not only individuals ("agitators") but organizations as well. This expansion of coverage led to covert intervention through informer infiltration, a development strongly influenced by the operational style of private detective agencies. Another consequence of the police attack on organizations was the raid, typically conducted at times and in a confrontational manner intended to maximize intimidation.[193]

The official lexicon for these tactics expanded. At first, the police said that they were repressing political dissenters because they were authorized to "keep the peace." This justification, according to Donner, served as "a blanket excuse for a virtually unbounded range of activities, and the enforcement of such common law offenses as 'unlawful assemblage,' 'incitement to violence' and 'riotous conduct.'"

To expedite repression, a host of state statutes and local ordinances were put into play. During the Progressive Era, for instance, permits were required and the police used various pretexts (discriminatory enforcement of fire codes, intimidation of meeting hall owners, rulings that only English be spoken at meetings, etc.) to prevent or intimidate gatherings.

Ideology increasingly replaced behavior as a police concern and the earlier focus on individuals such

---

193 op cit. p2.

as strikers and union organizers was given less priority than "subversion" and "political conspiracies." The increasing emphasis on "subversion" covered a spectrum of peaceful dissent and produced models for political suppression by agencies on all levels of government including local law enforcement agencies. Moreover, police units especially in large cities eventually formed national networks and backed their historic social class allies and corporate protectors with state and federal support.

By the 1950s and 1960s, the police provided, for many Americans, countersubversive relief from the fear and panic cultivated by media depictions of urban riots, civil rights protests, campus disturbances, and antiwar protests. Police units, as in the past, were especially venerated by right wing Americans when they were perceived as the heroic "thin blue line" guarding national security against the onslaught of foreign and domestic enemies. "At root the embrace of the protection of national security as a prime mission reflected the thrust of almost a century of police repression to define protest in such a way as to warrant the most freewheeling target selection and the most punitive modus operandi," Donner concludes.[194]

The Miami Model

The arch-conservatives who controlled the government during the Bush years appeared to have learned a lesson or two from the Vietnam era. They

---

194 op cit. p5.

knew that the massive use of force against political dissidents might backfire. Therefore, until thousands of protesters hit the streets, it was more advisable to respond to critics flexibly—with secrecy, limited engagements, stonewalling, and demagoguery. As a result, the emergence of "friendly fascism" on a federal level has generally remained—for now, at least—more "friendly" than "fascist"—even though the Justice Department is headed by zealots and fanatics who won't be satisfied with anything less than a wiretap, surveillance camera, or microphone in every home, office, and alley.

Nonetheless, the warfare conducted by police has undergone calculated changes. In November 2003, for instance, about 10,000 protesters in Miami opposed the Free Trade Area of the Americas (FTAA) pact with "free trade" agreements being negotiated by ministers from thirty-four American nations. The protests, ranging from civil disobedience to a prearranged march organized by the AFL-CIO, were met with official intimidation, terror, and violence. Operating in the shadows of our Janus-faced government, the officials previously responsible for the police brutality in Philadelphia and Washington, DC, sent their in-house reports to Miami officials, who conducted yet a third "training exercise," aimed at preparing police for repression rather than the defense of the Constitution.

The peaceful protesters were subjected for days to unjustified force. Miami Police Chief John Timoney used 2,500 police from 40 police agencies to assault 10,000 union members, elderly retirees, and young people. Chief Timoney was also the Philadelphia police commissioner responsible for the brutal treatment of people who demonstrated against the Republican National Convention on August, 2002. Here, Timoney's police smashed heads, conducted "preemptive arrests" on phony charges as well as destroying puppets and floats being constructed by demonstrators. Civic leaders and the *Philadelphia Inquirer* applauded Chief Timoney's tactics. In 2003, he was rewarded with the top position in Miami.

During the Miami protests, armored personnel carriers prowled the streets and police helicopters hovered overhead. Police arrested over 250 people, some for nothing more than walking near the protests. Many faced trumped-up charges and shockingly high bail. "We'll try to do as many arrests as we can," boasted Chief Timoney to the South Florida *Sun-Sentinel* on the biggest day of protests. "If we don't lock 'em up tonight, we'll lock 'em up tomorrow." Reporter Jeremy Scahill, a producer and correspondent for the nationally syndicated radio program, *Democracy Now*:

> My colleagues and I spent several days in the streets, going from conflict to conflict. We saw no attempts by any protesters to attack a business or corporation. With the exception of some graffiti and an occasional garbage can set on fire, there was very little in the way of action not aimed directly at the site of the FTAA meetings. Even the Black Bloc [anarchist] kids,[195] who generally have a rep for wanting to

---

195 These protesters were anarchists dressed in black ski masks and clothing.

smash everything up, were incredibly re-
strained and focused.[196]

There was no need for any demonstrator to hurl
anything at the forces to spark police violence. It was
clear that Chief Timoney's men came prepared to
crack heads. Which they did—over and over.

Scahill called the Miami police force by their true
name:

> After last week, no one should call what
> Timoney runs in Miami a police force. It's a
> paramilitary group. Thousands of soldiers,
> dressed in khaki uniforms with full black body
> armor and gas masks, marching in unison
> through the streets, banging batons against
> their shields, chanting, "back... back... back."
> Police fired skin-piercing rubber bullets and
> concussion grenades into unarmed crowds.
> Thousands were gassed and electric tasers
> shocked people. Retreating demonstrators
> were shot in the back. When one demonstrator
> held his fingers in a peace sign, the police fired
> [a rubber bullet] at him – hitting him in the
> stomach at point blank range.

Florida *St. Petersburg Times* columnist Robin
Blumner also linked Miami police tactics with names
commonly associated with low-intensity warfare:
"Timoney has a well-deserved reputation for using
paramilitary tactics to turn any city where large
protests are planned into a place where the Constitution has taken a holiday . . . The result was a show of

---

196 Jeremy Scahill. Nov. 4 2003. "The Miami Model: Paramilitaries,
   Embedded Journalists, and Illegal Protests. Think. This is Iraq? It's
   Your Country." *CounterPunch.*

force that would have made a Latin American dictator blush." Regarding Chief Timoney himself, she wrote:

> His anti-protester philosophy is a fitting sign of the times and intersects nicely with the new FBI protocols established by Attorney General John Ashcroft. Ashcroft recently junked FBI guidelines that prevented agents from monitoring groups without evidence of criminal wrongdoing, saying it was vital for antiterrorism operations. But in a J. Edgar Hoover redux, it turns out that this flexibility is being used to spy on and collect intelligence on antiwar protesters.

> When men like Timoney and Ashcroft are on the A-list of the nation's law enforcers, free speech doesn't stand a chance. It is open season on dissent. A vignette reported by the Miami Herald says it all: During the FTAA action, Timoney came upon a protester who was pinned against a car being arrested; without knowing anything about the circumstances, he pointed a finger at the demonstrator's face and said, "You're bad. F—you!" People exercising their First Amendment rights are now considered the enemy.[197]

Miami's police presence included sadists who took pleasure injuring female protesters. Nikki Hartman, a 28-year-old Florida resident, was shot with rubber bullets. A police officer fired point-blank at her buttocks when she stooped to pick up a bandanna she'd dropped. (The officer kicked it her way before firing.)

197 Robyn E. Blumner. Nov. 30 2003. "Miami Crowd Control would do Tyrant proud." *St. Petersburg Times.*

She was also shot in the back while retreating from the police. While trying to help her to her feet, a friend was shot seven times. According to Indymedia reports, at least 10 detainees were beaten at the jail and four women were sexually assaulted while in custody.

Journalists reported that protesters were attacked and arrested for doing nothing more than publicly expressing their opposition to the FTAA. Over 100 protestors were treated for injuries; 12 were hospitalized. Small groups leaving the protests were harassed, arrested, and beaten. People clearly identified as medics, legal observers, and journalists were jailed. In jail, police doused people with cold water, and refused to provide them with food and necessary medications.

Criminologists have used the term "police riot," to characterize brutality perpetrated by officers who defy their commanders' call for discipline and restraint. But the Miami police did not engage in a police riot. They were not out-of-control. When they maliciously and without provocation attacked protesters, they were operating as a vicious paramilitary force.

Weeks before the demonstrations occurred, Florida officials encouraged this paramilitary escalation of low-intensity political warfare. The State Supreme Court temporarily suspended the right to a speedy trial. The Miami City Commission passed a sweeping anti-protester ordinance. Storeowners were pressured to take down anti-FTAA posters. Activists were arrested for leafleting in downtown Miami. City officials in collusion with the feds—after publicly smearing the protesters as terrorists—withdrew 8.5 million dollars from the $87 billion Iraq appropriations bill to finance their criminal assaults.

Elderly protesters were treated cruelly. Despite age, heart conditions, asthma, emphysema, arthritis, bad knees, and exhaustion from participation in the demonstration, they were forced to walk blocks around the police cordons that intentionally cut-off the shortest accesses to their vehicles and buses. Although a number of organizations had previously negotiated parade routes and drop-off points for buses, city officials reneged on their promises. The police had promised safe passage to 25 busloads crammed with elderly people who had tried to attend a prearranged AFL-CIO rally against the FTAA at the Bayfront Amphitheater. Every bus had displayed the name *Florida Alliance for Retired Americans* on the front windshield. Every passenger's name and phone number had been given to police in advance. But Tony Fansetta, president of the Florida Alliance for Retired Americans, said 13 busloads were turned away. Many of the others were diverted and their passengers forced to walk up to two miles to attend the rally. Only five buses were allowed to park at the prearranged drop-off point near the Amphitheater. Fansetta compared Chief Timoney to vicious dogs used for guarding junkyards. He furiously condemned Manuel Diaz, mayor of Miami, and Alex Penelas, a top County official. He said:

> [Both of] you had the responsibility for this junkyard dog that you brought in here [from Philadelphia] by the name of Timoney. You cannot have a dog in your yard acting like they

[the police] did and not yourself accept accountability. And that's what this is going to be about. You cannot treat the greatest generation [that served the nation in World War II and Korean War] this way and not expect to be held accountable.

AFL-CIO President John Sweeney declared, "It is clear that the protesters' basic right to have their voices heard was severely restricted, and that all Americans' civil liberties took a one-two punch in Miami." Amnesty International announced that Miami police violated various international laws and covenants on civil rights and use of force when they crushed the FTAA protests.

Chief Timoney's tactics employed undercover police and *agents provocateurs*. Indymedia published photos of young men and women who appeared to be members of the Black Bloc—dressed in black with ski masks—but these men, unlike authentic members of the Bloc, were sauntering alongside uniformed officers behind police lines. Scahill observed:

> At one point during a standoff with police, it appeared as though a group of protesters had gotten into a brawl amongst themselves. But as others moved in to break up the melee, two of the guys pulled out electric tasers and shocked protesters, before being liberated back behind police lines. These guys, clearly undercover agents, were dressed like any other protester. One had a sticker on his backpack that read: "FTAA No Way."

Richard Margolius, a 60-year old circuit judge who witnessed the police response, said in open court that it was a disgrace for the community. "[I saw] no less than 20 felonies committed by police officers," Margolius added. "I probably would have been arrested myself if it had not been for a police officer who recognized me."[198]

Copying the Pentagon's use of "embedded" correspondents in the Iraq War, Chief Timoney invited dozens of major news organizations including the Associated Press, CNN, Fox News, and the *Miami Herald*, to embed reporters with police units. He equipped each correspondent with protective clothing, riot helmets, gas masks, and police press credentials. Fearless, the correspondents marched in lock-step to promote Chief Timoney's cowardly stance toward the demonstrators.[199]

While embeds were treated paternalistically, journalists and photographers from independent media and civil liberties organizations were arrested. Celeste Fraser Delgado, a 36-year-old reporter from the alternative weekly *Miami New Times*, *was* arrested while interviewing protesters. Miles Swanson, 25, a legal observer for the Lawyers Guild, was punched numerous times for pointing out undercover police dressed up as protesters. Eight of 60 Lawyers Guild observers were arrested; they wore green hats and were targeted. When Swanson was grabbed by three Broward County sheriff's deputies—two were undercover agents and wore Black Bloc ski masks—they told him "this is what you get when you fuck with

198 Robin E. Blumner. Jan. 18 2004. "Making the Right to Counsel Vanish." *St. Petersburg Times*.

199 Francisco Alvarado. December 4 2003. "Press Pass and Gas Mask." *Miami New Times*.

us." Swanson said the deputies then drove him around while looking for another legal observer to arrest.[200]

Police brutality paused momentarily while the AFL-CIO, led by President John Sweeney, conducted a march that had a legal permit and was carefully co-ordinated with the police. And in fact, many unionists applauded as they marched by columns of police in body-armor and shields. But as soon as the unionists began to disperse, the police escalated their violence against the other protesters.

Scahill affirmed:

> One woman had part of her ear blown off. Another was shot [with rubber bullets] in the forehead. I got shot twice, once in the back, another time in the leg. My colleague, John Hamilton from the Workers Independent News Service, was shot in the neck by a pepper-spray pellet - a small ball that explodes into a white powder. After a few moments, John began complaining that his neck was burning from the powder. We doused him in water, but the burning continued. When I tried to ask the police what the powder was, they told me to "mind myself."

Apparently, the Miami police had fine-tuned their tactics, cherry-picking those protesters whose ability to raise hell with the media under these circumstances was easily controlled.

At a midday rally outside the county jail where more than 150 protesters were imprisoned, a peace-

---

200 He ultimately pleaded no contest to one charge of obstructing justice so he could return to law school in Washington, D.C.

ful crowd of about 300 people chanted, "Free the Prisoners, Not Free Trade," and "Take off your riot gear, there ain't no riot here!" They sang, "We all live in a failed democracy" to the tune of *Yellow Submarine*. Their leaders met with police officials and promised to remain in a parking lot across from the jail if the police were not reinforced. The police agreed but violated the agreement. More officers arrived, surrounding the gathering and giving its members three minutes to disperse from an "unlawful assembly." The police arrested five activists led by puppetista David Solnit when they refused to leave. Even people who were complying with the order to disperse were charged! Thirty people were chased into a corner, shoved to the ground, beaten, and gassed at close range.

Another *Democracy Now!* correspondent, Ana Nogueira, was videotaping the carnage. Despite her visible press card because she was not embedded, an officer shouted, "She's not with us, she's not with us." "Embedded" journalists wore clothing that imitated uniforms even though they were not police. Nogueira was arrested and, at the jail, guards made her remove her clothes because they were soaked with pepper spray. She was forced to strip naked in front of male officers and held in a roach-filled cell until three in the morning—despite calls from *Democracy Now!* and the ACLU. She was only released after Scahill posted a $500 bond. Other independent journalists were locked up much longer and faced more serious charges, including felonies. Nogueira was falsely charged with "failure to disperse."

Journalists and TV anchors employed by the Miami mass media had circulated for weeks. Chief Timoney's "Miami Model" adopted the same procedures being used by the Defense Department to propagandize the public. In a lengthy letter to South Florida AFL-CIO official Fred Frost, Chief Timoney wrote, "The Miami Police Department and its law enforcement partners, in training for the FTAA [conference], placed primary emphasis on avoiding the use of force. This goal was impossible to achieve due to the violent actions of unaffiliated protesters using labor events and membership as cover." To back up this shameless assertion, Chief Timoney claimed,

> A firm rapid response was necessary to prevent serious injuries and significant property damage" because the "criminals," hidden among crowds of unionists and senior citizens attending the rallies and march, repeatedly emerged and attacked police with "projectiles including rocks, bottles, slingshot-fired marbles and steel bolts, paint, unidentified white powder, unidentified liquids feared to be human excrement, powerful fireworks, and ignited road flares.[201]

Chief Timoney also alleged the protesters "set fires and erected roadblocks."

However, numerous eyewitnesses testified that Chief Timoney's claims were barefaced lies. Tristam Korten of Miami *New Times*, for example, reported that many people said the five scheduled union

---

201 Tristam Korten. December 4 2003. "Pick Your Reality: Either FTAA Protesters Viciously Assaulted Police, or Police Viciously Assaulted Protesters." *Miami New Times*.

events, a union march through downtown Miami, and a senior citizens' rally, were peaceful. (Korten had observed the union march himself.) Also televised news footage taken from helicopters showed no disturbances at these events. At other times there were minor incidents involving activists who hurled rocks and paint-balls at police who, in return, quickly quelled them with concussion grenades, rubber bullets, and tear gas. These incidents were utterly insignificant considering how outgunned the protesters were by marauding police.

When confronted with the reports of police brutality, Sweeney demanded a congressional investigation and called the 8.5 million taken from funds slated for Iraq, money for "homeland repression." (Perhaps the phrase, "homeland fascism," might be more appropriate.) Of course, no investigation ever took place. And no one was held accountable for the crimes committed by the law enforcement officers.

WHO WERE THE TERRORISTS?

And what about the triumphant cheers from the local establishment after the demonstrations were over? When the FTAA ministers left town, Miami officials happily suggested that their Miami Model be used nationwide. Miami Mayor Manny Diaz touted Chief Timoney's tactics as "a model for homeland defense." And Alex Penelas, a top Miami-Dade County official who competed in the 2004 Democratic primary for the US Senate, backed him up.[202] His chief

---

202 Penelas competed in the 2004 Democratic primary for the U.S.

of staff, Javier Alberto Soto, declared that all forty participating police agencies providing security for the FTAA had done an "exemplary" job. He also recommended Chief Timoney's Miami Model to the Office of Homeland Security.

Given the coordination, information sharing, and planning among law enforcement agencies, even a one-eyed conspiracy theorist could see the writing on the wall. After every demonstration in Seattle, Los Angeles, Washington, DC, Philadelphia, and Miami, metropolitan police and federal agencies held seminars, scrutinized videos, and read reports evaluating their ability to suppress protests. Covert operations and surveillance were also analyzed. Identities of leading activists, revealed by this surveillance, were shuttled from one police department to another.

The surveillance found, for instance, that protesters had been managing their actions with cell phones. As a result, John Sellers wasn't simply targeted, beaten, and charged with unlawful conduct in Philadelphia because he was the head of the Ruckus Society. He was subsequently confronted with an enormous $1 million dollar bail because an "instrument of a crime," a cell phone, was clipped to his belt. The enormous bail was imposed because activists coordinated actions and relayed information via cell phones. Paramilitary propagandists and hardassed federal judges had transformed cell phones into assault rifles.

By 2003, police departments as well as the feds

Senate.

were engaging in on-the-spot surveillance of police tactics. With regard to Miami, several cities had arranged to send law-enforcement observers to conduct field studies of the "training [model] for the FTAA"

"To every action there is an equal and opposite reaction," according to Isaac Newton. But the Miami protesters' reactions were far from equal. They did pick up gas grenades and throw them back. And, although Chief Timoney claimed that they also threw glass bottles, in reality, they carried water in plastic bottles to quench their thirst and, when provoked, tossed them half full at the police. Furthermore, even though the anarchist Black Bloc in 1999 was reputed to have smashed windows of Seattle stores selling goods produced by third-world sweatshops—such as Nike, Addidas, and GAP—the Bloc in Miami showed notable restraint. This time, they marched in disciplined rows, with arms firmly linked, holding PVC pipes wrapped with barbed wire in front of them to fend off police with flailing clubs. They were defiant but they were not fools.

So outrageous was the Miami repression that Amnesty International also called for an independent investigation. Amnesty stated that the Miami police had violated the United Nations' Basic Principles on the Use of Force and Firearms by Law Enforcement Officials, the Universal Declaration of Human Rights, and other covenants as well. But the police were never investigated or punished for their crimes.

While paramilitary violence in Miami was still occurring, a federal official leaked a confidential FBI memo to The *New York Times*. The memo showed that the FBI had initiated a major surveillance of the anti-war movement in advance of the October 25 protests against the occupation of Iraq. Nonetheless, FBI officials smugly denied they were spying on legitimate protest activities. They insisted that their surveillance was restricted to actual or potential terrorists and others involved in "criminal activities."

How much further can paramilitary commanders like Chief Timoney go? How about rounding-up protesters and imprisoning them in penal colonies? From 1942 to 1945, more than one hundred and twenty thousand persons of Japanese descent (two thirds of whom were American citizens) were interned in penal colonies. They lived in cheaply constructed barracks behind barbed wire with armed guards under humiliating and unhealthy conditions. As it turned out, only 10 people during the war were convicted of spying for Japan—and all of them were Caucasian. Yet the government claimed the internment was justified because people of Japanese descent on the West Coast might possibly be traitors.

Achtung! Pay Attention! Chief Timoney! The land used for the penal colonies is still available. Cheap tarpaper barracks can again be built alongside the Mess Hall preserved at Manzanar, California, to provide homeland quarters for political prisoners.

PART FOUR

UNC HECKS & IMB ALANCES

— ◇ —

11 | Decapitating the Judiciary

We can have democracy in this country, or we can have great wealth concentrated in the hands of a few. But we can't have both.

—Justice Louis Brandeis,

1941

FIGHTING THE NEW DEAL

The Supreme Court prior to the Great Depression challenged congressional legislation less than a dozen times. However, the challenges increased during the Depression because of its opposition to New Deal reforms. It decided in 1932 that a New York minimum-wage law for women was unconstitutional and in 1935 three more decisions further validated its opposition to the New Deal.

Still, the necessity for progressive reforms was

obvious. Millions were dying from starvation, malnutrition, stress, and the lack of medical care. Given the loss of earnings, familial support for the elderly among the poor declined. Corporations were still using armed force to crush attempts by organized labor to improve wages and working conditions. The Congress of Industrial Organizationss led by militant leaders such as John L. Lewis had come into being and members of the United Auto Workers forced their way into factories—conducting "sit-down strikes" that prevented General Motors from using scabs to resume production.

Sit-down strikes in the auto industry broached the possibility of violence. The strikers threatened to smash the machines they normally operated if the police or the National Guard attempted to enter the factories and forcibly replace them with scabs.

Spurred by the shattering crisis, veteran's organizations, labor unions, and left-wing organizations challenged the unchecked corporate control of all branches of government as well as the legitimacy of capitalism itself. Unlike Herbert Hoover, who had used federal troops to repress veterans demanding relief, FDR responded decisively with programs that put millions to work. The Public Works Administration constructed dams, schools, hospitals, and highways. Publicly employed musicians and actors provided free concerts and plays for families in poverty-stricken communities. Young men employed by The Civilian Conservation Corps planted millions of trees in eroded land.

Eventually, immense political pressure and FDR's judicial appointments altered the Supreme Court. It rejected precedents and legitimized New Deal reforms. The Social Security and National Labor Relations Acts were enacted in 1935 to provide support for the elderly, prohibit unfair labor practices, and impose elections to resolve conflicts over union representation.[203]

But the industrial and financial networks that opposed the New Deal never surrendered. Nor did their succeeding counterparts calmly accept the campaigns led by organized labor, civil-rights, and antiwar movements during the post WWII period. Toward the end of the Seventies, they quietly adopted a long-term strategy for suppressing the welfare state and the political organizations that supported it.

This trend is evocative of Nazi attacks on the German welfare state and its *Sozialpolitik* leading to the collapse of parliament (the Reichstag) and the suppression of independent labor organizations. Of course, the opposition to the American welfare state and organized labor in recent decades has by comparison been predictably "friendly."

More than 33 per cent of employed workers in America belonged to unions in 1945; by 1979 union membership had fallen to 24.1 per cent of the US work force. In 1981, the Reagan administration attacked organized labor by illegally firing striking air traffic controllers and then supporting corporate attacks on unions. In the Eighties and Nineties, fewer

---

203 The Act outlawed the stockpiling of arms (rifles, machine guns, and tear gas) by corporations and the use of police and thugs to break unions. The Act also compelled corporations to recognize unions instead of machine-gunning employees when they demonstrated outside factory walls.

and fewer strikes were conducted. By 1998, as the economy deindustrialized, union membership dropped to 13.9 per cent. In 2010, about 12 per cent of the American workforce belonged to unions—and the government grudgingly employed half of this force.

The catastrophic fall of organized labor in the US, of course, was prefigured by the successful suppression of left-wing union leaders during the McCarthy period. But the *coup de grace* was administered by law firms and consultants who advised corporations on ways to avoid lawsuits and prosecution for unfair labor practices as they smashed unions and fired union activists.[204] Also the political corruption of the National Labor Relations Board (NLRB) greased the decline of organized labor. Tens of thousands of employees who backed organizing drives were fired in the last decades and entire factories have been shut down and relocated to avoid unions from taking hold.

In addition, even expenditures for people who face food shortages and hunger came under attack. For example, while the Bush administration was spending billions on the war, the US Department of Agriculture reported that since 1999 more than 7 million had joined the ranks of people experiencing hunger and food insecurity. By 2004 more than 138 million Americans, including 14 million children, lived in households with insufficient funds for food. Nevertheless, the House Agricultural Committee in

---

204 See *American Rights at Work* website and Steven Greenhouse. Dec 14 2004. "How do you Drive Out a Union? South Carolina Factory provides a Textbook Case."

October 2005 recommended budget cuts taking food stamps away from about 300,000 people and cut-off school lunches and breakfasts for 40,000 children. The assaults on the welfare state have targeted its costs, its regulatory agencies, and its services. Regulatory agencies were established to sustain minimum wages, working conditions, and public health. They also attempted to minimize stock-market fraud, urban sprawl, and environmental pollution. But these agencies were under-funded, corrupted and eliminated.[205]

Also, long-standing welfare-state programs were cut in order to offset the colossal sums expended on empire building, corporate welfare, and tax cuts for wealthy Americans.[206] Some public health, public transportation, and education services, for instance, were privatized in spite of the fact that this has meant actually paying more for these services while enduring the increased fraud, environmental degradation, and anti-union policies that privatization normally entails.

In 2005, Bush launched an aggressive campaign to privatize Social Security, "the crowning jewel" of the welfare state. In his 2005 State of the Union speech before Congress, Bush declared, "By the year

205 Eliminating Glass-Steagall paved the way for Enron. Also, Gov. Jeb Bush eliminated Florida's annual pollution test for autos. Enron's frauds destroyed its pension funds and Florida's inhabitants are breathing polluted air.

206 Also, imperial expansion requires colossal expenditures that are either extracted directly from the population at large (via the exploitation of the labor force in the armament industries, for instance) or extracted from the taxpayers indirectly via public revenues spent to expand the American empire.

2042, the entire [Social Security] system would be exhausted and bankrupt." However, the facts branded this declaration as yet another Big Lie. Social Security would actually be able to pay elderly retirees every dime they were promised—until a half-century from the day he made his speech.[207] After that date, minor modifications would enable it to pay full benefits until the end of the century.

But the new conservatives who echoed Bush's Big Lies didn't really care about facts. As syndicated journalist Cynthia Tucker, noted:

> Before the invasion of Iraq, Bush and his minions predicted that combat would be a cakewalk, that Saddam had not only WMD but also ties to al-Qaeda and that nation-building would be paid out of Iraqi oil resources. Two years later, more than 1,400 US troops are dead, there were no ties to al-Qaeda, the nuclear program turns out to be in Iran, and US taxpayers are paying nearly $4.5 billion a month for our presence in Iraq. Do you dare believe them about Social Security?[208]

In his eagerness to enrich bankers and stockbrokers by privatizing as much of the Social Security program as he could get away with, Bush disregarded the loss in benefits for the people who remain in the program. Furthermore, the effects of this loss would not be restricted to the elderly. It would tear

---

207 The Congressional Budget Office said no change was necessary until 2052.

208 Cynthia Tucker. Feb. 7 2005. "The Administration That Cried Wolf: Campaign against Social Security is Full of Falsehoods." *Universal Press Syndicate*. (our emphasis).

families apart because children and other close relatives would have to assume an even greater burden unless they had sufficient funds to commit their elderly to "assisted living" agencies.

TERRY SCHIAVO & "JUDICIAL ACTIVISTS"

Bush's attempt to privatize Social Security increased popular disillusionment with his administration. Even the media prostitutes could not dissuade citizens that they could get the brass ring if they opted for his ideological and conservative "reforms." The disillusionment with the Bush administration had also surged in 2005 when Bush's brother (Florida's Governor Jeb Bush) and a potpourri of Republicans and Democrats fought to keep Terry Schiavo alive. For 15 years, Schiavo had been in a vegetative virtually brain-dead state; and years of litigation and unanimous judicial reviews had ratified her husband's right to respect her wishes by having her support system removed. Most people regarded the tactics used by Jeb Bush, G. W. Bush, and members of Congress to keep her on a life-support system as unwarranted government intrusion into family affairs. Significantly, the opinion shared by the majority was not diminished by the mass media as thousands of newspaper articles and countless television broadcasts supported right-wing "pro-life" demands.

Disillusionment was particularly acute for the people who were repelled by the grotesque events during the final week of Schiavo's life. Bush and members of Congress rushed from their homes back to Washington to exploit the media coverage and hysteria surrounding the Schiavo case. They bragged about their commitment to preserving her life despite her vegetative state. But their real values surfaced when people discovered that Bush, during his term as governor of Texas, had signed into law a "cost saving measure" permitting the withdrawal of life support measures if a Medicaid patient appeared to have an incurable illness. In fact, during the national uproar over the Schiavo case, Houston doctors were pulling a breathing tube from the throat of an ailing infant in a Texas children's hospital even though his grief-stricken mother wanted him kept alive. Neither the media nor right-to-life groups and government officials raised a ruckus about the withdrawal of the child's life support system because, in addition to being impoverished, the boy and his mother—unlike the white, middle-class Schiavo and her parents—were African-Americans. Sen. Tom De-Lay, the Republican whip who led the Republican pack that flew back to Washington provided another example of the hypocrisy associated with the Schiavo case. In the Eighties he had personally consented to the withdrawal of his own comatose father's life-support system.

Since the courts without exception had ratified Schiavo's right to respect her wishes, Republican Party officials mocked and threatened the judges who had ruled in her husband's favor. They claimed that unlike so-called "strict constructionists" these judges were "judicial activists" because they grossly misinterpreted the Constitution and ignored "the letter of the law" even though nothing in the Constitution justified this charge.

The phrase, "judicial activists," is an ideological term. It was manufactured by rightists to discredit legitimate interpretations of the Constitution that favored social equality and individual liberties. Consequently, the so-called "strict constructionists" have been the real "judicial activists." They have deliberately interpreted the Constitution wrongly in order to support conservative causes and ignore its historical development.

The sources of constitutional texts were never restricted to the "founding fathers." Mitchell Franklin's scholarly writings demonstrate that the Constitution has undergone significant changes.[209] He said the first version of the Constitution, expressed by the 1787 Articles of Confederation, for instance, legitimated "federalist principles" that imposed a political and economic system based on a market economy and slavery. But subsequent versions, dubbed the "Second" and "Third Constitutions," were generated by the original Bill of Rights and the 14th and 15th Amendments. These versions abolished slavery and represented open-ended amendments that were in later years interpreted by members of the Warren Court—which was "packed" by FDR—to designate universal rights rather than the rights and privileges of property owners, white racists, and tyrants. (Eventually, its members notably included William O. Douglas and, the first African-American Supreme Court Justice, Thurgood Marshal)

209 Mitchell Franklin. 2000. *Dialectics Of The US Constitution: Selected Writings Of Mitchell Franklin.* (Edited by James M. Lawler.) Minneapolis, Minnesota: MEP Press.

Mitchell Franklin's writings actually anticipated some of the liberal thought behind the Warren Court decisions.[210] Furthermore, after the decisions were written, he claimed that they were based on *authentic* readings of the Constitution. They did not represent a capricious political intrusion into the judicial process because the Second and Third Constitutions were purposefully written as safeguards to be expanded by future generations in support of civil liberty and political freedom. He believed these safeguards defended the *democratic* form of our republican government and not just any government.

We know that Justice Thurgood Marshal deplored the compromises made historically with slave owners at the first Constitutional Convention; nonetheless, he insisted that the Civil War amendments repudiated these compromises. The Constitution, in his view, represented "living law" and not the words of dead men immutably carved in stone. It did not represent the fictitious entity fabricated by "strict constructionists" and right-wing demagogues.

Stacking the Courts

While the Republicans exploited the Schiavo case and condemned "judicial activism," Bush asked the Senate Judiciary Committee to approve his nominations for Federal Appellate Court vacancies. Although the Democrats had previously confirmed *98 per cent* of his nominations when they controlled the Committee, the President deliberately recommended

---

210 In fact, Justice Douglas cited Franklin.

10 individuals in 2005 that had been rejected by the Democrats. After the 2004 election, Bush knew that the Democrats on the Committee could no longer summon enough votes to block his nominations.

The filibuster was the only tactic left to the Democrats. Historically, this tactic had been useful to reactionaries as well as progressives depending upon the issues at stake. (Dixiecrats, for instance, had used it to keep the South racially segregated; however, in later years, the tactic had stopped right-wing extremists from being appointed to the federal courts.) To prevent the Democrats from using the filibuster, the Senate and House majority leaders, Bill Frist and Tom DeLay, called for reducing the votes required to block a filibuster. (The existing rule for nullifying a filibuster required 60 per cent of the Senate vote but these leaders wanted it reduced to 50%.) Vice President Cheney, President of the Senate as well, called Frist's proposal a "nuclear option" because it would effectively silence the Democratic opposition and ensure the lifetime appointments for Bush's nominations.

By this time, the political stakes had skyrocketed. The fight over Bush's appellate nominations represented the opening battle for control of the Supreme Court. Judge Rehnquist, who chaired the court, had throat cancer. Bush was lining up the pins to guarantee that Rehnquist's replacement would be an arch-conservative.

The Warren Court had represented a profound break with the past because Justices Douglas, Marshal, and Brennan had nudged the court to the left and rendered the so-called "activist" decisions that remain milestones in the history of American jurisprudence to this very day.

But the Republicans had changed the court. When Thurgood Marshall, the first African American to serve on the court, announced his retirement, the elder Bush in 1991 proposed Clarence Thomas as Marshall's substitute even though he opposed principles that Marshall had espoused. Marshall had successfully represented the NAACP in the groundbreaking *Brown vs. Board of Education (of Topeka)* case and the NAACP, Urban League, and National Organization for Women opposed Bush's appointment because Thomas had criticized affirmative action policies and they believed that he would not support *Roe v. Wade*. Topping it off, the American Bar Association didn't consider him fully qualified for the position and, finally, two women, who had been supervised by Thomas, accused him of sexual harassment.

When G. W. Bush exploited the opportunity to determine the court's composition, right-wing Republicans controlled the executive and legislative branches; consequently; stacking the court would also place the judicial branch firmly under their control. Thus, capitulation to Bush's nominations would go a long way toward ensuring a *de facto* one-party dictatorship.

All of Bush's judicial candidates for the federal appellate courts represented the far right. They included William Myer III, a mining and cattle industry lobbyist, and Judge Terrence Boyle of the US District Court for the Eastern District of North Carolina whose rulings had been overturned by conservative appellate Courts 120 times for errors in judgment or incompetence. (These reversals, moreover, included his attempts to reverse federal laws prohibiting job discrimination by race, gender, and disability.)

Alabama's Attorney General William Pryor Jr., was another nominee. He reportedly took money from Phillip Morris and undermined an anti-tobacco lawsuit until it was almost over. He had cost Alabama billions in settlement money for its healthcare system and had fought against civil rights for minorities, women, the disabled, and lesbian and gay couples. He had declared that *Roe vs. Wade* was "the worst abomination of constitutional law in our history."

Bush also nominated Priscilla Owen. According to Senator Edward Kennedy, Owen was previously elected to the Texas Supreme Court with donations from Enron and other big companies, she had systematically ruled against workers, consumers, and "the most vulnerable members of our society." In fact, as Kennedy added, "Judge Owen's activism and extremism has manifested itself in cases dealing with business interests, malpractice, access to public information, and employment discrimination, in which she rules against individual plaintiffs time and time again." Senator Charles Schumer exclaimed:

> If there was ever a judge who would substitute her own views for the law, it is Judge Owen . . . [S]he thinks she knows better than 100 years of legal tradition and clear legislative intent. There is no question that when you look up 'judicial activist' in the dictionary, you see a pic-

ture of Priscilla Owen.

Sen. Arlen Specter—a so-called "moderate Republican"—chaired the Senate Judiciary Committee. His speech before the Senate emphasized that Judge Owen should be confirmed because she was a Texas Supreme Court judge and had graduated cum laude from Harvard Law School. Bush had originally ordered the Republicans on the Committee to keep Specter from being the chairman unless he promised to toe the line. In May 2005, Specter lived up to the promise.

Sen. Patrick Leahy's speech before the Senate made mincemeat of Sen. Specter's disingenuous defense of Judge Owen's qualifications. He told the Senate that the Republicans in 2003 had staged a 40-hour filibuster on judicial nominees. When it ended the Democrats discovered that the Republicans had been repeatedly forewarned about Democratic tactics—because their aides had been stealing files for three years or more from Judiciary computer servers.[211]

Furthermore, when Leahy was the Democratic chair of the Judiciary Committee, its members reduced federal judicial vacancies to their lowest level since President Reagan. To make sure that even the most biased Republican recognized this point, Leahy

---

211 What measure of respect for their privacy could ordinary Americans expect? The Republicans had no qualms about stealing confidential information from Democrats and they continued to steal information even though they had almost nothing to gain. Astonishingly, the Democrats had confirmed 169 of Bush's nominations by November 2003. They had refused to confirm a mere four.

held up a large sign with the numbers, "*208—5*," showing that 208 of Bush's nominees had been confirmed by 2005. Only five had been unconfirmed. Apparently, however, the Republican Party's need for power—like a corporation's greed—had no bounds. Leahy remarked with sadness:

> if the vote on the Republican leader's nuclear option were by secret ballot, we all know that it would fail overwhelmingly. That is because Senators know that it is wrong—wrong in terms of protecting the rights of the American people, wrong in terms of undercutting our fundamental system of checks and balances, and wrong in destroying minority protection in the Senate in favor of a one-party rule system. Democratic Senators will not be able to rescue the Senate and our system of checks and balances from the breaking of the Senate rules that the Republican leader [Frist] is planning to demand. If the rights of the minority are to be preserved, if the Senate's unique role in our system of government is to be preserved, it will take at least six Republicans standing up for fairness and for checks and balances. I believe that a number of Republican Senators know in their hearts that this nuclear option is the wrong way to go. I have to believe that enough Republican Senators will put the Senate first, the Constitution first, and the American people first, and withstand the momentary political pressures when they cast their votes.

DELETING CHECKS & BALANCES

Senator Leahy passionately opposed Senator Frist's threat of the "nuclear option" to stop a filibuster because it prevented a Senate minority from making a last-ditch stand to check the executive branch. However, Frist's threat was withdrawn when a small but critical number of Senators announced their intention to support Bush's first three nominations. They made Frist's threat irrelevant by proposing to increase the margin of votes to that which could shut down a filibuster.[212]

This small bi-partisan group claimed that its Democratic and Republican party representatives had made a deal that met the interests of Democrats as well as Republicans. The Democrats, according to the group's reasoning, would have been irreparably harmed if the Republicans succeeded in reducing the votes for blocking a filibuster. But, if the Senate did not change the rule, the filibuster would be saved as an eleventh-hour option that could be used by Democrats on another day.

This claim was preposterous. The necessity for making a deal was demolished when Sen. Frist promptly announced that he had not been a party to the deal. He promised to use the "nuclear option" if the Democrats threatened to filibuster Bush's nominations in the future. (Frist reserved the option because he knew that Senate Republicans would never allow the Democrats to check Bush when they were asked to confirm candidates for the Supreme Court.)[213]

---

212 This incident occurred on Tuesday May 24 2005.

213 Again, in the current struggle for democracy, form replaced substance because the filibuster could be challenged if it was employed for Supreme Court nominations. Meanwhile, the concentration on preserving the rules veiled the issue of what kinds

Ironically, Frist himself had used the filibuster option in 2000 to try to stop one of President Clinton's court nominees. In addition, Bush had already nominated 225 people to federal judgeships and all but 10 had been confirmed despite the fact that the last handfuls, as Jim Hightower declared, were "political hacks and extremist ideologues that consistently push for unfettered corporate power, while working against consumers, workers, and ordinary folks." Preserving the 60 per cent filibuster rule may have enabled the bipartisan group to believe that they retained the Senate's formal independence, but the confirmation of three more staunch defenders of corporate interests indicated how far Bush had gone in packing the federal judiciary and how far, in the fight for democracy, a demagogic obsession with *form* (i.e., Senate rules) had replaced *substance*.

The so-called "deal" made by the "bipartisan" brokers led to the confirmation of three right-wing judges. The phony "deal" cut the ground from under the Democratic opposition to the Bush candidates and undermined the judiciary's role as an independent force.

Subsequently, Bush nominated John Roberts Jr. as Chief Justice of the Supreme Court. On September 20 2006, when the Senate hearings on Roberts' candidacy were over, the Senate Democratic leader, Harry Reid, issued a passionate statement denouncing the nomination: "We should only vote to confirm this nominee if we are absolutely positive that he is the right person" for the post. Roberts had served in

---

of politics these appointments implied and how far Bush had gone in stacking the courts.

the Solicitor General's office; yet the Bush administration refused to release memos that he had written. So even though the hearings had other information that disclosed Roberts' right-wing stands on civil rights, privacy issues, and other matters, he was confirmed as Chief Justice.

Roberts was nominated as a replacement for Rehnquist. In addition, to replace Justice Sandra O'Connor, who had retired, Bush nominated Samuel Alito. (Like the Christian rightist, Clarence Thomas, Alito was not a legal authority or noted government official—although Thomas who had been a bureaucratic nonentity was even less qualified.) Alito's record indicated that he would strip Congress of its authority and increase the power of the executive branch to determine how laws are to be interpreted. His disdain for ordinary people and his support for corporate interests were also distinctive. (He had even ruled against a 14 year old child's infraction of a law against eating an ice cream cone in the subway.) Corporate media, of course, ignored this record and immediately proclaimed him an eminently qualified jurist.

Senators Ted Kennedy and John Kerry regarded Alito as the last straw, and decided to filibuster his appointment—asking Senate democrats to support their effort and to do the right thing. But they did not succeed in getting enough Democrats to back them. *Bad News*.

Within months, the new Supreme Court set the clock way back—prohibiting voluntary efforts in Seattle and Louisville to desegregate schools, overruling the medical community by upholding late abortion bans, blocking citizens—whose taxes were being unlawfully spent to subsidize religion—from bringing a complaint to court. The court undermined the government's responsibility to uphold the Endangered Species Act, allowed corporations to pay for political ads (for candidates that served their interests) during elections, and ensured that women suffering from pay inequities would have a harder time getting justice in court.

Predictably, the new members of the Supreme Court have tried to destroy all the contributions to school desegregation, free speech, privacy rights, a women's right to choose, and other pioneering decisions of the Warren Court. The liberals who fought to put teeth into the Bill of Rights are long gone. Right wing judicial activists, who will negate the court's role in the system of checks and balances, have replaced them. (More on this later.)

How About Neo-Fascism?

Bush's attempts to destroy checks and balances call to mind Allen Dulles's remarks about the importance of this system in the fight against totalitarianism.[214] During the Second World War, Dulles headed the clandestine counter-intelligence agency, Office of Strategic Services (OSS) in Berne, Switzerland.[215] As

---

214 Allen Welsh Dulles. 2000 (orig. 1947). *Germany's Underground: The Anti-Nazi Resistance.* (Intro. Peter Hoffman). New York: DaCapo Press Edition. Dulles' grandfather and uncle had been Secretaries of State. His elder brother, John Foster Dulles, served in that position from 1953 to 1959.

215 The OSS reportedly was the precursor to the CIA.

an OSS chief, he had personal contact with a conspiracy largely composed of highly placed German officers that attempted to kill Hitler, seize control of their government and negotiate peace with the Western powers. The assassination attempt occurred in 1944 but failed. Hitler, though wounded, survived the conspiracy's bomb and the Gestapo arrested and executed about 2,000 co-conspirators. Some, such as the celebrated "Desert Fox," Field Marshall Erwin Rommel, were allowed to commit suicide rather than face a firing squad because of their notoriety and because Himmler wanted to hide the scope of the conspiracy from the armed forces and public.

Dulles reports that he began to gather the information about the conspiracy in 1943; but, as his inquiry progressed, he became convinced that it illuminated fundamental issues about the conditions that supported totalitarianism. He said:

> In Germany, at least, there were no defenses in depth against totalitarian attack. When the line was broken at a vital point, the battle was lost. It should make all of us consider how adequate our own institutions are for democracy's preservation and how far its survival must depend upon the devotion to these institutions by men and women ready and willing to act in time to defend them.

He also wrote that his insight into the "anatomy" of Hitler's ascent to power, gained from his own experiences and the Nuremberg trial had provided lessons that would help Americans defend themselves against the same forces that created Hitler's regime. He said:

The fatal weakness of the political system of the Weimar Republic lay in the ease with which absolute power could be taken from the people and entrusted to one man. When constitutional safeguards are so frail that a single thrust can overcome them, the people may be deprived even of the opportunity to make an effective fight to preserve democracy. Yet today in many European countries there are bitter struggles over inserting in the new constitutions the checks and balances that delimit political power. These checks and balances may at times seem frustrating, and appear to make democracy less efficient than dictatorship. But they are really beyond price.

Dulles didn't live long enough to witness the subordination of America's Senate to the "friendly fascists" who command the executive branch of government. But when Bush's nominations to the appellate and Supreme Court were evaluated, their obsequious deference to the executive branch stood out.

The House of Representatives also deferred to the executive branch. Congressional support for Bush's fraudulent "state of emergency" (and domestic "reforms") count heavily when neo-fascism is considered. Historically, "states of emergency" adopted by governments with parliamentary systems were regarded as "exceptional states." These states were limited in certain respects and were considered *temporary expedients* when a regime was faced with war, natural disaster, or economic crisis.

In contrast, Bush's state of emergency had been justified by the necessity to fight a perpetual war against terrorism (epitomized by North Korea, Russia, China, Cuba, Venezuela, Afghanistan, Iran, Libya and all other predictable and unpredictable enemies). His initiation of an "endless war" and its policies had cleverly *normalized* an 'exceptional state' in the public's mind. As a result, it has obtained Congressional support for a step-by-step strategy that is replacing with neofascism the democratic form of our republic and its constitutional safeguards.

12 | Changing Drivers and Moving On

Question: *How many Bush Administration officials does it take to screw in a light bulb?"*

Answer: *None. There is nothing wrong with the light bulb; its conditions are improving every day. Any reports of its lack of incandescence are a delusional spin from the liberal media. That light bulb has served honorably, and anything you say undermines the lighting effect. Why do you hate freedom?*

—Uncertain Origin[216]

---

216 Reportedly, Doug Simmons relayed this gag sent to him by Don Flood, who got it from someone else, who saw it in a column by Eric Alterman.

"LYING LIARS"

At the beginning of his second term in office, Bush promoted Alberto Gonzales, Condoleezza Rice, and John Negroponte to key offices. Ashcroft had become a civil libertarian lightning rod but he reportedly resigned for health and family reasons. As indicated, Gonzales replaced him. Prior to confirmation as Attorney General, Gonzales (as well as Bush) had written ambiguous memos giving the American military and "private contractors"—i.e. mercenaries—the latitude to outsource torture. Jailors were authorized to chain Guantanamo prisoners in fetal positions, attach electrodes to their genitals, deprive them of food and water, and beat them pitilessly. Nevertheless, despite denunciations from the Democratic side of the Senate, Gonzales' appointment was confirmed.

Two years later, Deputy Attorney General, James B. Comey, testified before the Senate Judiciary Committee that Gonzales had rushed to Ashcroft's bedside in George Washington Hospital. Ashcroft had had a gallbladder operation and was in pain, sedated, and "barely articulate," according to Comey. But his signature was needed by the next day in order to renew the National Security Agency's unconstitutional surveillance program, which was still secret at that time. "I was very upset," Comey informed the Committee: "I was angry. I thought I had just witnessed an effort to take advantage of a very sick man, who [actually] did not have the powers of the attorney general because they had been transferred to me."

National Security Advisor Condoleezza Rice replaced Colin Powell as Secretary of State. Although the CIA had told Rice that Iraq had no active nuclear program, she had appeared on TV talk shows to con Americans into believing otherwise. Despite the fact that the military never found the weapons, she continued long after the war started to promote the WMD deception. During the Senate Foreign Relations Committee hearing, she shamelessly contradicted the testimony Clarke had given to the National Commission on the 9/11 attacks. She tried to create the impression that neither she nor any other top official shared any responsibility for the 9/11 catastrophes. Senator Christopher Dodd, the Connecticut Democrat, asked Rice about transfers of detainees to countries for the purpose of being tortured. Rice denied that prisoners were being *intentionally* transferred for this purpose. "We make efforts to ascertain that this will not happen and you can be certain that we will continue to do so," she added. Despite the fact that thousands of documents, hundreds of photographs and a growing number of individuals were testifying otherwise, she assured the Committee that "anything that is done is done within the limits of the law."

Even though on-the-spot journalists, ex-CIA operatives, heads of UN investigation teams, and government documents contradicted Rice's claims, the Senate Committee, also confirmed her promotion with only two dissensions. As Secretary of State, Rice assumed the highest cabinet position in the government.

With regard to Bush's 2005 appointments, Nat

Hentoff asserted: "Under this new attorney general, this new secretary of state—and the president . . . the twists and turns of the American rule of law will accelerate during the next four years while the administration preaches our need to spread democracy throughout the world."[217] Yet neither Gonzales nor Rice's appointments were as alarming as John Negroponte's appointment as Director of the National Security Service.

THE AMERICAN SS

During the weeks following his 2004 reelection, Bush obtained congressional approval for a far-reaching bill to reform the country's intelligence system. Leading Republicans had stalled the bill's passage until the Pentagon was assured that it would retain control of most of its own intelligence operations including the National Security Agency (NSA), the country's largest intelligence unit.[218] (The NSA is limited to intelligence and foreign communications but its work includes some domestic surveillance.) Nevertheless, the final version of the bill permitted the biggest revamping of the intelligence community

217 Nat Hentoff. Jan. 28 2005. "Condi Rice: Misrule of Law: The New Secretary of State, the President's Confidante, Plays by His Code of Justice." Village Voice.

218 The bill included little-noticed provisions expanding the government's policing power and broadening the Patriot Act. These provisions also loosened standards for FBI surveillance warrants and allowed the DoJ to more easily detain people without bail. They also enabled the FBI to obtain secret surveillance and search warrants even if individuals had no connection with a foreign government or terrorist group.

in half a century. It enabled Bush to create the National Security Service by Presidential decree and appoint Negroponte as the Director.

And like the creation of the Homeland Security Department, which tightened presidential control over 22 federal agencies, the creation of the National Security Service tightened control over 15 intelligence agencies. Since Negroponte reports directly to the President, Timothy Edgar, an ACLU consultant observed, "The FBI is effectively being taken over by a spymaster who reports directly to the White House." He added, "It's alarming that the same person who oversees foreign spying will now oversee domestic spying, too." Strangely, the administration claimed that the National Security Service was to become an office within the FBI so that it could consolidate the FBI's clandestine counter-terrorism duties. But some people had suggested that being submerged in the FBI would enable it to avoid Congressional oversight.

It is important to recall in this context that President Lyndon B. Johnson secretly obtained FBI files that he used against his political opponents. (Hoover, too, broke the law when he gave Johnson the files.) The National Security Service, on the other hand, is authorized to provide this sort of service lawfully—yet it remains a clandestine agency. As a result, journalist Mike Whitney called the National Security Service, the "National SS" and an "American Gestapo" because it functioned as Bush's personal secret police. [219]

219 Mike Whitney. July 16 2005. "Genesis of an American Gestapo." *dissidentvoice.org*. (We have italicized the letters, *SS*.)

"The formation of the Bush Gestapo," Whitney insisted, "overturns long held precedents for maintaining the independence of law enforcement agencies." The National SS, according to Whitney, will be independent of congressional oversight and beyond the media's reach. "It will provide the requisite muscle for maintaining America's one-party system; spying, harassing and intimidating those dissident elements who dare to challenge the status quo."

Whitney's 2005 prediction was offset by Obama's election. Nevertheless, the assumptions underlying the prediction seemed reasonable. After all, Negroponte was associated during the Reagan years with covering up Iran-Contra.[220]. He was ambassador to Honduras from 1981 to 1985. In early 1984 he helped US mercenaries Thomas Posey and Dana Parker make arrangements to supply arms to the Contras after Congress had banned governmental aid. The operation was exposed nine months later, at which point the Reagan administration denied any US government involvement—despite Negroponte's role earlier that year.

Negroponte had falsified State Department human-rights reports. He oversaw operations creating the elite Honduran Special Forces unit, Battalion 3-16, which murdered up to 184 people, including an American priest, Father Carney. Negroponte told a

---

220 Another is Elliott Abrams. In 2001 he was appointed as G.W. Bush's senior adviser on Middle East and African affairs. He was made the National Security Council's senior director for democracy, human rights, and international operations in 2005. He had pled guilty to two counts of lying to Congress during the Iran Contra hearings and was subsequently pardoned by George Bush, Sr.

team of investigators headed by Sister Laetitia Bordes in 1982 that his embassy knew nothing about the whereabouts of 32 Salvadoran nuns and women of faith who fled to Honduras in 1981 after the assassination of Archbishop Oscar Romero in San Salvador. (Romero had begged for international intervention that would stop the killing of civilians by the Salvadoran military. In 1980 the cadavers of thousands who were tortured or killed outright were clogging streams and thrown on garbage dumps and on the capital's streets.) In 1996, however, Negroponte's predecessor Jack Binns reported that the women had been captured, tortured, and then crammed into helicopters from which they were tossed to their deaths.

The Human Rights Ombudsman in Honduras, Leo Valladares, also investigated the atrocities committed by Battalion 3-16. Valladares concluded that the CIA had supported this unit to fight leftists in Honduras and to sustain the Contra war. Declassified documents from the Iran-Contra scandal showed Negroponte had provided support for the Contras and Honduran cooperation—even after the US Congress terminated official support for the Contra war. In his confirmation hearings as U.N. Ambassador to Iraq in 2001, Negroponte testified that the death squads were not due to deliberate Honduran government policy. He said, unbelievably, "To this day, I do not believe the death squads were operating in Honduras."

Bring On the Troops

When the National SS was being put on the table, Deputy Defense Secretary Paul Wolfowitz's testimony before the Senate Armed Services Committee showed that the fear of terrorism was once again being exploited to formally revoke the Posse Comitatus Act and expand the role of federal troops in domestic policing. Recall that the employment of federal troops in domestic conflicts had with rare exceptions been banned since 1878. But the Posse Comitatus Act had been breached during the Clinton administration. Federal armed forces had engaged in surveillance and provided logistical support for domestic police forces. One particularly horrifying instance of this was the 1993 assault on the Branch Dravidian compound in Waco, Texas in which Special Forces personnel trained FBI agents, flew choppers, reviewed the plans, and supervised the use of military equipment. The Feds used tanks provided by the Army to smash the exterior walls and shoot inflammable tear gas canisters into the compound. At least 86 men, women, and children were engulfed by flames. The FBI falsely accused the Davidians of setting the fires themselves and committing mass suicide—but motion pictures of the final stages of the assault, taken from a helicopter and from ground level, proved that the FBI and Special Forces caused the fires. Although the Pentagon did everything possible to hide its complicity in the assault, on-sight observations and photos of military observers and tanks showed that it was lying.

Previous chapters noted that in 2002 the Pentagon began to mobilize its resources and turn its attention on Americans. The corporate media deliberately ignored military plans for dealing with domestic dissent. On the other hand, the media paid attention when Bush proposed to use armed forces in domestic crises after Hurricanes Katrina and Rita had devastated New Orleans. Louisiana's National Guard failed to provide sufficient help because it was mismanaged, had little or no training in relief work, and its resources were tied up in Iraq. In addition, federal and local governments had provided insufficient funds for rebuilding the levees despite repeated warnings before the hurricanes occurred. Severe cuts in FEMA's budget prior to the hurricanes ultimately compromised its ability to cope with the disaster. Finally, the corrupt, incompetent, and inhumane policies adopted by local, state, and federal agencies had for decades worsened the devastating effects of the hurricane by digging a channel to Lake Pontchartrain and refusing to revitalize the wetlands that prevented New Orleans from sinking further below sea level.

And what a disaster this was! *Almost an entire city under water*. Structures collapsed, old people fleeing on foot through water up to their necks, babies and infirm adults being carried by younger men and women. Thousands carrying whatever they could save from their homes—leaving behind their lives as they had known them—all being herded toward highways and buses wherever the vehicles were scheduled to go. Families being split up and shuttled to Texas, Oklahoma, Colorado—older children forced to go in one direction and parents in another.

"You're doing great Brownie" applauded President Bush to the head of FEMA. These two smiling officials were photo-opted days after the hurricane hit while looking at mostly black survivors who hadn't been provided with food, water, soap, or life-saving medical supplies for four or five days of this obscenity. More than a week after the hurricane hit, dead bodies were still lying in plain view alongside city streets and interstate highways.

One year later thousands of homes were still abandoned. Over 200,000 people had not made it back to the city. An incredible number of homes were shattered and covered with mold. Clean-up crews were still finding bodies. Seventy thousand families lived in 240 square foot FEMA trailers reeking with formaldehyde from cheap building materials. A fraction of the houses had electricity. The one big public hospital was closed and a year after the hurricane hit, hardly anyone knew whether it would be reopened. Suicide rates had skyrocketed. Six thousand criminal justice cases had not been tried. As the human rights lawyer and law professor, Bill Quigley, declares, "It has occurred to us that our New Orleans is looking more and more like Baghdad."

Corrupt Louisiana officials were in Nirvana. Public services were being privatized. Four public schools remained out of the preexisting 115. Most of the rest were sliced into charter schools that were publicly funded but run by private groups. Teachers were fired and, even though they had had the largest labor union in the state, denied the right to bargain collectively. Public housing was left in ruins or boarded up. Thousands of families in public housing were not allowed to return. The federal housing authority planned to demolish 5,000 apartments and allow corporations to build houses, office building, and malls on the sites.[221]

The incompetent, inhuman, and selfish responses to one of the greatest so-called "natural" disasters in the US were evident from day one. Sending national guardsmen from surrounding states as well as Louisiana was inexcusably delayed and federal troops finally filled the gap. They were dispatched to assist relief efforts and help bring some order to chaotic conditions in the city. Nevertheless, addressing the nation in his New Orleans photo op, President Bush did not mention that federal troops would have been unnecessary in the first place if these conditions had been addressed.

Bush said, "It is now clear that a challenge on this scale requires greater federal authority and a broader role for the armed forces—the institution of our government most capable of massive logistical operations on a moment's notice." What was Bush talking about? Using federal armed forces that are primarily trained to annihilate foreign enemies to do the job that state militias have done for over a century? What else did federal troops do besides herd the inhabitants of New Orleans into the Superdome —an enclosed stadium—at the point of a bayonet without adequate supplies of food, water, and medical services?

Of course, leaders of emergency-relief groups

221 Bill Quigley. June 29 2006. "Ten Months after Katrina: Gutting New Orleans." *CommonDreams.org.*

doubted that giving the federal armed forces police power in such situations would actually make Americans safer. "With images of soldiers in New Orleans carrying M-16s but no medical or relief supplies fresh in the public memory, the president would still have us believe that a military response is the preferred response," said Mary Ellen McNish, General Secretary for the American Friends Service Committee.[222] This Quaker agency, with experience in disaster relief and war zones for almost 90 years, believes the military is no substitute for trained relief and reconstruction personnel and it accused the president of chasing after more money for the Pentagon. According to McNish:

> Relief work cannot be a military add-on. Public safety is too important to be used in a ploy to prop up ballooning military expenditures and a failed foreign policy of global dominance. The answer is not to embed disaster response even more deeply in the *"war on terror"* bureaucracy but to return FEMA to its former independence and its focus on helping Americans in times of need.

Furthermore, a 2009 court ruling demonstrated that Bush's faith in the army was questionable. A landmark federal court ruling—in a lawsuit brought by thousands of storm victims—blamed the Army Corps of Engineers' for its "monumental negligence" in constructing the levees that were supposed to guard New Orleans against Katrina. The victims had

---

222 McNish's statements were issued as a Sept. 16 2005 press release posted on the Committee's Web site, *afsc.org/news/2005/military-relief.htm.*

claimed that their losses and suffering were largely due to a man-made disaster, especially caused by the government's failure to maintain levees on a channel called the Mississippi River-Gulf Outlet, and their suit was upheld by a federal court.

But Bush had no doubts about using the military to deal with catastrophes. After 9/11, the president pushed through a legislative program broadening federal authority, slashing civil liberties and militarizing public safety. Even after Mississippi Senator Trent Lott admitted that it was a mistake to place FEMA under the Department of Homeland Security, Bush still was committed to his militaristic agenda. And why not? Wouldn't a professional military force be more reliable *politically* in policing Americans than a citizens' force like the state militia?

Bush reiterated his New Orleans proposal when the avian flu scare made headlines. He asked Congress to reevaluate the Posse Comitatus Act. Without a trace of insincerity, he said, "I'm concerned about what an avian flu outbreak could mean for the United States and the world." To prove his point, he added, "One option is the use of a military that's able to plan and move." *Plan and move.* Isn't that what the guys who race on the Indiana Speedway do all the time? Was Bush testing the waters? Was he using a well-known political tactic that would help his Orwellian spinmeisters by checking on the public's response to martial law?

NEW REVELATIONS

By May, 2006, amidst scandalous new revelations about the corruption in government, the media blew the administration's spin on its secret programs. For more than five years, Bush, Cheney, Rumsfeld, and other top officials had lied about their unconstitutional policies in order for their lawlessness to appear legitimate.

In 2004, Porter Goss replaced Tenet who resigned from the CIA.[223] By May 2006, Gross had purged the CIA and got rid of the employees who refused to squat on demand for the Bush administration. Then he was caught up in a sordid Washington corruption scandal whose participants held poker games serviced by prostitutes. To assure the public that the administration had nothing to do with his scandalous behavior, Negroponte got rid of him.

At the Office of National Intelligence, Air Force General Michael Hayden—who had previously headed the Pentagon's National Security Agency's (NSA) surveillance and data mining operations—was assisting Negroponte. On May 8, 2006, Hayden replaced Goss as Director of the CIA. After the Senate approved his appointment, a crack investigative reporter, Tom Engelhardt, observed:

> Republican and Democratic Senators, having questioned the credibility of a military man

---

223 Goss had been a CIA operative during the Cold war but he was elected to Congress in 1989 and served as chair of the House Intelligence Committee. He co-sponsored the Patriot Act and served as co-chair of the Joint Intelligence Commission on 9/11.

who had overseen a patently illegal surveillance program on American citizens for years and then defended it vigorously, promptly collapsed in a non-oppositional heap of praise, and rubber-stamped him director by a vote of 78-15.[224]

Engelhardt crashed through the barriers constructed by Bush to keep journalists from the truth. He pointed out that an incredible amount of money was being spent by the administration on intelligence agencies and Congress was not monitoring most of it. For instance, among these agencies, the Pentagon's NSA had an annual budget estimated at six to ten billion dollars while the CIA had a five billion dollar budget (and 16,000 employees). Actually, an estimated 80-85 per cent (or possibly more) of the total US intelligence budget was being controlled by the Pentagon, and that proportion was increasing.

Engelhardt boldly contended that administrative lawlessness, bureaucratic turf wars, and bloated expenditures meant that billions were being spent on unnecessary, unlawful, and redundant programs. Also, the size of the black box concealing domestic surveillance was increasing. In 2006 the Supreme Court reduced the protections for whistleblowers, while Attorney General Gonzales and other federal officials were threatening to prosecute reporters who got their hands on so-called "classified information" for the purpose of making the public aware of the lawless intelligence programs being authorized by

---

224 Tom Engelhardt. May 30 2006. "Thirty Flew into the Cuckoo's Nest. The Tangled Web of American 'Intelligence'." tomdispatch.com.

the administration.

In May 2006, Democrats uncovered further evidence of Bush's contempt for democracy and denounced him for claiming that he had the authority to defy more than 750 statutes enacted since he took office. Sen. Edward Kennedy, for instance, said that Bush was rejecting the system of checks and balances by asserting that he can ignore laws that disagree with his reading of the Constitution. Astonishingly, Bush did not veto a single bill but, after signing his acceptance of one out of every 10 bills, he quietly appended "signing statements" to these bills adding his own legal interpretation for officials to follow when implementing these new laws. The statements, rarely mentioned by Congressional representatives or the media, were quietly inserted in the federal record.

A president who has an opinion about the worthiness of a law can issue a "signing statement." Traditionally, these statements were often composed of rhetorical comments issued by a president upon signing a bill into law. However, actually, Bush's signing statements were deliberate attempts to modify the meaning of laws enacted by Congress. Because he used these statements to usurp powers assigned to Congress and the courts, a task force of the American Bar Association in July 2006 said that Bush's statements reflected contempt for the rule of law and our constitutional separation of powers. Instead of using a veto, Bush, for instance, would assert that a law can be ignored because it is constitutionally defective in order to make executive agencies limit its implementation. The Detainee

Treatment Act of 2005, for example, prohibited cruel, inhuman, and degrading treatment of detainees in U.S. custody. Nevertheless, Bush's statement asserted:

> The executive branch shall construe... the Act, relating to detainees, in a manner consistent with the constitutional authority of the President to supervise the unitary executive branch and as Commander in Chief and consistent with the constitutional limitations on the judicial power.

This statement says that any law or Congress cannot bind the President, because he is Commander in Chief.

In a January 30, 2008, editorial, the *New York Times* declared, "Over the last seven years, Mr. Bush has issued hundreds of these insidious documents declaring that he had no intention of obeying a law that he had just signed." Former Vice-President Al Gore wrote, "One of President Bush's most contemptuous and dangerous practices has been his chronic abuse of what are called 'signing statements.'" He adds, "This helps explain why Bush has vetoed only one bill during his entire term in office [at the time]. Why bother, if he can simply decide on his own whim which provisions of a law apply to him and which ones he'll simply ignore." Recognizing that most of Bush's "signing statements" had nothing to do with ensuring national security, legal scholars have noted that his statements went far beyond those of any previous president in US history. *Moreover, no other president had ever applied signing statements to over 750 new statutes.*

However, the Republicans controlled Congress. And Democrats still committed to preserving democracy did not have the power to follow up their denunciations and conduct hearings on Bush's arrogant attempt to "pick and choose" which laws he deemed appropriate to follow. Previously, Rep. Conyers had tried to get support in Congress for an investigation into US war crimes at secret detention facilities in Iraq, Afghanistan, and Guantanamo Bay but his attempt was equally fruitless. He could not get the votes to launch an investigation. The Congress for all practical purposes was in Bush's pocket.

On the other hand, when criticism of Bush's devious strategy for neutralizing new bills mounted, he repeatedly used the "war on terrorism" as a pretext. He said that he had the right to ignore Congress especially when it sought to regulate the military and spy agencies. He insisted that the Constitution grants him that power as commander in chief during a state of emergency. Given an emergency, he could, among other things, legitimately authorize torture, limit Congressional oversight into the Patriot Act, and refuse to cooperate fully with Congressional investigations into unlawful domestic wiretapping.

Clearly, the Bush administration didn't give a damn about preserving the balance of power. An open-ended "state of emergency" was being used to justify the suspension of constitutional liberties and restrictions imposed by other branches of government. This suspension was accompanied by administrative decrees that had the "force of law" despite the fact that they were not enacted by Congress.

Similar suspensions of constitutional laws under

the guise of a national emergency had enabled Hitler to make the transition from a parliamentary regime to a dictatorship. *Actually, the Weimar Constitution had never been formally repealed by Hitler's regime;* it was kept as a parallel system of law even though its constitutional safeguards for individual liberties and balance of power were not implemented.

Despite the questions that could have been raised, Congressional majorities, like Pavlov's dogs who salivated at the sound of a bell, immediately backed Bush's "endless war against terrorism." When 9/11 occurred, almost no one questioned whether his "state of emergency" and all the trade-offs it implied was necessary to cope with terrorism.

13 | Widening Terrorism

In its annual global survey of terrorism ... the State Department says about 14,000 attacks took place in 2006, mainly in Iraq and Afghanistan. These strikes claimed more than 20,000 lives—two-thirds in Iraq. That is 3,000 more attacks than in 2005 and 5,800 more deaths.

—MSNBC.com

After commanding the invasion of Iraq, General Tommy Franks returned to Florida. He told Robyn Blumner of the *St. Petersburg Times* in 2003 that another terrorist strike with massive casualties could cause "our population to question our own Constitution and begin to militarize our country." Blumner agreed, adding, "Pundits and prognosticators are saying out loud what anyone who has been following the government's actions since 9/11 already senses . . . If terrorism's sting is

379

felt again fascism may be its aftermath."[225]

Was it a possibility? Well, Bush had pushed the pedal to the metal and scores of writers indicated that any credible pretext—intended or unintended—for toughening his state of emergency would make this possibility a reality. Who could be relied on to block this possibility? Democratic Party leaders were obvious candidates but most were veering wildly. In 2005, they were trying to overtake Bush's motorcade, force it to the same side of the road and leave it behind but without changing their direction.

What was wrong with these leaders? The answer was simple. In key respects, they were no different from their opponents. They collaborated with Republicans in cultivating a rightward shift in popular thinking about left-of-center politics. As a result, neoliberals in the Democratic Party were now called "moderates" while "liberal" had become a derogatory metaphor for all sorts of slightly left-of-center alternatives. And, in turn, New Deal Democrats were being bracketed with the traditional left in the style of the Thirties when conservatives routinely called FDR and other liberals "socialists" and "communists."

In recent decades, moreover, corporate interests and anti-tax movements had turned leading Democrats into salt-and-pepper haired skateboarders shooting down the slope and up a sharp incline to somersault in midair and go back again. No American politician could help but admire their ability to give lip service to welfare state policies and organized labor while encouraging policies that oppose

---

225 Robyn E. Blumner. Jan. 7 2003. "From Tommy Franks, a Doomsday Scenario." *St. Petersburg Times.*

these aims.

Clinton, for example, rock and rolled into FDR's Hyde Park estate on his 1991 campaign trail playing his saxophone while promising to undo Reagan's damage to New Deal reforms. He titled his campaign *Put People First*. Then, after his election, he ditched New Deal populism. He introduced an austerity program that eliminated the federal deficit at the expense of working-class families whose real incomes hadn't changed since 1970.[226] To carry out his neoliberal program, Clinton trashed the New Deal by cultivating the image of a "vampire state" sucking the American people's blood. Aided by the Republicans, he deregulated the banking industry and abolished another product of the New Deal, the Glass-Steagall Act. The Act insured savings accounts, controlled speculation, and prohibited bank holding companies from owning other banks.[227]

Predictably, corporate fraud and stock-market manipulation ballooned and intensified the 1998-1999 collapse of the so-called 'new economy'. Millions of shareholders and employees lost investments, pensions and jobs when the market bubble burst and corporations like Enron, WorldCom, Adelphi, Tyco, SBC Communications, Global Crossing,

---

226 The collapse of the USSR provided an opportunity to brake the growth of the American empire and its military industrial complex. But Clinton used the small savings from cutting military expenditures to lower the deficit. He did not try to make it less dependent on the industrial complex or improve education and other social programs.

227 Robert Scheer. 2010. *The Great American Stickup: How Reagan Republicans and Clinton Democrats Enriched Wall Street While Mugging Main Street*. New York: Nation Books.

ImClone, Qwest, Dynegy, Sunbeam, Anderson, and others tanked.

Finally, Clinton didn't even pretend to fight for a universal health care system. Instead, he blamed his shameful capitulation on the Republicans—and supported the privatized and costly health-maintenance proposals offered by future presidential aspirant Hillary Clinton and her secret committee.[228] Moreover, while Clinton surrendered to Republicans on health care, he twisted the arms of Congressional Democrats to vote for the North American Free Trade Agreement (NAFTA)—despite the righteous condemnation by organized labor and liberal economists of its inescapably destructive effects on domestic job markets and environmental conditions.

INSURGENCY OR TERRORISM?

After 9/11, moderate Democrats joined their conservative colleagues in Congress in providing billions for the military industrial complex. A few years later, Senate and House committees were drafting the 2006 defense authorization bill planning to fund increased troop levels. In fact, a group of moderate Democrats attempted to outdo the Republicans by eagerly stepping forward and proposing to jump-start the bill. In 2005, Senators Lieberman, Clinton, Tauscher, and Udall proposed a United States Army Relief Act that would begin to more rapidly increase

---

228 The committee met secretly and, although the media misinformed the public about Canada's, France's, or Scandinavian universal health care systems, they were superior alternatives.

the size of the Army.[229] They justified the increase by emphasizing the stresses experienced by the Army due to the fighting in Iraq and Afghanistan and the deployment of soldiers in hundreds of other nations throughout the world.[230]

In a press release, Lieberman even brought up the *unforeseen* military costs of empire-building: "We are concerned that if other crises occur elsewhere in the world in the years ahead we won't have the appropriately sized Army trained and ready to go there to deal with these other crises."[231] But would their defense bill really help the armed forces defeat terrorism? Or would it just increase the threat?

Professor Robert Pape of the University of Chicago provides some answers. His book, *Dying to Win: The Logic of Suicide Terrorism*, was discussed in an interview with American Conservative's Scott McConnell.[232] In the interview, Pape reported:

> Over the past two years, I have collected the first complete database of every suicide-terrorist attack around the world from 1980 to early 2004. This research is conducted not only in English but also in native-language sources— Arabic, Hebrew, Russian, and Tamil, and others—so that we can gather information not

229 They were either members of the Senate's Armed Services committee or the House's committee.

230 Lieberman's press release mentioned 118 nations but the authentic figure was much higher.

231 Senator Joseph Lieberman. July 13 2005. Remarks for Troop Increase Press Conference. (See his web page.)

232 Robert Pape. 2005. *Dying to Win: The Strategic Logic of Suicide Terrorism.* New York: Random House. Also, *American Conservative* (July 18 2005 Issue).

> only from newspapers but also from products from the terrorist community. The terrorists are often quite proud of what they do in their local communities, and they produce albums and all kinds of other information that can be very helpful to understand suicide-terrorist attacks.

Pape's findings contradicted myths cultivated by neo-cons and the corporate media. He did not find Islamic fundamentalism to be correlated as tightly with suicide terrorism as people were being led to believe. In fact, a secular group that recruited terrorists from families of the Tamil regions in Sri Lanka "invented the famous suicide vest for their suicide assassination of Rajiv Ghandi in May 1991." The Palestinians, Pape notes, got the idea of the suicide vest from the Tamil Tigers.

What, then, are the Middle Eastern terrorists trying to accomplish? After analyzing the data, Pape found that their suicide attacks were primarily driven by an unambiguous strategic objective:

> Since 1990, the United States has stationed tens of thousands of ground troops on the Arabian Peninsula, and that is the main mobilization appeal of Osama bin Laden and al-Qaeda. People who make the argument that it is a good thing to have them attacking us over there are missing that suicide terrorism is not a supply-limited phenomenon where there are just a few hundred around the world willing to do it because they are religious fanatics. It is a demand-driven phenomenon. That is, it is driven by the presence of foreign forces on the territory that the terrorists view as their homeland. The operation in Iraq has stimulated sui-

cide terrorism and has given suicide terrorism
a new lease on life.

Since foreign occupation—rather than Islamic
fundamentalism—is primarily at fault, Pape reck-
oned that increasing occupation forces would only
increase the number of suicide terrorists. "Osama
bin Laden's speeches and sermons run 40 and 50
pages long. They begin by calling tremendous attention to the presence of tens of thousands of American combat forces on the Arabian Peninsula."

Religion has some influence on suicide terrorism
but not in the way most people think. "In virtually
every instance where an occupation has produced a
suicide-terrorist campaign," Pape writes, "there has
been a religious difference between the occupier and
the occupied community. That is true not only in
places such as Lebanon and in Iraq today but also in
Sri Lanka, where it is the Sinhala Buddhists who are
having a dispute with the Hindu Tamils."

To emphasize the causal importance of occupying
forces rather than religion, Pape pointed out that al-
Qaeda suicide terrorists haven't come from Iran—
even though it is one of the largest Islamic fundamentalist countries. He also listed other countries
that support fundamentalism. Sudan, with 21 million
people, for instance, is one of these countries—
Osama bin Laden found its Islamic fundamentalism
and government so congenial that he spent three
years in Sudan during the Nineties. "Yet there has
never been an al-Qaeda suicide terrorist from Sudan," Pape observed.

Pape also used Iraq to back his thesis. Before the

invasion, Iraq never had a suicide-terrorist attack. Since the invasion, suicide terrorism has escalated. Twenty suicide attacks occurred in 2003, 48 in 2004 and more than 50 in the first five months of 2005. "Every year that the United States has stationed 150,000 combat troops in Iraq, suicide terrorism has doubled." Furthermore, most of the suicide terrorists were, as Pape termed them, "walk-in volunteers." He noted, "Very few were criminals. Few are actually longtime members of a terrorist group. For most suicide terrorists, their first experience with violence is their very own suicide-terrorist attack."[233]

Pape's information about al-Qaeda's post 9/11 targets is equally disturbing. He reported that an al-Qaeda document (uncovered by Norwegian intelligence) advised its agents not to attack the US in the short term. The document went on to state that attacking Spain, Britain, or Poland had greater priority. This plan was designed to split the coalition fighting the war in Iraq and it has had some success. Spain withdrew from the coalition as a result of a terrorist attack in Madrid. Other nations followed.

When asked about the possibility that a weapon of mass destruction might be employed against an American city, Pape speculated:

> I think it depends not exclusively, but heavily, on how long our combat forces remain in the Persian Gulf. The central motive for anti-American terrorism, suicide terrorism, and catastrophic terrorism is response to foreign

233 Pape's conclusions were based on examination of about 462 records of suicide terrorists who killed themselves from 1980 to 2004.

> occupation, the presence of our troops. The longer our forces stay on the ground in the Arabian Peninsula, the greater the risk of the next 9/11, whether that is a suicide attack, a nuclear attack, or a biological attack.

After Pape summed up his research on suicide bombers, he proposed that the US could secure its "vital interests in oil" without employing sizeable occupation forces and stirring up "a new generation of suicide terrorists." Despite the astonishing number of civilians who lost their lives and despite terrorist reactions to American offshore bombing raids prior to 9/11—he recommended that the US should resume its reliance on aircraft carriers, air power, and military bases to bomb targets anywhere in the Arabian Peninsula or to rapidly dispatch ground forces if a crisis emerges. "That strategy, called 'offshore balancing,' worked splendidly against Saddam Hussein in 1990 and is again our best strategy to secure our interest in oil while preventing the rise of more suicide terrorists," Pape concluded.

Sadly, Pape's suggestions spark more questions than answers. Will terrorists actually stand down in the face of "offshore balancing"? Offshore balancing is a cool phrase but it says nothing about the "collateral damage" due to air strikes. Besides, whose "vital interests in oil" would actually be served by his proposal? How many sons and daughters from wealthy families will die to defend these interests? And who will pay the fuel prices driven skyward by the continued attempt to dominate the Arabian Peninsula? Whose children will be saddled with the trillion-dollar debts imposed regardless of how the government's criminal policies are carried out? By May 12, 2007, the US government had spent more than 425 trillion dollars on the Iraq war. Furthermore, Bush's "war on terrorism" by that time had increased the number of terrorist attacks abroad by more than 600 per cent!

Besides, additional research suggests that offshore bombing would never decrease terrorism. Consider Marc Sageman's research, for instance. In the 1980s, Sageman originally obtained an undergraduate degree at Harvard and an MD and doctorate in sociology at New York University. He was a flight surgeon in the US Navy. He left the Navy for the CIA in 1984, spending a year with an Afghan Task Force. He also ran U.S. unilateral programs with the Afghan Mujahedin from 1987 to 1989. After 1989, he began a medical career in forensic and clinical psychiatry. He is a counterterrorism consultant as well.

Sageman based his research on biographical material obtained from al Qaeda terrorists. Most of these biographies are derived from voluminous trial records and his analysis of this data is published in *Understanding Terror Networks* (2004) and *Leaderless Jihad* (2008). Sageman found that three quarters of the terrorists in his study were young adults with upper or middle class status. They were born and raised in caring, intact families. They were mentally stable, with more than sixty-percent having a college background (compared to a 5-to-six percent average for third world populations). They were married and most had children. Although terrorists who were captured in the most recent wave of terrorism were poorly educated and lacked religious training, over seventy percent of the terrorists in Sageman's total sample were professionals, or semi-professionals—mostly scientists, engineers, architects, and civil engineers. Consequently, unlike stereotypes of terrorists circulated nationwide, most of the terrorists were not poverty-stricken, unemployed, uneducated, and mentally unstable individuals who hailed from broken families. Furthermore, none of them had a criminal record!

Sageman also found that the terrorists were affected by moral outrage over the violent treatment of Muslim nations by US policies. This outrage was mediated by their fundamentalist religious ideology and further intensified by interacting with small groups of friends who they met at mosques, Internet chat rooms, or in living quarters where they shared costs. Seventy-percent of Sageman's sample joined the jihad while they were living in another country from where they grew up. Sageman adds:

> When they became homesick, they tried to congregate with people like themselves, whom they found at mosques. They moved in to apartments together in order to share rent and eat together following Halal, the Muslim dietary laws. These cliques, often in the vicinity of mosques that had a militant script advocating violence to overthrow corrupt regimes, transformed alienated young Muslims into terrorists. The process of radicalization is very much a function of group dynamics. You cannot understand the 9/11 type of terrorism by focusing primarily on individual characteristics.

Sageman believes that in recent years al Qaeda serves a source of inspiration for terrorist acts committed by independent local groups that adopt the al Qaeda name. But—and this is an important point— they are not incorporated within al Qaeda's organizational framework. He states:

> The Al Qaeda social movement was dependent on volunteers, and there are now huge gaps worldwide in the volunteer network. The movement has now degenerated into something like the Internet. It is now self-organized from the bottom up, and is much decentralized. Networks function more like street gangs than a "high-minded" mission-driven terrorist network.

With regard to the kinds of terrorists in his study, Sageman suggests that the "zeal of jihadism" is "self-terminating." Eventually its followers will turn away from violence as a means of expressing their discontent. However, this termination is dependent on ending the sources of the moral outrage that stimulates the spontaneous "bottom-up" formation of terrorist networks. These sources include the wars of aggression, occupation of Islamic nations, Islamophobic policies, and killing innocent people by troops on the ground or aerial bombardment.

SHOCK & AWE

For three days in April, 1937, the German Luftwaffe supported Franco's fascist armies in Spain by dropping tons of bombs and incendiaries on the Basque town of Guernica. Only civilians occupied the town and about 1,700 individuals—a third of its inhabitants—were killed or wounded. Villagers who escaped the bombs and fled to nearby fields were machine gunned from the air. Survivors recall people crawling and dragging broken limbs; parts of animals and human bodies were found everywhere. Yet the German Condor Legion squadron commander gloated in his diary that the attack on Guernica was a great success.

Seventy years later, before Iraq was invaded, environmentalist Gar Smith compared the Guernica attack with the Pentagon plan to use offshore vessels and bases to pound Baghdad.[234] He also remarked, "Now, like the 9/11 terrorists, Bush and Co. are planning a similar act of almost unparalleled ferocity—a devastating premeditated attack on a civilian urban population." Over a two-day period 800 cruise missiles were sent to Baghdad. *A missile hit the city every four minutes.*

Driving through Baghdad a few months later reporter William Van Wagenen wondered why some of the missiles had targeted government shopping malls, which resembled the huge Wal-Mart stores in the States. The targeting of major markets also puzzled him: "The bombing of the Rashid market in downtown Baghdad was so precise that no other buildings next to it, including a mosque, seemed to be harmed."[235]

---

234 Gar Smith. Jan. 27 2003. "Shock and Awe: Guernica Revisited." *alternet.org*. Smith is the former editor of *Earth Island Journal*, edits eco-zine *The-Edge* (*earthisland.org/the-edge*) and co-founded Environmentalists Against War. *envirosagainstwar.org*.

235 William Van Wagenen. July 6 2005. "Shock and Awe: Aerial Bombardment, American Style." *Electronic Iraq* (*electroniciraq.net*).

Asked Wagenen rhetorically, "This begs the question, why did the US bother to bomb markets and shopping malls? In war, don't armies kill other armies, and weapons destroy other weapons?" He answered his question by referring to witless statements expressed before the bombing by Pentagon officials, news media, and consultants. Remarked a Pentagon official, "There will not be a safe place in Baghdad." After a government briefing, CBS News declared, "The sheer size of this [plan] has never been seen before, never been contemplated before." Like the atomic weapons dropped on Hiroshima and Nagasaki, the use of "Shock and Awe"—the code name for the [Iraqi bombing? Or Hiroshima?] bombing tactic—was said by consultant Harlan Ullman to "convey the unmistakable message that unconditional compliance is the only available recourse."

Undoubtedly millions of Iraqis were "shocked" by the bombardment, but many were overcome with rage rather than "awe." And it is not hard to understand why this rage fueled the resistance against the American occupation. During the invasion and occupation, about 100,000 Iraqis were killed, primarily by bombing, according to researchers at the School of Public Health at John Hopkins University.[236] Professor Ira Chernus, from the University of Colorado at Boulder, noted sarcastically:

> If all this leaves you in shock and awe, you

---

236 John Hopkins University Bloomberg School of Public Health. "Mortality Before and After the 2003 Invasion of Iraq: Cluster Sample Survey." *The Lancet*, Volume 364, Number 9445, 30. October 2004.

have had your vision raised several levels too. You see what Ullman, Powell, and all the Bush- ies see: the US frightening the whole world so badly that no one will dare fire a single bullet at us. Let them be as angry as they like, just so they know who is the meanest, toughest son of a bitch on the global block.[237]

Chernus adds, "That now represents US foreign policy. And the Bushies seriously believe it will put an end to war. The Romans may have believed it too."

Picasso's painting, *Guernica*, memorialized the horror committed by the Luftwaffe in 1937. Millions of people protested around the world at that time. In 2003, however, few voices were heard in the U.S. When the cruise missiles pounded Baghdad, the American media triumphantly televised dazzling explosions illuminating the nighttime sky. At the same time, the media rarely showed heart-breaking photos of "collateral damage"—of Iraqi civilians whose bodies had been blown apart by these same bombs.

Yet the Democratic candidate for the highest office in the land, Sen. Kerry, despite his reservations, continued to back the Iraq war even though he surely knew what was really happening.[238] He had served in Vietnam where the US dropped more bombs than were dropped on the entire European theatre during World War II. Also, when Kerry campaigned against

---

237 Ira Chernus. Jan. 27 2003. "Shock & Awe: Is Baghdad the Next Hiroshima?" *CommonDreams.org.*

238 George Lakoff wrote, "Kerry stepped in to help Bush, basically supporting the President's position but offering policy-wonk modifications. The message: Bush is basically right, except for some minor twiddles." The Rockford Institute.

Bush's war crimes, he defended his own legislative record on the war with Orwellian "doublespeak." He denounced Bush for starting "a wrong war in the wrong place" but he had voted to authorize the invasion and when confronted with this fact inexplicably said he would have cast the same vote even if he had known that Bush's reasons for going to war were lies.

Kerry stonewalled the critics who accused him of being a traitor because he had in 1971 told a Senate Foreign Relations Committee that 150 veterans (who were members of Vietnam Veterans Against the War) had gathered and testified to war crimes committed "on a day-to-day basis with the full awareness of officers at all levels of command in Southeast Asia." He himself had testified:

> They told stories that at times they had personally raped, cut off ears, cut off heads, taped wires from portable telephones to human genitals and turned up the power, cut off limbs, blown up bodies, randomly shot at civilians, razed villages in fashion reminiscent of Genghis Khan, shot cattle and dogs for fun, poisoned food stocks, and generally ravaged the countryside of South Vietnam in addition to the normal ravage of war and the normal and very particular ravaging which is done by the applied bombing power of this country.

The corporate media pilloried Kerry during the 2004 election campaign for having given this testimony. But he never fought back by steadfastly and courageously defending his irrefutable claim that American troops in Vietnam had routinely committed appalling crimes.[239]

Representatives Conyers and Kucinich, on the other hand, bravely opposed the war in Iraq from the beginning, and Sen. Kennedy had asked Bush to provide a withdrawal plan as early as 2004. Later, in May 2005, Rep. Lynn Woolsey, a Democrat from California, introduced a withdrawal bill in Congress, while Barbara Boxer and Russ Feingold introduced another in the Senate. What's more, Rep. Maxine Waters created the "Out-of-Iraq Congressional Caucus" that included about 40 members.

But Sen. Kerry still refused to support his fellow Democrats publicly. During his presidential campaign he had promised to increase troop strength and "stay the course" until the terrorists were killed and the Iraqis' could rebuild their government. Furthermore, although Bush's popularity dropped sharply during the first half of 2005, speeches by other "illustrious" Democrats such as Senators Biden, Clinton, Edwards, Dodd, and Reid also refrained from publicly supporting demands for an early withdrawal.[240] Americans were becoming aware that the war was unwinnable—but these Democrats were silent. They waited opportunistically on the sidelines, hoping perhaps to capitalize later on the growing dissatisfaction with Bush in general and the war in particular. (More on this later.) In July 2005,

---

239 See, above all, Vietnam Veterans Against The War. 1972. *The Winter Soldier Investigation: An Inquiry into American War Crimes.* Boston: Beacon Press.

240 The group's agenda (prosecuting the global "war on terror," democratizing the Middle East, and increasing the military's ground forces) was echoed by likely Democratic presidential candidates, including Senators Joe Biden and Hillary Clinton.

Sherle R. Schwenninger, a Senior Fellow at the World Policy Institute, wrote:

> Rather than seizing the moment to point us in a more constructive direction, much of the Democratic leadership is reinforcing a foreign policy agenda that has divided us from the world, inserted us more deeply into an Islamic civil war and drained us politically and economically, all the while distracting us from many of the real challenges to our security and well-being. The party—indeed, the nation—deserves a better alternative.[241]

Ironically, the 2006 elections demonstrated that the Democratic leadership had underestimated the anger experienced by millions at the mounting American casualties and the failure to find weapons of mass destruction in Iraq. The Democratic leaders also underestimated Bush and his crafty advisor, Karl Rove. After all, Rove knew that Richard Nixon won the 1972 election by promising to pull the troops out of Vietnam. (Kissinger backed him up by declaring, "Peace is at hand!") Bush, like Nixon, could have promised to pull troops out sooner than later and enabled his party to win the 2006 election—while the Democrats were left behind trying to convince people that they can fight a war more vigorously and provide more security against terrorism than the Republicans.

But the signs indicated that the US couldn't win the war in Iraq. So what did its commander-in-chief

---

241 Sherle R. Schwenninger. July 18 2005. "Reconnecting to the World." *The Nation*. (The World Policy Institute is at the New School University).

do? In July 2005, Bush consulted Nixon's ghost and told Gen. George Casey, Commander of US forces in Iraq, to inform the public that substantial reductions of troop levels could be expected in the following year if the political reforms in Iraq continue to go forward and if the build-up of its security forces is successful. Given the astonishing drop in popular support for the war, how else could he have saved the Republicans who were up for reelection?

Apparently, however, Casey's announcement was merely aimed at damage control. General Abizaid, the head of Central Command, just one month earlier had warned that the Pentagon might (1) keep about 138,000 American soldiers in Iraq *throughout* 2006, (2) *increase* the number of in December 2005 to provide security for Iraqi elections (3) and *keep* the troops leaving Iraq as a reserve at military bases on its border. Neither Bush's lies nor Pentagon propaganda had made it less difficult to sell a war that continued to cost American lives and that could not be completed rapidly. Noting the unstoppable rise of the Iraqi insurgency, the *New York Times'* Frank Rich wrote, "Someone Tell the President the War Is Over."[242]

Predictably, the Senate Democrats sent Bush two messages. The first was more pleasing to the moderates because it waffled. It proposed a "phased redeployment" of US forces by the end of 2006 but it indicated that this deadline could be ignored if Congress felt that a continued "continued redeployment" was necessary. It also suggested steps that the Iraqi

---

242 Frank Rich. August 14 2005. "Someone Tell the President the War Is Over." *New York Times*.

government must take to become a democracy and requested an international conference to help Iraq overcome its problems. (Did this suggestion imply that the US hasn't had innumerable discussions with other powers about the Iraq war?)

The second message was more specific and it demonstrated that Sen. Kerry had finally stepped away from the hawks in his party. He joined the growing number of Democrats in 2006 calling for a withdrawal. Senators Kerry, Feingold, and Boxer proposed a Congressional resolution calling for the withdrawal of all combat troops from Iraq by July 1, 2007, leaving only troops for training Iraqi security forces, counterterrorism operations, and protecting US personnel and facilities. The resolution did not hedge the deadline even though neither the Iraqi puppet government nor US counterterrorism operations could survive this withdrawal.

Bush carefully orchestrated his response to the Democrats. He waited until the Pentagon announced that an Al-Qaeda leader, Abu Musab al-Zarqawi, was slain. He then informed America that the killing was a "promising development." Although US casualties had reached another 500 increment (2,500 troops had been killed since the war began), Bush grossly exaggerated the import of Zarqawi's death. He invited his band of merry men—his top military and political aides—to a "summit" at Camp David where they struck up the *Danse Macabre*. When their ghoulish photo-op concluded, Bush announced his determination to "stay the course" even if the Iraqi violence escalated, because Al-Qaeda will make every effort to prove that it can survive without Zarqawi.

Whether the violence escalated or whether it represented "business as usual," two US soldiers were found tortured and murdered by Zarqawi's successor immediately after Bush said he would "stay the course." Moreover, during the week following Bush's optimistic take on Zarqawi's death, the media described a memo sent two days before the death of Zarqawi by the US ambassador, Zalmay Khalilzad, to Secretary of State Condoleezza Rice—stating that the Iraqi guards in the Green Zone were threatening Iraqis who worked for the US embassy and that the conditions outside the Zone were deteriorating.

Predictably, while Gen. Casey was casting about to find cannon fodder to reinforce the US troops already employed in Iraq, the Republicans in the Senate loudly rejected the demands for a withdrawal. They passed a non-binding resolution to continue a "perpetual war" until the US troops had suppressed the insurgents with the aid of an Iraqi government.

Yet the Republican precision goose-steps did little to offset the drop in Bush's popularity ratings. Democratic leaders like Nancy Pelosi, who had voted in 2002 against authorizing Bush to invade Iraq, refused to join the parade. She exclaimed, "This war is a failed policy of the Bush administration." She considered the war "a mistake, a grotesque mistake."

Evidently, Bush and his empire builders never got the message sent by the Vietnam Communists in the Sixties, because they hadn't a clue about how much suffering an anti-colonial force will endure and how long it will "stay the course" in its fight for independence. The Viet Minh had been hardened by 30 years of struggle against France's armed forces. Yet, three American presidents believed that any resistance to America's imperial demands could be overcome. Well, their "mistake"—as it's termed in Robert McNamara's memoirs—eventually ended in a catastrophe that sent 58,000 Americans home in coffins.

PART FIVE

RIGHT-WING
CULTURE WARS

—◇—

14 | Culture Wars

"Through clever and constant application of propaganda people can be made to see paradise as hell, and also the other way around, to consider the most wretched sort of life as paradise."

—Adolf Hitler,

Mein Kampf, 1923

RIGHT-WING DEMAGOGUES

Thomas More, in 1516, described an imaginary society epitomizing perfection in social and political relationships. He called it "Utopia" and criminologists would find it notable because it upheld the rule of law. Although *Utopia* does not explicitly reveal More's motives, it tacitly underscored the sordid realities of his time. Subsequently, the word "dystopia" was adopted to label works about dreadful societies. These works include H. G. Well's

Time Machine (1895), Jack London's *The Iron Heel* (1908), Aldous Huxley's *Brave New World* (1932), George Orwell's *1984*–or *Nineteen Eighty Four*– (1949) and Ray Bradbury's *Fahrenheit 451* (1953).

Orwell's *1984* is one of the finest English novels of the 20th century. It depicts a superpower, called *Oceana*. Engaged in a perpetual war against two other superpowers, *Eurasia* and *Eastasia*, *Oceana's* regime legitimizes its policies by convincing citizens that they operate in the interest of the greater good. To stop deviations from its sexual prohibitions and prevent political dissent the regime employs surveillance, intimidation, conditioning, and torture as well as propaganda.

The heart of Orwell's novel concerns Winston Smith and Julia who fall in love even though *Oceana* proscribes their love. The omniscient surveillance conducted by *Big Brother*, who personifies the state, discovers their defiant behavior. They are tortured, humiliated, brainwashed, and exposed to unending attacks on their sanity. They finally betray each other as *Big Brother* transforms their mutual love into mutual hatred.

Orwell described himself as a "democratic socialist." He said *1984* was not intended to be an attack on socialism or the British labor party, which he supported. He wrote the novel to expose the totalitarianism realized under communism and fascism. But, he added, "The scene of the book is laid in Britain in order to emphasize that the English speaking races are not innately better than anyone else, and that totalitarianism, if not fought against, could triumph anywhere."

Terms introduced by Orwell when describing Oceana's management of popular thinking, such as *Big Brother, doublethink, thought crime, thought police, Newspeak, and Memory hole,* were adopted by writers throughout the world. The word "Orwellian," itself, which symbolizes the manipulation of language by demagogues became entrenched into the English vernacular. Orwell's description of Oceana included a "Ministry of Truth" (Minitrue in *Newspeak*) which operated in an "enormous pyramidal structure of glittering white concrete, soaring up, terrace after terrace, three hundred meters into the air." On the face of this gigantic edifice, *Big Brother* had carved in "elegant lettering" the three slogans of his political party: "WAR IS PEACE," "FREEDOM IS SLAVERY," and "IGNORANCE IS STRENGTH."

Smith is paid by Minitrue to update past newspaper articles so that the historical record is consistent with changes in official propaganda. Today, corporate interests and wealthy families finance politicians, journalists, academics, celebrities, and other "spinmeisters" who, like Smith, continuously update an Orwellian armament for fighting culture wars. [243] Their weapons have—regardless of brazen contradictions—not merely altered established ways of thinking. They have also reduced right-wing discourse to shameless lies, sloganeering, and sound bites, such as "FREE TRADE CREATES JOBS," and "WAR ENSURES DEMOCRACY."

---

243 For example, see Ernest Partridge. April 20 2011. "Shameless GOP Lies: Is There Any Limit to What Republicans Will Say—And What People Will Believe?" *Alternet.org.*

CHRISTIAN RIGHT

The right-wing Christian evangelical movement has also supported creeping fascism. The US has an electoral system in which the 'winner takes all' and a mere one per cent of the vote has spelled victory or defeat for the Republicans. Estimates indicated that the right-wing evangelicals only represented 7 per cent of the entire evangelical population but they have provided a critical mass that has at times tipped the outcomes of elections in favor of conservative candidates. Sadly, the Christian right has become the political face of Christianity. Personified by Pat Robertson, the late Jerry Falwell, and James Dobson, this facet of the culture wars stood for bigotry, intolerance, and violence. When people were trying to comprehend why terrorists had killed thousands of Americans on 9/11, Falwell told them,

> I really believe that the pagans, and the abortionists, and the feminists, and the gays and the lesbians who are actively trying to make that an alternative lifestyle, the ACLU, People For the American Way, all of them who have tried to secularize America. I point the finger in their face and say "You helped this happen."

Falwell at that time was pastor of the 22,000-member Thomas Road Baptist Church. He declared that 9/11 was God's judgment on America for "throwing God out of the public square, out of the schools." "The abortionists have got to bear some burden for this because God will not be mocked," he added angrily.

In 2005 Robertson called for the assassination of Hugo Chavez, the democratically elected President of Venezuela.[244] Also, Jerry Vines, another Christian rightist and a former president of the Southern Baptist Convention, made the news at its 2002 annual meeting. He denounced Mohammed as "a demon-possessed pedophile."

The expressions of violent rage against "satanic enemies" of Christianity signified a distinct shift among American evangelicals. Traditional fundamentalists like Billy Graham had called on believers to shun the contaminants of secular society and avoid an obsession with political life. But the evangelical movement led by Robertson, Falwell, and Dobson damned every religious and nonreligious outlook but their own. "This is a new movement," Chris Hedges declared. Since its leaders wanted to attain secular power and create a theocratic state, he suggested that they should be called "Christian Reconstructionists" or "Dominionists" because they are not traditional fundamentalists or traditional evangelicals. In fact, according to Hedges,

> They [have] fused the language and iconography of the Christian religion with the worst forms of American nationalism and then created this sort of radical mutation, which has built alliances with powerful rightwing interests, including corporate interests, and made tremendous inroads over the last two decades into the corridors of power.

---

244 Robertson also declared that the Israel's Prime Minister Ariel Sharon had a stroke because God was punishing him for giving up part of the Gaza Strip to the Palestinians.

In addition to being a former *New York Times* Mideast bureau chief, Hedges had achieved a Master of Divinity from Harvard Divinity School. Fortified by his religious background, he spent two years observing Christian far right rallies, sermons, and radio broadcasts. He attended evangelical events across the nation and interviewed the leaders of this Christian movement.

Hedges was so shocked by the movement's antidemocratic goals that his book was titled: *American Fascists: The Christian Right and the War on America*. The book shows that right-wing preachers condemned New Deal policies, public schools, and welfare for the poor. But they never attacked law enforcement and the military. Movement leaders, Hedges demonstrates, want a theocratic regime installed by "holy warriors" who are fighting an apocalyptic battle against "secular forces," composed of liberals, humanists, homosexuals, pro-abortionists, and Islam, depicted as a "satanic" religion. Armed with a vision of Armageddon and rapturous ascent to heaven by God's chosen people, the movement's impact on the rightward shift in American politics has been astonishing.

Hitler orchestrated gigantic rallies filled with thousand of storm troopers arranged in disciplined formations to impress ordinary Germans and invoke their adoration. But far-right American evangelical leaders had substituted military rituals with rallies composed of thousands of adoring worshippers fixated on every word uttered by their infallible preachers. These rallies were also orchestrated for young people. Hedges found that BattleCry, an evangelical youth movement, attracted as many as 25,000 people to Christian rock concerts in San Francisco, Philadelphia, and Detroit. Dazzling light shows, ranks of Navy SEALS, militaristic rhetoric, and images of embattled American soldiers in Iraq were used to urge audiences to heed the call to arms and fight the secular forces everywhere. (And "everywhere" meant *everywhere*—in suburban communities where county governments and local schools insist on the separation of church and state as well as in Iraq.) At a BattleCry concert in Philadelphia, an audience of thousands, aided by lyrics projected on huge screens sang: "We are an army of God and we're ready to die... Let's paint this big ol' town red . . . We see nothing but the blood of Jesus..." In unison, they shouted, "*We are warriors!* "[245]

Hedges describes evangelical preacher, Pastor Russell Johnson, praising Dr. Martin Luther King Jr. and Rosa Parks while speaking against the backdrop of a huge American flag with a Christian cross superimposed on the Stars and Stripes. King and Parks had urged their followers to engage in non-violent civil disobedience, but Johnson declared, "We're on the beaches of Normandy, and we can see the pillbox entrenchments of academic and media to liberalism." He urged his worshipers to heed the call to arms and take back our country for Christ.

Now Johnson may have been speaking figuratively—but his fusion of Christian, patriotic, and warlike symbols express his, and presumably his

---

245 The examples used in these paragraphs can be found in Chris Hedges. 2006. *American Fascists: The Christian Right and the War on America*. New York: Free Press, pp.148–151.

congregants', passionate craving for a state religion. Hedges called this state religion "a Christo-fascism." Liberals, in Johnson's sermons, are dubbed secular "jihadists" who have "hijacked" America.

Reverend Timothy F. Simpson, a Presbyterian minister, personifies a different Christian tradition. He contends that the truth can be spoken by Muslims, Jews, and atheists. He says,

> An atheist who stands for the interests of the neighbor, an atheist who stands for the interests of poor people at the margins, for the oppressed, is worth more than a hundred Christians who have made their bed with the fat cats, because that atheist is actually articulating the ends of the kingdom of God.

The binary world constructed by the radical evangelicals, on the other hand, has no room for compromise. Nonbelievers are stereotyped as enemies who oppose the kingdom of God.

EVANGELICAL ISLAMOPHOBIA

Although Islamophobia is by no means restricted to Christian Dominionists, Muslims are especially stereotyped as the enemies of God. Evangelicals who share this bigoted standpoint have exploited the post-9/11 increase in anti-Muslim bigotry. In fact, the justifications for the "preemptive strike" against Afghanistan and Iraq were reminiscent of Nazi propaganda about the necessity of forcibly oppressing or expropriating the resources belonging to inferior or evil races. Reminiscent because these measures allegedly dealt with the violent "clash of civilizations" being instigated by barbarous "Muslim fundamentalists" against enlightened "Judeo-Christian" traditions.

However, Professor Mamdani, the Director of the Institute of African Studies at Columbia University has asked if it is true that a Muslim who takes his or her religion seriously is a potential terrorist. Where does one find the literal reading of the Koran translate into hijacking, murder, and terrorism? In the last century, myths about the "Yellow Horde", and slant eyed "*gooks*" were used to justify imperial policies. But, nowadays, government officials and corporate media are too sophisticated to employ this outdated rhetoric. Instead, as Mamdani observed, "We are told that there is a fault line running through Islam, a line that divides moderate Islam, called genuine Islam, and extremist political Islam. The terrorists of September 11, we are told, did not just hijack planes; it is said that they also hijacked Islam, meaning *genuine* Islam!" [246]

Mamdani knows that Islam and Christianity share a messianic orientation. But, whether or not force should be employed to accomplish this mission is debatable. He doubts that political behavior can be predicted from a person's religion or national culture. "Remember, he said, "it was not so long ago that some claimed that the behavior of others could be read from their genes." Is an orthodox Muslim or

---

246 Mahmood Mamdani, op. cit. (our emphasis). The quotes are taken from Chapter 3 (e.g., pp.119-132) which deals chiefly with the role of the Reagan administration and CIA in the creation of Afghan terrorism.

an orthodox Jew a potential terrorist? He asked, "How do you make sense of politics that consciously wears the mantle of religion? Take, for example the politics of Osama bin Laden and al Qaeda, both of whom claim to be waging a *Jihad*, a just war against the enemies of Islam?" Did Islamic teaching create this politics or does it have a contemporary origin? Chapter 4 answered this question. The so-called Islamic fundamentalists were created during the Cold War and their current jihad is a terrorist blowback that was expanded by administration policies.

RIGHT WING POPULISM

Primeval culture warriors carrying "Nativist" banners also play a significant role in contemporary American politics. Their big sticks are waved threateningly at Latin American, Caribbean, Middle Eastern, and African immigrants. And their impact is symbolized by the billions being spent to wall off undocumented immigrants who enter the US from Mexico.

Nativists and their racist views are not the only cultural representatives of right-wing populism. Prior to the Sixties and Seventies, corporate media used Bobbysoxers, gray flannel suits, conspicuous consumption, tract houses, and Cadillacs to symbolize styles of life favored by "middle class" America. However, the Sixties witnessed an unparalleled counter-cultural assault on traditional values, political agendas, and life styles. Then, in the following decade, the media discredited this assault. Its backlash equated the assault with irresponsible unwashed and longhaired hippies, dopers, and pacifists who had wrongly rejected traditional values, the commercialization of everyday life, and imperial dreams.[247]

In addition to condemning counter-cultural politics, ersatz populists who supported the right-wing backlash disseminated myths about a new "class war" conducted by a virtual Nixonian enemies' list of government bureaucrats, technocrats, academics, tree-huggers, faggots, commies, lesbos, tax-and-spend liberals, and other domestic fauna. Like the Nazi fabrication of a worldwide Jewish and Communist conspiracy, these populists contended that their comic-strip characters constituted ruling elites that ran the government at the expense of ordinary people.

During the first year of Obama's term in office, these populists were being rejuvenated and funded by right wing foundations and lobbyists. They appeared at "town hall" meetings and shouted down people in the audience and democratic legislators who were attempting to discuss controversial issues. They displayed signs at demonstrations that depicted Obama as Hitler and implied that armed resistance could be justified when responding to Democratic Party attempts to provide health care for all Americans.

However, despite these culture warriors, a fundamentally different populist tradition had survived, traceable back to the late 19th and early 20th century *progressive movement*. Members of this movement

247 Ironically, clothing firms and advertising agencies eventually co-opted counter cultural styles of life.

believed that a ruling class composed of "robber barons"—finance capitalists and industrialists—was using the government to promote the exploitation of middle-class and working-class Americans. Later, in the Sixties, progressives had expanded their vision of America's social hierarchy. They targeted "power elites" in command of political, military, and economic institutions.

The overwhelming majority of Americans, the progressives said, were wage-earners, self-employed, or owned small businesses. But right-wing populists envisioned a very different social hierarchy. Even though most Americans are actually wage earners, they positioned the vast majority of Americans in a "middle class." Although a mere ten per cent of the nation's families owned 80 per cent per cent of the wealth, and most of the remaining families barely earned enough to own their own homes without a mortgage, the great majority of Americans were called "stakeholders" and "shareholders." *Twenty* per cent of the children in the United States were being reared in families with incomes at or below the poverty line, but right-wing populist views of class realities shrunk these families until they filled a barely noticeable niche at the bottom of the social hierarchy.

Right-wing populists joined the chorus of neoliberals who attributed God-like powers to a fictitious Free Market in which consumers were sovereign. They equated the geopolitical expansion of this Market with a worldwide growth of democracy. Allegedly, this Market gave everyone an equal chance to "get ahead"—if it was not hampered domestically by organized labor, corporate taxes, "politically correct" affirmative action policies, and other government regulations.

Media stars like Bill O'Reilly, Rush Limbaugh, Pat Robertson, and Pat Buchanan also coupled their bilious messianic and reactionary utopianism with attacks on legal and illegal immigrants, corruption in government, offshore displacement of American jobs, the role of "big money" and "special interests" in Washington. Bill O'Reilly—whose Fox News contract was rumored to be in the neighborhood of 50 million dollars—became a celebrity after posing as the loud-mouthed champion of the "little man" and an uncompromising foe of "vested interests."

JUSTIFYING INEQUALITY

Paradoxically, contemporary culture wars are being fought by social Darwinists as well as sincere right-wing populists. The shift toward the right has refreshed America's legacy of nativism, racism, and sociopathic class standpoints. This legacy has for more than a century justified inequality because it claimed that a society cannot function properly unless it is ruled by vastly superior individuals. Notions of "superiority," in this context, were usually based on eugenic, ethnic, and class distinctions. Male chauvinists, for instance, believed men were more qualified to rule society while social Darwinians encouraged Americans to regard poor and unemployed people as "*born* losers." The Darwinians, in particular, emphasized a individualistic stance toward property rights that undermined beliefs in the ability of common people to deal with social problems *collectively.*

As a result, social Darwinians provide a receptive audience for neoliberal pundits and politicians who, despite decades of contrary evidence, espouse "trickle down" or "voodoo economics" because they claim that *free market* policies safeguard individual liberty and that *unregulated* monopolies (and their wealthy CEOs) benefit ordinary people. These pundits and politicians include thousands of demagogues whose material welfare depends on support from extremely wealthy networks. Their performance at this time is updating Orwell's *1984*. They are probing newsworthy sensations, political polls, and opinion groups in order to cover *all bases* with their propaganda. Employing both right-wing populism and social Darwinism, for instance, they rely on whatever they deem effective regardless of logical consistency and rationality in order to market their policies and candidates.

Millions of ordinary Americans are economic and political illiterates. They have never acquired the educational experiences that enable them to distinguish between "commonsense" interpretations—involving, for instance, how to keep their credit card expenditures under control—and an informed grasp of the Keynesian policies that have dealt with federal deficits during the Great Depression and beyond. These Americans do not have the intellectual exposure that enables them to properly evaluate the claims being made by mainstream media and corporate pundits. Given their exposure to a never-ending demagogic stream of propaganda, it is not surprising to find them being conditioned emotionally. They were furious about left-wing attempts to deal with the Recession as well as the "bail outs" of the corporations that created the Recession.

PARALLEL CULTURES

Milton Mayer was an American correspondent of German descent who was in Berlin during the Thirties. After the war, he spent a year observing and interviewing ten law-abiding, hard-working, lower middle-class men in Kronenberg, a conservative Hessian town.[248] The town had been but lightly scarred during the war and although he told them that he had fought against Germany; he did not tell them that he was Jewish.

He selected the men because they were sufficiently different from one another in background, character, intellect, and temperament to represent a broader population of lower middle-class Germans. (They worked during the Thirties in the respective trades of baker, cabinetmaker, high-school student, bill-collector, teacher, policeman, bank clerk, tailor, tailor's apprentice, and unemployed salesman.) Yet they had been Nazis. They were patriotic, dutiful, and politically conservative. They readily accepted authority and believed in the racial superiority of German blood.

Mayer found that economic circumstances and political ideology had more to do with the embrace

---

248 Milton Mayer. 1955. *They Thought They Were Free: The Germans 1933-1945*. Chicago: University of Chicago Press.

of fascism than congenital defects or deep-seated personality traits. In fact, until the men in his study realized the war was lost, some said that under the Nazi regime they had experienced the best years of their lives. Mayer also found that, at the beginning, when fascism began to take hold, the men he interviewed hadn't a clue as to where the small group of Nazis at the head of government was taking them. He observed,

> This separation of government from people, this widening of the gap, took place so gradually and so insensibly, each step disguised (perhaps not even intentionally) as a temporary emergency measure or associated with true patriotic allegiance or with real social purposes. And all the crises and reforms (real reforms, too) so occupied the people that they did not see the slow motion underneath, of the whole process of government growing remoter and remoter.

Mayer returned to the US feeling that similar circumstances—authoritarian changes in government, right-wing media, exploitation of economic and political crises, nationalism, and racial chauvinism—could generate fascism here. In fact, he titled one of his concluding chapters, *"Peoria über Alles,"* because it depicted an imaginary small American city whose residents, like the men in Kronenberg, believed that their country is awesomely superior to all others on earth.

Nationalism and racial chauvinism are among the social forces that have made ordinary Americans indifferent to other people's suffering. During the Vietnam War, American soldiers repeatedly demonstrated this kind of indifference. In one appalling instance, as described by the First Air Calvary Division's Captain John Mallory, companions used Vietnamese skulls as candleholders or conversation pieces. They burned buildings and killed two small children after dropping incendiary grenades on the village of Sa Troc from a helicopter. Summarized Captain Mallory,

> In general, US attitudes towards Vietnamese civilians were not inhumane per se, but they were certainly not human. The Vietnamese civilians were regarded much as America regards her own minorities—a pat on the head for a tick, a kick in the ass for an imagined fault, and invisible the rest of the time.[249]

On March 16, 2008, the *Washington Post*'s Steve Vogler reported on the shocking stories told by former soldiers before several hundred people in Silver Spring, Maryland. Vogler entitled his article, "War Stories Echo an Earlier Winter", because the Silver Spring event was modeled after 1971's Winter Soldier Investigation. (This 1971 event was organized by the Vietnam Veterans Against the War and it exposed the atrocities committed by American forces. Soldiers, civilian contractors, medical personnel, and academics testified about war crimes they had committed or witnessed during 1963-1970.) As photos and videos were displayed on a large screen, veterans described firing indiscriminately at Iraqi vehicles

---

249 Capt. John Mallory. Testimony, 1972. *The Winter Soldier Investigation: An Inquiry into American War Crimes.* New York: Beacon Press, p.94.

filled with civilians and gunships shattering apartment buildings filled with families. "During the siege of Fallujah," said one, "we changed our rules of engagement more often than we changed our underwear."

Joe Bageant's book, *Deer Hunting with Jesus: Dispatches from America's Class War,* focuses on additional forces that have brutalized ordinary Americans. His book is about the author's working-class friends and relatives in a Southern town whose lives are being threatened by plant closings, declining wages, and rising cost of living. The people in Bageant's town are called "rednecks" because they descend from Scotch and Scotch-Irish immigrants—typically farmers and workers whose skin became leathery and tough and whose necks were reddened by the harsh southern sun. Rednecks, Bageant notes, "have shown a preference for demagogues selling fear, hatred and ignorance since the Civil War." They voted Democrat decades ago but they abandoned the Democratic Party when it supported the civil-rights movement. They now vote Republican even though they face the same dismal economic outlook as black southerners who vote Democrat.

Bageant describes a relative, Tommy Ray, who cannot get 40 hours work at a living wage but who never stops trying—because he kids himself that opportunity is knocking at his door. The relentless, autocratic blue-collar American workplace has ground people like Tommy down. "Their concept of personal freedom has now been reduced to a pale facsimile," concludes Bageant, "to the symbolism of gun ownership or the freedom to express their individuality by buying and squirreling away more meaningless junk."

Throughout much, if not most, of America, gun ownership is a matter of pride. Liberals made a cardinal mistake, Bageant insists, when they advocated gun control. He notes that over 70 million Americans own and enjoy more than 200 million guns; consequently, it seems more reasonable to reform the conditions that generate crime—rather than use gun control to "blow another political toe off American liberalism during each election cycle." Notes Bageant mordantly,

> [With] Michael Savage and Ann Coulter openly calling for putting liberals in concentration camps, with the CIA now licensed to secretly detain American citizens indefinitely, and with the current administration effectively legalizing torture, the proper question to ask an NRA member these days may be, "What kind of assault rifle do you think I can get for three hundred bucks, and how many rounds of ammo does it take to stop a two-hundred-pound born-again Homeland Security zombie from putting me in camp?" Which would you prefer, 40 million gun-owning Americans on your side or theirs?[250]

However, rednecks can be receptive to using camps, detention, and torture to deal with liberals. In fact, some of Bageant's friends and relatives might give the Homeland Security Zombie a hand—or a gun—if the price is right. As Bageant painstakingly,

---

250 Joe Bageant. 2008. *Deer Hunting with Jesus: Dispatches from America's Class War.* New York: Crown p.133

and painfully, points out, the rise of religious fundamentalism—and its condemnation of everyone but
true believers—has contributed to the hardening of
his people's hearts. Yet there are class experiences,
especially among the men, that have made weightier
contributions. Sadly, observes Bageant, "the tide of
our national meanness rises incrementally, one brutalizing experience at a time, inside one person at a
time in a chain of working-class Americans stretch-
ing back for decades." Examples of these experiences
include his neighbor's 80-year-old father, who recalls "getting paid $2 apiece for literally cracking
open the heads of union organizers at the local textile and sewing mills during the days of Virginia's
Byrd political machine." Other examples enumerate
experiences acquired while fighting in Vietnam,
Afghanistan, and Iraq—and torturing prisoners in
Abu Ghraib. Traditionally, violent peer relations during adolescence provide further examples of class experiences that have brutalized the men in Bageant's
town.

> The Tom Henderson who once loved to play
> folk guitar on the porch at night did not mutate
> into the iron heart he is today of his own voli-
> tion. Nam did part of it; the increasing brutal-
> ity of the American workplace and being pitted
> against every other working American did
> most of the rest.

Bageant points out that nearly half of the 3,000
killed in Iraq in the early years were from small
towns with fewer than 40,000 inhabitants even
though they only contain 25 per cent of the nation's
population. Most of the young recruits were fleeing

economically dead-end jobs or deteriorating economic conditions. Despite their patriotic rationales, these recruits were drawn by the economic benefits. Count the rewards: If he or she isn't killed, the recruits get a bonus when they sign up, a salary of $1300 a month, free room and board, and money for college. All of these benefits "sure beats hell out of yanking guts through a chicken's ass" in a local chicken processing plant, Bageant bluntly observes.[251]

Bageant recognizes that recruits also sign up because "they want to do that which they, in their ignorance, have been persuaded is right and good, to fight for their country and freedom." As a result, he primarily blames

[P]eople who see principles as a weakness to be exploited, and have eagerly convinced an entire class of Americans, through their radio stations, preachers, sportscasters, and cable news channels, that their country is under siege from liberals and our 'allies,' homosexuals, immigrants and Islamic terrorists. Wickedly manipulative people like Cheney and Rove, and the scads of others willing to fan the flames and ride the wave for their own selfish ends are at the root of this.

Nevertheless, Bageant also recognizes other forces at work. He describes a "parallel culture" created by the Scots-Irish in small towns. The infusion in this culture in recent decades of Christian fundamentalism hasn't only promoted a theocratic state. It has weakened the commonsense reluctance to engage in

---

251 Op.cit. p.200.

a nuclear holy war. "Conquer the world! Impose democracy on the *towel-headed niggers.*" "If you don't force them to accept liberty, they'll steal it from us!" "If they fight back, *nuke 'em!*" These words are not merely produced by boilermakers (i.e., with a shot of bourbon and a beer chaser) consumed loudly in the local bar. They also reflect a way of thinking and stereotypes upheld by a huge number of American men regardless of their national heritage. Bageant believes that we have ignored brutal experiences historically undergone by America's hardest-working folks—and how these folks were forced to internalize "the values of a gangster capitalist class." In his view, the American "political and economic system has hammered the humanity of ordinary working people." After stripping illusions about the inherent nobility of working class Americans, Bageant concludes:

> The people doing our hardest work and fighting our wars are not altruistic and probably never were. They don't give a rat's bunghole about the world's poor or the planet or the animals or anything else. Not really. The people [in his town] like cheap gas. They like chasing post-Thanksgiving Day Christmas sales. And if fascism comes, they will like that too if the cost of gas isn't too high and Comcast comes through with a twenty-four-hour NFL [National Football League] channel.

NEOLIBERALISM & INEQUALITY

In the Sixties and Seventies progressive academics

scrutinized the strands of liberalism framing social science discourse. They recognized that changing historical conditions had produced distinctly different liberal standpoints. Classical liberalism, for example, was generated when mercantile capitalism gradually replaced feudalism. Laissez-faire liberalism distinguished itself later when liberals supported the unchecked power of early manufacturers and traders. Corporate liberalism, on the other hand, was shaped by class wars accompanying the rise of monopoly capitalism toward the end of the 19th century. Corporate liberals did not limit the growth of monopolies but they aimed to preserve capitalism by ameliorating class conflicts and opposing anarchist and socialist ideas.[252]

To unravel neoliberalism, we must go back in time and recall the class conflicts in Germany during the 1920s over a *Sozialpolitik* supporting welfare state policies, favorable-wage settlements, workmen's compensation, and other costly legislation that reduced economic inequality and improved working-class living standards. During the Depression, the parliamentary coalitions supporting these policies and legislation unraveled. At that time, tax policies, protectionism, and economic concessions achieved by trade unions became particularly divisive issues. Manipulated by powerful interests and Nazi demagogues, small farmers and small business owners raged at having to pay taxes for programs that appeared to benefit urban workers only.

---

252 Herman Schwendinger and Julia Schwendinger. 1974. *Sociologists of the Chair, A Radical Analysis of the Formative Years of American Sociology, 1883–1922.* New York: Basic Books.

FORWARD
with
ROOSEVELT

Vote

DEMOCRATIC ⊠

In the US, however, FDR succeeded in ameliorating the class conflicts that could have shattered his administration. Ironically, he accomplished this goal by boldly borrowing socialist ideas in order to keep capitalism alive. FDR's reforms succeeded because he was backed by the American labor movement. To combat unemployment, he sponsored the Public Works Administration (WPA) and its employment programs for manual laborers and skilled workers. To increase employment by constructing buildings, highways, dams, and other projects, an enormous number of public works were funded by the WPA during his administration. He also created a public agency, the Homeowners Loan Corporation which granted loans that helped more than a million people keep their homes. Even huge publically funded projects were created such as the Tennessee Valley Authority which generated electricity and modernized a poverty stricken region.

FDR also encouraged the creation of the Civilian Conservation Corps (CCC), a massive public program for young, unemployed and unmarried men whose families were on welfare. The CCC was dedicated to the preservation of natural resources in rural lands owned by the government and it eventually employed about 2.5 million men who cleared swamps, planted nearly 3 billion trees to reforest the nation and constructed more than 800 parks. These men also upgraded public roadways in remote areas.

FDR also promoted the United States Housing Authority which provided funds to cities for replacing slums with low-rental housing projects for low-income families. His administration introduced banking reforms that included the Glass-Steagall Act which, among other things, prevented collusion between investment banks and commercial banks. His New Deal reforms also included The Securities and Exchange Commission (SEC) which regulated the stock market and restricted financial speculation. (Abolishing the Glass-Steagall Act and gutting the SEC during the Clinton and Bush administrations paved the way for the 2008 recession.) Finally, FDR's reforms included a lynch pin of the modern American Welfare State, namely, the Social Security Act of 1935, which provided for unemployment insurance and old-age pensions.

But the American Masters of the Universe never accepted these New Deal reforms. As the labor movement declined during the 1980s, wealthy right-wing families invested heavily in culture wars aimed at annihilating FDR's reforms. Their hired guns drew eclectically upon the legacy of liberal thought and became known as "new" liberals (neoliberals) and "new" conservatives (neoconservatives).

Neoliberals claimed that free (unregulated) competitive markets enhanced economic growth. They supported "free trade" agreements (e.g., NAFTA,

CAFTA) that had little or no protectionist and currency restrictions such as tariffs and value-added taxes. They advocated privatizing state agencies (e.g., public schools) and outsourcing their services to community shareholders or corporate enterprises. To undermine taxing the rich to reduce the effects of a crisis on the middle and working classes, they opposed the accumulation of fiscal debt and advocated "balanced budgets." They maintained that private enterprises operate more efficiently than government agencies and insisted that putting social security under Wall Street control would increase pensions and save taxpayers a great deal of money. Medicare should also be controlled by private interests even if this meant Americans might die if they couldn't afford the care that would keep them alive.

Since neoliberals borrowed most of their ideas from laissez-faire doctrines, they did not represent a new variant of liberalism. Instead, these hired guns created eclectic justifications for stripping the costs incurred by the welfare state and enabling the government to further enrich the American Masters of the Universe.

The neoliberals were employed as mercenaries in class wars. And we know that they helped win these wars because the wealthiest families in the U.S. experienced a new Gilded Age. During the Fifties and Sixties annual incomes over $200,000 were taxed at 91 per cent. But the right-wing propaganda (that had promised prosperity and a better quality of life if taxes were cut for ordinary Americans) recast the standards of economic justice prevailing since the Great Depression. Beginning with Reagan the tax rate for incomes over $200,000 plummeted. By 2004, as a Princeton professor of economics and *New York Times* columnist, Paul Krugman, pointed out, the average federal tax rate imposed on the top one per cent of all families in the US was merely 31.1 per cent.

Discovering the results is a no-brainer: Today, too many ordinary Americans believe that the rich always get richer but they are wrong. Certain conditions make them richer and other conditions do not. Sam Pizzigati's award winning book, *Greed and good: Understanding and Overcoming the Inequality That Limits Our Lives* points out that only 1% of all the families in American had acquired 23.9% of the nation's income before the Great Depression. By 1976, their share had plummeted by nearly two-thirds to 8.86%. In 2005, however, their share had skyrocketed and it stood at 21.93%.[253] Furthermore, recently, research conducted by the Congressional Budget Office found that the after-tax income received by the top 20% of Americans alone from 2005 to 2007 was more than the rest of the 80% altogether.[254]

For three decades, neoliberal "free market" doctrines, supported by voodoo economics and adulation of the rich and famous, reduced the human spirit to its most selfish qualities. These doctrines

---

253 Sam Pizzigati. 2004. *GREED and good: Understanding and Overcoming the Inequality That Limits Our Lives*. New York: The Apex Press.

254 Linette Lopez. Oct 25 2011. "The Congressional Budget Office Just Jumped Into The Debate About Inequality, And It Definitely Picks A Side." *Business Insider*. (*businessinsider.com/the-congressional-budget-releases-a-report-on-inequality*.)

operated like the Abrams tanks did when Iraq was invaded.

Pizzigati is an outstanding labor historian and the title of his book mimics the actor Michael Douglas who, in the role of a Gordon Gekko, attacks the CEOs who run a corporation called Teldar Paper. Gekko denounces their attempts to enrich themselves even though the company isn't profitable. In a keynote scene, Gekko histrionically points out that the interests of the shareholders come first because their "[G]reed—for lack of a better word—is good." Gekko extols human selfishness, declaring:

> Greed is right! Greed works! Greed clarifies, cuts through, and captures the essence of the evolutionary spirit. Greed, in all of its forms—greed for life, for money, for love, for knowledge—has overcome all the obstacles that prevented the upward surge of mankind!"

Pizzigati provides a thoroughgoing analysis of the correlation between greed—when it sparks economic inequality—and the conditions affecting ordinary Americans. He demonstrates that the unchecked pursuit of greed is decidedly not good. The wealthiest families have increased their share of wealth at the expense of an overwhelming majority of Americans. The super-rich got richer while the incomes of ordinary Americans stagnated. And when inequality increases, there follows a deterioration of longevity, health, quality of life, housing conditions, job opportunities, and wages and salaries of ordinary people.

In the 1990s, when welfare for the poor was being gutted, corporations were receiving more than $100 billion a year in corporate welfare, $53 billion in tax breaks and another $51 billion from direct subsidies to industries. After 9/11, the airline industry faced bankruptcy and more than 100,000 workers lost their jobs, health care, and severance pay. A $15 billion government bailout provided no help for these workers, while the airline CEOs raked in millions in disguised salary increases and stock options.

Equally important, in a prescient chapter entitled "Dying Democracy," Pizzigati spells out the harmful impact of growing inequality on America's democratic institutions.[255]

Pizzigati's proposals for turning things around begin with increasing taxes imposed on wealthy families, lowering taxes on the remaining Americans, and increasing the minimum wages. Other options include legislation aimed at preventing outsourcing jobs should be considered. Most certainly, updating and reinstituting FDR's New Deal would help ensure Social Security, preserve living wages, health care, and other necessities of life. These options would provide antidotes to the Snake Oil that neoliberal quacks have sold to Americans over the last decades.

---

255 Get Pizzigati's iconoclastic book. It is an eye-opener and its chapters can be downloaded without cost at *greedandgood.org*.

15 | Mainstream & Alternative Media

Freedom of the press is limited to those who own one.

—A. J. Liebling

INFORMING THE PUBLIC

Who will really inform the public about the deterioration of democratic institutions? As a rule, one can't depend on the mainstream media, because seven huge global conglomerates—Disney, AOL Time Warner, Sony, News Corporation, Viacom, Vivendi, and Bertelsmann—control most media options in America. Almost all of these conglomerates are listed among the largest firms in the world. They also own the major US film studios and most of the US television networks. They control 80-85 per cent of the global music market, most of the satellite broadcasting worldwide and a considerable percent of book publishers and commercial magazines. They own the bulk of the commercial cable-TV channels in the US as well as a significant number of European television stations. Only three of these firms are truly US corporations!

In February and March, 2007, we tried to obtain news about the massive anti-war demonstrations occurring in the US and beyond. The only opportunities to actually witness the demonstrations were provided on YouTube with individual photos of European demonstrations and a brief video of the demonstrators in Washington. The US television media blackout was so effective that the millions who were not at the demonstrations did not know that they had taken place.

As a foremost expert on the media, Professor Robert McChesney, says, "Regardless of what a progressive group's first issue of importance is, its second issue should be media and communication, because so long as the media are in corporate hands, the task of social change will be vastly more difficult, if not impossible, across the board." We do not have to recap corporate media's support of customary repression to validate McChesney. He reminds us:

> American political culture . . . has virtually precluded public discussion of the fundamental weaknesses of capitalism, forcing media reformers to argue defensively that commercial broadcasting is a special case of market failure. This constraint has been reinforced by the near-absence of a viable Left, and by the dominant culture's sanitized images of capitalism.[256]

---

256 Robert McChesney. 2008. *The Political Economy of the Media:*

In addition, McChesney observes:

> Today, the weapons of global media conglomerates include their sheer financial resources and their ability to use cross-promotional synergy, brand-name recognition, distribution muscle, high entry costs, and economies of scale. Oligopolistic markets give them the power to marginalize or take over smaller players. They also have the ability to pre-empt or co-opt politically troublesome opposition through token concessions.

The "privatization" (think "piratization") of publicly owned airwaves is another problem. It began in 1996 when the Clinton administration increased the number of local radio stations that could be owned by a single corporation. The proponents of this deregulation claimed that expanding the private ownership of the airwaves would produce greater diversity and competition; but, later, two federal communication studies were suppressed because they showed that deregulation had *lowered* rather than increased competition and diversity. Clear Channel, Viacom, and other right-wing corporate giants, which minimize local events and maximize commercialized content, had devoured the radio stations.

Bush appointed Gen. Powell's son, Michael Powell, as the head of the Federal Communication Commission (FCC). Although faced with thousands of protests, Powell immediately attempted to further gut public ownership of media resources—attempting to loosen regulations preventing corporations

---

Enduring Issues, Emerging Dilemmas. New York: Monthly Review Press.

from unlimited ownership of TV and radio stations and cable franchises in the same market. Regarding Powell's attempts to deregulate the communications industry, two media experts, John Nichols and Robert McChesney, in 2002 predicted:

> This deregulation, should it proceed, will result in an explosion of corporate deal making that will make the past decade of unprecedented media conglomeration look like a Wednesday-night bingo game at the local old-folks home. For the first time, media giants that control TV station empires—Disney, News Corp., Viacom, General Electric—would be able to merge with or acquire media empires built on cable franchises, such as AOL Time Warner and AT&T-Comcast. As Blair Levin, a former FCC chief of staff, puts it, the ruling "allows for a powerful new entity we have never seen before—something that combines both cable and broadcasting assets."[257]

The fight to privatize public communications markets is still going on and, if it succeeds, may eventually engulf the Internet.

To support the democratization of communication industries and offset the media blackouts, progressives are urging people to bring their video recorders and smart phones when they attend a demonstration. Some of these instruments will be smashed, but hundreds more may still be on hand to identify instances of police brutality for more democratized, progressive media websites such as YouTube, Real

---

257 John Nichols and Robert W. McChesney. 2005. *Tragedy & Farce: How the American Media Sell Wars, Spin Elections, and Destroy Democracy*. New York: New Press,

News, and Indymedia.

In 2007, televised screams and images of a tortured student on YouTube recorded an Iranian-American UCLA student being repeatedly shocked with high-voltage tasers in the library by campus police—who alleged that he refused to show them his library card. A crowd of student onlookers, who had caught the spectacle on their cell phone video cameras, immediately distributed their content online for millions throughout the world to witness.

In addition, a daily radio and TV news program, *The War and Peace Report* (aka *Democracy Now!*), hosted by Amy Goodman and Juan Gonzales, was being transmitted across the nation by over 500 radio and TV stations. Aaron Russo's *America: Freedom to Fascism* and Robert Greenwald's *BraVeNew Films* embody the proliferation of markets for documentaries produced by progressives. *Fox Attacks, Yes Sir! No Sir!*, *The Endless War*, *Real McCain*, *Impeach Gonzales*, and *Wal-Mart: The High Cost of Low Price*—as well as Michael Moore's blockbusters, *Fahrenheit 9/11, Sicko, and Capitalism: A Love Story*—signify that liberals and leftists are attempting to expand media options for the public at large.

A politically unrestricted Internet is providing a revolutionary expansion of mass media along with an ever-growing number of progressive writers, artists, composers, and musicians communicating their works to countless people throughout the world. This expansion and its diverse offerings have grown far enough to justify the installation of search engines devoted to websites and articles genuinely supporting free speech and assembly. The existing websites have become essential in the fight for democracy because they provide articles and chat rooms that uncover political hoaxes, spot disinformation, and unearth further attempts to assemble weapons of mass repression.

Alternative Media

Americans since 9/11 have had little success at blocking assaults on the Constitution. For example, a broad coalition organized by the ACLU, and The Coalition in Defense of Freedom in Time of National Crisis, tried to block the Patriot Act.[258] Unfortunately, the Act passed and the coalition was defeated. However, since law-enforcement agencies used the Act as cover for investigating and prosecuting criminal cases having nothing to do with terrorism, principled conservatives as well as liberals continued to protest that the agencies were circumventing the greater burden of proof required by the criminal law.

In addition, local governments went on the offensive, condemning the Act. By March 2005 more than 407 cities and counties across the country had passed anti-Patriot Act resolutions that claimed security need not come at the expense of civil liberties. The big cities included Philadelphia, Detroit, San Francisco, and Seattle. (A small California city, Arcata, took a largely symbolic but significant step. Its

---

258 The coalition among others included The Center for Constitutional Rights, Free Congress Foundation, American Friends Service Committee, Gun Owners of America, NAACP Board of Directors, Rutherford Institute and Amnesty International.

City Council adopted an ordinance that made cooperation with the Patriot Act a crime. Any city department head, including the police chief, who voluntarily complied with investigations or arrests under the Patriot Act, was fined.)

State legislatures in Alaska, Colorado, Hawaii, Idaho, Maine, Montana, and Vermont also condemned the Act. Hawaii's legislature declared that it "poses significant threats to Constitutional protections" and instructed law-enforcement officers employed by the state to uphold civil liberties and human rights. It urged Hawaii's representatives in Congress to work toward repealing sections of the Act as well as negating executive orders that violated personal freedoms under the guise of national security.

Concurrently, the numbers of periodicals, newsletters, and websites opposed to Bush's policies grew astronomically. In 2006, an astonishing number—61 —Indymedia internet websites were operating in America alone, and they were informing the public, exchanging news with each other, and communicating with Indymedia sites in Europe, Asia, and Africa.

The publication of online "white papers" also increased. These kept track of the shocking number of unconstitutional practices supported by Ashcroft, Gonzales, Chertoff and other officials. ACLU's Action Network used this information to encourage more than 30,000 messages from American citizens to their senators expressing their objections to Gonzales' nomination.

In 2005, an ACLU "white paper" had urged the Senate to take care before approving Chertoff's appointment as head of the Department of Homeland Security. The ACLU claimed:

> Chertoff has demonstrated a very limited view of civil liberties: he played a leading role in the crafting of the USA Patriot Act, the relaxation of internal DoJ guidelines that now permit the FBI to secretly spy on public religious, social or political gatherings and the blanket 'voluntary' interviews of thousands of Arabs and Muslims that have sown distrust between law enforcement and these communities.

The ACLU had also urged senators to ask Chertoff about the FBI's aggressive detention of suspects, since he had primary authority over these detentions and decided who would be released and who would be held in solitary confinement, for instance.

To prove its point, the ACLU summarized a lengthy Department of Justice Inspector General report about the 1,200 citizens and non-citizens who were detained and questioned in the two months following 9/11. The department had used shallow excuses to justify the detentions—including criminal charges, even though none of these people was ever charged with a crime that had anything to do with terrorism and many were imprisoned for months. Furthermore, Alice Fisher, Chertoff's deputy at the time, said, "[T]he Department was detaining aliens on immigration violations that generally had not been enforced in the past." Yet, Chertoff had previously deceived a Senate Judiciary Committee in November, 2001. He had stated "nothing that we are doing differs from what we do in the ordinary case or what we did before September 11th."

In addition, websites maintained by bloggers, political organizations, newspapers, magazines, radio programs, and research institutes produced email alerts, forceful commentaries, in-depth essays and domestic and international news releases. They inform the public about the dates and times of the rallies and demonstrations held throughout the nation by peace and social-justice movements. Official and unofficial attacks on the Bill of Rights are counterattacked overnight with acerbic commentary, interpretive essays, concise summaries, and riotous satire. (The magnitude and diversity of information being produced by these sites is so large that a new breed of committed individuals, called "website hosts" and "list managers," perform an invaluable service by scanning the Internet for timely information and forwarding it to their subscribers.)

A Foot in the Door

Progressives also used the Internet as an organizational tool. In addition, the Internet helped set new records in electoral campaign fundraising. At that time, the Republicans predictably raised millions almost overnight from extremely wealthy supporters while the Democrats lagged far behind in the race for resources. Suddenly, however, a progressive website, MoveOn.org, appealed for campaign funds. Millions of small contributors responded and, afterwards, other websites adopted this tactic. Progressive Democrats were running neck and neck with Republicans in the most heavily financed election campaign in American history.

But before progressives celebrated their achievements, they were confronted with the suppression of the Phil Donahue nightly MSNBC show. The day before MSNBC canceled his show, he interviewed actress and author Rosie O'Donnell. Instead of going through a standard celebrity interview and talking about sex, betrayal, and money, Donahue asked O'Donnell's opinion about whether the US should go to war with Iraq. She replied:

> Well, I think like every mother, every mother that I've spoken to, every day when I go to pick up my kids from school, every person I've spoken to has said they're against this war, for basic reasons. I don't want to kill innocent mothers and children and fathers in another country when there are alternate means available, at least at this point.

When Donahue then asked O'Donnell why anyone should take what celebrities say about war seriously, she responded:

> Nobody wants to interview the mother of the two kids in my daughter's class who feels the same way. I stand with 36 women every day outside the elementary school. And if any newscaster wanted to speak to any member of the PTA across America, I have a feeling they would say the same thing I'm saying. I'm not speaking as a celebrity. I'm speaking as a mother and I'm speaking for the mothers who don't have the option of an hour on the Phil Donahue show.

The Donahue show was abruptly canceled, and a rare forum for progressives on cable TV was silenced. Donahue had interviewed Congressman Bernie Sanders, Bishop Desmond Tutu, the Rev. Jesse Jackson, Institute for Policy Studies foreign-policy analyst Phyllis Bennis, and Global Exchange director and "Code Pink" anti-war activist Medea Benjamin.[259] In addition, his ratings had actually been ticking upward when his show was canceled. But, according to media analyst Rick Ellis, Donahue's fate was sealed because NBC News executives were alarmed by a study that suggested his show would become "a home for the liberal antiwar agenda" while NBC's competitors were waving the American flag at every opportunity. Supposedly, Donahue's show sounded like it might actually enable NBC to credibly argue that it was "fiercely independent." However, in reality, according to Ellis:

> Donahue was sent to battle Fox's Bill O'Reilly and CNN's Connie Chung with one lobe tied behind his brain. Pressured by desperate MSNBC executives to fit into the contemporary talk-TV mold ("Be like O'Reilly, only nicer—but not too nice"), Donahue was never allowed to be Donahue. For every program that featured Ralph Nader and Molly Ivins, there were ten where Donahue was forced to ask polite questions of second-string conservative pundits.

Ellis notes that Donahue's ratings dropped when MSNBC executives forced him to weigh his show down with apologists for Bush. When Donahue was given the freedom to exercise greater control of

259 John Nichols. March 2 2003. "Donahue's Demise." *The Nation.com.*

choices of guests and responses to questions from his audiences, however, his ratings rose. In its final days, *Donahue* was actually averaging a nightly audience of 446,000 people. (It was beating the much more strongly promoted MSNBC program, *Hardball With Chris Matthews.*)

After *Donahue* was tossed in 2003, few talk shows comparable to Bill O'Reilly and Sean Hannity's right-wing shows routinely featured progressive voices on television. Jon Stewart's popular *Daily Show* and Bill Maher's comedy hours held interviews and debates between liberals and conservatives. But they were exceptions not the rule.

Suddenly, in the face of growing disillusionment with the war, NBC upset about the size of its audience, executed a left turn. Keith Olbermann, who had been a sportscaster, began to host a nightly weekday newscast, *Countdown with Keith Olbermann,* on MSNBC. Olbermann provided fast-paced, hard-hitting, and incisive political commentaries that thoroughly discredited the Bush administration. Ridiculing Bill O'Reily at every opportunity, his show became the highest-rated program on MSNBC, averaging over 700,000 viewers in January 2007. In 2009, his program was being preceded by the hard-hitting, liberal "Ed Show" and followed by Rachel Maddow's insightful news-commentaries and interviews.

PROPAGANDA TSUNAMI

Recall Goebbels' jubilation when Hitler became

Reichschancellor: "Now it will be easy," he wrote, "to carry on the fight, for we can call on all the resources of the State. Radio and press are at our disposal. We shall stage a masterpiece of propaganda."

William L. Shirer was a foremost American journalist and historian who lived in Berlin during the 1930s when Goebbels' produced his "masterpiece of propaganda." He wrote communiqués for the American press and teamed up with Edward Murrow in the first news broadcasts sent to the US from Germany and other parts of Europe. Shirer experienced the power of Goebbels' campaigns. Despite his access to foreign sources of information and his distrust of Nazi sources, he found that "a steady diet over the years of falsifications and distortions made a certain impression on one's mind and often misled it." To drive this point home, he said, "No one who has not lived for years in a totalitarian land can possibly conceive how difficult it is to escape the dread consequences of a regime's calculated and incessant propaganda."

> Often in a German home or office or sometimes in a casual conversation with a stranger in a restaurant, a beer hall, a cafe, I would meet with the most outlandish assertions from seemingly educated and intelligent persons. It was obvious that they were parroting some piece of nonsense they had heard on the radio or read in the newspapers. Sometimes one was tempted to say as much, but on such occasions one was met with such a stare of incredulity, such a shock of silence, as if one had blasphemed the Almighty, that one realized how useless it was even to try to make contact with

a mind which had become warped and for
whom the facts of life had become what Hitler
and Goebbels, with their cynical disregard for
truth, said they were.

The fit between Shirer's experiences and post 9/11
developments in the US is uncanny. The German fascists believed that if you tell a lie often enough, it becomes accepted as truth. Bush linked al Qaeda to
Saddam Hussein in almost every speech on Iraq. His
underlings alluded to a 9/11-Hussein link after the
attacks. (In late 2001, for instance, Vice President
Cheney said it was "pretty well confirmed" that the
attack mastermind Mohamed Atta met with a senior
Iraqi intelligence official.) Almost two years after
9/11 a *Washington Post* poll found that 69 per cent
of Americans thought that Hussein had a role in the
attacks on the Twin Towers and the Pentagon.[260]
When people who voted for Bush in 2004 were interviewed, the majority indicated that weapons of mass
destruction were found in Iraq despite the fact that
there were none. They said that Saddam supported
al Qaeda even though he did not. Others said that
Social Security faced an imminent crisis even though
it will not face a shortfall until 2045 or later.[261] Still
others admitted that they voted for Bush because
they believed he would fight terrorism more effectively than Kerry. Yet his policies increased the
threat of terrorism. They did not diminish it.

---

260 Dana Milbank and Claudia Deane. Sept. 6 2003. "Hussein Link
to 9/11 Lingers in Many Minds." *Washington Post* p.A01.

261 Even that shortfall could be rectified easily by eliminating the
cap on social security taxes so wealthy families would pay more to
support a universal program than other families.

During the 2004 election, the Americanized version of the *Dolchstoss* ('stab-in-the-back) legend reappeared. An innovative and thought-provoking sociologist, Jerry Lembcke, found stories circulating in several cities about military personnel being spat on or otherwise mistreated. "In Asheville, North Carolina," he notes, "two Marines were rumored to have been spat upon, while in Spokane, Washington, a threat to 'spit on the troops when they return from Iraq' was reportedly issued." The leader of the Vermont National Guard told local Burlington television audience that "spitting incidents" had occurred and that antiwar teenagers had stoned one of his Guardswomen.[262]

After investigating these stories, Lembcke found that none of them panned out. (The Spokane "threat" actually misrepresented a letter published in the local newspaper that said the anti-war protesters would *not* spit on returning soldiers.) Nevertheless, the dissemination of these falsehoods stoked pro-war rallies.

Tales about anti-war protesters spitting on Vietnam veterans accompanied these falsehoods. Lembcke traced the story of spitting in Asheville, for example, "to a local businessman who says he is a veteran who was also spat upon and called a 'baby killer' when he returned from Vietnam." Also, an Associated Press article reported incidents of people spitting at Vietnam veterans in several cities including Spicer, Minnesota where the mayor claimed someone spit at him in the San Francisco airport

---

262 Jerry Lembcke.1998. *Spitting Image: Myth, Memory, and the Legacy of Vietnam*. New York: New York University Press.

while returning in 1971 from Vietnam.

Lembcke, who had served in Vietnam, had previously investigated the legend about anti-war protesters who spat on Vietnam veterans. He tracked down one unfounded incident after another reported by the media and individual veterans.

The incidents played the same role as the "stab in the back" legend created by the German Officer Corps after the First World War. Consequently, Lembcke writes, "The fact that we seldom, if ever, hear stories about soldiers in winning armies returning home to abuse suggests that these tales function specifically as alibis for why a war was lost."[263]

Lembcke analyzed more than 100 films that portrayed relations between Vietnam veterans and the anti-war movement. Did the films present an accurate picture? Despite one or two exceptions, he reports, "Anti-war GIs and veterans made it to the screen in very small numbers and then almost always as characters whose mental and physical disabilities overshadowed their political identity." The films perpetuated myth that political dissidents as well as other Americans treated the Vietnam veterans badly. Lembcke concluded: "The image of warriors betrayed and then forgotten has been the centerpiece of paramilitary cultures throughout the twentieth century." "Unless it is laid to rest," he insisted, "the myth of the spat-upon Vietnam veteran will continue to feed the politics of division and violence."[264]

---

263 Op cit. p89.
264 Op. cit. pp142-43.

This myth should also be evaluated in light of the millions who were displaying yellow ribbons with the words "Support our Troops" on their front doors and automobiles. As Lembcke observes, "Everyone supports the troops and wishes them a safe and speedy homecoming. It's the mission they have been sent on that is dividing the nation and it is the mission that we have a right and obligation to question." Today, when used against anti-war protesters, the spat-upon veteran stories and imputation of disloyalty are being used to replace debate about what got us into the war with the phony issue of who supports our troops.

Who Pays the Tab?

Another significant development is the degree of funding public-relations agencies and advertising firms by wealthy individuals, corporations and "philanthropic" foundations. This funding has been aimed at increasing public support for administration proposals and discrediting individuals and organizations opposing these proposals. For example, USA Next, a GOP front group that contributed millions in support of Republican proposals, adopted plans in 2005 to spend 10 million on discrediting senior citizens' organizations opposing Bush's attempt to privatize Social Security. USA Next had backed all the usual suspects from the deceitful 2004 "Swift Boat" campaign.[265] It hired the consultants and ad-

---

265 Bush's proposal was backed by Big Lies expressed in the "Swift Boat Veterans" TV ads that accused Kerry of faking circumstances justifying a medal for bravery and Purple Heart awards. None of

vertising agencies behind the original Kerry attacks. Shortly afterwards, a website, The Daily Kos, found an ad posted on the *American Spectator* that professed to show the "real" AARP agenda. It reported:

> The weird ad shows a photo of soldiers in Iraq – with a big "X" through it – next to one of two men kissing – with a big green check. The group doesn't even pretend to provide the rationale behind the ad; clicking on the "click here for details" merely brings you to USA Next's home page, with nothing about either troops or gay marriage. Thus the ad exists just to spread the implication that AARP hates US troops but loves gay marriage.[266]

Americans not deceived by the privately funded propaganda tsunami were appalled. But most of them were unaware of the plainly illegal use of public revenues to pay syndicated journalists, public relations firms, advertising agencies, and other media resources to promote Bush's policies. Even the Pentagon was hiring advertising agencies to drum up

---

these "veterans" served under Kerry. Nevertheless, their ads were displayed endlessly. Few Americans were exposed to Kerry's crewmen who fought with him and publically supported his bravery.

266 USA Next, which poured millions into Republican policy battles, admitted planning to spend as much as $10 million on commercials and other tactics assailing AARP (formerly the American Association of Retired Persons), an organizational lobby opposing the private investment accounts at the center of Mr. Bush's plan. "They are the boulder in the middle of the highway to personal savings accounts," said Charlie Jarvis, president of USA Next and former deputy under secretary of the interior in the Reagan and first Bush administrations. "We will be the dynamite that removes them."

popular support.

Furthermore, the Pentagon introduced exceptional restrictions on journalists in Iraq. Its practice of "embedding" journalists in military detachments is one example. Another is deliberately blocking newsgathering about civilian casualties. Still another is the attempt by the government to make Freedom of Information requests so expensive that grass roots movements cannot afford to find out what crimes are being committed by the government.

With the aid of marketing experts and its corporate supporters, the Bush administration diligently explored every avenue to control the hearts and minds of Americans. In March 2004, Ben Austin, a sociologist, asked his academic colleagues:

> Did anyone else watch Anderson Cooper's report on CNN tonight! Secretary Ridge of the new Department of Fatherland Security is looking for someone to fill a newly created position for someone to educate and screen Hollywood in any cinematic representation of the war on terror. Too bad Goebbels and Leni Riefenstahl aren't available. If they were, they would have been hired to help Bush recreate the Third Reich's "Ministry of Illusion.[267]

---

267 Ben Austin posed this question on the *Progressive Sociology Network.*

PART SIX

REVIVING THE INQUISITION

—◇—

This contemporary painting is attributed to
Florence Siegel. It is an adaptation of a
progressive-era cartoon.

16 | The New Inquisitors

To be patriotic is to be able to question government policy in times of crisis. To be patriotic is to stand up for the Bill of Rights and the Constitution in times of uncertainty and insecurity.

—Dr. Sami Al-Arian

The Customary Heretics

For more than a century, academics have been targeted in right-wing shooting galleries. Furthermore, although they were often involved in on-campus political activities, classroom teaching itself was with notable exceptions not used to justify the firings, harassment, denial of promotions, unfair workload assignments, inability to obtain research funding, and other customary practices that threatened their jobs and suppressed academic freedom. Moreover, despite the First and Fifth Amendments

455

to the Constitution, mere membership in left-wing parties and a refusal to answer questions about potentially self-incriminating political associations led to loss of employment.

As a result—and contrary to fanciful conservative myths about the undue influence in universities of "liberals" and other "left-wingers"—the long-term effects of customary political repression have been clear. Generally, politically relevant debates in universities and academic publications have epitomized the political conformity that Thorstein Veblen condemned in 1918. Despite its boisterousness, mainstream academic discourse has been anchored anywhere but at the left of the political spectrum.

Thorstein Veblen had complained that economic and political discourse among his academic peers had produced a "calamitous conformity" that shut out dissenting voices.[268] His pioneering writings exposed the degree to which *engineers* (who had a major role in creating American corporations) had been replaced by *finance capitalists*. Today, he is considered one of the period's great American economists even though he spent 14 years teaching at the University of Chicago and was never given tenure. He ended his life in poverty because he had exposed the

---

268 Thorstein Veblen coined these words as well as the phrase, "conspicuous consumption" but he was never advanced beyond an assistant professorship even though he worked at the University of Chicago for 14 years. He couldn't even get a temporary position later at another university because of his scathing critiques of finance capitalism, leisure class styles of life and institutions of "higher learning." See, for example, Veblen. 1973. *The Theory of the Leisure Class*. (Intro. by John Kenneth Galbraith.) Boston: Houghton Mifflin.

corporate liberalism that had overwhelmed thinking among economists during his lifetime. His works satirized the lifestyles of the newly rich (*nouveau riche*) who had become "robber barons." And he originated the phrase "conspicuous consumption" that never went out of style.

THE NEW MCCARTHYISM

From the late Fifties to the Eighties, civil rights, anti-war and feminist movements undermined customary repression in academic institutions. They introduced student representation within university departments and expanded teaching opportunities for women, left-wing scholars and ethnic and/or racial minorities. Academic minors were also introduced in "ethnic studies," "women studies," "labor studies," and "peace studies" programs. Students in these programs probed deeply into how governments encouraged economic, racial, and gender inequality as well as wars of aggression and social injustice.

However, after the Vietnam War, the forces that rule the dark side of our Janus-style government mobilized to take back what they had lost. They encouraged networks of wealthy foundations, right wing journalists, academics, politicians, and trustees to oppose the curriculum reforms and suppress academic freedom.

Although this suppression became particularly vicious following 9/11 when Ashcroft headed the Department of Justice, it relied on FBI investigations conducted during the Nineties.

For example, consider the events preceding Prof. Sami Al-Arian's dismissal from the University of South Florida in December 2001 in spite of the fact that his professional credentials were exemplary. In 1992 he had achieved tenure as an associate professor in computer science. He won the USF College of Engineering Outstanding Teaching Award in 1993 and a Teaching Incentive Program Award in 1994. He had also obtained over a million dollars in research grants and published 46 articles by 2002, exceeding most of his peers. But Al-Arian was a devout Muslim and an imam in his mosque.[269] He had helped found an Arab-Muslim youth league in 1977, the Islamic Community Center in Tampa, and the Florida Islamic Academy, a school for Muslim students.[270] He co-founded the Islamic Association for Palestine (IAP) in 1981 and an offshoot, The Holy Land Foundation for Relief and Development. The Feds highlighted these institutions after 9/11 because they tied Al-Arian to charities that reportedly included among their numerous recipients some families of deceased suicide bombers.

Also, Al-Arian had been one of most active North American lecturers dealing with the Palestinian-Is-

---

269 Al-Arian was born in Kuwait and emigrated with his family to Egypt in 1966. He traveled to the US when he was 17 and completed his doctorate in electrical engineering in 1985. He obtained employment in the USF Computer Science Department in 1986.

270 Al-Arian also co-founded the Islamic Association for Palestine in 1981. Its daughter organization is the Holy Land Foundation for Relief and Development. An organization affiliated with IAP, InfoCom Corporation, had its offices raided by the government.

raeli conflict and Islamic-versus-Christian culture wars from Palestinian and Islamic points of view. He had helped found the World Islamic Study Enterprise (WISE) and the Islamic Committee for Palestine (ICP).[271] These think tanks were established when the First (Palestinian) Intifada was about three years old. (Although the meaning of the word "intifada" is ambiguous, it was typically used in Arabic for "uprising" aimed at ending Israel's military occupation.)[272] Televised views of the intifada in America initially featured Palestinian teenagers throwing stones at Israeli bulldozers that were leveling Palestinian homes as well as armed clashes between Palestinian guerrilla forces and Israeli infantry units supported by tanks.

The Intifada lasted from 1987 to 1993 until the Palestinian National Authority was founded and the Oslo Accords signed. Before this period, however, the US government had adopted the term "terrorism" to brand guerrilla forces opposing its imperial partners and client fascist regimes. It supported this policy by deliberately ignoring the critical distinction between the armed uprisings directed at *military forces* and the armed attacks conducted by *terrorists* against civilians.

The political climate in the US strongly backed Israel during the Intifada and created a market for outrageous films and articles about Islamic terror-

---

271 Over a period of five years, WISE and ICP issued 20 volumes, several books and sponsored some conferences

272 Unfortunately, the territorial boundaries stipulated by the Accords were rejected by the Israeli conservatives when the labor party lost the election.

ism. In 1994, for instance, a self-styled authority on terrorism, Steve Emerson, produced an inflammatory documentary "Jihad in America," which alleged that Muslims living in the US posed a greater threat to Americans than Muslim terrorists abroad did. In April 1995, his friend, Michael Fechter, launched a career as a so-called 'terrorism expert' by insinuating in the *Tampa Tribune* that the *Oklahoma City* bombing was perpetrated by Islamic militants.[273] ("More and more, terrorism experts in the United States and elsewhere," he wrote, "say Wednesday's bombing in Oklahoma City bears the characteristics of other deadly attacks linked to Islamic militants.") The public hysteria sparked by the growing fear of terrorism enabled Fechter to market nearly 70 articles and appear on TV as an "expert" over the next six years even though the FBI found that the Oklahoma bombing was committed by two right-wing *American* terrorists, Timothy McVeigh and Terry Nichols.[274]

Then, in May 1995, the *Tampa Tribune* began to publish a rambling series of articles by Fechter claiming that Al-Arian had raised funds for Islamic terrorists abroad and that WISE, his USF think tank, had associates who were terrorists and had invited terrorists to conduct research or speak at the campus. Emerson supported Fechter's allegations by publishing recorded excerpts from Al-Arian's

---

273 His previous experience was limited to writing *Tampa Tribune* articles on local crimes, city council politics and neighborhood groups.

274 The FBI was still unsure about their identities when Fechter's article was published.

speeches and thereby invigorating his reputation as a 'media expert' by accumulating and misinterpreting this kind of data. Eventually, CNN dropped him because they felt that his interpretations were unreliable. (Later, the possibility that Fechter had collaborated secretly with Emerson was firmed up by the fact that Fechter had to leave the *St. Petersburg Times* and was hired by Emerson.)

Al-Arian was a militant defender of Palestinian rights. He condemned Israel's policy of Apartheid and the ethnic cleansing it imposed on the Arabic population who lived in territories controlled by Israel. But Al-Arian repeatedly insisted that he never advocated terrorism (e.g., the indiscriminate killing of innocent civilians). He also said that he had at first supported the Palestinian Islamic Jihad (PIJ), an organization that participated in the intifada. However, he disassociated himself from the PIJ when it adopted terrorist measures.

While speaking in Arabic at mosques, Al-Arian had used inflammatory rhetoric that had become fashionable among Muslims during the 1980s and early 1990s to rally support for the intifada. Excerpts from this rhetoric that were recorded furtively showed that he damned American foreign policy and shouted "Death to Israel." But he insisted that his defense of armed struggle did not imply that Palestinian guerrillas should attack *civilians*.[275] Besides, this kind of rhetoric had been protected by the First Amendment to the Constitution.

Even so, after the alarming *Tribune* articles ap-

---

275 The excerpts of Al-Arian's speech were reported by Emerson who had slipped into a mosque and recorded the speech.

peared, the university president, Betty Castor, suspended Al-Arian with pay while a committee headed by William Reese Smith, a former president of the American Bar Association, investigated him. The committee cleared Al-Arian of wrongdoing and he was allowed to resume teaching.

During the Nineties, the FBI also reacted to the media-induced hysteria surrounding Al-Arian's devotion to Palestinian causes. For several years, FBI agents taped tens of thousands of phone conversations between Al-Arian and his pro-Palestinian associates. It also spied on his political activities. Indeed, after examining the FBI's data, Attorney General Janet Reno concluded that Al-Arian did not support terrorism.

The Lynch Mob

Prior to 9/11, Bush courted Muslim voters because they apparently supported his candidacy. At a conference sponsored by Muslim leaders, in fact, he paused for a photo-op with Al-Arian. Even a contretemps involving Al-Arian's son, who was a Congressional aide, did not disrupt their cordial relationship. (The son was barred from a White House meeting with 20 leading Muslims who walked out when they discovered that he could not join them. Bush apologized to Al-Arian for the Secret Service's "mistake" and, in June 2001, Al-Arian was invited to a briefing with Karl Rove and 160 Muslim leaders.)

However, fifteen days after 9/11, right-wing media

demagogue Bill O'Reilly invited Al-Arian to appear on his TV talk show, *The O'Reilly Factor*. Al-Arian may have felt that he had been asked to comment on 9/11 because he was an expert on Middle-Eastern developments but when the interview was televised, O'Reilly abruptly cited fraudulent allegations made 15 years before the interview and accused Al-Arian of assisting terrorists and using his think tanks as fronts for terrorist organizations. Al-Arian was stunned. He repeatedly denied O'Reilly's accusations. He insisted that neither the FBI nor courts had found him a threat to national security. However, O'Reilly, in characteristic fashion, ended the interview by insisting that Al-Arian and his associates were terrorists—and stated that the CIA should stalk Al-Arian at all hours of the day and night.[276]

O'Reilly's remarks inflamed the Southern Florida public when it was still in shock from the devastating attacks on 9/11. As a result, Al-Arian was flooded with hate mail and death threats. Some of these messages were sent along with malicious media items to USF whose president, Judy Genshaft, announced that her obligation to ensure campus security superseded Al-Arian's right to speak freely. She placed him on paid leave and barred access to the campus.

About three months later, Genshaft initiated measures revoking Al-Arian's tenure in order to terminate employment without risking a lawsuit. Then, in December, the Board of Trustees recommended dis-

---

276 O'Reilly said sarcastically, "Yeah. Well, Doctor, you know, with all due respect—I appreciate you coming on the program, but if I was the CIA, I'd follow you wherever you went. I'd follow you 24 hours..."

missal. Al-Arian was sent two letters. The first said he was fired. But a second letter delayed his dismissal because it informed him that he was subject to being fired but not actually fired. While the university president's office was turning handsprings in order to fire him without making USF subject to a lawsuit, Fechter's slanderous allegations and Al-Arian's employment status received greater notoriety.

Nationwide and regional professional societies responded immediately. The American Association of University Professors condemned the USF administration "for grave departures from Association-supported standards" which resulted in "serious professional injury" to Al-Arian. In addition, the American Federation of Teachers (AFT) and the United Faculty of Florida, protested Al-Arian's dismissal because it violated the AFT's contract with USF, the principle of academic freedom, and the First Amendment to the Constitution.

In February 2003—without advance notice—Ashcroft and his Department of Justice zealots donned their hooded robes, mounted their white steeds and staged a "'legal lynching." Astonishingly, at a press conference, Ashcroft charged Al-Arian with being the North American leader of the Palestinian Islamic Jihad (PIJ) and the secretary of its international network. Al-Arian was arrested and imprisoned. Along with seven associates, he was indicted on 50 charges, most having to do with terrorism.

After the arrest, Al-Arian was placed in solitary confinement. Although he was imprisoned on February 20, 2003, the federal district court judge, James

Moody delayed the trial date until May 16, 2005. Al-Arian's lawyers immediately objected. They complained that the delay violated his Constitutional right to a speedy trial. But Moody refused to shorten the delay which meant that Al-Arian remained in *solitary or near-solitary confinement for almost two years and three months* before the trial began.

The federal prosecutors did not have a shred of evidence to tie Al-Arian to an act of terrorism either in Israel or the US. To compensate, they attempted to overwhelm the jury by presenting them with 80 witnesses including 21 from Israel whose families, friends, and other civilians had been killed or injured by Palestinians terrorists. The witnesses were used in a cynical attempt to inflame the jury by implying that Al-Arian was guilty of terrorism because he, like the Palestinian terrorists, also opposed Israeli policies.

Al-Arian's trial in Tampa finally commenced in June 2005. He was tried with three co-defendants and estimates indicated that the government spent $50 million dollars to get convictions. However, after deliberating for 13 days, the jury acquitted Al-Arian on 8 counts. It was overwhelmingly deadlocked— 10 to two—in favor of *acquittal* on the other nine counts. Al-Arian and his co-defendants had been originally charged with having committed altogether 51 violations of the criminal code but, in the end, no defendant was found guilty of any violation.

The government, at this point, had ample justification for ending this juridical farce and dropping the remaining charges in order to avoid the strong possibility of facing another acquittal or hung jury.

But it refused. Unless he pled guilty to one or more charges, the government threatened to keep Al-Arian in solitary confinement while it attempted to save face by setting up another trial. Faced with additional years of solitary and near-solitary confinement and the agony of being separated from his wife and five children, Al-Arian accepted the Feds' "plea bargain."[277]

On March 2, 2006, Al-Arian pled guilty to having conspired to provide financial support for the Palestinian Islamic Jihad (PIJ) and the Feds agreed to dismiss the remaining charges. The Feds declared that Al-Arian's plea provided undisputable proof that he was a terrorist. But the plea merely stated that Al-Arian had helped people who supported the PIJ with immigration matters. Given the nationwide notoriety associated with the case, the plea was pathetic. Al-Arian's so-called "terrorist acts" consisted of (1) hiring a lawyer for his brother-in-law who had in the late 1990s contested a ruling by the immigration bureau, (2) sponsoring a Palestinian historian in 1994 to conduct research in the U.S., and (3) withholding information from a journalist during a 1995 interview. Nothing in the plea agreement indicated he had supported violence or committed an illegal act Nevertheless, the agreement also forced Al-Arian to agree to being deported even though he and his wife were naturalized citizens and his five children were born in the US.

Al-Arian had lived in the US more than 25 years,

---

277 "Near solitary" means confinement with one other person in a cell that is governed otherwise by solitary confinement restrictions (e.g., regarding exercise, etc.).

but he preferred being set free even if it meant being deported. As indicated, he had spent more than three years in prison and was being threatened with another trial on the remaining charges, more years of solitary confinement and 23 hours-a-day lockdowns. His family, as the award winning documentary, *USA vs. Al-Arian*, demonstrates, had suffered enormously while he was being persecuted. Their emotional life, finances, and everyday relationships in their communities had been battered. His children had been deprived of their father and, his wife, of her husband. It is not surprising that his family favored leaving the US so that they could be with him despite the fact that they were citizens.

After a plea bargain is concluded, judges normally accept a prosecutor's recommendation. But Judge Moody flatly refused. Moody—like the Nazi judges who turned their trials of political dissidents into media events—accused Al-Arian of committing crimes that, despite all the money and efforts expended by the DoJ, could not produce a conviction. The federal prosecutor had recommended "a sentence at the low end of the applicable guideline" which meant that he would be released shortly after signing the agreement. However, Moody angrily rejected the recommendation. He sentenced Al-Arian to the maximum 57 months in prison with credit for time served—leaving him with a balance of 11 months in solitary confinement. Moody justified this extremely harsh sentence by exclaiming outrageously, "You lifted not one finger. To the contrary, you laughed when you heard of the bombings." Despite the lack of evidence and a plea bargain that did not tie Al-Arian directly to violence, Moody shouted: "You are a master manipulator. The evidence is clear in this case. You were a leader of the PIJ!"

Close scrutiny of the evidence in this case proves that Amnesty International was right. Amnesty had condemned the trial and Al-Arian's imprisonment emphasizing that the FBI spent more than a decade investigating, wiretapping, and seizing files in homes and organizations tied to Al-Arian. (The FBI had recorded almost a half million phone calls in a futile attempt to prove that Al-Arian was a terrorist or aided terrorists.) Also, federal prosecutors had spent another three years in trial preparation followed by a six-month trial. *Millions* of dollars had been expended to imprison him on unsubstantiated charges and to tear him away from his family.

Furthermore, Al-Arian had been conned by the federal prosecutors. He was led to believe that the plea agreement would finally get him out of prison and stop further persecution. But after he had undergone additional months of solitary confinement and 23 hour-a-day lockdowns, Assistant US Attorney Gordon Kromberg in the Eastern District of Virginia deliberately disregarded the agreement. He subpoenaed Al-Arian to appear before a grand jury in Virginia where Kromberg was investigating an Islamic think-tank. Kromberg had been identified as a racist and religious bigot who abused the grand-jury system by indicting Middle Easterners for perjury if he disagreed with what they said at a grand-jury hearing. [278]

---

278 Arian's lawyers had arranged to see Kromberg and, while listening to his ranting about "the Islamization of America," pointed

Federal grand juries are notorious for being used as "rubber stamps" for prosecutors. This abuse of the grand-jury system is particularly evident when political dissidents are being investigated. Nevertheless, Judge Moody ordered federal marshals to transport Al-Arian to Virginia where he was confronted by Kromberg at the grand jury hearing. Al-Arian refused to testify and was held in contempt of court on January 22, 2007. He faced a new prison sentence that could add another 18 months in solitary confinement.

To grasp Al-Arian's desperate response to these developments, we must briefly note the punitive conditions imposed on him *before* the jury acquitted him in the original trial. Despite the fact that he was a pre-trial detainee, Al-Arian had been placed in a small cell in the maximum security wing of the Federal prison in Coleman Florida. The wing, called the "Special Housing Unit," housed prisoners considered the worst—murderers, terrorists, drug traffickers, racketeers, rapists, and armed robbers—apart from other prisoners. Again, *Al-Arian was merely a pretrial detainee* but his conditions were so outrageous that Amnesty International wrote to the prison authorities calling his prison conditions "gratuitously punitive" and "a breach of international standards."

In addition, unlike privileges convicted felons enjoy with almost no red-tape, Al-Arian was denied any contact or visits with his wife or family unless his lawyers petitioned the court. He was denied the right

---

out that the plea agreement would never have been concluded if Al-Arian had known that the government would continue to persecute him.

to purchase the same food items that other prisoners could purchase from the commissary such as tea or cheese or tuna. He had difficulty getting more than pencil stubs and obtaining adequate stationary to take notes (while listening to FBI wiretaps of telephone conversations in Arabic) to work on his case.

And while he was not beaten with rubber hoses or otherwise assaulted, the guards manacled his hands in back of his body (instead of in front) and refused to carry his paperwork and publications when he met with his lawyers. As a result, he was forced to walk a considerable distance to the building in which the conference room was located, bent over, like a beast of burden with a pile of documents strapped to his back.

Because of his political beliefs, Dr. Al-Arian on January 22, 2007 faced another 18 months of physical harassment. When he appeared before a federal judge in Virginia on the charge of contempt, he said that he been transported to four prisons in three weeks. He had spent 14 days in a roach infested cell in the Atlanta penitentiary where the rats also shared his food. While being transported, his guards only permitted him to wear a t-shirt in freezing weather during long walks. He purchased a thermal undershirt from the prison but a guard threw it in the garbage. In Petersburg, a guard forced him to discard his clean underclothing and replace it with dirty and worn out clothing. During an airlift, a marshal kept him in pain by over-tightening his handcuffs. When he complained, he was met with indifference or told that he was being mistreated because he was a terrorist.

Although a diabetic, he finally went on a hunger strike to protest the government's refusal to honor it's assurance that he would not have to cooperate with federal authorities who threatened him with further prosecution. After six weeks, he collapsed, injured his head when he fell and was transferred to a federal prison medical ward in North Carolina.[279] After he had lost more than 50 pounds on the water-only diet, the prison authorities said that if his condition worsened he would be force fed despite the danger of injury.[280] Appalled by these events, Peter Erlinder, his attorney and former president of the National Lawyers Guild, said, "We're hopeful that there can be resolution before that. Gonzales could end this all with a stroke of a pen."

Attorney General Gonzales was Kromberg's boss. Consequently, Erlinder believed that Gonzales was responsible for either violating the explicit agreement upon which Al-Arian's plea was based because Gonzales either refused to rein in Kromberg, a rogue Assistant US Attorney, or intentionally violated the plea agreement himself. "In either case," Erlinder declared, "this is a direct violation of the ruling of the 4th Circuit in *US v. Garcia*, a 1992 case that makes clear that grand jury subpoenas *are* covered in [Al-Arian's] non-cooperation agreement."

During this time, Gonzales and Michael Mukasey, the Attorney General who replaced Gonzales could have ended this vicious misuse of the federal justice

---

279 Alexander Cockburn. March 4 2007. "A Federal Witchhunt: The Persecution of Sami Al-Arian." *CounterPunch*.

280 The reader can visit *freesamialarian.com/home.htm* to find out if Arian is still alive and/or protest his treatment.

system and deported Al-Arian. But they did not. After further litigation, a federal judge on January 16, 2009 ruled that Al-Arian should be tried by Kromberg on March 9, 2009 for contempt-of-court charges. The judicial ruling, moreover, said that he could not use his prior plea agreement with the government to justify his refusal to testify or cooperate with Kromberg's investigation. Jonathan Turley, a famous civil liberties lawyer, affirmed:

> They have indicted him despite the fact that the prosecutors admitted that he is a minor witness in the IIIT investigation and he has already given two detailed statements under oath to the government and offered to take a polygraph examination to prove that he has given true information about his knowledge of IIIT.[281]

February 20, 2010 marked the seventh anniversary of the arrest of Al-Arian. The Obama administration had replaced Bush's and, on June 4, 2011, Al-Arian still refused to be caught by Kromberg's perjury trap. Fortunately, when Al-Arian was finally arraigned before the federal district judge, Leonie Brinkema, she questioned the validity of Kromberg's charge, released Al-Arian from prison and placed him under house arrest until his trial takes place. He is a political prisoner but he is finally living with his family.

---

281 Turley had noted that the evidence advanced at his trial was almost entirely based on speeches, articles, books, attendance at conferences and other activities protected by the Bill of Rights. For media coverage, useful links, etc., see: "Free Sami Al-Arian," Political Prisoner Since Feb. 20, 2003. *freesamialarian.com*.

When taken as a whole, Moody's refusal to grant Al-Arian the right to a speedy trial, the cynical strategy employed by the federal prosecutors, and the cruel and inhuman punishment imposed on Al-Arian by the US gulag, cannot be attributed to careerism or fanaticism alone. The Bush administration had publicly promised to hunt terrorists who lived in America but the result of that hunt had been bizarre. That administration had arrested more than 6,400 Muslim "terrorist suspects" and, despite the mainstream media's complicity, the outcome had been pitiful.

Nevertheless, Al-Arian's persecution and imprisonment undoubtedly prevented him from becoming a major critic of U.S. foreign policies toward Israel. And his case must have played an important role in restricting support for Palestinian movements and charities that would have been provided by millions of Muslims in the US. In these two respects, the U.S. government and its bureaucratic menials succeeded in achieving these outcomes.

17 | The Counter Reformation

One of the most salient features of our culture is that there is so much bullshit.

—Harry G. Frankfurt, 2005

THE RIGHT-WING INSURGENCY

As indicated, from the late Fifties to the Eighties, civil rights, anti-war, and feminist movements undermined customary repression in academic institutions. In addition, their reforms encouraged student representation within university departments and expanded teaching opportunities for women, left-wing scholars and ethnic and/or racial minorities. "Ethnic studies," "women studies," "labor studies," and "peace studies" were introduced and students enrolled in these programs probed the underlying causes of economic, racial, and gender inequality as well as wars of aggression and social injustice.

Nevertheless, the reforms introduced during this turbulent period made no truly fundamental changes in how universities operated. In fact, after the Vietnam War, the forces that rule the dark side of our government mobilized to take back what little they had lost. Networks of wealthy foundations, government officials, right-wing journalists, and even "traditional" academics, attacked the curriculum reforms and suppressed academic freedom.

While the FBI investigated Al-Arian—in the Nineties, for example, the far-right culture warriors, David Horowitz and Peter Collier, founded the Center for the Study of Popular Culture (CSPC) reportedly to create "a conservative presence" in Hollywood as well as expose the influence of "leftists" on popular culture. To accomplish this goal, the Center actively recruited a network of conservatives and promoted rabid right-wing writers in addition to Horowitz's own racist and anti-liberal works. The Center also obtained funds for the "Wednesday Morning Club," a weekly forum for right-wingers in the entertainment industry. The Club's speakers in 1999 featured George W. Bush (then Governor of Texas), Dick Cheney, Newt Gingrich, Robert Bork, Tom DeLay, Christopher Hitchens, Henry Hyde, Trent Lott, Bill Frist, George Will, and Joseph Lieberman. The budget for the forums was steep but far-right sugar daddies—like the billionaire and newspaper publisher, Richard Mellon Scaife—

bankrolled the Center. Horowitz also founded an on-line publication called *FrontPage Magazine*. When the far-right columnist, Ann Coulter, was fired from *National Review Online* for the vicious anti-Muslim comments she made after the September 11th attacks, *FrontPage* picked up her regular column.

In September 2006, one of Horowitz's projects moved out of the shadows in the form of ABC's *Path to 9/11*, a televised miniseries that claimed Clinton did not prevent 9/11 because he was distracted by (1) the Lewinsky sex scandal, (2) his top officials were unwilling to act decisively (when bin Laden could have been killed), and (3) his anti-terrorism measures were absurd. Even though the House Intelligence Committee, intelligence officials, and terrorism experts had blamed the Bush administration for not preventing 9/11, the miniseries shamelessly turned history upside down in order to promote a Republican victory in the 2006 elections.

In the *Huffington Post*, Max Blumenthal exposed the secret network behind the ABC miniseries. He said,

> In fact, *The Path to 9/11* is produced and promoted by a well-honed propaganda operation consisting of a network of little-known right-wingers working from within Hollywood to counter its supposedly liberal bias. This is the network within the ABC network. Its godfather is far right activist David Horowitz, who has worked for more than a decade to establish a right-wing presence in Hollywood and to discredit mainstream film and TV production. On this project, he is working with a secretive evangelical religious right group founded by

> *The Path to 9/11's* director David Cunningham
> that proclaims its goal to "transform Holly-
> wood" in line with its messianic vision.[282]

Clinton, his former top officials and Senate
Democrats, denounced the miniseries and called it a
fraud. Horowitz responded with a broadside. He declared that their accusations "are easily the gravest
and most brazen and damaging governmental attacks on the civil liberties of ordinary Americans
since 9/11."[283]

Path to 9/11 was costly but far-right foundations
had deep pockets. It had a $40 million dollar price
tag and its showing on ABC was not supported by
advertising. Furthermore, reportedly, thousands of
copies were sent without charge to high school
teachers.

Around 1999, the Center also began to attack progressives in colleges and universities, eventually creating a nationwide network of students
unapologetically called Students for Academic Freedom (SAF). This network was demagogically
shielded by a self-professed allegiance to the principles of free speech and academic freedom. The SAF,
however, monitored, harassed, and discredited
teachers and administrators who justifiably enjoyed
protection by these principles.

In 2006, the Center for the Study of Popular Culture changed its name to the David Horowitz Freedom Center. It created another spin-off called the

---

282 Max Blumenthal. Sept. 8 2006. "Discover the Secret Right-Wing
   Network Behind ABC's Deception." *The Huffington Post.*
283 See *frontpagemag.com/blog/BlogEntry.asp?ID=718*

Students and Parents for Academic Freedom in K-12 Schools (PSAF). Reportedly modeled after the college and university student network (SAF), this new organization recruited parents and students linked with elementary schools, middle schools, and high schools.[284] Accordingly, PSAF expanded Horowitz's front groups and grass roots networks. It also is designed to censor and purge educational institutions.

Campus Watch is yet another nasty Horowitzian enterprise. Its mission statement claims that it "reviews and critiques Middle East studies in North America, with an aim to improving them." (It asserts that it "fully respects the freedom of speech of those it debates while insisting on its own freedom to comment on their words and deeds.") The real mission of *Campus Watch*, however, is to discredit, suppress and sack faculty associated with Middle East studies who opposed US and Israeli policies.

The wide-ranging task of identifying progressive groups and individuals and their "organizational interlocks" was handed over to Discover the Networks, a voluminous Horowitzian website providing a "guide to the political left." This website covers individuals, organizations, fundraisers, radical agendas, front groups, and networks of affiliations. It provided a history of the US left and a variety of leftist causes that are associated with civil rights, feminist,

---

284 It also intends to encourage parents and their children to spy on teachers. The Students for Academic Freedom website featured an "advertisement" titled, "Is Your Professor Using the Classroom as a Platform for Political Agendas? This is a Violation of Your Academic Rights." The ad concluded, "If your professor is abusing his or her teaching privilege or is confused about the professional obligations of an education, please contact us."

democrat, socialist, communist, anarchist, environmentalist, animal rights, homosexual, and other "anti-capitalist" and "anti-American" causes. According to Horowitz's Center, Discover the Networks is designed to be "the largest publicly accessible database defining the chief groups and individuals of the Left and their organizational interlocks." (This database undoubtedly was created to identify likely candidates for academic and publishing blacklists and to block their job placements and promotions as well.)

One subdivision in Discover the Network was entitled, Leftwing Millionaires Club, and it flatly informed online visitors "all socialist movements are the creation of intellectual elites, liberally pollinated by millionaires." The opening page of this subdivision displayed a list of 60 names including, among others, Jimmy Carter, Tom Brokaw, Bill Moyers, Dan Rather, Yasser Arafat, Jay Leno, George Clooney, Ramsey Clark, Pol Pot, Bill Clinton, Hillary Clinton, Barbara Streisand, Fidel Castro, Martin Sheen, Louis Farrakhan, Al Gore, George Soros, Jane Fonda, Danny Glover, Bill Maher, Noam Chomsky, and Ted Turner. (Why Fidel Castro, Yasser Arafat and Pol Pot were included in this wacky list is anyone's guess. But don't expect to get a rational explanation from Horowitz.)

Horowitz's Center also conducted a nationwide anti-academic freedom campaign. It was called, unbelievably, the "Academic Bill of Rights" (ABOR) campaign and it allegedly supported academic freedom for *conservative* students in order to "liberate" American universities from "liberal bias." According to the Center, its version of the Academic Bill of Rights provided model legislation for lawmakers and administrative guidelines for university trustees and administrators. (In August 2006, the Center boasted, "All public institutions of higher learning in Colorado have adopted a version of the Academic Bill of Rights. South Dakota and other states have followed suit.")

In 2007, Horowitz' propaganda factory promoted an "Islamo-Fascism Awareness Week" centered around campus forums featuring far-right luminaries, including Ann Coulter, Rick Santorum, and, of course, Horowitz. Essentially, the propaganda consisted of scarcely concealed racist and bigoted attempts to inflame fear of Muslims—suggesting that the war on terror is actually a war on Islam—and to discredit academics who truly support academic freedom. Bush had used the term "Islamofascism" (rather than Islamo-Fascism) and by 2007, other neocons including a founding neoconservative, Norman Podhoretz, an editor of *Commentary* and advisor to Rudy Giuliani (a Republican presidential candidate in favor of bombing Iran as soon as possible) were also accusing Islam of fomenting terrorists to create a world ruled by Islamofascists.

Meanwhile, *Obsession: Radical Islam's War Against The West*, a DVD containing a documentary video was mailed to millions of Americans and distributed to advertisers even though it was condemned as bigotry by some Christian, Jewish, and Muslim leaders because it compared radical Muslims to Nazis and portrayed Islam as a demonic force aiming at world-wide domination. The individuals and foundations that provided the millions for the creation and distribution of the DVD were not disclosed.

Still other candidates used the Orwellian buzzword, *Islamofacism*, to instigate fear by implying that Muslims generally posed a greater threat than Hitler's Panzers or Soviet missiles ever did. In response, Krugman remarked that

> ...there isn't actually any such thing as Islamofascism—it's not an ideology; it's a figment of the neocon imagination. The term came into vogue only because it was a way for Iraq hawks to gloss over the awkward transition from pursuing Osama bin Laden, who attacked America, to Saddam Hussein, who didn't.[285]

The war on terror is not a war on Islam. No matter how *Islamofascism* is spelled, it shoves the standpoints of Sunni insurgents, al-Qaeda, Hamas, Hezbollah, Taliban, and a host of other divergent standpoints into a magician's top hat. Although it may be a buzzword, it has little to do with the fascist ideology that developed in Germany or Italy. As conservative journalist Eric Margolis declares,

> There is nothing in any part of the Muslim World that resembles the corporate fascist states of western history. In fact, clan and tribal-based traditional Islamic society, with its fragmented power structures, local loyalties, and consensus decision-making, is about as far as possible from western industrial state fascism. The Muslim World is replete with brutal

---

285 Paul Krugman. Oct. 29 2007. "Fearing Fear Itself." *New York Times*.

dictatorships, feudal monarchies, and corrupt military-run states, but none of these regimes, however deplorable, fits the standard definition of fascism. Most, in fact, are America's allies. [286]

Of course, Middle Eastern terrorists, as Mamdani points out, have created their ideological reconstructions to claim that they are fighting the enemies of Islam. But neither Osama Bin Laden nor Horowitz should be considered an authentic authority on what version of Islam these terrorists are fighting for.

HEAVY ARTILLERY

The Horowitz Center's organizational spin-offs, propaganda arsenal, and legislative campaigns were not the only far-right enterprises aimed at controlling the minds of Americans. His assault troops were supported by a battery of big guns that also laid siege to colleges and universities.

In 1995, the American Council of Trustees and Alumni (ACTA) also began to stifle freedom of thought. (It was originally called The National Alumni Forum when it was founded by Lynne Cheney, Vice-President Dick Cheney's wife, and Senator Joseph Lieberman.) ACTA at first attacked

---

[286] The head of the Islamic Society of North America, Ingrid Mattson, said that recasting the war on terrorism as "a war against Islamic fascism" (by US President George W. Bush and other Republicans) was inaccurate and added to a misunderstanding of the religion. Mattson acknowledged, however, that terrorist groups "do misuse and use Islamic concepts and terms to justify their violence."

affirmative action, multiculturalism, and "political correctness" in colleges and universities but it expanded its mission after 9/11 to provide support for Horowitz's campaigns and to gag academics opposed to Bush's "war on terrorism." Familiar far right foundations also backed ACTA because it offered advice to large donors interested in using their millions to influence university courses and departments.[287]

ACTA reiterated Horowitz's malicious fabrications to justify its goals. It deceitfully alleged for instance that (1) university faculties are "the weak link" in America's response to 9/11 and that (2) politically intolerant professors posed the "main threat to academic freedom" on campus and that (3) professors and students want to support the US government but they are afraid that their liberal colleagues might shout them down.

ACTA used these lies to enable radical-right organizations and their representatives to dominate institutions of higher learning. For instance, *Nation* correspondent Annette Fuentes reported that "conservative Republican governors have appointed trustees who are their political allies, rather than independent advocates for the university system." She noted that in Florida ACTA worked with Governor Jeb Bush in abolishing a statewide Board of Regents —which had prevented Bush's allies from deciding who would be university presidents—and replaced them with 12-member boards of trustees at each university.[288] When Betty Castor—whose position as

---

287 ACTA in 2000 claimed that its members included wealthy donors who had contributed 3.4 billion to higher education.

288 An October 5, 1998 article entitled, "Trustees of the Right's

president had been approved by the original statewide Board of Regents—left the University of South Florida, Judy Genshaft, who was selected by the trustees appointed by Jeb Bush, replaced her. Castor, as indicated, had allowed Al-Arian to return to the campus after an investigative committee (headed by a former president of the American Bar Association) had exonerated him. But Genshaft banned and dismissed him when the right-wing *Tampa Tribune*, Bill O'Reilly, and other media personalities smeared him.

President Bush's Secretary of Education Margaret Spellings also joined the right-wing gang. Alan Jones, a dean of the faculty and Professor of Psychology and Neuroscience at Pitzer College, reported that Spellings set up a commission calling for scrapping the current system of accreditation conducted by independent regional bodies, in favor of a National Accreditation Foundation created by Congress and the President. In addition, Jones wrote,

> The current system of institutional review through independent accreditation boards is one of the hallmarks of American higher education and is one of the most important structural safeguards of the academy's ability to ensure academic quality and intellectual excellence. The introduction of oversight by an inherently partisan political body in lieu of the currently independent accreditation process is a peculiar remedy if the perceived ailment in the academy is political bias. Carol Geary Schneider, president of the American Associ-

---

Agenda," in *The Nation* by Annette Fuentes exposes ACTA's underlying goals.

ation of Colleges and Universities, has said that "the commission is sending out fire bolts, one after another." To chair this extraordinary committee Secretary Spellings chose Charles Miller, a former chairman of the University of Texas Board of Regents and, historically, a large contributor to the President's election campaigns.[289]

The ABOR Campaign

As indicated, the Horowitz Center promoted the adoption by state and federal governments of the Academic Bill of Rights (ABOR). Unsurprisingly, the legislators who sponsored the passage of this Bill represented far-right constituencies.

Dennis Baxley, a former funeral director, provides a bizarre illustration. In 2002, Florida's Republican leaders had asked him to run for the state legislature. According to James Vanlandingham, a staff writer for the *Alligator* (an independent University of Florida Gainesville student journal), Baxley reportedly hesitated in order to think and pray about the decision. "After weeks of introspection, he called his family together and said he felt God calling him to public service." Baxley agreed to run and won. He immediately voted to overturn a Constitutional amendment requiring smaller public-school class sizes. He sponsored bills aimed at increasing public subsidies (i.e. "vouchers") for students in religious schools. He also sponsored a bill that freed Floridi-

---

289 Alan Jones. May 16 2006. "Connecting the Dots." *Inside Higher Education.*

ans from criminal or civil liability if they shot anyone whom they believed threatened them.

Baxley chaired the House Education Council in 2005 when he introduced ABOR to the Florida legislature. University of Florida faculty members immediately accused him of advocating the kind of repressive legislation passed in 1956 that allowed police to actually enter classrooms while they were in session and interrogate students and teachers in order to uncover and purge left-wingers and homosexuals. However, Baxley said that comparing ABOR to the 1956 anti-communist and homophobic legislation was not justified. He insisted that ABOR was only trying to stop "liberals," "leftists," and "communists" who were persecuting conservatives in the university system. To convince his legislative colleagues and the public about the need for ABOR, he scheduled a 90-minute promotional workshop that featured Horowitz as an authority on academic freedom and as the founder of SAF. (Baxley, in fact, had admitted that the Students for Academic Freedom had inspired the bill.)

A Florida legislative analyst informed Baxley that ABOR would encourage lawsuits. Since universities were also responsible parties, the analyst had recommended that $4.2 million be set aside to hire lawyers to defend the universities if the bill passed. However, this sticky possibility hardly deterred Horowitz. With regard to ABOR, he insisted, "This bill is not to start lawsuits, but to give a kick in the pants to administrations to get their houses in order." Besides, he contended, even if lawsuits did occur, $4.2 million would be a small price to pay.

A March 2006 report issued by the Florida Office of Program Policy Analysis & Government Accountability highlighted the irony characterizing Horowitz and Baxley's campaign.[290] Despite the availability of academic freedom statements in school catalogs and student handbooks, this report found that, less than one per cent of the formal grievances, submitted by all students in Florida higher educational institutions from 2004 to 2006 had anything to do with academic freedom.

The Pennsylvania legislature had also held hearings on the bill. Split along party lines, the legislature passed a watered-down version even though the academic crisis that Horowitz invented didn't exist there. Pennsylvania colleges and universities had provided every student with the opportunity to make a complaint against the system's 8,000 professors. Penn students, however, only lodged 13 bias-related complaints over 5 years, a complaint rate of only *three hundredths of a per cent* (0.03%) per professor per year! Evidently, Horowitz assumed that a Big Lie is more believable than a little one and depended on Republican legislators to deliver the goods.

THE "DANGEROUS ACADEMICS"

In his malevolent book, *The Professors: The 101 Most Dangerous Academics in America,* Horowitz maintained that liberal and leftist professors have inflicted terrible damage because of "the unrelenting

---

290 Report No. 06-22. March 2006. The Office of Program Policy Analysis and Government Accountability.

malice so many of them hold in their hearts for a country that has given them great privileges and freedoms they enjoy as a birthright."[291] Without a shred of credible evidence, Horowitz claimed that the 101 dangerous professors were the tip of an iceberg: He believed that they typify 25,000-30,000 professors who control American institutions of higher learning. (The estimates given in public appearances went as high as 60,000) His wild assertions—and the deceptive statements used to support his estimations—indicate how far he is willing to go in order to purge educational institutions.[292] In addition, Horowitz's list of "dangerous professors" implicates the hiring policies of the foremost universities, including Harvard, Columbia, Princeton, Massachusetts Institute of Technology, U. C. Berkeley, and New York University, among others. These renowned universities despite their first class standards were on his hit list because they employed (and, in some cases, promoted) "dangerous" professors.

Grasping what Horowitz was up to does not require a familiarity with the indictments disseminated by Nazi student organizations in 1933. To show that Sami Al-Arian is dangerous, for example, Horowitz quotes an unidentified reporter, who flatly asserts,

---

291 David Horowitz. 2006. *The Professors: The 101 Most Dangerous Academics in America*, Washington DC: Regnery Publishing, Inc., p. xlvii.

292 Horowitz implies that his estimates of academic bias are based on a "representative sample." His Master's degree in English may have acquainted him with Orwell's *1984*, but his knowledge of statistics is abominable.

> The [Al-Arian] trial exposed the professor as having been enmeshed in the internal workings of Palestinian Islamic Jihad, a terrorist group that has killed well over a hundred people mostly through its favored technique of suicide bombings.[293]

This reporter (or ghostwriter) is a liar. Neither the jury nor Al-Arian's plea bargain proved that he was "enmeshed in the internal workings" of the PIJ or supported suicide bombings. The jury did not find him guilty of a single crime and the plea bargain actually signified both the Fed's attempt to save face and Al-Arian's desperate desire to be set free and rejoin his wife and children.

While describing Al-Arian's political activities, Horowitz stated,

> Professor Al-Arian supported the civil liberties coalition that formed to oppose the Patriot Act, which was in effect [merely] an extension of the Clinton anti-terrorism law. Professor Al-Arian's coalition partners included the National Lawyers Guild, the American Civil Liberties Union, and the Center for Constitutional Rights, whose lead spokesperson in the coalition was David Cole, professor of law at Georgetown University and the lawyer for Professor Al-Arian's terrorist brother-in-law, Professor Mazen al-Najjar.[294]

Thus, Horowitz claims that Al-Arian supported a

---

293 Horowitz, op cit. p 20. However, in the footnote [fn. 44] at the end of this sentence, Horowitz does not identify the source of these words.

294 Op. cit., pp. 18-19. The word "merely" (in brackets) is ours.

civil liberties coalition (composed of the ACLU and CCR) in opposition to the Patriot Act, and that David Cole—a professor of law at Georgetown University and the lawyer for Al-Arian's "terrorist" brother-in-law, Professor Mazen al-Najjar—is a "spokesman" for this coalition.[295] In this Horowitzian stream of consciousness, Al-Arian was associated with civil liberties organizations that were presumed dangerous because they opposed the Patriot Act and because they were represented by a law professor who is defending a "terrorist." Since Cole can be found in the roster of 101 scary professors, Horowitz heads back in the direction he started from—implying that Cole is assisting terrorism because he represented the anti-Patriot Act coalition and defended al-Najjar.

But the inclusion of al-Najjar unhinges Horowitz's convoluted use of guilt by association to make this bullshit fit together. Professor Mazen al-Najjar, an industrial engineer and part-time language instructor at USF, was never convicted of being a terrorist even though the Feds imprisoned him for more than three-and-a-half years before deporting him.[296] Furthermore, al-Najjar never saw the charges leveled against him. Shockingly, the Feds conducted his trial in secret. His lawyers were not allowed to see the evidence against him nor were they given an opportunity to confront his accusers.

---

295 Ibid.

296 Al-Najjar said that his prison experience was devastating: "I did not know when this nightmare could end. Is it a month, is it a day, is it a week, is it a year or is it years? I did not know. It took too long. It took three years and seven months." When he was set free, he said he lived one day at a time. He was cursed by other prisoners and only received one blanket to protect him from the cold.

Al-Najjar was finally acquitted and set free. Nonetheless, the Immigration and Naturalization Service deported him—even though he had, like his brother, married an American citizen and his daughters had been born in America.

Another Political Lynching

Unsurprisingly, Horowitz especially objects to ethnic, women's, and peace studies programs. He claimed that "activists" rather than "scholars" are ensconced in these programs and, to prove it, used Ward Churchill—who had chaired the Colorado University Ethnic Studies Department—as the poster boy for all the perilous things occurring in American colleges and universities.

In a brief essay hastily written the day after 9/11, Churchill tied the attacks on the World Trade Center and the Pentagon to a war perpetrated by the "Christian West" beginning with the Crusades, against the "Islamic East." According to Churchill, the war had had a thousand-year history but the Gulf War, US Overflghts, and economic sanctions resurrected it after a lull. By the beginning of the new millennium, these events had already led to the deaths of a half-million children and over a million and a half Iraqis, because the 1991 US "surgical bombing" had destroyed Iraqi water purification and sewage facilities, as well as other "infrastructural" targets upon which Iraqi civilians depended for their survival. For a full decade, periodic bombing raids, the embargo and other US-imposed sanctions ratcheted-up the death toll by blocking the import of nutrients, medicines, and other life-saving materials.[297] This ideological warfare, Churchill declared, is a crime against humanity, "entailing myriad gross violations of international law, as well as every conceivable standard of "civilized" behavior." The attacks on 9/11, in Churchill's view, represented a response "in kind" to the genocidal policies the US has long dispensed "as a matter of course" on the Iraqi people.

Churchill's indictment included such offenders as the corporate managers, stock brokers, bond traders, finance, and systems analysts" and other members of "a technocratic corps at the very heart of America's global financial empire" that operated as causal agents behind the scenes. In his opinion, this corps was indirectly responsible for the 9/11 attacks because they fulfilled their imperial functions "both willingly and knowingly." Astonishingly, he said they were comparable to the "Good Germans" who administered the Holocaust. They, too, served as "little Eichmanns" even though they inhabited "the sterile sanctuary of the twin towers." Churchill added:

> To the extent that any of them were unaware of the costs and consequences to others of what they were involved in—and in many cases excelling at—it was because of their absolute refusal to see. More likely, it was because they were too busy braying, incessantly and self-importantly, into their cell phones, arranging

---

297 The original 2001 article was reprinted on the website, *Political Gateway.* (*politicalgateway.com/index.html.*). Churchill's book provides greater support for his original article. See Ward Churchill. 2003. *On the Justice of ROOSTING CHICKENS— Reflections on the Consequences of U.S. Imperial Arrogance and Criminality.* Oakland, CA: AK Press.

power lunches and stock transactions, each of which translated, conveniently out of sight, mind and smelling distance, into the starved and rotting flesh of infants.

Churchill's reference to Adolph Eichmann in his essay implicitly evoked Hannah Arendt's refusal to depict Eichmann as a pathologically cruel individual. After observing Eichmann at his trial, she concluded that his record signified the "banality of evil." Eichmann had been a bureaucrat who had helped engineer the holocaust because of a sense of obligation and loyalty to the state. He was ambitious and opportunistic but he was a "good German" too who followed orders faithfully. Consequently, the phrase "little Eichmanns" referenced the corps of "faceless bureaucrats and technical experts" who profited by managing the financial workings of "America's genocidal world order." This corps, in Churchill's opinion, helped create the conditions that gave rise to terrorism. Americans, he declared, should recognize that "the chickens came home to roost" on 9/11 because the "little Eichmanns" had been morally responsible for these conditions.

Academic critics have responded to Churchill's interpretation of the events behind 9/11 but their criticism illustrates what can happen when a colleague proposes politically controversial ideas. His phrase "little Eichmanns" was brilliant and despite the flaws associated with his essay, it draws attention to numerous examples of war crimes and crimes against humanity perpetrated, for instance, by US troops in the Philippines a century ago when they followed orders to slaughter every male Filipino over the age of ten, resulting in the death of one in every six inhabitants on the island of Luzon.

As a result, academic disagreements with Churchill's essay do not detract from his central theme, first expressed in his 2001 article and then expanded in a 2003 book, *On the Justice of Roosting Chickens: Reflections On the Consequences of US Imperial Arrogance and Criminality*. Other academics had previously exposed the war crimes and crimes against humanity perpetrated historically by US government policies. Furthermore, two years after the publication of Churchill's book, a shocking memoir, *Confessions of an Economic Hit Man*, by John Perkins, provided evidence that makes Churchill's use of the phrase, "little Eichmanns," credible.

John Perkins revealed that "hit men" like himself aided the International Monetary Fund, the World Bank, and the US State Department by offering leaders of South American nations the options of taking "bribes or a bullet" if they refused to cooperate with these agencies. The NSA had secretly recruited Perkins for this job although he was officially employed by an international consulting firm and assigned to Indonesia, Panama, Ecuador, Saudi Arabia, and other strategically important countries. Under the cover of providing consultation that would diminish poverty, he pressured governments, banks, and corporations to adopt policies that inadvertently gave rise to anti-Americanism and terrorism.

Almost two years after the publication of Churchill's 2001 essay, a conservative student at Ball

University, Virginia, protested a forthcoming visitation (and speech) by Churchill. This student wrote an article in the student-run newspaper that misquoted and misrepresented Churchill's essay. He accused Churchill of using the phrase "little Eichmanns" to smear all the victims of the 9/11 massacre. This student was obviously unaware of the fact that Churchill's analogy referred to the behavior of a bureaucrat, Eichmann, who, despite the demands for railroad cars from military forces during the war, commanded the transportation of Jews in box cars from all parts of Nazi occupied Europe. Churchill's essay never said that 9/11 was payback time for all the people killed that day—especially not the firefighters, janitors, clerical, and food service workers!

Nevertheless, the media's ultra-right attack dogs exploited the student's ignorance and called for a political lynching. O'Reilly, Hannity, and other right-wing talk-show hosts immediately charged Churchill with treason. To avert further scandal, Ball University canceled his speech and its president resigned.

Colorado Governor Bill Owen, a right wing Republican who opposed abortions, gay and lesbian rights, affirmative action and "the left," and who demanded that universities employ "patriotically correct" professors, declared hypocritically, "No one wants to infringe on Mr. Churchill's right to express himself. But we are not compelled to accept his pro-terrorist views at state taxpayer subsidy nor under the banner of the University of Colorado." Owen noted that Churchill had responded to the political hysteria by resigning as Ethnic Studies Chair; but he urged Churchill to resign his faculty position as well and leave the University. The Colorado House of Representatives joined Governor Owen's lynch mob, called Churchill a traitor, and demanded his dismissal.

Naturally, publications or speaking engagements that exposed the murderous policies of the US government drove right-wingers (like Horowitz, Owen, and their academic toadies) up-the-wall. These enemies of free speech and academic freedom believed that neither Churchill nor others who accuse the government of engaging in genocide, among other things, have the right to speak their minds. They also believe those teachers in elementary schools, middle schools, high schools, colleges, and universities—or anywhere else for that matter—that refuse to be silenced should be harassed, censored, dismissed, and blacklisted.

Long-lasting effects of customary repression, especially among right-wing politicians, backed their play. From the 1950s onward, civil rights movements and increasing numbers of Americans have experienced success in struggling for equality. But even though Jim Crow laws have been shattered, racism survives—especially in job markets, housing markets, and law enforcement. A foremost facet of this repression includes a black hole that sucks the chronicle of oppression of Native and African Americans into an invisible dimension and leaves behind a collective memory afflicted with Alzheimer's disease.

Predictably, a politically significant constituency of right-wing Republicans and Reagan Democrats remained in Colorado and their racist spokespersons eagerly formed the lynch mob that sacked Churchill.

While the vigilantes were chasing Churchill, legal counselors told Owen and Philip P. DiStefano, the Colorado University Chancellor, that the university could be sued if the actual text of Churchill's article (rather than its misrepresentation) was used to justify the dismissal. As a result, DiStefano dropped the original charges because they could be hard to prove in court. He appointed a committee composed of academic Keystone Kops and a staff member who probed Churchill's personal history and his numerous and highly annotated books, essays, and reviews to find anything that would support the decision to fire him. Every one of the Committee's findings and indictments has been challenged and, as Noam Chomsky, Howard Zinn, and other notable progressives believe, none of them justifies his dismissal.

18 | Behind the Scenes

Money Talks, Bullshit Walks

—Popular Saying

Bullshit as Modus Operandi

Many writers have called the campaigns launched by David Horowitz and ACTA, "The New McCarthyism." But this label in certain respects is too mild. Granted, the word "McCarthyism" refers to a nation-wide repressive movement, operating during the Fifties and Sixties, but the current attempts at thought-control go beyond anything Sen. McCarthy had in mind. When McCarthy attacked the State Department, he held a single sheet of paper aloft at the Republican Women's Club of Wheeling, West Virginia, and declared, "I have here in my hand a list of 205 people that were known to the Secretary of State as being members of the Communist Party, and who, nevertheless, are still working and shaping the policy of the State Department." McCarthy had plucked this number out of thin air when the Korean War was going badly in order to discredit Truman's administration.[298]

Still, compared to the current crop of far-right inquisitors, McCarthy was crude. He played the game of "naming names" (of Communists and fellow travelers) and identifying "front groups" that were not what they seemed. However, the fabrications employed by today's ideologues like Horowitz, Collier and (Lynn) Cheney conceal their true intentions more effectively.

Horowitz, for instance, insisted that he wanted to unshackle academic freedom so that students and faculty alike can speak their minds. Actually, he was trying to destroy academic freedom. He is adept at naming names and engaging in character assassination yet denies any interest in a political purge. He persistently attacks university administrators who believe that progressives should have right to speak freely—but he rarely admits publicly that these administrators should be replaced or that they should do everything in their power to shift the academic workforce rightward. Above all, while bullshitting about his "righteous" desire to provide academic freedom for students and faculty alike, he wants lawmakers to produce laws that will help the far-right forcibly silence or purge dissidents from thousands of educational institutions.

In an article entitled, "David Horowitz' War on

---

298 McCarthy named as subversives leading Democrats associated with FDR's New Deal policies. He considered President Truman a dangerous liberal and his campaign helped the Republican candidate, Dwight Eisenhower, win the presidency in 1952.

Rational Discourse", Graham Larkin, a humanities fellow at Stanford University—where he teaches in the Department of Art and Art History—pointed out that Horowitz employed bullshit as a modus operandi and therefore his wily statements were not restricted to outrageous lies, cooked statistics, race baiting, guilt by association, and editorial foul play.[299]

Larkin clarified this point by referring to Harry G. Frankfurt's book, *On Bullshit*. (Frankfurt is a renowned moral philosopher and University of Princeton professor emeritus.) While differentiating a liar from a bullshitter, Frankfurt observes that a liar knows the truth while trying to pass off information that is not true. ("Someone who lies and someone who tells the truth," Frankfurt writes, "are playing on opposite sides, so to speak, in the same game.") The bullshitter, by contrast, doesn't give a hoot about whether anything is true or false. "The fact about himself that the bullshitter hides, in contrast to the liar, is that the truth of his statements are of no central interest to him; what we are not to understand is that his intention is neither to report the truth nor to conceal it."

Let us restate these ideas in familiar terms. If a traveling salesman is selling snake oil, he might be telling the truth when he claims that it will reduce pain because it contains laudanum, a tincture of opium. However, while he is actually telling the truth, the truth or falsity of his claim is irrelevant. What counts is his appearance of sincerity. He will

---

299 Graham Larkin. April 25 2005. "David Horowitz's War on Rational Discourse." *Inside Higher Ed* (*insidehighered.com*).

use anything—truths, half-truths, little lies, big lies— to make a sale. Furthermore, the pitchman does not even have to know *when* he is lying *while* he is bull-shitting. Certainly, he does lie when he markets snake oil as a universal remedy but excessive bull-shitting can undermine his ability to tell the truth and *he may actually believe his own bullshit regardless of how false it may be.*

Of course, Horowitz never forgets to indict the usual suspects. A professor is dangerous if he has ever been a member of the Socialist or Communist Party or, for that matter, so is any organization that has opposed the imperial and racist policies of the US government such as Students for a Democratic Society. But Horowitz also contends that academics do not have the right to share their thinking about political repression at professional conferences. To show that the radical left has "colonized a significant part of the university system", he reports that the Political Science Association's 2005 annual meeting had a panel (on the Bush administration) entitled, "Is It Time to Call It Fascism?" Horowitz contends that the panel *should not have been scheduled*. To justify his stand, he merely says, "Given the vibrant reality of American democracy in the year 2005, this was obviously a political rather than a scholarly agenda."[300]

"Vibrant reality of American democracy?" Not according to Harvard Professor Neil Gross who surveyed social science professors in 2006 and found that about one-third felt their academic freedom was threatened. In contrast, Columbia University's Prof.

---

300 Op. cit. p.xxv.

Paul Lazersfeld did a similar survey in 1965 and discovered only one-fifth of the professors felt that they were affected by attacks on their academic freedom.[301] Evidently, Horowitz's slick criterion for a valid scientific inquiry was tailored opportunistically to the current political circumstances and, if one line of bullshit in any given instance is not appropriate for censoring scientific inquiries, another replaces it.

Money Talks

In the late Eighties, right-wing philanthropic foundations stepped-up funding for the production of "knowledge" specifically designed to influence popular thinking in the United States. By the Nineties, they synchronized their grants for national and regional think tanks, legal service centers, magazines, scholastic journals, and other publications that reached millions. The infrastructure created by their grants turned publications into best-sellers, promoted conservative academics, monitored liberals and leftists and stage-managed the traditional media.

Hard cash set-off the avalanche of bullshit and the spin-offs produced by Horowitz's Center. A memo prepared by Trent Douthett for the American Association of University Professors about the Center's funding sources reported that it received over three and a half million dollars from 2001 to 2003 from the Bradley, Scaife, and Olin foundations. The Ja-

---

301 Scott Jaschik. Aug 15. 2007. "Pessimistic Views on Academic Freedom." *Inside Higher Ed.*

cobs Foundation provided another $20,000 for 2002 and 2003. The Krebble Foundation gave $55,000 in 2003. Still other foundations could be counted but Douthett could not determine their contributions.[302]

Yet Horowitz's grants were comparatively small potatoes. Sally Covington, in a 1998 report commissioned by the National Committee for Responsive Philanthropy (NCRP), indicated that 12 foundations over a two-year period (1992-1994) gave conservative causes a total of $210 million (out of grants totaling $300 million). Unlike middle-of-the-road and liberal philanthropies (e.g., the Ford Foundation), nearly half the money covered operating costs, which allowed conservative agencies to devote less energy to fundraising and gave them greater control over how to spend the money. "[G]rants were focused on building institutions, not programs, with foundations remaining faithful to their grantees year after year, sometimes for decades at a time."[303] Covington also reported,

> The vast majority of grants was awarded to institutions which make an aggressive and presumptive case for industrial and environment-

---

302 See, for instance, Trent Douthett. April 6 2005. "Horowitz Funding Sources." [Memo to Senator Fedor.] AAUP.

303 Horowitz's Center for the Study of Popular Culture or the Heritage Foundation, Cato Institute, Washington Legal Foundation, *American Spectator*, *Weekly Standard*, Fox News Channel, and Clear Channel networks would never have come into existence without these grants. Furthermore, was it not for the Milwaukee Foundation, the pioneering attempts to privatize public school education, and subsidize religious schools through "school vouchers" may have not succeeded.

al deregulation, the privatization of government services, deep cuts in government programs serving low income constituencies, reductions in capital gains and corporate income taxes and the transfer of social programs from government to the charitable sector.

Eighty per cent of the 12 foundations funded academic sector organizations and programs. "Tens of millions of dollars have been invested in the Law and Economics movement, which has gained immense influence in leading law schools as a pseudo-scholarly crusade against regulation."[304] Funding conservative projects at Yale, Harvard, Stanford, and the University of Chicago, for instance, created a corps of scholars who make conservative media celebrities seem credible because academic specialists back them up.

Conservative legal organizations have also opened the way for a radical transformation of the American legal system. The Federalist Society for Law and Public Policy Studies, for instance, has a membership exceeding 40,000 lawyers, policy experts, and business leaders. It largely promotes education programs for judges and lawyers that discredit liberal precedents. Its publications and forums assault the foundations of civil- and voting-rights legislation. It resists legal protections for labor and celebrates juridical rejection of laws opposing age and gender discrimination and sexual harassment in the workplace. It undermines the separation of church and state by advocating public support for "faith-based" welfare programs, "vouchers" for religious schools, teaching creationism, and distributing religious publications in public

304 Jedediah S. Purdy. January-February 1998. "The Chicago Acid Bath: The Impoverished Logic of Law and Economics." TAP.

schools.

The Federalist Society insists that it is politically "non-partisan" but this claim is bullshit. The Departments of Justice during the Reagan and Bush administrations filled their ranks with Federalists.[305] Although the Society keeps its membership rolls secret and Chief Supreme Court Justice John G. Roberts claimed that he was not a member after 2001, when Bush appointed him to the US Court of Appeals, he was on the Society's Washington Chapter Steering Committee according to its 1997-1998 Leadership Directory. As Jerome Shestack, a former American Bar Association president (ABA) indicates, the Society has become extraordinarily successful in politicizing law schools, the courts, and the selection and confirmation of federal judges. C. Boyden Gray, a longtime leader of the Federalist Society, was Bush's former White House Counsel and employed a co-founder of the Society to screen candidates for the federal bench. And Shestack reveals that former Iran-Contra special prosecutor Lawrence Walsh has written that he was "especially troubled that one of White House Counsel Boyden Gray's assistants had openly declared that no one who was not a member of the Federalist Society had received a judicial appointment from President Bush."

Predictably, leading Federalists have succeeded in blocking the ABA from providing the Senate Judiciary Committee with genuinely nonpartisan evaluations of the candidates for juridical appointments. The ABA is the largest and oldest voluntary organization of

---

305 Supreme Court Justice Antonin Scalia was a faculty adviser to the University of Chicago's Federalist Society chapter in the 1980s.

American lawyers, law students and judges. It was formed in 1878 and it has over 400,000 members today. It has played a major role in providing law-school accreditation, maintaining professional ethics, continuing legal education, and advising legislators about lawyers and policies that can improve the legal system. It has been accused of giving lower rankings to Bush administration appointees than Clinton's but this so-called "bias" may have actually reflected unbiased evaluations of professional worth.

Traditionally, the Senate Judiciary Committee has considered ABA recommendations for appointments to federal courts. However, Supreme Court Justice Clarence Thomas, denounced the ABA in the keynote address on "judicial independence" at the 1999 Federalist Society Convention. After claiming that the ABA was incapable of reforming itself, Thomas juxtaposed the ABA, which he called "an interest group," with the Federalist Society. He candidly stated, "The Federalist Society, by the way, should be commended for maintaining the wall of separation between law and politics."[306] Subsequently, Senator Orrin Hatch, Senate Judiciary Committee Chair and Co-chair of the Federalist Society Board of Visitors, announced that he would defy tradition by refusing to invite the ABA to participate as a consultant in the Senate judicial confirmation process" even though Bush's appointments were being vetted by Federalists.

The reasons for Hatch's abhorrence of the ABA

---

306 Shestak observes, "Shortly thereafter, the Federalist Society announced that it would develop 'voter guides' for ABA elections —an unprecedented effort to influence the governance of the ABA. This is reminiscent of the Christian Coalition's allegedly partisan efforts to influence elections by regularly issuing voting guides."

were obvious. In July 2006, for example, an ABA task force released a report that concluded George W. Bush's use of "signing statements" violates the Constitution. (Again, these are documents attached by the President to bills he signs, in which he states that he will enforce the new law only to the extent that he feels the law conforms to his personal interpretation of the Constitution.) So-called "liberal" stands on gun control and abortion also provoked Hatch and other Federalists to discredit the ABA.

While the Federalists and other conservative institutions were tearing democratic jurisprudence apart, academics—whatever their party affiliation—tended to be conservative when teaching economics. An economics professor, Mike Meeropol, indicates, "Left perspectives are ruthlessly excluded from most economic departments, so that research and teaching in the field has a distinct right-wing bias." Meeropol backs this point with sales figures for economic textbooks. Four left-leaning textbooks combined sold at most 8,000 copies in 2005. "Meanwhile, just to name one mainstream text, McConnell's and Brue's *Economics* sells about 215,000 copies annually." *Economics* merely contains one mention of Marx and a reference to an online chapter devoted to his theory of surplus value.[307] Meeropol uses another leading textbook, written by N. Gregory Mankiw—who is on the Harvard economics faculty and served as chair of Bush's Council of Economic Advisors. Notes Meeropol, "[It] is a measure of extreme rightward

---

307 McGraw-Hill's marketing department estimates that the textbook has a 23.2% overall market share in a market of about 930,000.
Mike Meeropol. July-August 2006. "Dangerous Academics." *Dollars and Sense.*

drift of economics education that Mankiw's textbook sidelines even Keynes."

CREEPING FASCISM

Previously, we asked, "How do we know that neo-fascism is waiting in the wings—when the curtain opens or when it is onstage and confronting an American audience?" Finding a clear-cut answer is difficult because the widespread approval of customary repression obscures the search for fascist precursors—especially when the precursors themselves have customary features. In Al-Arian's case, for instance, the University of South Florida and the Department of Justice Department desecrated academic freedom and the First and Fifth Amendments; however, these outrageous violations by themselves did not make his case a harbinger of neo-fascism. In fact, when historical precedents are recalled, his persecution is in line with standard operating procedures for suppressing academics.

Neither did neo-fascism appear on the horizon when additional cases are considered. Brigham Young University jerked Prof. Stephen E. Jones out of his classrooms and put him on paid leave, assigning other professors to teach his physics courses. Despite the fact that Jones had taught at Brigham U since 1985, he was forbidden to teach because he had posted essays on a website (called Scholars for Truth) contending the US government had staged 9/11. Since his writings were restricted to a website, a university spokesperson was asked if other faculty members would find their jobs threatened if they wrote op-ed pieces or spoke at rallies. She responded by dismissing the question and insisting that Brigham Young was "committed to academic freedom." Jones, she said pathetically, was on paid leave because his writings (on the website) had not been cleared by a professional review.

Brigham Young, as you would have thought, had a dumpster overflowing with sorry excuses because the AAUP had censured the university in 1998. The university's assaults on academic freedom and constitutionally protected speech were found to be "distressingly common." And its continuing assaults had kept it on the AAUP's censure list.[308]

In March 2005, Prof. Jonathan Cole, a Columbia University provost and dean of faculties from 1989-2003, protested the new inquisition.

> Today, a half century after the 1954 House Un-American Activities Committee held congressional hearings on communists in American universities, faculty members are witnessing once again a rising tide of anti-intellectualism and threats to academic freedom. They are increasingly apprehensive about the influence of external politics on university decision making. The attacks on professors like Joseph Massad, Thomas Butler, Rashid Khalidi, Ward Churchill, and Edward Said, coupled with other actions taken by the federal government in the name of national security, suggest that we may well be headed for another era of intolerance and repression. The United States paid a

---

308 Scott Jaschik. Sept. 11 2006. "Frays on Academic Freedom," *Inside Higher Education*. See file entitled, "Academic freedom cases."

heavy price when the leaders of its research universities failed in the 1950s to defend the leader of the Manhattan Project J. Robert Oppenheimer; the double Nobel Prize chemist Linus Pauling; and the China expert Owen Lattimore. But a wave of repression in American universities today is apt to have even more dramatic consequences for the nation than the repression of the Cold War.

Cole believes that the current violations of academic freedom are undermining the international preeminence of American universities and threaten scientific innovation, as well as the welfare and prosperity of the nation. According to Cole, German universities still haven't regained scientific ground lost from purging researchers accused of engaging in "Jewish science." Japanese universities deteriorated after purging dissident intellectuals in 1935. And Soviet genetics never fully recovered from Lysenkoism, imposed by Stalin.

Cole also recalls that Darwin's theory has been purged from the high school science curriculum in at least 13 states because of political pressure to include (as alternatives) religious theories dubbed "creationism" and "intelligent design." What's next? A return to 1925 when Tennessee tried John T. Scopes—a high school football coach who had substituted for the principal in a science class—for illegally teaching Darwin's' theory? The intrusion of political or religious criteria for determining truth is not the only reason why government policies represent a throwback to the dark ages. Foreign students are harassed and even denied entry into the United States without any evidence that they are security risks. As a result,

American professors cannot work with gifted foreign scientists and students. Open scholarly communication is impeded by policies designed to isolate nations accused of supporting terrorism; library and computer records are searched; political litmus tests were used by the Bush administration to decide who will serve on scientific advisory committees; and scientific reports whose content is inconsistent with the Bush administration's ideology have been altered. Even though the National Institutes of Health supported the research, some members of Congress almost succeeded in rescinding funding for projects on HIV/AIDS. Another bill, House Resolution 3077, almost succeeded in mandating direct government oversight of university geographical "area studies" programs devoted to interdisciplinary study of geographical or cultural areas such as Middle Eastern studies or ethnic studies. (The bill passed the House but died in the Senate).

Of course, some things remain the same. According to Cole, the FBI indicted Dr. Thomas Butler, a leading expert on plague bacteria, for violating the Patriot Act's requirement for reporting on the use and transport of specific biological agents and toxins that in principle could be used by bioterrorists. (Butler failed to obtain a transport permit for moving the bacteria from Tanzania to his Texas laboratory, as he had done for the past 20 years.) Although he was acquitted of all charges related to the Patriot Act, the FBI searched his lab at Texas Tech University, scrutinized his accounts, and then added on 54 counts of tax evasion, theft, and fraud unrelated to the Patriot Act. The FBI eventually convicted him on the basis of some of these additional counts and Cole reported that "the upshot of all of this was that he [Butler] lost his medical license, was fired from his job, and now, if he loses his appeal, faces up to nine years in jail."

What about Butler's ability to conduct research that would protect Americans from bioterrorists? Forget it! Obviously, the FBI is no different from prosecutors at every level of government who justify their existence by winning at all costs regardless of the consequences.

During the anthrax scare following 9/11, Ashcroft publicly smeared Dr. Steven J. Hatfill of Louisiana State University (LSU) as "a person of interest." Although Hatfill was never charged with any crime, LSU fired him. Furthermore, faculty members at other institutions also suffered unannounced and intimidating visits from the FBI to their homes or campus offices. "These crude efforts to enforce the Patriot Act have already had serious consequences. Robert C. Richardson, whose work on liquid helium earned him a Nobel Prize in Physics, has described the atrophy of bioterrorism research at Cornell." Richardson painfully reports,

> The Patriot Act, which was passed after 9/11, has a section in it to control who can work on "select agents," pathogens that might be developed as bioweapons. At Cornell [before 9/11], we had something like 76 faculty members who had projects on lethal pathogens and something like 38 working specifically on select agents. There were stringent regulations for control of the pathogens—categories of foreign nationals who were not allowed to handle them, be in a room with them or even be aware

of research results. So what is the situation now? We went from 38 people who could work on select agents to two. We've got a lot less people working on interventions to vaccinate against smallpox, West Nile virus, anthrax and any of 30 other scourges.[309]

In "Academic Freedom Under Fire," Cole questioned whether America's security is protected when the government turns our best immunology and biodefense laboratories into ghost towns. He adds,

Periodically, often during times of national fear, political leaders and ideologues on the Right and the Left have silenced dissent and pressured universities to abandon their most fundamental values of free and open inquiry. Most university leaders and faculty members fell easily into line during the First Red Scare of 1919 -1921 and during the reign of Joseph McCarthy. As historians Ellen Schrecker and Sigmund Diamond have shown, presidents and trustees of research universities often publicly espoused civil liberties, academic freedom, and free inquiry while privately collaborating with the FBI to purge faculty members accused of holding seditious political views.[310]

Does the new academic inquisition provide evidence of creeping fascism? A reaction to a speech made by Horowitz at a campus meeting raises this possibility. Jo Schaffer is a retired SUNY Cortland

---

309 Quoted in Claudia Dreifus. July 6 2004. "The Chilling of American Science: A Conversation with Robert C. Richardson." *The New York Times*.

310 Jonathan R. Cole. Spring 2005. "Academic Freedom under Fire." *Daedalus*,

professor who attended the meeting, which was sponsored by the Young Republicans and the national Young America's Foundation. After making copious notes, she reported, "What an experience! Had I closed my eyes and translated his phrases into German, I would have sworn I had been transported to Thirties Germany. He ranted; he raved; he rambled. He didn't support his statements with documentation."

Horowitz claimed, according to Schaffer, that a "University Communist Party" was undermining universities; that her campus had only one conservative on its faculty; and that he couldn't find a single statement about academic freedom in any published campus sources. (All of these claims were lies.) After accusing the Cortland faculty of getting unwarranted salaries and "lifetime jobs," he told students in the audience that their tuitions could be cut in half if their faculty taught more courses. The faculty listening to National Public Radio were called "Islamofascists." Schaffer said Horowitz even had the gall to claim that liberal and left-wing faculty members were responsible for failing inner-city schools, and that Democrats, Progressives, Marxists, unions, immigrants should be ground to dust. "The most pernicious moment of the evening was when he called a senior, distinguished professor unfit to teach because a political cartoon hung on his office door."

Some academics believe that Horowitz was merely interested in identifying individuals but they mistake his primary aim. Professors indicted by his work were labeled "dangerous" because their particular writings and speeches condemned the Bush administration, denounced the war in Iraq, or accused Israeli officials of war crimes. Editing *The Nation* or merely publishing liberal textbooks and articles is dangerous as well.

Further scrutiny also demonstrates that liberal and leftist ideas horrify him. The 101 professors threatened Americans because they protested McCarthyism, condemned neoliberalism, espoused Marxian notions, attributed poverty to the logic of capitalism, praised Cuba's public health program, affirmed women's reproductive rights, advocated gender and racial equality, supported women's, ethnic or peace studies programs, blamed the deaths of 1.5 million Iraqis during the Nineties on economic sanctions, expressed anti-religious prejudices, or advocated any and all conceivable notions, perspectives, affiliations, or acts that signify liberal or leftist inclinations.

TRAITOR BAITERS

Let us recall that traditional political labels were undergoing unprecedented changes. Buoyed by the rightward shift, neoliberals in the Democratic Party were called "moderates" while "liberal" has become a derogatory metaphor for left-of-center alternatives. In turn, New Deal Democrats were merged with the traditional left in the style of the Thirties when conservatives routinely called FDR and other liberals "Socialists" and "Communists." As indicated in Chapter 13, a variety of disparaging labels are being employed in myths about a new "class war" conducted by bureaucrats, technocrats, academics, tree huggers, hippies, faggots, commies, lesbos, and tax-and-spend liberals. Like the Nazi fabrication of a worldwide Jewish conspiracy, American right-wing populists contend that their comic strip characters constitute ruling elites that run the government at the expense of ordinary people.

Consequently, by 2006, old-fashioned interpretations of liberalism were hardly recognizable. The di-

[Image via www.worldcantwait.org]

verse world-views represented in Germany prior to 1933 by republicans, social democrats, independent socialists, communists, and anarchists were now being dismissed as "liberalism" or "leftist." Furthermore, broad right-wing categories like "liberalism" defied singular definitions. They could be expanded until they occupied all the space besides the far-right wing of American politics or collapsed so they filled a hallway closet stuffed with the Marx brothers—who tumbled hilariously into the hallway when the closet door was jerked open.[311]

The Al-Arian case illustrated how right-wing institutions were treating intellectuals. Of course, such illustrations can reach back to Socrates although the modern inquisition is more effectively evoked by the imprisonment of Galileo Galilei, whose theories and methods represented a turning point in the evolution of modern science. Galileo's rejection of the celestial mechanics imposed by the Roman Catholic Church was the classic instance of how academic freedom enables scholars to expand humanity's understanding of natural and social relationships. In Galileo's case, a counter-reformation movement led by 16th-century Jesuit scholars at the Collegio Romano, in Rome, had campaigned against scientists who denied that the Earth was the center of the universe and thus undermined their dogmatic interpretation of biblical events. Working covertly at first, these inquisitors gradually mounted a campaign that convicted Galileo as a heretic and for all practical purposes put him in near-solitary confinement by

---

311 This madcap scene took place in the movie Night at the Opera.

sentencing him to house arrest.[312] His health deteriorated while he was confined. His mail was censored and he was afflicted with almost total blindness until he died in 1638.

In *Banana Republicans: How the Right Wing is Turning America into a One-Party State*, Sheldon Rampton and John Stauber chronicle the growing repression of political dissent and the degradation of democracy. Conservatives, they cogently argue, routinely accuse liberals and leftists of treason—especially if Bush's invasion of Iraq was opposed. Substituting the phrase, "Traitor Baiter" for "Red Baiter," Rampton and Stauber show how the new-fangled witch-hunters bait their political opponents. For instance, Horowitz warns everyone, "If the word 'traitor' has any meaning at all, Noam Chomsky is an American traitor, and in fact the leading advocate of the call for all progressive citizens of America to betray their country."[313]

Right-wing radio shows feature traitor baiters. Take Melanie Morgan who in 2006 co-hosted the fourth-highest-rated morning show in the San Francisco Bay area. Despite all evidence to the contrary, she still insisted that Saddam Hussein had weapons of mass destruction and that global warming may not be taking place. She raised money for an advertisement before the 2006 election that dumped the

---

312 Pietro Redondi. 1987. *Galileo Heretic.* (trans. Raymond Rosenthal) New Jersey: Princeton University Press.

313 Sheldon Rampton and John Stauber. 2004. *Banana Republicans: How the Right Wing is Turning America into a One-Party State.* New York: Jeremy P. Starcher/Penguin, p.181.

blame for Bush's failure to prevent 9/11 on Clinton.[314] She called for the jailing and possible execution for treason of *New York Times* editor Bill Keller because he had approved articles exposing the administration's clandestine surveillance of international bank transfers to track terrorist financing. She told the *San Francisco Chronicle* in June 2006 that if Keller was actually convicted of treason, she would have no problem if he was sent to "the gas chamber" because he revealed classified secrets in time of war.

Morgan, true to form, did not mention the fact that *The Los Angeles Times*, *Wall Street Journal*, and *Washington Post* had also disclosed the information immediately after the *New York Times* article appeared, because the massive data mining operation behind the so-called "classified information" represented an abuse of power and an invasion of privacy rights. Other professionals felt so strongly that the public had a right to know about the classified project that they awarded the *New York Times'* article the Pulitzer Prize for outstanding journalism.

Anonymous sponsors of the Internet website, *AmericanTraitor.US*, represent another genus of traitor baiting.[315] This website appeared online a few

---

314 Morgan provided propaganda that helped to remove smog checks and other curbs on toxic emissions in California. In addition, as Joe Garofoli pointed out in an October 8 profile of Morgan in the *San Francisco Chronicle Magazine*, "Morgan and then-California Republican Party chair Shawn Steel first publicly launched the idea to recall the Gov. [Gray] Davis," which ultimately led to the election of Arnold Schwarzenegger as Governor. See, also, Bill Berkowitz, Oct. 18 2006. "The mouth that roars," *Media Transparency. (mediatransparency.org)*.

315 AmericanTraitor.US. (*americantraitor.us.*)

weeks before the 2006 election and it is purportedly devoted to "revealing American traitors for what they are." The website displays names, photos and justifications for its traitor baiting. For instance, to explain why Jaime Gorelick is awarded first place on its list of "political traitors," *American Traitor.US* asserted,

> Ms. Gorelick shares a huge chunk of responsibility for making the US of A vulnerable to a terror attack on 9/11. In fact, she may be the most responsible of any government figure. See, she's the one who put a halt to the sharing of information between different agencies charged with national security. To her it was a conflict of interest at best and "entrapment" at worst, and would unfairly "railroad" criminals. To see her on the 9/11 commission and condemn those same agencies for not sharing info was the ultimate insult—perhaps she has premature Alzheimers? The blood of nearly 4000 Americans is on her hands! If anyone should apologize to the American people, it is Jaime Gorelick. If she had one moral fiber in her being she'd take the blame (and her own life if we were lucky).

This vicious slander simply resurrected Ashcroft's lies, expressed during the 9/11 Commission hearings, when he tried to discredit the Commission and distract attention from the failures of the Bush administration by blaming Gorelick (and other Clinton officials) for 9/11. (As indicated, Ashcroft invented a fairy tale at the hearings about an unassailable "wall"—allegedly constructed during the Clinton administration when Gorelick had been Deputy Attorney General—that prevented the FBI and CIA from sharing information about terrorists.)

American Traitor.US also called Sen. John Kerry a traitor. It accused him of betraying America by informing a Senate subcommittee that American soldiers had raped women, slaughtered civilians, and executed prisoners of war during the Vietnam War. Its list included other Democrats as well—Rep. John Murtha, Sen. Ted Kennedy, former President Jimmy Carter, retired General Wesley Clark, Rep. Charlie Rangel, Sen. Hillary Clinton, and former governor of Vermont and Democratic National Committee chairman, Dr. Howard Dean. Another list, entitled "Academic Traitors," includes, among others, Noam Chomsky, Ward Churchill, Jay Bennish, and Patricia Sonntag as well as The National Education Association and Scholars for 9/11.

ProBush.com targeted celebrities. Its "traitors" include George Clooney, Sheryl Crow, Johnny Depp, Danny Glover, Mike Farrell, Janeane Garofalo, Whoopi Goldberg, Madonna, Sean Penn, Julia Roberts, Susan Sarandon, Martin Sheen, and Barbara Streisand.

Granted, most Americans today would probably laugh at this traitor-baiting but they should heed observations made at a 2002 conference called Roundtable organized by far right philanthropies.[316] As a panelist in a Roundtable forum devoted to right-wing think tanks and the importance of ideas, Christopher Demuth of the American Enterprise In-

---

316 Roundtable notably sponsored conferences that provided opportunities for synchronizing the impact of right wing foundations.

stitute observed that school vouchers and Social Security privatization were at first considered radical but they eventually acquired nationwide currency.[317] Another member of the Institute felt that a radically new idea required at least two decades to become commonly accepted. Yet it hasn't taken that long to get patriotic attack dogs to ignore the lies, inequities and crimes perpetrated above all by the Republicans blindly accepting their Great Leader's simple-minded dictum: "You are either with us or you are against us!"

How far along the road to neo-fascism have the Banana Republicans and their Democratic collaborators, taken the United States? Answer: *As far as they can.* The cumulative number of despotic measures—rather than each measure taken by itself—makes this conclusion credible.

Furthermore, this credibility was implanted in rock-hard soil when Bush signed the Military Commissions Act in October 2006. The Act legitimated torture such as "water-boarding" in which prisoners are forced to experience drowning or to stand for 40 hours or more in one place while they are being exposed to 50-degree temperatures without clothing and drenched with cold water. US tribunals had convicted Japanese officers in 1947 for war crimes because they used water-boarding and other forms of torture.

Simultaneously, the Act eliminated *habeas corpus,* the right of suspected terrorists, or anybody else —including innocent American citizens—to know

---

317 Rampton and Stauber, op. cit., pp.25-26

why they have been imprisoned, provided Bush or Rumsfeld decides that they are "enemy combatants." Any American—including Chomsky, Gorelick, Kennedy, Kerry, and Streisand—could be smeared as enemy combatants merely because they oppose unjust wars and, in the eyes of the Bush administration, commit treason by "giving aid and comfort to the enemy."

Obviously, the remaining distance to neo-fascism where the host of traitors are rounded up and imprisoned in the detention camp contracted in 2006 by Halliburton (for 385+ million dollars) will require a bit more than the Military Commissions Act. It will require a genuine or fabricated crisis and the collaboration of high-ranking uniformed officers such as those standing behind Bush when he was photographed as he signed the Act into law.

PART SEVEN

FASCISM OR
DEMOCRACY

—◇—

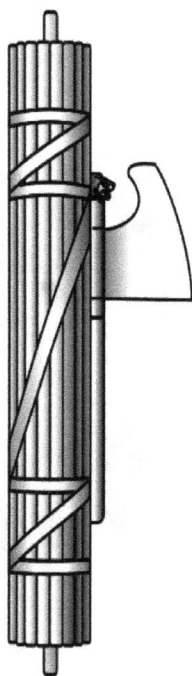

Fasces. "Fascist symbol",
Wikipedia Commons
version [by Direktor,
CC-BY-SA 3.0]

19 | Reassembling the *Fasces*

When a legislature undertakes to proscribe the exercise of a citizen's constitutional rights it acts lawlessly and the citizen can take matters into his own hands and proceed on the basis that such a law is no law at all.

—Supreme Court Justice

William O. Douglas

Mussolini adopted the word "Fascism" because it was derived from the Latin word *Fasces*, a malevolent bundle of wooden rods tied together with an axe, forming a cylinder with a blade protruding from one side.[318] The axe symbolized the power to decapitate enemies of the state and, since the tightly bound rods were much stronger than a single rod, the *Fasces* symbolized strength in unity

---

318 The axe at times would protrude from an end of the cylinder rather than the side.

as well. *Fasces* were carried by lictors (i.e., body-guards) who attended dictators and magistrates, and by executioners or heroic soldiers who marched past Janus' gates in Rome after a military conquest.

Is the whole more than the sum of its parts? If customary forms of repression plus neoliberal expansionism (by contemporary Americans) were bundled like *Fasces*, would they confirm our doubts about the survival of American democracy?

This question was posed when we acknowledged that the steadily increasing surge of customary forms of repression could jump-start neo-fascism. Obviously, this possibility depends on formative developments and it grants that the US has not experienced anything like the 1932 Nazi campaign of terror. As indicated, the U.S. has not seen fascist storm troopers beating, torturing, and killing thousands of political dissenters or pounding the ground with their heels while goose-stepping down Main Street, USA, singing *America the Beautiful.*

Furthermore, the increases in repression have not reached the levels of violence imposed during the Vietnam War. At that time, millions of people were protesting the war and police officers and National Guardsmen had notched their rifle butts with the clubbing, maiming or killing of Black Panthers, Kent State demonstrators, and uncounted numbers of dissidents who fought for peace and social justice.

Even so the question we posed remains. Does the use of the word *neo-fascism* to describe the changes taking place in America seem reasonable? Is it valid? Especially when we take stock of what Bush's so-called "endless war" was about and when we consider the range and magnitude of repressive policies instituted by his administration?

Before answering this question, recall again that neo-fascism is not wedded to its classical costume. Take John Strachey's work, *The Menace of Fascism*, published in 1933.[319] This British parliamentarian's opening chapter is devoted to one terrifying incident after another committed earlier that same year by Nazi terrorists in Germany and reported by the *London Times*. Although these terrorists did not wear velvet gloves, Strachey acknowledged that fascism would appear in "a less openly aggressive guise" if it occurred in America. A half century later, Gross reaffirmed and expanded Strachey's thought in *Friendly Fascism*.

SELECTING THE RODS

Most of the notable repressive tactics being employed after 9/11 had exhibited customary features. Peaceful demonstrators had been beaten and arrested. Exorbitant bails (and the denial of their right to bail) had kept protesters in prison, and felony charges threatened or punished them with loss of voting rights and jobs. Laws created originally to cope with organized crime and terrorism were targeting protesters.[320] Organizing committees could not get permits to assemble on public property. Law

---

319 John Strachey. 1933. *The Menace of Fascism*. New York: Covici, Friede.

320 The organized crime laws usually include the Racketeer Influenced and Corrupt Organizations Act (RICO).

enforcement agencies fabricated grounds for arrests and charges, secretly monitored anti-war organizations and made use of *agents provocateur*.

On the other hand, the sheer number of weapons of mass repression fabricated during the Bush administration raised doubts about their customary status. Was the administration secretly assembling American-style *Fasces*? If so, the "rods," that is, the repressive components being selected for the *Fasces*, begin with fabricated threats to national security and false arrests. (No American who truly believes in democracy would ever equate civil disobedience with terrorism; yet Americans were being arrested for this form of resistance and detained in overcrowded and substandard prisons.) The authorities had also expanded their targets by including religious profiling, by demonizing Islam, and by imprisoning thousands of Middle East Muslims in addition to ambiguous "extremists," "radicals," and other "usual suspects."

When selecting the rods for the *Fasces*, consider, too, the extraordinary lengths to which the Bush administration had gone in tightening its control over the federal bureaucracy by creating the Homeland Security Department and the National SS. Concurrently, domestic intelligence agencies had been taken over by people who allegedly monitored the CIA—or worked for the "Agency"—and allowed it to commit a shocking array of crimes. Meanwhile scientific evidence was being suppressed while scientists were threatened for speaking honestly in public about research on global warming, evolution, and stem-cell research. Advisory committees that did not fit political agendas had been dismantled and funding for research was cut. To further consolidate its control, the Bush administration packed the bureaucracy with conservative sycophants and cronies who proceeded to disorganize as well as purge one department after another. [321] As Thomas Frank demonstrates, in *The Wrecking Crew*, Bush's policies made the efficient operation of the government impossible.[322]

Similar changes took place in the Department of Justice (DoJ). In December, 2006, Attorney General Gonzales summarily fired well-regarded prosecutors for political reasons rather than their job performance. Two prosecutors, for instance, were dismissed after refusing to pursue a bogus indictment that would influence an election. Others were removed to discourage indictments against Republican officials for corruption and influence peddling and prostitution paid for with government funds. And then, in 2007, House hearings began to uncover further dismissals as well as evidence suggesting that Carl Rove, Gonzales, and other top-level officials had especially targeted prosecutors who refused to harass Democratic Party officials.

---

321 See, for example, Joel Havemann. 3/19/2007. Scientist accuses White of 'Nazi' tactics. *Los Angeles Times*. Havemann states: "A government scientist, under sharp questioning by a federal panel for his outspoken views on global warming, stood by his view today that the Bush administration's information policies smacked of Nazi Germany. James Hansen, director of the Goddard Institute for Space Studies in the National Aeronautics and Space Administration, took particular issue with the administration's rule that a government information officer listen in on his interviews with reporters and its refusal to allow him to be interviewed by National Public Radio."

322 Thomas Frank. 2008. *The Wrecking Crew: How Conservatives Rule*. New York: Henry Holt & Co.

In January 2009, days after President Barack Hussein Obama assumed office, an internal DoJ report came to light. It revealed that Bradley Schlozman for three years starting in 2003 politicized hiring policies in the Civil Rights Division. Schlozman lied to Congress when he claimed that politics had nothing to do with his hiring decisions. He had routinely hired Republicans, Federalist Society members, and "Right Thinking Americans." He pressured supervisors at the DoJ to reject applicants who were considered liberal. His email and voice mail messages revealed efforts to shape the political composition of the Civil Rights Division by "doing away with 'pinko' and "crazy lib" lawyers and others he did not consider "*real Americans.*"[323]

Additional rods for bundling *Fasces* include link-up of federal intelligence agencies with local police departments—utilizing the spin-offs from creation and recreation of surveillance projects with huge databases and software for data-mining names, ages, addresses, political affiliations, health records, credit card expenditures, and every conceivable personal item stored in electronic form. The Bush Administration had tirelessly hacked and trimmed rod after rod from the branches of the neo-fascist tree in order to create information networks for spying on individuals and groups. Its efforts had relentlessly ignored popular protests, congressional hearings, and criminal codes. His measures represented an unmistakable neofascist strategy for roping in every individual and organization that contributed to

---

323 Eric Lichtblau. 1/14/2009. "Criticism of Ex-Official in Hiring at Justice Dept." *New York Times*.

progressive causes at home or abroad. The Al-Arian case symbolized the degree to which these measures could hunt American progressives and bring them down.

The fracas over the unchecked spying permitted by the updated versions of the Foreign Intelligence Act (FISA) was merely a temporary stop on the highway to fascism. For five years, the American clones of the Gestapo had been reading email and tapping phones without a warrant, even though these actions at that time were explicitly forbidden by the Foreign Intelligence Surveillance Act of 1978. Moreover, in 2008 whistleblowers and civil liberties organizations disclosed that Verizon, AT&T, Sprint, and other telecommunications companies had violated the 1978 FISA Act by secretly providing intelligence agencies with millions of email messages. When the violations were exposed, Bush demanded indemnity for the telecom agencies, and his congressional collaborators acquiesced. So called "moderate" Democrats as well as Republicans passed a new FISA bill that gutted privacy safeguards incorporated in the 1978 Act. How can any defender of democracy—whether they are ordinary citizens, law enforcement officials or criminal justice students—go along with this attempt to indemnify the telecoms retroactively even though they had violated the law?

On January 21, 2009, Keith Olbermann interviewed a former US intelligence official, Russell Tice, who said that the NSA during the Bush regime illegally eavesdropped without warrants on millions of Americans. The NSA had accessed faxes, phone calls, computer communications, etc. It monitored *all* communications—not merely contacts between Americans and foreign sources. It had also solved the technical requirements for identifying politically significant groups among the millions of Americans who were communicating with one another. To conduct a detailed analysis of a subset composed of journalists, anti-war or civil libertarian groups, for instance, the NSA computer programmers had developed programs that were capable of isolating a significant subset of their immense databases in order to conduct a detailed analysis of the subset.

InfraGard provided another rod for Bush's *fasces*. We reported that the Office of Homeland Security (OHS) had originally proposed an experimental program entitled Terrorism Information and Prevention System (TIPS) in ten cities during the winter of 2002. But TIPS was dropped like a hot potato after it was denounced nationwide as a device for spying without a warrant on people's mail, homes, and conduct. Nevertheless, in 2003, the FBI quietly dealt with this set-back by expanding a preexisting program, called InfraGard, which had become a corporate TIPS program.

The potentially dangerous use of the massive databases required by the neofascist infrastructure being created by Bush's administration was further represented by the FALCON project. FALCON stood for "Federal and Local Cops Organized Nationally." Touted as a crime-fighting tactic targeting terrorists as well as violent criminals, it had been "tested" in three massive sweeps carried out by almost a thousand law-enforcement agencies. As freelance journalist, Mike Whitney, pointed out, not one of the more than 30,000 individuals swept up by these dragnets was charged with a terror-related crime. Furthermore, although FALCON produced the largest number of arrests ever recorded in the US, most of the people arrested were not violent criminals. (Thousands, for instance, were illegal immigrants and individuals with outstanding warrants.) Consequently, Whitney asks, "So, what was the real impetus for the Falcon raids? Was it just a bean-counting exercise to see how many people would fit in the back of a Paddy-Wagon or are they a dress rehearsal for future crackdowns on potential enemies of the state?"

How about the administration's criminal efforts to legitimize and outsource torture and to indemnify Bush, Cheney, Rumsfeld, and others from being indicted for war crimes and crimes against humanity? These efforts certainly would contribute to the *Fasces* being assembled by Bush and Co. The legalization of COINTELPRO tactics via the Patriot Act would provide another candidate. Wasn't COINTELPRO a *covert* program because of its illegality?

Add the Military Commissions Act to the number of rods being bundled. The Act legitimates torture, eliminates *habeas corpus* and enables the government to declare innocent Americans as "enemy combatants," and send them off to the detention camp being quietly constructed out west by Halliburton.

What about the revisions to the 1807 Insurrection Act? This ancient act had governed the President's deployment of armed forces within the US to put down lawlessness, insurrection, and rebellion. When conjoined with the 1878 Posse Comitatus Act, the Insurrection Act in principle limited the powers of the Federal government to use the military for law enforcement. However, on October 27, 2006, Bush—in the dark of the night during a private Oval Office ceremony—signed a new version of the Insurrection Act. This version allowed him to declare a state of emergency and take control (without the consent of Congress, governors, or local authorities) of the armed forces, state militia, and local law-enforcement agencies to suppress "public disorder" anywhere in the US.

And there's more! Consider an executive order issued on July 17, 2007 that unquestionably repealed the right to political dissent. The Order entitled, "Blocking Property of Certain Persons Who Threaten Stabilization Efforts in Iraq," enables the President to confiscate the assets of people opposing the war in Iraq. Bush's Order plainly stated,

> Pursuant to the International Emergency Economic Powers Act, as amended (50 USC. 1701 et seq.)(IEEPA), I have issued an Executive Order blocking property of persons determined to have committed, or to pose a significant risk of committing, an act or acts of violence that have the purpose or effect of threatening the peace or stability of Iraq or the Government of Iraq or undermining efforts to promote economic reconstruction and political reform in Iraq or to provide humanitarian assistance to the Iraqi people.[324]

---

324 President George Bush. 7/17/2007. "Message to the Congress of the United States Regarding International Emergency Economic Powers Act: Executive Order: Blocking Property of Certain Persons who Threaten Stabilization Efforts in Iraq." Office of the Press

If this Order was activated it would criminalize everyone who participated in the antiwar movement. It allowed the Pentagon to "block" (freeze? confiscate?) the assets of anti-war protesters and their organizations. It even targeted the assets of people who opposed the administration's efforts to privatize Iraq's oil resources (on behalf of Anglo-American corporations) as well as the humanitarian organizations who weren't approved by the Iraqi puppet government.

The Order represented an unmistakable fascist strategy for roping in every individual and organization that contributed to progressive causes at home or abroad. The Al-Arian case symbolized the degree to which this repressive strategy could hound American progressives and bring them down. Bush's Order violated the First, Fourth, and Fifth Amendments of the US Constitution. It repealed one of the fundamental tenets of US democracy, which is the right to free expression and dissent. It was devised to intimidate anti-war protesters as well as anyone else opposed to government foreign policies and suppress them before the order could be rejected by a judicial challenge.

Bush & Co., without doubt, knew that an attempt to activate this order would trigger a massive response from Americans. But that's why this order was quietly introduced and put on the back burner. At this writing, it had been stored among the options that had been available for him or that could be available for any president who thinks that he or she can get away with it.

Secretary.

Meanwhile, to support these kinds of executive decrees, the US military had devised unprecedented plans for guarding against and responding to so-called terrorist attacks in the United States. It had drafted plans that envisioned 15 potential crisis scenarios. How many of these scenarios targeted anti-war protesters included in Bush's decree? The answer to this question is unavailable. No *one—including Congress—had demanded an answer!*

Earlier, in 2002, Sen. Joseph R. Biden Jr., Delaware Democrat who in 2008 became the Vice President of the United States, strongly endorsed giving soldiers the power to arrest American civilians. He was interviewed on "Fox News Sunday." Mr. Biden, a member of the Judiciary Committee, said the Posse Comitatus Act of 1878, which prevents the military from exercising police powers in this country, should be re-examined and "has to be amended." Such a change will happen soon, he said. However, Tom Ridge, who was director of the OHS in 2002, declared that the Biden proposal should be considered but that he thinks it's "very unlikely" such a change will be made. Both Biden and Ridge's statements may have been coordinated and calculated to measure public reaction. Eventually, Bush was empowered to use federal troops in domestic policing.

The Department of Defense Civil Disturbance Plan 55-2- (code-named: "Operation Garden Plot") planned to supply prison camps for US citizens as well as illegal aliens. This Pentagon plan would have enabled Ashcroft to order the indefinite incarceration of US citizens in abandoned army bases and summarily strip them of their constitutional rights and access to the courts by declaring them "enemy combatants."

Jose Padilla's case is important in this context. He is an American citizen and, in 2005, the 4th US Circuit Court of Appeals ruled that Bush had the authority to detain him without charges. Padilla had attended an al-Qaeda training camp before 9/11 and, despite skimpy evidence he was found guilty of conspiring to kill people in an overseas jihad and to fund and support overseas terrorism. He had been put in solitary confinement for more than two years without recourse to legal representation and a hearing. His attorneys, plus civil liberties organizations, claimed his treatment could lead to the military holding anyone, from protesters to people who check out what the government considers the wrong books from the library.

Frank Morales is an Episcopal priest, independent researcher, and New York activist. His extraordinary historical portrayal of US military civil disturbance planning points out that Operation Garden Plot actually originated during the Vietnam War in 1968. But it had been updated over the last three decades. He also contended that plans to employ federal troops in "civil disturbances" were primarily created to suppress the aims of social justice movements. Consequently, these plans assumed that an enemy lurks within the body politic that the military might have to fight, or at least be ordered to fight. Morales added,

> Equipped with flexible "military operations in urban terrain" and "operations other than war" doctrine, lethal and "less-than-lethal" high-

> tech weaponry, U.S. "armed forces" and "elite" militarized police units are being trained to eradicate "disorder," "disturbance" and "civil disobedience" in America. Further, it may very well be that police/military "civil disturbance" planning is the animating force and the overarching logic behind the incredible nationwide growth of police paramilitary units, a growth which coincidentally mirrors rising levels of police violence directed at the American people, particularly "nonwhite" poor and working people.[325]

What a legacy! By 2008, the administration had installed the Patriot Acts, the Department of Homeland Security, the Joint Terrorist Task Forces, the National Security Service, the InfraGard, the Military Commission Act, the revised Insurrection Act, a decree enabling Bush to control the assets of political dissenters, and other malevolent segments of a growing repressive infrastructure.

On November 21, 2008, the ACLU distributed a leaked Homeland Security Document revealing how the Bush administration planned to suppress protests at the 2008 Republican National Convention (RNC). In addition to the involvement between federal, state, and local organizations, the document exposed military participation that had been shielded from public view because the military was prohibited from domestic intelligence data gathering. The document mentioned the National Geospa-

---

325 Frank Morales. 2002. "U.S. Military Civil Disturbance Planning: The War at Home." In Tom Burghardt (ed.). *Police State America*, (pp.59–101). Toronto, Montreal, San Francisco: Arm the Spirit/Solidarity Publishing. (The quote is on p.59.)

tial Intelligence Agency (NGA), which provides intelligence data provided by military spy satellites. The NGA can use the satellites to monitor journalists, activists, and demonstrators and relay this information to local officials. Alarmingly, the ACLU discovered,

> A second agency that was involved in the planning [to suppress protests at the RNC] is the Pentagon's Northern Command, NORTHCOM. Having NORTHCOM at the table, assisting in the planning is troubling because it could mean that the military was involved in the crowd control strategies and dealing with potential civil unrest. According to a report in Army Times, it said that an active military unit has been deployed by NORTHCOM in the United States. This deployment marks the first time an active unit has been given a dedicated assignment within U.S. Borders.

Still other incremental additions have backed qualitative changes that exceed customary repression. For instance, take Tom Burghardt's account of the so-called "preemptive arrests" conducted in St. Paul, Minnesota, during the 2008 Republican National Convention (RNC). FBI agents accompanied by 30 St. Paul police armed with tasers, pepper spray, and automatic weapons, invaded a house containing five members of the I-Witness Video team and the *Democracy Now* journalist, Elizabeth Press. Displaying a warrant, they arrested, photographed, and recorded the residents' names and addresses and confiscated their cameras, video equipment, cell phones, privileged notes, and computers. Later, police detained five other members of I-Witness Video who were not present during the home invasion that lasted over three hours, preventing them from documenting three other simultaneous raids in Minneapolis and St. Paul. Additionally, members of still another video group, the Glass Bead Collective were also illegally detained and had their notes and equipment confiscated by the police.[326]

Nevertheless, were it not for the security and intelligence agencies coordinating the repression in St. Paul, these First Amendment violations would not—by themselves—have exceeded customary repression. Burghardt reports that a leaked planning document showed that the agencies carrying out this repression—among others—included the Federal Bureau of Investigation (FBI), the Department of Homeland Security (DHS), the Minnesota Homeland Security, the Emergency Management agency (HSEM), the United States Secret Service (USSS), the National Geospatial Intelligence Agency (NGA), and the Pentagon's Northern Command (NORTHCOM).

During the RNC, a "working group" operated round the clock at a centralized communications and coordination center. This center was called a Multi-Agency Communications Center (MACC) and, during the convention, it included representatives from Pentagon agencies (as well as local, state, and federal law enforcement agencies). MACC tracked cell phones, email messages, individual activists, groups of demonstrators, and so on, with the aid of US telecom corporations, undercover agents, on-the-ground

---

326 Burghardt's website, Antifascist calling… (*antifascist-calling.blogspot.com*) offers timely and trenchant online essays on neo-fascist developments in the US.

reports, and military satellites. It then relayed its intelligence data to the police who were intimidating and beating protesters and accusing them of engaging in criminal conduct. Given the Pentagon's participation, the repression coordinated by MACC can be justifiably termed "low-intensity urban warfare."

At first glance, Bush's anti-welfare state policies may not seem relevant in this frightening context. But he had relentlessly opposed the rights and liberties of Americans—returning us to the days when labor unions and environmental, wage, and safety standards were outlawed as "illegal restraints" on trade. Also, despite his demagogic recognition of the reality of global warming, environmentalists still had to plead for funds to oppose the administration's plans to back the corporate destruction of the Alaskan Wildlife Refuge. Bush refused to support the Kyoto Protocol and had done nothing to alleviate catastrophic climate change. The failed promises to invest in schools and college grants; the demagogic attempts to stop jobs from leaving the US; the attacks on Social Security and other welfare-state programs such as Medicaid or Medicare and tax cuts for millionaires—were illustrative of the willingness to use trillions of public revenues to promote the lives of the rich and powerful at the expense of everyone else.

WHAT ABOUT THE AXE?

The Bush administration has made unprecedented efforts to privatize military services. During his administration, Blackwater USA, headed by Erik

Prince, a multi-millionaire and radical right-wing Christian—who said his company is a patriotic extension of the U.S. military—had been awarded numerous government contracts to supply mercenaries for guarding military transports, political officials, military bases in Iraq, and patrolling New Orleans after Hurricane Katrina's devastation. Advertising itself as "the most comprehensive professional military, law enforcement, security, peacekeeping, and stability operations company in the world," Blackwater had opened a domestic operations division that sold services to the Department of Homeland Security. Moreover, Blackwater had applied for operating licenses in all U.S. coastal states, at the same time expanding its military facilities (storage, armories, and training grounds) in Arizona, Illinois, and California.[327] With regard to Backwater's forces, Michael Ratner, President of the Center for Constitutional Rights, declared,

> Unlike police officers they are not trained in protecting constitutional rights and unlike police officers or the military they have no system of accountability whether within their organization or outside it. These kind of paramilitary

---

327 Jeremy Scahill. 2007. *Blackwater: The Rise of the World's Most Powerful Mercenary Army*. New York: Nation Books. Scahill reports Blackwater had "2,300 personnel deployed in nine countries, with 20,000 other 'contractors' at the ready. In 2006, it owned more than twenty aircraft, including helicopter gunships and a private intelligence division, and it is manufacturing surveillance blimps and target systems." Blackwater provided "security personnel" and patrols for the Bush administration in Afghanistan and Iraq as well as in New Orleans during the Hurricane Katrina disaster where it billed the Feds more than $250,000 a day (at $950 per man, per day).

groups bring to mind Nazi Party Brownshirts, functioning as an extrajudicial enforcement mechanism that can and does operate outside the law. The use of these paramilitary groups is an extremely dangerous threat to our rights.

Mercenary units in Iraq, including Blackwater, contained some 120,000 fighters. A correspondent for *Democracy Now,* Jeremy Scahill observed,

> They unleash indiscriminate and wanton violence against unarmed Iraqis, have no accountability and are beyond the reach of legitimate authority. The appearance of these paramilitary fighters, heavily armed and wearing their trademark black uniforms, patrolling the streets of New Orleans after Hurricane Katrina, gave us a grim taste of the future. It was a stark reminder that the tyranny we impose on others we will one day impose on ourselves.[328]

When the Roman Republic became a dictatorship, 24 bodyguards called *lictors* attended a dictator with the *axes* protruding from their *Fasces*. These *axes*—symbolizing the state's juridical power to decapitate "public enemies"—were prominently displayed in grand processions. Originally that power was turned over to a single person—because the Roman Senate

---

328 Scahill notes that "The firm was also eager to stake out a role in crafting the rules that would govern mercenaries under US contract." Blackwater's lobbyist Chris Bertelli indicates, "There are now several federal regulations that apply to their activities, but they are generally broad in nature. One thing that's lacking is an industry standard. That's something we definitely want to be engaged in." By May 2007, Blackwater was leading a lobbying effort by similar types of corporations to try to block Congressional or Pentagon efforts to place their forces under the military court martial system.

felt that emergency conditions warranted appointing a *dictator* for a short time who was called the *Magister Populi* ("Master of the People"), *Praetor Maximus* ("The supreme Praetor"), or *Magister Peditum* ("Master of the Infantry"). A *dictator* was given absolute power to suppress the enemies of the state—no one opposed to his decisions could appeal to the Senate or any other body!

Today, American mercenaries and homegrown Freikorps units would supply the axes for decapitating "enemies of the state" and the people that offend our "unitary executive." On the other hand, when Hitler seized power in 1933, it was with the tacit collaboration of the German Officer Corps. Likewise, the fast-track to U.S. fascism would undoubtedly require the collaboration of the nation's officer corps or at least sizeable representation thereof.

This collaboration may seem impossible today but Chris Hedges' *American Fascists* shatters conventional beliefs—insisting that the radical Christian right has penetrated the American military. He contends that far-right evangelicals have converted American officers with the intention of co-opting the country's military and law enforcement. Hedges further insists that the mass movement being built by the Christian radicals is promoting military forces willing and able to aggressively silence political heretics. Its leaders hold special services and ceremonials to attract law enforcement and military personnel. They advised young men and women to join law enforcement and military forces. Sympathetic officers are encouraged to attend church events, where they are applauded and feted for their Christian pro-

bity and patriotism. Hedges concludes: "All this befits a movement whose final aesthetic is violence. It
also befits a movement that, in the end, would need
the military and police forces to seize power in
American society"

There are no scientific studies that provide trust-
worthy and substantial data about the political inclinations of law-enforcement and military personnel.
This kind of data is simply unavailable—despite its
critical importance for safeguarding democracy. Certainly, the repressive tactics implemented by police
departments in a variety of cities and towns speaks
volumes about how reactionary these departments
can be. Yet as a whole, the public is only aware of an
infinitesimally small number of instances revealing
the impact of the right-wing movements on the
armed forces.[329] Hedges predicts:

> The drive by the Christian right to take control
> of military chaplaincies, which now sees radic-
> al Christians holding roughly 50 per cent of
> chaplaincy appointments in the armed services
> and service academies, is part of a much larger
> effort to politicize the military and law enforce-
> ment. This effort signals the final and perhaps
> most deadly stage in the long campaign by the
> radical Christian right to dismantle America's

329 Americans know little or nothing about the political inclinations
  of law enforcement and military officers in the US. Reportedly, a
  considerable number if not majority of US military chaplains in
  Iraq were evangelicals, but how many are actually radicals cannot
  be validated. The US Deputy Undersecretary of Defense for
  Intelligence, General William Boykin, was chastised in 2004 for
  publicly framing the war in Iraq as a war against Satan. He was also
  criticized for sending emails to air force officers recommending the
  election of a candidate who had "Christian qualifications."

> open society and build a theocratic state. A
> successful politicization of the military would
> signal the end of our democracy.

On the other hand, despite the mounting criticism of its bureaucratic bumbling and incompetence, Bush & Co. is composed of right-wingers who have learned the lessons of the Vietnam War. When state militia and local enforcement agencies used violence, they were at times met with a massive surge in protests. A fascist regime change in the US—backed by a congressional majority or not—would require force and inevitably provoke violent opposition in return.

In addition, regardless of the fact that the customary tactics for repressing dissidents are rarely ever contextualized by the media and that anti-war demonstrations are blacked out or relegated to small articles on back pages, millions of people in other countries—in Canada, Europe, the Middle East, Southeast Asia, and South America—protested the war in Iraq. Demonstrations occurred in London, Oslo, Madrid, Vienna, Copenhagen, Paris, Rome, Athens, Prague, Budapest, Istanbul, and many, many other cities in February and March of 2007. Almost a half-million people protested in Berlin. Canada experienced protests in 70 cities and towns despite extremely cold temperatures. London saw the largest political demonstration in the United Kingdom's history: More than three quarters of a million people demonstrated on the streets of London! BBC News estimated that between six and ten million people protested the war in 60 countries.

Given the memories of the horrors inflicted by

Nazi Germany, one can only imagine how Europeans would respond to the revival of fascism—this time in America!

"A Better World is Possible"

Photo by Ela Orenstein, Atlanta
Independent Media Center. (Posted on
la.indymedia.org, Sunday January 12,
2003.)

20 | Turning Points

I am upset with those who prefer to remain spectators until it may be too late. I am shocked by those who seem to believe—in Anne Morrow Lindbergh's words of 1940—that "there is no fighting the wave of the future" and all you can do is "leap with it."

—Bertram Gross,
Friendly Fascism

After a period of silence, the hawks came out of the closet during the summer of 2005. Senators Clinton, Lieberman, Bayh, and Biden astonishingly called for increasing the number of troops in Iraq and stepping up the war. To assuage Americans appalled at this suggestion, they proposed that our armed forces should also be employed abroad for "humanitarian purposes." (At a conference sponsored by the Democratic Leadership Council in

July 2005, Senator Clinton ominously declared, "Having the strongest military in the world is the first step, but we also have to have a commitment to using our military in smart ways that further peace, stability, and security around the world.") Then, like a ventriloquist's dummy in Bush's lap, Biden added his voice to the demagogic bipartisan bluster. He wanted to restore alliances with other nations but, at the same time, he insisted that the US should continue to reserve the right to use force without asking anyone's permission.

Also, a report—endorsed by the House and Senate minority leaders, Nancy Pelosi and Harry Reid—encouraged Americans to regard a preemptive strike against Iran or North Korea to be a suitable option. In spite of investigations and negotiations being conducted by the International Atomic Energy Agency and five nations, the report shockingly recommended threatening Iran and North Korea with "the possibility of repeated and unwarned military strikes" to compel their compliance with US demands.

"Unwarned military strikes?" Like Japan's attack on Pearl Harbor? Were these Democratic leaders serious? Had they forgotten that Chinese soldiers overwhelmed American troops when they came to North Korea's defense and forced the Americans back to the 38th parallel? How would bombing Iran *ever* make Americans safe from terrorism?

TURNING AROUND

Fortunately, tens of thousands of Americans had refused to follow these Democratic hawks. During the second anniversary of the invasion of Iraq, in March 2005, Americans called for demonstrations that would support our troops by bringing them home. Iraq Veterans Against the War and Gold Star Families for Peace (whose sons and daughters had died in Iraq) marked the anniversary by demonstrating near army bases. In Fayetteville, North Carolina —the home of Fort Bragg, the 82nd Airborne and Special Forces base—over 4,000 protesters carried banners saying *Show Real Support for the Troops: Bring Them Home Now!* The protesters conducted the largest anti-war demonstration in Fayetteville's history.

More than 15,000 New Yorkers marched from Harlem to Central Park, where thousands were already gathered. As the demonstrators merged in the Park, the police were arresting protesters who lay down next to cardboard coffins, a couple of miles south in Times Square near a famous armed forces recruiting station.[330] In Los Angeles, 20,000 demonstrators marched in the rain through Hollywood, chanting, "End the Occupation—Bring the Troops Home Now!" In San Francisco, over 25,000 anti-war protesters marched for over three-quarters of an hour on wide streets before entering the Civic Center

---

330 Abid Aslam. March 21 2005. "US Rallies Mark Iraq Anniversary, Reflect Anti-War Groups' Growth, Challenges." *OneWorld.net*. The numbers were derived from the United for Peace and Justice Events Calendar (*unitedforpeace.org*).

Plaza.

Chicago was an armed camp filled with 2,000 cops in full riot gear. The Democratic Governor and Democratic Mayor had tried to stop the protests by denying permits for a peaceful march and a federal judge supported them. Defying arrests and beatings, thousands of mostly young demonstrators formed "feeder marches" spanning the city and conveyed anti-war messages that were being suppressed at prominent downtown places. Although one of these places, located on Michigan Avenue, was finally designated a "no-free-speech zone," young protesters dodged police lines and handed out flyers to onlookers anyway.[331]

A Chicago anti-war coalition reported that the Mayor did permit a rally at Chicago's Federal Plaza, but the police had copied the 2002 Washington DC police tactics by surrounding it on all sides and blocking several entrances. Nevertheless, the rally was packed to overflowing and its list of prominent speakers included Georgia Congresswoman Cynthia McKinney who in 2002 had voted against the resolution to go to war in Iraq. She declared,

> They tell us that this is a war for democracy, but that is a joke because George Bush came to power by stopping democracy at home, denying the opportunity to vote to Blacks and Latinos in Florida. In countries like Haiti they arrested President Aristide and forced him at gunpoint to leave his own country.[332] While

331 The police tactics made it hard to get an accurate count of the protesters but estimates ranged from 3,000 to 5,000.

332 Randall Robinson. 2007. *An Unbroken Agony: Haiti, From*

they purport to cherish democracy, they really have a disdain for it.

The Chicago coalition also reported that the speakers included Fred Hampton Jr., whose father was murdered decades ago when COINTELPRO turned federal and local police into assassins. (He spoke on behalf of Aaron Patterson, a political prisoner.) Juan Torres, whose son was killed in Afghanistan, spoke out against the war, as did Leila Lipscomb who lost her son in Iraq. Maria Salgado, a high school student, told of the struggle students, teachers, and community had waged to keep the federal and city governments from turning part of their school into a US Navy training academy. Aiyinde and Aisa Jean Baptise spoke of the role of the US in Haiti and Africa; and Gustavo Vasquez of the Bolivarian Circle spoke of US imperialism's attacks on the people of Venezuela, Cuba, Colombia, and other Latin American nations. Speakers from Iraq, Iran, and other countries joined veterans and community activists in a program chaired by a Palestinian woman and man.

Anti-war demonstrations were held in 765 cities and towns across the nation. On the first anniversary of the war, only 319 cities and towns had conducted anti-war rallies. On the second anniversary, the number had more than doubled!

In other communities (including the deep South) small groups of brave souls had for two years held silent nocturnal vigils with burning candles to com-

---

Revolution to the Kidnapping of a President. New York: Basic Civitas Books.

memorate soldiers who had died in Iraq. On the second anniversary, however, they reported dramatic changes in responses from drivers and passengers in passing cars who smiled, waved, and honked horns or signaled "Thumbs-up!" to the protesters at the side of the road. These groups, despite being cursed, spit upon, and called "traitors," had conducted their demonstrations during the day at busy intersections and government buildings.

By the summer of 2005, the AFL-CIO passed a resolution demanding the rapid withdrawal of US forces from Iraq. The resolution represented the first time the AFL-CIO had opposed an ongoing US war.

Surprisingly, spontaneous eruptions of anti-war protests in the summer of 2005 marked a new phase in growth of the anti-war movement. After being denied a meeting with Bush to tell him that her 24 year-old son, Casey, was killed in Baghdad, and that American troops should be withdrawn from Iraq, Cindy Sheehan of Vacaville, California, flew to Crawford, Texas. She erected a tent on the side of a hot, dusty road a few miles from Bush's vacation home. In the middle of his war, Bush had taken a six-week vacation and even though his limousine drove down that road on several occasions, he refused to stop and talk to her.

Sheehan's brave action snowballed. The media descended in hordes on "Camp Casey," the name given to the ground occupied by her tent. Anti-war groups such as Code Pink and Gold Star Mothers Against the War traveled to Crawford and signaled their support by camping nearby. After the news of her protest spread through the Internet, Moveon.org succeeded almost overnight in sparking more than 1600 vigils in 50 states and Washington, DC. The Internet gave the anti-war movement new legs. Within a day or two, it had expanded this single anti-war incident into a nation-wide protest.

Simultaneously, anti-war activists packed Camp Casey with tents, trailers, and a refrigerator truck with generators and electric ranges. Joan Baez, the renowned folk singer who had opposed the Vietnam War, sang before an audience of 500 people. Colleen Rowley, the whistle blower who had testified about incompetent handling of intelligence reports before 9/11, provided on-spot interviews. And camp residents set up rows of 264 crosses symbolizing Americans who died in Iraq.

Then, on October 29, 2005, over 200,000 demonstrators converged on Washington, DC and held the largest anti-war demonstration since the Vietnam War.[333] Six months later, on April 29, 2006, at least 350,000 protesters assembled in New York City. Mobilized around the calls to end the war in Iraq, to "Say No" to any attack on Iran, and to support the rights and dignity of all people, including immigrants and women, the demonstrators brought a renewed urgency to the demand for change.

THE "THIRD PARTY" DEBATE

Subsequently, American protests dropped-off sharply. After four years, demonstrators were affected by their inability to stop the wars in

---

333 Some estimates reported as many as 500,000 demonstrators.

Afghanistan and Iraq. Their inability to sustain the same level of anti-war activities was based on many factors. But one fact involved the Bush administration's awareness of the role that the compulsory draft had played during the Vietnam War when millions of Americans had fought to prevent their sons, loved ones, or companions from being *forced* to risk their lives in an unjust war. To curb the size and intensity of the anti-war movement, the Bush administration did not draft young people to fight its wars. Instead, it relied on "voluntary" recruitment policies that appealed to patriotic sentiments or "GI Bill" incentives. It also relied on offsetting a lack of volunteers by funding the massive privatization of military services and mercenaries.

The declining level of anti-war movement activities was also affected by the lack of backing from the Democratic Party. As a result, United for Peace and Justice declared that it was time to hold pro-war Democrats as well as Republicans accountable for the deaths in Iraq and the toll on American communities.[334] An "Anybody but Bush" tactic had failed to stop the war as well as the assaults on the Constitution. And these failures sparked questions about why the Democratic Party was handed a blank check for the Party's platform in 2004.

As indicated, the so-called "endless war against terrorism" served as the raison d'être for installing

---

334 It also called for "three days of action against the war" in Washington, DC, starting with a gigantic march, rally, and festival; an interfaith religious service and grassroots training; and a grassroots lobbying day and training sessions in nonviolent direct action and civil disobedience. But this "action" did not meet expectations.

the Patriot Acts, the Department of Homeland Security, Joint Terrorist Task Forces, the National SS, the Military Commission Act, the Insurrection Act, and other components of the Apparat. Furthermore, these developments were influenced by organizational and personnel changes that consolidated power in the hands of top officials. Wracked with cronyism and corruption, they increased the executive branch's power to control government agencies; yet, as the years passed, the Katrina disaster and the threat of global warming signified their inability to avert catastrophes—now and in the future.

In addition, the House Ethics Committee and federal grand juries were scrutinizing the scandalous behavior of key members of the Bush team, including Cheney, Rove, "Scooter" Libby (Cheney's chief of staff), plus Tom Delay and Bill Frist (the senate and house whips). By January 2006, the mass media was headlining the corruption of GOP Senators and Representatives who had been paid-off by Jack Abramoff and other lobbyists.

However, unlike the parliamentary systems in Europe, political destabilization did not produce a new election or prime minister. The U.S., as indicated, favors a two-party system that preserves the status quo and encourages anti-war movements to remain captives of leading hawks in the Democratic Party.

The "Anybody but Bush" campaign showed how far such captivity could go. The Green Party was almost wiped out in 2004 because it refused to compete with Democratic presidential candidates especially in the "swing states" where Kerry and Edwards ran neck-to-neck with Bush and Cheney. After the election, progressive writers dared to raise questions that they had refused to ask earlier. They dissected Kerry and Edward's pro-war stand and asked whether these candidates, if elected, would have been able to finance the war and have enough left over for health, education, job training, public housing, and other programs that elevate middle and working class living standards.

Similar questions were raised about civil liberties. Bush could never have introduced the Patriot Act and reorganized government agencies so rapidly without his exploitation of 9/11. What's more, he had successfully caged the "moderate" Democrats by playing on the fear of terrorism. Would a Democratic administration break out and still turn things around if the US kept fighting in Iraq or in another war—with Iran, Syria, North Korea, or Venezuela, for instance?

These questions implicated the century-old quandary facing American progressives. If the Democratic Party can't break away, can a "third party" take its place and alter the course of American imperialism? Or is any opposition doomed unless it works within the framework of the two-party system? When answering these questions, two progressives, Joshua Frank, a contributor to such magazines as *Counter-Punch*, *Z Magazine*, and *Green Left Weekly*, and William Domhoff, a noted sociologist, took opposing stands.

FRANK'S PROPOSALS

Frank claimed that progressives should not expect meaningful support from leading Democrats such as

Clinton, Gore, Lieberman, Kerry, Edwards, Dean, or Obama.[335] After examining their 2004 pre-election records, he concluded that their liberal reputations were undeserved. These legislators despite their rhetoric did not represent the Democratic Party base that remained devoted to New Deal economic policies, environmental justice, and civil liberties. They had done little or nothing to stop the decline of organized labor and the passage of the North American Free Trade Agreement. They had supported notable anti-environmental legislation and deregulation but their political rhetoric masked a hidden contempt for civil liberties. The progressives who backed these Democrats, Frank said, ignored the fact that neoliberal principles had determined their politics.

Frank also insisted that the Greens and other progressives had inadvertently helped Bush by giving Kerry a "get-out-of-jail-free" card. "If the Greens had put more pressure on Kerry," Frank claimed, "the Democrat may have taken stronger positions and effectively differentiated himself from the Republicans."[336]

Accordingly, Frank condemned the tactic of accommodating to the "lesser of the two evils" because it encouraged wishful thinking. It ignored the possibility that Kerry and Edwards would have followed in Bill Clinton's footsteps if they had won the election and betrayed the progressive members of the party. Frank concluded: "Whether it is the Green Party or another third party that rises to challenge

---

335 Joshua Frank, 2005. *Left Out! How Liberals Helped Reelect George Bush*. Monroe, Main: Common Courage Press.

336 Op. cit. pp.207-208.

the Democrats and Republicans, an unyielding force must be cultivated if we ever want to see a political entity in Washington represent our concerns."

DOMHOFF'S PROPOSALS

In our second example of opposing views, William Domhoff provided evidence showing that third parties have failed to get their candidates elected to national offices. Consequently, progressives, in his view, cannot win major elections unless they work within the Democratic Party. Domhoff's conclusion is supported by the degree to which electoral rules are stacked against third party candidates.

Obviously, the Greens have the capacity to field candidates who can win state and local elections and raise vital issues that are ignored by the media. (After all, Green Party organizations are still comparatively young. The oldest party only dates back to 1987 and who knows how large they may eventually become especially in states being devastated by global warming?) But almost all of their campaigns have been fought successfully only in local elections. (The Green Party of the United States in 2005, for example, had about 221 Greens in 27 states and Washington, D.C., serving on local levels in elected office.)

The Greens advocate electoral reforms such as proportional representation and instant run-off voting because they know that the rules governing elections restrict their chances drastically. Proportional representation would enable parties to obtain legislative seats roughly in proportion to their overall vote in elections. As a result, proportional representation is far more democratic than the "winner takes all" system that currently operates in the US

Sadly, neither the Democratic nor the Republican Party would ever support proportional representation without overwhelming pressure. In 1993 President Clinton, for example, nominated Lani Guinier to head the DoJ Civil Rights Division. (Guinier was an eminently qualified lawyer who had been a civil rights attorney for more than ten years and had served in the Civil Rights Division during the Carter Administration.)[337] But Clinton *instantly* withdrew her nomination when conservatives pointed out that she believed proportional representation could prevent the widespread disenfranchisement of racial minorities.

Domhoff, as indicated, disagreed with Frank. He observed that third parties have been small and ephemeral. They rarely win more than a per cent or two of the vote and rarely last more than one or two elections. Just two "third parties" in the first quarter of the 20th century made it to the US Congress. When compared to legislatures around the world, only South Africa had fewer parties opposing the government than the US.[338] To underscore his main

---

337 In 1998 she became the first female African-American tenured professor in Harvard Law School's history.

338 The rules governing the election of a president are more restrictive. Some room for the creation of post-election coalitions between two parties exists in parliamentary systems. But hardly anyone believes that Republicans or Democrats will overturn the rules that have allowed two parties to determine who will be president.

point, Domhoff writes,

> [M]ore leftists were elected to Congress in the Thirties and early Forties as Democrats – from California, Washington, Montana, Minnesota, and New York – than were ever elected earlier as socialists. They weren't fully open about their socialism or their sympathy for the Communist Party, but their views were well known to everyone involved in politics at the time.

Nonetheless, the question remains. Can progressives realistically wrest control of the Democratic Party away from conservatives? Answering affirmatively, Domhoff notes that Southern Dixiecrats have in the past ensured conservative domination of the Party—but the Civil Rights Movement in the Sixties had forced southern white racists (who controlled the Democratic Party) into the Republican Party. This change in party loyalties, Domhoff suggests, had created a political vacuum that can be filled by a nationwide liberal-left-labor coalition.

For Domhoff, building Democratic clubs headed by "egalitarian" Democrats at the local level and competing for candidates in primaries offers still other opportunities for sending progressives to national Democratic conventions. The Republicans had used this strategy successfully. "Starting with the 1964 presidential candidacy of Senator Barry Goldwater of Arizona," Domhoff observes, "right-wing Republicans began using primaries at all levels to increase their leverage within their party." Also, beginning in the 1980s, the Christian rightists sponsored candidates for the Republican primaries. Bush won these primaries because they had neutralized the

Northeastern Republican "liberals" and moved the Republican Party radically toward the right.

TO THE RESCUE?

In later years, progressive Americans still wondered if the Democratic Party could move to the left. The Party certainly didn't lack intellectuals who could advise voters about rectifying the damage done since the end of the 70s. Paul Krugman's *Conscience of a Liberal,* for example, takes note of the rightwing shift in American politics. His work, and the articles and books of an increasing number of other critics of federal policies, have charted the damage done to our democratic institutions and scrupulously proposed what to do about it.

But the Democratic Party will *never* move to the left if some of its leaders have their way. Before he left his office as Obama's chief of staff, Rahm Emanuel, for instance, strongly influenced what kinds of support (including funds) would be provided to congressional candidates by the Democratic National Committee. In 2006, for instance, progressives discovered that Emanuel represented a Democratic Party fraction that devoted (and, in some cases, wasted) the Party's efforts in securing funding for so-called "moderate" candidates. These efforts were opposed to progressive Democrats who might have actually been elected and influenced Party decisions.

The Progressive Democrats of America (PDA) recognized the conservatizing role played by Emanuel and other Democratic "moderates" in the party. These progressives in April 2005 attempted to form coalitions and networks that countered these moderates. But the PDA was not a branch of the Democratic Party. It was being organized around autonomous local "chapters" tied together by state and national coordinating committees. Nor was the PDA a third party although it was eager to caucus with Greens and other independents as well as Democrats. Its members identified themselves first as Progressives and, second, as Democrats, Greens, or Independents.

As Will Rodgers once quipped, "I am not a member of any organized political party. I'm a Democrat." Since hundreds of disparate progressive groups exist within the United States, the PDA attempted to provide a big tent under which these groups were brought together in order to get progressive bills passed and back progressive candidates regardless of their party affiliation. Allied with Representatives John Conyers, Jesse Jackson Jr., Dennis Kucinich and others, the PDA protested the 2004 Republican National Convention in New York City. Working with the grass roots organization, United for Peace and Justice, the PDA also brought over 1,000 activists to lobby Congress about ending the war.

The PDA opposed candidates who supported war crimes, environmental degradation, social inequality, and the destruction of living standards. In September 2005, for instance, the Massachusetts PDA in consort with other organizations published a scorecard (based on the Democratic Party platform) that identified Democratic legislators whose voting records were worse than some Republicans because they had voted against abortion rights, gay rights, or environmental safeguards. Some of these legislators had even voted for bills (e.g., NAFTA, CAFTA) that destroyed American jobs, working-class health benefits, and unions.

After the scorecards were published, Democratic Party hacks accused the PDA of "beating on" moderate Democrats and undermining the Party's "diversity." The Massachusetts PDA, however, rejected these demagogic accusations. Their scorecard had identified the legislators who upheld the Party platform as well as those who had sold out to the Republicans. In addition, the people who were leading the PDA included distinguished progressives who had served as Democratic legislators, cabinet officers, and legislative assistants—a list including Robert Reich, Tom Hayden, and Joe Segal. As indicated, Congressional Democrats who were working closely with the PDA include John Conyers, Dennis Kucinich, and Jesse Jackson, Jr.

PDA leaders proposed, "The PDA should boycott, not vote for, or oppose any Democrat running for office in 2006 and 2008 if they support the war in Iraq." They also suggested, "the PDA should be building forces on the ground to attack Bush's supplemental Iraq request—expected to be $100 billion —this coming January [2006]." The PDA intended to help progressive office holders communicate with each other, learn more about policy initiatives, receive campaign assistance and find support to counteract their political isolation. PDA staffers were attempting to build an "Elected Progressives Network", consisting of mayors, city councilors, and members of municipal and state legislative bodies, county officers, school committees, boards, and the like. In 2006, a progressive columnist, Norman Solomon, observed,

> PDA combines progressive idealism with tough-minded pragmatism. During its first ten months, this national organization has jumped into key battles on Capitol Hill while starting to build a grassroots network that has the potential to transform the Democratic Party. Whether pro-war corporate boosters continue to dominate the Party may depend, in large measure, on whether PDA can keep growing. [339]

Joshua Frank, on the other hand, stuck to his guns. He contended that the PDA's efforts would fail because the Democratic Party is a dead end. Howard Dean, in his opinion, was a demagogue whose call for "realigning Democratic values is all for naught, because Dean is only talking about changing the failing rhetoric not the failing policy." As far as Frank is concerned,

> Dean's promise to change the way the Democrats talk about issues is a sure sign his party will never ever genuinely embrace the issues that matter most to progressives. They'll only talk about the issues differently. The Democrats will never be anti-war. They will never be pro-living wage. They will never be in favor of

[339] Norman Solomon is the author of a trenchant 2006 work, *War Made Easy: How Presidents and Pundits Keep Spinning Us to Death*. Hoboken, New Jersey: John Wiley & Sons.

real universal health-care; they'll only pretend they are. So don't believe the hype, for nothing could be more damaging to building a left alternative than believing Howard Dean and the PDA are avenues for legitimate change in the US.

Therefore, Frank concluded, the PDA cannot empower the progressive wing of the Democratic Party —and its coalitions with the Green Party will merely weaken attempts to build that Party.

Unfortunately, the PDA at this point has not shown that it fully grasps the nature of the neo-fascist infrastructure being instituted by the Bush administration. None of its programmatic statements employ such terms as "police state," "creeping fascism," or "neo-fascism." To find these terms, we have to turn to another emerging organization.

In June 2005, the student organization, *The World Can't Wait: Drive out the Bush Regime (WCW)*, explicitly compared Bush to Hitler when it launched a movement to drive Bush from power. After listing the unconstitutional and criminal policies being instituted by the regime, the proclamation for a November mobilization stated,

> Before I get into all we need to do, I want to really stress that we have to keep in mind exactly WHY we are doing all this. The Call [for mobilizing on November 2, 2005] captures this in a very powerful way: "People look at this and think of Hitler - and they are right to do so. The Bush Regime is setting out to radically remake society very quickly, in a fascist way, and for generations to come. We must act now; the future is in the balance."

On the anniversary of Bush's "re-selection," WCW sponsored protests in San Francisco, Atlanta, Chicago, New York, Seattle, Los Angeles, and other cities. Although it is difficult to gauge the strength of this organization, it's list of endorsers includes Harold Pinter, Jane Fonda, Gore Vidal, Cornel West, Russell Banks, Eve Ensler, Jonathan Kozol, Studs Terkel, Cindy Sheehan, Howard Zinn, Edward Asner, Ed Begley, Jr., and others.[340]

The WCW primarily consists of young adults including university and college students. Although it would not surprise people who protested during the Vietnam War, the organizers encouraged high school students to leave school for the day and join the demonstrations. More than 800 Los Angeles Unified students walked out of their high schools, for instance, and joined the protest. Reportedly, adults accompanied students as they left from 10 high schools.

---

340 The list includes Harold Pinter, Jane Fonda, Gore Vidal, Cornel West, Russell Banks, Eve Ensler, Jonathan Kozol, Studs Terkel, Cindy Sheehan, Howard Zinn, Edward Asner, Ed Begley, Jr., Kate Clinton, Sam Hamill, Leland Yee (Speaker Pro Tem, CA State Assembly), Tom Ammiano (SF Board of Supervisors), Deborah Glick (NY State Assembly), former US diplomat Ann Wright, Michael Eric Dyson, Cal. State Assemblyman Mark Leno (author of gay marriage bill), Not In Our Name, ACT UP, Code Pink, Progressive Democrats of America; musicians Anti-flag, Grammy Award Winning Ozomatli, Axis of Justice, the Hip Hop Caucus, and so on. (See worldcantwait.org for others.) An endorsement by Nobel Laureate playwright, Harold Pinter, stated: "The Bush Administration is the most dangerous force that has ever existed. It is more dangerous than Nazi Germany because of the range and depth of its activities and intentions worldwide. I give my full support to the Call to Drive out the Bush Regime."

By February and March, 2007, a variety of student organizations participated in the anti-war demonstrations. Radicalized by the political events, students even resurrected the Students for a Democratic Society (SDS) to fight once again for free speech, civil rights, and against imperial war. The National Youth and Student Peace Coalition, the Campus Antiwar Network, and the Hip Hop Caucus,[341] among others, joined the demonstrations marking the fourth anniversary of the war.

DESTABILIZATION

When the November 2006 election came in sight, the government's inability to crush the Iraqi insurgents—and the astonishing eruption of a sectarian civil war—at last convinced a decisive number of voters that Bush had lied to them and that the Republican Party had abused their trust. As the political climate shifted toward the Democrats, the anti-war demonstrations and rallies, the anti-Bush websites, bloggers, journalists, articles, and books were finally getting their messages across. Nationwide polls finally reported that a majority of Americans opposed the war and Bush's approval rates had plummeted.

In addition, a growing number of leading Democrats were changing their tune. They had insisted that they could do better than Bush and promised to bring the troops home after crushing the Iraqi insurgency and establishing a democratic gov-

---

341 An organization founded (2004) by Rev. Lennox Yearwood Jr., See http://www.hiphopcaucus.org/

ernment. But the popular demand to end the war forced these Democrats to line up behind their more courageous colleagues who had condemned Bush's war of aggression earlier.

Simultaneously, popular discontent with such issues as stagnant wages, huge federal debt, corporate profiteering, Tom Delay's money laundering, Mark Foley's sexual exploitation of Congressional pages, and other outrageous incidents committed by Republicans, finally pushed conservative voters as well as independents into the Democratic camp. When the 2006 election was over, the Democrats narrowly won control of both the Senate and the House of Representatives. Despite cold-blooded Republican measures aimed at keeping ethnic minorities from voting, six governors and more than 300 Democratic candidates for state legislative seats were added to the number of Democrats in state offices who were not up for election.

Impeachment

In 2004 a former Democratic senator from Florida, Bob Graham, who headed the Senate Intelligence Committee when 9/11 occurred, said any one of Bush's serious presidential crimes, abuses of power, and obstructions of justice would justify impeachment. "Taken together," he added, "they are a searing indictment of a president who, despite lofty words to the contrary, has not been a leader, has not been honest, and has not made America safer."[342]

---

342 Senator Bob Graham and Jeff Nussbaum. 2004. *Intelligence*

In *The Case for Impeachment*, the award winning journalist, Dave Lindorff, and the Deputy Director for the Center of Constitutional Rights, Barbara Olshansky, angrily asserted:

> One thing is alarmingly clear: the threats posed to the constitutional tradition of separation of powers and of checks and balances in government, to the various supposedly inalienable rights enumerated in the Constitution's Bill of Rights, and to the rule of law in a dangerous world, are all in grave danger if the American people do not take a stand in their defense against an administration that is clearly intent on eroding or destroying all these things.[343]

John Nichols, in *The Genius of Impeachment: the Founders' Cure for Royalism*, provides historical evidence that justifies impeaching Bush and Cheney. The evidence includes Jefferson's insistence that impeachment is a recourse for challenging "an elected despotism" and for rectifying a "corrupt republic." As Nichols indicated,

> the crafters of the Constitution did not leave to chance the question of how abusive executives might be removed. The threat of what our third president referred to as "electoral despotism" was so feared that multiple steps were taken to provide citizens and their elected rep-

Matters: The CIA, the FBI, Saudi Arabia, and the Failure of America's War on Terror. New York: Random House.

343 Dave Lindorff and Barbara Olshansky 2007. *The Case for mpeachment: The Legal Argument for Removing President George W. Bush from Office*. New York: Thomas Dunne Books, St. Martin's Press, p.14.

> resentatives with the power to check it. As was
> his practice, Jefferson explained the need for
> the fettering of the executive with a question:
> "What country can preserve its liberties if its
> rulers are not warned from time to time that
> this people preserve the spirit of resistance?"[344]

Prior to the installation of a Democratic Party majority in Congress, a small number of representatives had raised the issue of impeachment. (In addition, three dozen Vermont towns by March 2007 had actually supported resolutions calling for impeachment.) Nonetheless, Senator Nancy Pelosi ordered fellow Democrats in Congress to stop fighting for impeachment because it would distract from their efforts to end the war in Iraq. (Every newspaper in the country quoted her when she told her progressive colleagues that impeachment was "off the table.") But impeachment hearings—successful or not— could actually provide extraordinary opportunities for discrediting Bush's 'electoral despotism' and its corruption of democratic principles. (By 2007, national polls found a majority of Americans favoring impeachment and wishing the Bush administration was over.) Yet, despite all the Democratic Party resources for exploiting these opportunities, Pelosi decided that the Party should not raise the issue of impeachment.

Pelosi's decision was bizarre because a progressive, Sen. Conyers, chaired the Senate Judiciary Committee—the very committee that would hold impeachment hearings. After all, the Republicans would have joyfully exploited any opportunity to

---

344 Nichols, op cit., p.121.

gather votes for the 2008 election by impeaching a Democrat President if they had been in Pelosi's position and if a Republican (instead of Sen. Conyers) headed the Senate Judiciary Committee. Their attempts to impeach Clinton, despite its unpopularity, cost them little or nothing. Bush moved into the White House in the next election and most of the Republicans who led the impeachment campaign improved their electoral support. Republicans continued to control the House and Senate in 1998 and their setback in 2000 was in the Senate, which had refused to use the impeachment process to punish Clinton. David Swanson observes,

> In every election back to 1842 where House members of an opposition party to a sitting president have—as a whole or a significant caucus within the party—proposed impeachment of the president, that opposition party retained or improved its position in the House at the following election. There is no instance of voters responding to a significant impeachment effort by sweeping its advocates out of office. In fact, history points in a different direction—suggesting that voters frequently reward parties for taking the Constitution and the rule of law seriously.[345]

Sadly, during the spring of 2007, Pelosi and other Democratic Party leaders refused to capitalize aggressively on the anger and disillusionment over the war, shared by a majority of voters. The moderates once again ignored their progressive colleagues who refused to fund the war and thereby save lives by *un-*

---

345 See davidswanson. Feb. 19 2007. "Is Impeachment Politically Smart or Dangerous?" *AfterDowningStreet.org.*

equivocally bringing the troops home in a short period. Supported by MoveOn, they amended a 400-billion-dollar war funding House Bill that would pay for the war until March 2008 or September 2008 or the next century—depending on what form of the bill was selected by these politicians to justify their stand. Obviously, the closest deadlines were determined opportunistically because they occurred just before the 2008 election. But, significantly, the Democratic amendments to the proposal justified funding American troops and military bases in Iraq for "security purposes" *indefinitely*.

MoveOn's support of Pelosi's tactics stunned anti-war activists.[346] Howard Zinn succinctly exposed why MoveOn's tactic repelled progressives:

> There is an understandable predisposition for reasonable people to compromise, but there are compromises which are real, and others which are surrenders. See the new movie *The Wind that Shakes the Barley*. The Irish rebels were offered a compromise, which gave them the Irish Free State, something palpable, a ledge to stand on from which to fight for more, which they have done. There is nothing palpable in this [Democratic] "compromise," only a promise whose fulfillment is in the hands of George Bush, and meanwhile funds the ongoing slaughter in Iraq.[347]

346 MoveOn tried to justify its support by conducting an online poll of legislative options that excluded voting for a proposal by progressive Congressional representatives that requested the immediate withdrawal of troops from Iraq and funded the means necessary for carrying it out.

347 Howard Zinn. March 23 2007. "Howard Zinn Replies to MoveOn's support for the Supplemental." *Information Clearing*

Zinn concluded, "To me [the Democratic legislation] is tantamount to the abolitionists accepting a two-year timeline for ending slavery, while giving more money to enforce the Fugitive Slave Act."

A few days later, a narrow Senate majority backed the House by recommending no withdrawal until March 2008. However, since both of their recommendations amended a bill that would provide billions for continuing the war, Bush was furious. He could have accepted the amendment without any intention of honoring it by responding deceitfully to its requirements for proving the war was reaching its goals. But he decided that Congress had no right to tell him what to do and threatened a veto.

Nevertheless, the Senate Majority whip, Harry Reid, announced his intention to cut off funding for the Iraq war regardless of Bush's threat to veto any proposal setting a deadline for ending combat. The House proposal had ordered all combat troops out as of Aug. 31, 2008, whereas the Senate ordered some troops to leave right away with a nonbinding proposal for ending combat by March 31, 2008. Sadly, Reid was silent on funds for keeping some American troops in Iraq for "security purposes."

In the midst of this political ambiguity, Bush's attempts to colonize the richest oil-producing region in the world turned up new imperial possibilities. Instead of abandoning his "Armed Madhouse" and leaving everyone in peace, he secretly encouraged the bloody creation of powerless and ethnic-cleansed Sunni, Shiite, and Kurdish partitions in Iraq. In ad-

---

House.

dition, the Iraqi parliament was pressured to privatize roughly 80 per cent of the oil produced in Iraq—thereby enabling Exxon-Mobil, Shell, British Petroleum, and other gigantic oil and gas corporations, to get their share of the oily pie.

Oil is the single important Iraq natural resource and for 36 years the Iraqi government controlled its production and distribution. In 2008, America's colonizing efforts and its Iraqi collaborators began to return this natural resource to the Western corporations that originally owned it. Concurrently, leaks about a pending US assault against Iran, another major oil producer, began to appear! If they actually proved true, then Pelosi's refusal to call for Bush's impeachment could become a serious tactical error. Republicans would undoubtedly make any withdrawal of troops from Iraq appear treasonous—because Iraq would become an important staging area for invading Iran. On the other hand, impeachment hearings could produce grand opportunities to discredit an invasion plan. It would make millions of Americans choke with rage if a new war of aggression occurred.

Finally, impeachment, as the Founders intended, did not preclude prosecuting public officials for violating criminal codes. Keenly aware of this option, Vincent Bugliosi boldly summarized evidence demonstrating that Bush was accountable for the deaths of thousands of American troops and Iraqi civilians. His book, *The Prosecution of George W. Bush for Murder*,[348] advocated prosecuting Bush and

---

348 Vincent Bugliosi. 2008. *The Prosecution of George W. Bush for Murder*. Cambridge, MA: Vanguard Press.

his co-conspirators in federal courts. Bugliosi's qualifications for making this suggestion are impeccable. In addition to the prosecution of the infamous Charles Manson, Bugliosi had successfully prosecuted 105 out of 106 felony jury trials, including 21 murder convictions, without a single loss. In the book, Bugliosi adopts the stance of a prosecutor who refutes every argument that might be used by the defense to exonerate Bush. His refutations demonstrate that Bush is guilty because he *knowingly lied* to obtain congressional and popular support for invading Iraq. By 2008, for instance, investigative journalists, scrupulous officials, and Congressional committees had established that US intelligence agencies had told Bush before 9/11 that there were no ties between al Qaeda and Saddam Hussein—and that Hussein did not possess weapons of mass destruction that posed an *imminent threat* to the US.

On the other hand, the use of criminal sanctions would not deal adequately with the attacks on democratic institutions—conducted while Bush and his cronies controlled the government. Since Bush cannot be impeached after he leaves office, Kucinich took to the floor of the House of Representatives in June 2008 and audaciously spent more than four hours reading aloud 35 articles justifying Bush's impeachment.[349] The articles, among other things, spelled out Bush's abuse of power, incompetence, corruption, lying to the public, violations of international laws, and contempt for the legislative and judicial branches of the American government. The 35

---

349 Murder does not have a statute of limitations but impeachment does.

articles made a powerful case for impeachment and Kucinich's reading became one of the top political stories circulating the next day on the Internet. His own webpage experienced slowdowns due to the volume of traffic. But the corporate media simply shrugged its shoulders and provided minimal coverage. And the House of Representatives quickly referred the articles to Conyer's judiciary committee where they were fated to remain buried—ignored while "more important issues" were to be considered.

Republicans jumped with joy because they could count on the opportunistic and spineless responses from "moderate" Democrats. In the summer of 2008, everything was fluid—but it looked like the street fighters in the Republican Party and their Democratic Party collaborators still outclassed the progressive Democrats in spite of the lessons acquired from the 2006 election.

Nothing would change unless, of course, millions of progressives took to the streets, roused their neighbors, gave Bush the finger, kicked the corporate democrats in the butt, called for impeachment and supported the troops by bringing them home straight away. *Wow!* Sadly, every one of these possibilities appeared to be a pipe dream. Congress continued to fund the war, impeachment was "not on the table," and progressives were still challenging Democratic Party leaders to do the right thing. In June 2008, the peace movement was subdued—perhaps from exhaustion and despair—and most of the public was mesmerized by election year battles between Clinton, McCain and Obama even though none of them rejected Pelosi's stand on impeachment.

Then, surprisingly, the House Judiciary Committee—with Pelosi's agreement—began to hold a hearing entitled "Executive Power and Its Constitutional Limitations." House Democratic leaders absurdly insisted that the proceedings would allow witnesses to make a case for impeachment but the proceedings would not actually try Bush in order to remove him from office. When the first, June 2008, version of *Homeland Fascism* (posted as *Big Brother is Looking at You, Kid!*) was posted online, eleven witnesses had testified at a six-hour hearing, including Kucinich, who was loudly cheered, and legal experts such as Bugliosi, Fein, and Holtzman. Conservative law professors Stephen Presser from Northwestern University and Jeremy Rabkin of George Mason University also testified. The former Georgia Republican and current Libertarian presidential candidate Bob Barr also added to the litany of "high crimes and misdemeanors" committed by Bush.

The struggle continued.

Statue of Liberty in a Casket
[Image: demo video still]

21 | Fighting Customary Repression

*Pray for the dead and fight like hell
for the living!*

—Mother Jones

The anti-war movement in 2007 faced volatile political conditions and huge obstacles. But, even if an early withdrawal call could be successful, it would sooner or later be confronted by another imperial war and a renewed surge in the repression of domestic dissent. Whatever happens, Americans needed to adopt strategies for uninstalling the enactments, decrees, agencies, and other components of the *Fasces* assembled by Bush & Co. They also required tactics for fighting customary repression more effectively.

CRIMINALIZE REPRESSION

Disassembling the *Fasces* required support for the "Benjamin Franklin True Patriot Act," sponsored by Rep. Kucinich along with 20 other Congressmen. Aimed at restoring constitutional liberties, the Act would strip the Patriot Act of its search-and-seizure provisions, unconstitutional incarceration clause, denial of attorney-client privilege, Justice Dept. secrecy orders, egregious anti-immigrant provisions, and authority to search private records without probable cause. It would also restore transparency to Justice Dept. and Homeland Security administrative procedures and revoke the secrecy orders that have crippled the Freedom of Information Act. Conferences sponsored by the ACLU, National Lawyers Guild, EPIC, Center for Constitutional Rights, and other civil rights organizations also proposed step-by-step strategies for dismantling the neofascist infrastructure created by the Bush administration.

However, abolishing customary repression requires atypical methods. When coping in the short term with repression, for instance, the normal strategies for fighting such abuses as illegal surveillance, police brutality, "preemptive" arrests, "no fly lists," and indefinite detention are justified. But these strategies chiefly rely on civil rather than criminal law; and when the victims really win their day in civil court, government officials usually dip into public revenues to make restitution. In most cases, the public pays—*not* the wrongdoers themselves.[350]

---

350 See, for example, Dylan M. Nearly (2002). "Police Aggression is Costing You Money." *Earth Times News Service*. (Also,

What a deal! As a result, Chief Timoney and his Philadelphia officers had nothing to fear. They had beaten the people who demonstrated against the Republican National Convention in 2002 and conducted unconstitutional "preemptive arrests" of demonstrators. They had raided and destroyed the construction equipment, floats, and puppets stored in the *Puppetistas'* warehouse because the puppets dramatically portrayed the aims of the protest and the kinds of people who were destroying constitutional liberties. Like the enraged plainclothes officer who bloodied the environmentalist, Rob Fish, and tried to smash his camera, they too assumed any claim for justice in criminal courts would be futile. Traditionally, the government routinely attempts to use the criminal law to repress political dissent—but civil libertarians turn to the civil law for their defense.

In addition, civil libertarians, who actually demand criminal prosecutions, routinely rely on *conventional* criminal codes even though these codes do not take a fundamental characteristic of "crimes of repression" into account. They overlook the fact that political repression is especially harmful because it subverts *elementary rules for democratic* life.[351] Noting how the US Constitution conserves these rules, in 1975 Congressman Don Edwards observed:

> Regardless of the unattractiveness or noisy militancy of some private citizens or organizations, the Constitution does not permit federal interference with their activities except

justdissent.org, Feb. 5 2002.)

351 Again, see *icdc.com/~paulwolf/cointelpro/copapprf.htm*

through the criminal justice system, armed with its ancient safeguards. There are no exceptions. No federal agency, the CIA, the IRS, or the FBI, can be at the same time policeman, prosecutor, judge and jury. That is what constitutionally guaranteed due process is all about. It may sometimes be disorderly and unsatisfactory to some, but it is the essence of freedom. . . . I suggest that the philosophy supporting COINTELPRO is the subversive notion that any public official, the President or a policeman, possesses a kind of inherent power to set aside the Constitution whenever he thinks the public interest, or "national security" warrants it. That notion is a postulate of tyranny.[352]

How do we distinguish ordinary crimes (e.g., against persons or property) from a crime against democratic life? Judging violations of the elementary rules requires thinking about conditions distinguishing them from conventional crimes calling for different sanctions. For instance, the Senate Church Committee, which investigated FBI abuses in 1975, found that 40 per cent of 290 COINTELPRO actions from 1968 to 1971 violated the Constitution because they aimed at keeping activists from speaking, writing, and publishing. [353]

Yet the Committee *failed* to recommend policies

---

352 Edwards is quoted in the Preface to Churchill and Wall's *COINTELPO Papers*, op. cit.

353 The phrase, "Church Committee" refers to the United States Senate Select Committee to Study Governmental Operations with Respect to Intelligence Activities. This committee was chaired by Senator Frank Church (D-ID _ Idaho) and it investigated illegality by the CIA and FBI after Watergate.

that would actually disarm the government's weapons of mass repression and enable political dissidents to fight back. Furthermore, since no oversight committee rectified this failure, civil libertarians still had to consider the limitations of their own deterrence strategies. They should at least have advocated passage of crime-fighting legislation penalizing the *individuals* responsible for *political* repression. By "penalize" we actually mean *criminalizing* the usage of information technology and law enforcement practices that suppress political dissent and subvert the Constitution.[354] The Washington, DC and Miami police chiefs and every police officer who followed their paramilitary directives were guilty of felonies that would net any civilian a long sentence.

Furthermore, since Chief Ramsey's and Chief Timoney's police "training exercises" subverted the Constitution, political dissidents should have demanded legislation—akin to the Civil Rights and Voting Rights Acts of the Sixties—authorizing federal intervention to defend demonstrators from police brutality. The Sixties were evidence of how crucial federal intervention was in protecting the Freedom Riders in Montgomery, Alabama, after mobs beat them and firebombed their busses at the Anniston,

---

354 Libertarians cannot rely on legislative oversight committees to initiate this process. As both Donner and Glick point out, these committees have repeatedly turned a blind eye or whitewashed the repressive policies of government intelligence agencies. Donner adds that Hoover collected information about the private lives of subjects—sexual activities, drinking habits, gambling proclivities, and similar items—and traded this information for increased budget appropriations and protection from oversight committees and Congressmen who used it against their opponents.

Birmingham, and Montgomery Trailways terminals. In 1961, Federal marshals were ordered to protect the Riders.[355] Also, in 1963, when defending a group of Freedom Riders (including Martin Luther King), the marshals were greatly outnumbered by a mob because Alabama Governor John Patterson did not provide the protection he promised. Attorney General Robert Kennedy "federalized" state troopers and the National Guard to reinforce the marshals.[356] Later, in Mississippi, 160 marshals supported the struggle against segregation, fighting a racist mob the night before James H. Meredith enrolled at "Ole Miss." Finally, in 1965, after pitiless beatings and gassing by police, Martin Luther King led civil rights demonstrators from Selma, Alabama, under the protection of a federalized National Guard, to Montgomery, the state capitol where they were greeted by a rally of 50,000 people.

We know that federal marshals, national guardsmen, and state troopers have victimized political dissenters. Guardsmen killed black students at Jackson State and white students at Kent State University. But, again, our Janus two-faced government is a paradoxical entity and, despite Ashcroft's or Gonzales' efforts, the American criminal justice system is not monolithic. Activists should explore strategies that will compel enforcement agencies to uphold the Constitution even if this means protecting demonstrators from fascists on the same police force.

---

355 Southern police also killed three Freedom Riders.

356 The Riders left safely on the next route in defiance of the segregated public transportation system but they were arrested in Jackson, Mississippi.

Furthermore, establishing civil liberties commissions at federal, state and local levels of government should be considered. They should have the power to monitor and audit law enforcement expenditures and the power to prosecute offending officers. To justify the creation of these commissions, let us provide examples underscoring the need for prosecuting officers who fit the bill.

PARAMILITARY VIOLATIONS

At first, reality appeared to imitate art when Chief Timoney's paramilitary forces playacted defending the American Empire. Like imperial Roman soldiers, beating swords on their shields and scattering barbarians in a Cecil B. Demille epic, his line of Miami police advanced toward the demonstrators, beating their batons in unison on their shields, chanting: *Back! Back! Back!* But, clubbing, gassing, and shooting rubber bullets at people who are old and weak and unable to flee the scene rapidly; or attacking groups leaving demonstrations in small numbers (after most of their compatriots are gone); or charging demonstrators with overwhelming force was abominable. Under the guise of "riot control," "curbing civil unrest," and "conducting training exercises," the Miami police slowly but surely refined their tactics for repressing domestic dissent.

Demonstrators have usually responded to this police brutality by fighting in courts to dismiss unjust charges and make the government pay wherever possible for its lawlessness. But they have failed to provide long-term solutions. Donner's final book,

Protectors of Privilege: Red Squads and Police Repression in Urban America, presents damning evidence for this failure. (Donner, as indicated, had been the Director of the ACLU Project on Political Surveillance.) He recalls numerous cases in which demonstrators initiated lawsuits charging police departments and city governments with false arrest, brutal treatment, planting informers, inciting criminal acts, conducting surveillance without warrants, suppressing First Amendment rights, and promoting illegal wiretapping. Nevertheless, Donner also points out that the customary strategy for curbing this lawlessness was limited to "pocketbook sanctions, civil damage actions against cities, their police departments, and individual malefactors." This "pocketbook" strategy, at best, only curbed repression temporarily. Even million dollar judgments in favor of demonstrators has not prevented the revival of covert surveillance, the exchange of surveillance data between agencies, the infiltration of lawful groups by police agents, and brutal attacks. (Furthermore, years passed after these lawsuits were initiated and final judgments rendered.)

The recourse to "pocketbook sanctions" hardly changed the mobilization of bias that governed the selection of political targets. Scrutiny of FBI files demonstrates that millions of individuals have been targeted because they opposed the nuclear arms race, the degradation of the natural environment, the death penalty, job discrimination, oppressive labor practices, US foreign policies as well as gender, racial, ethnic, religious, and economic inequality. Every organization attempting to defend civil liberties in general and privacy rights in particular (e.g. the ACLU, the National Lawyers Guild, the National Committee against Repressive Legislation, Amnesty International, the Quakers) has been monitored if not infiltrated, and harassed by law enforcement agencies.[357]

Anti-war activists and groups opposed to the government's criminal policies are also targeted because right-wing fanatics have largely controlled American intelligence services as far back as the late 19th century struggle for an eight-hour day. Furthermore, after the demise of the Cold War, files obtained by FOIA requests have continued to demonstrate that officials who have contempt for democracy still control intelligence agencies.

Anyone reading Frank Donner's earlier book, *The Age of Surveillance*, should also be appalled at the extent to which government officials have committed crimes with impunity. To cite just one example, no agent, officer, or informant who shared the responsibility for murdering Black Panther leaders, Fred Hampton and Mark Clark, has ever been brought to trial.[358] From 1960 to 1974 alone, FBI agents conducted more than *half a million investigations* of so-called "subversives" who, in their collective imagination, might have tried to overthrow the government by force. And what did they find? According to Don-

---

357 The passage of the Freedom of Information Act (FOIA) in 1966 enabled people to request their files from federal, state and local law enforcement agencies. But the DoJ under the Obama administration is blocking the availability of these files. (More on this later.)
358 Regarding FBI and police complicity in the murder of Black Panther leaders, see Donner 1980, op. cit. pp. 221-232.

ner, not a single individual or group was prosecuted under the laws prohibiting the planning or advocating an action to overthrow the government.[359] Dissidents, however, were imprisoned on unrelated or fraudulent charges in order to destroy their political influence.[360]

The facts are indisputable. Attempts to subvert political dissidents—whether they were composed of organizations led by anyone who has demanded significant changes in our corporate economy—have been so extensive, it is doubtful there is anything comparable to the US government's record in recent decades among the Western industrial democracies. Moreover, on the whole, the repression has been successful. As indicated previously, influential left-wing political parties are evident in virtually every European democracy. But customary forms of repression have not allowed any influential leftist party —or even a Green party—to provide alternatives to the two-party system in the USA.

Monitoring Repression

As indicated, political surveillance programs play a key role in the neo-fascist infrastructure installed

359 The COINTELPRO operations were officially discontinued in April of 1971, after public exposure, reportedly in order to "afford additional security to [their] sensitive techniques and operations." [https://web.archive.org/web/20060615083223/http://www.icdc. com/~paulwolf/cointelpro/blackstock30.jpg

360 For further information, among many other sources, see a website which was devoted to COINTELPRO: https://web.archive.org/web/20120125024603/http://www.icdc.com /~paulwolf/cointelpro/cointel.htm

by the Bush administration. These programs are ostensibly being created to protect Americans from terrorists and ordinary criminals but this justification cannot be taken at face value. Take, for instance, the National Counterterrorism Center's (NCTC) database on international terrorism suspects and people who aid them. This database is compiled from reports supplied by the CIA, FBI, National Security Agency (NSA), and other agencies. In 2006 NCTC's central database contained 325,000 names. Reportedly, US citizens made up "only a very, very small fraction" of that number" but an NCTC official refused to say how many citizens were actually on the list. After all, 325,000 is a big number and, if a mere five per cent of the names were used as an estimate, the database would contain more than 16,000 citizens. Is such an estimate believable? How many American citizens are actually in the database? Is their presence there justified?

Gonzales would not provide the number. He falsely assured the Senate Judiciary Committee in February 2006 that even though he could not discuss specifics, "Information is collected, information is retained and information disseminated in a way to protect the privacy interests of all Americans." The Director of National Intelligence, John Negroponte, was another unlikely source of information. Negraponte provided cover for the Iran-Contra campaign and, when he was ambassador to Honduras, falsified human rights reports. (As indicated, he told investigators that his embassy knew nothing about the Honduran Special Forces unit, Battalion 3-16, who killed up to 184 people, including an American priest and 32 Salvadoran nuns and women of faith who were thrown into the sea, alive, from a helicopter.)

To top it off, two *Washington Post* staff writers, Walter Pincus and Dan Eggen, reported that the NCTC database has been made available on a website to "about 5,000 analysts around the counterterrorist intelligence community."[361] Even though the analysts must have clearances, how can privacy rights of the players ever be ensured in a 5,000-seat stadium? Timothy Sparapani, legislative counsel for privacy rights at the American Civil Liberties Union, called the number of names in the database "shocking but, unfortunately, not surprising." Since every intelligence agency and counterintelligence program is constructing its own lists, he added, "We have lists that are having baby lists at this point; they're spawning faster than rabbits."

Since the NCTC database is compiled from a variety of intelligence agencies, Pincus and Eggen asked Shannon Moran, a spokeswoman for the FBI screening center, to answer detailed questions about her center's work, "including how many names are on its list, how many US citizens are included and whether the FBI database includes names linked to the NSA program." They were told that in 2005, the "FBI database alone contained more than 270,000 names, including a large number of people associated with "domestic terrorist movements" such as "radical environmentalists" and "neo-Nazi white supremacists."

---

361 Walter Pincus and Dan Eggen. Feb. 15 2006. "325,000 Names on Terrorism List: Rights Groups Say Database May Include Innocent People." *Washington Post.*

Are any other "domestic movements" included? The answer indisputably is "Yes." They have been uncovered previously in one law enforcement database after another.

Previous chapters have mentioned the severe "false positive" problems associated with names on the relentlessly expanding number of "watch lists," "no fly lists," and a host of other self-styled "counter-intelligence" lists. These chapters have also highlighted the Orwellian broadening of the term "terrorist" and its use by prosecutors to frame innocent people.

Yet, despite their potential for abuse, there is nothing in sight that has effectively evaluated the validity of these lists or their fidelity to Constitutional principles. NCTC and other intelligence agencies have ignored criticism expressed by civil liberties groups and at Congressional hearings. And these agencies have either lied or stonewalled civil-liberties groups such as the ACLU, Electronic Privacy Information Center, and the National Lawyers Guild about their lists. As a result, these groups have had to resort to lawsuits to force the NCDT, for example, to reveal that the names in its central database *quadrupled* between 2003 and 2006.

In July 2007, a federal appeals court ordered the dismissal of a lawsuit painstakingly pursued at great expense by the ACLU, lawyers, journalists, and scholars who claimed their jobs were handicapped by government monitoring. The court said that the plaintiffs had no standing to sue even though a lower court judge found that warrantless surveillance violated their constitutional rights.

The political abuse of databases has been mentioned repeatedly. Recall that almost a thousand law enforcement agencies utilized massive databases in the FALCON project. Will experience gained from these sweeps be used if government leaders wrap themselves in a flag and are willing to risk a coup carried out in the name of national security?

Surely, progressives can think of numerous ways to curb the weapons of mass repression that would back a fascist coup. One possibility could empower national commissions to monitor the people who construct these databases and their programmatic applications in order to ensure that they not be used to suppress civil liberties. These commissions should also when warranted be free to prosecute these people.

AUDITING REPRESSION

In addition to the millions in damages levied in lawsuits against local police, how much money and time are actually being spent to support political repression by the FBI, the CIA, the IRS, the JTTF, the old and new 'Red Squads' and all the other law enforcement agencies? How many billions or even trillions of dollars have been required just to investigate nonviolent outfits such as the NAACP, Clamshell Alliance, Greenpeace, the Sierra Club, the United Methodist Church, League of Women Voters, PTA, Catholic Interracial Council, Planned Parenthood Association, PUSH, the SCLC, the Black Panther Party, the Committee in Solidarity with People of El Salvador, United for Peace and Social Justice, United

Electrical Workers Union, Furriers Union, Memphis Sanitation Workers' Union, Mine and Smelter Workers, SOA Watch, Green Party, Socialist Workers Party, Communist Party, Families for Peaceful Tomorrows, the American Friends Service Committee, Upper NY State Area Office, Brooklyn Parents for Peace, the Buffalo War Resisters League, the Council on American-Islamic Relations, the Council on Peoples Organization, NY Immigration Coalition; Peace Action of Central NY, People for the American Way, People for Animal Rights, Veterans for Peace, the Western NY Peace Center, and other progressive organizations?

Chapter 6 described how the NYPD indiscriminately rounded-up thousands of demonstrators who protested the 2004 Republican Convention. New York police dumped these demonstrators in Pier 57, a condemned, filthy, asbestos-poisoned old bus depot, where they were imprisoned without charge for up to 24 hours or more! Two years later, lawsuits forced the City to reveal that undercover NYPD officers flew to cities across the nation as well as Canada and Europe for more than a year to engage in covert surveillance of progressives who protested the 2004 Republican National Convention in New York City. The records uncovered by civil liberties organizations found that the officers had traveled within the US to cities in California, Connecticut, Florida, Georgia, Illinois, Massachusetts, Michigan, Montreal, New Hampshire, New Mexico, Oregon, Tennessee, Texas, and Washington, D.C. as well as cities in Europe. They used any tactic imaginable to spy on progressives. They had attended meetings, posed as sympathizers, lied about their identities, made friends with anti-war activists, and shared meals with their families. And they had certainly hacked into their email.

The records provided by this massive surveillance supposedly spotted a small handful of people who expressed interest in breaking the law when the Republican convention took place. Actually, some protesters engaging in civil disobedience proved to be the only unlawful acts conducted during the convention. Furthermore, the reports on these possible troublemakers were overwhelmingly outnumbered by reports about people who never expressed any intention of breaking the law. The people being watched by undercover officers included members of street theater companies, music groups, church groups and antiwar organizations, as well as environmentalists and people opposed to the death penalty, globalization, and other ill-conceived government policies. Three New York City elected officials were also watched," according to Jim Dwyer, a *New York Times* correspondent.[362]

In addition, NYPD intelligence reports on lawful activities were shared with police departments in other cities. The identities of anti-war music or theatrical groups and the locations and dates of their performances in such municipalities as New York, Washington, Seattle, San Francisco, and Boston were sent to other police departments.

What did this unconstitutional intelligence operation cost? Who was responsible? Michael

---

362 Jim Dwyer. March 25 2007. "City Police Spied Broadly Before G.O.P. Convention." *New York Times*

Bloomberg, the Mayor, and his corrupt Police Commissioner, Bernard Kerik, were certainly guilty of managing this massive political surveillance program.[363] Shouldn't Bloomberg and Kerik have been impeached or fired? What other options do New Yorkers have to stop this extraordinary, illegal expenditure of their money?

It can be argued that congressional, state, or local legislative bodies provide "implied consent" for repressive policies when they fund the FBI or any other intelligence agency. But their repressive activities are unconstitutional despite Orwellian attempts to justify them; as a result, this argument is a distraction. Given the evidence gathered through FOIA requests, Congress, for instance, has the responsibility to correct its failure to monitor FBI policies adequately. At a minimum, therefore, it should pass legislation that requires the General Accounting Office (GAO) to conduct periodic audits of what the FBI is actually doing with the billions of dollars it receives. These audits should incorporate methods for distinguishing between genuine criminal investigations and unconstitutional ones. And, depending upon the proportion of time and money being spent on unconstitutional activities, Congress should, after reviewing the GAO report, *force the FBI to operate*

---

363 While his term in office, Kerik accepted thousands in illegal gifts. He copped a plea and paid 221,000 dollars in fines to stay out of jail and begin a new career as a security consultant in the Middle East. The gifts included 165,000 dollars in renovations to his apartment from a construction company seeking to do business with the city. Kerik violated an ordinance by failing to report this gift as a loan.

within constitutional limits by cutting its funds.[364]

Imposing this budgetary strategy on all intelligence agencies including the CIA would be a wise move. There is no good reason why federal, state, and local governments should not conduct periodic audits with this aim in mind.

CIVIL DISOBEDIENCE

Understandably, actualizing the previous suggestions would require massive shifts in popular standpoints. In the meantime, a number of intellectuals are attempting to probe the current threats to democracy. Shortly before 9/11 a hard-hitting book, David McGowan's *Understanding the F-Word: American Fascism and the Politics of Illusion*, attacked the far-right shift in government policies. Mc-Gowan points out that powerful Americans, including Bush's grandfather and great-grandfather were among the principals in a Wall Street powerhouse—Brown Brothers/Harriman—which had its assets seized after World War II under the Trading with the Enemy Act.[365] He proposed that after the Second World War, fascism was "deconstructed" in America—it acquired a democratic façade. Behind the façade is a one-party dictatorship, organized by

---

364 We are aware of GAO audits required by the Patriot Act but we are not referring to these audits. Furthermore, Congress does not need award-winning legal experts or social scientists that specialize in organizational behavior to create these methods.

365 David McGowan. 2001. *Understanding the F-Word: American Fascism and the Politics of Illusion.* Lincoln, NE: Writers Club Press.

Republicans and Democrats whose joint efforts forcibly prevent the rise of an effective political opposition.

Gerry Spence's book—aptly entitled *Bloodthirsty Bitches and Pious Pimps of Power: The Rise and Risks of the New Conservative Hate Culture*—is primarily devoted to an attack on far-right cultural icons such as Bill O'Reilly, Ann Coulter and Pat Robertson. It also reiterates points made by McGowan. As trial attorney for more than five decades, Spence has fought successfully for the families of Karen Silkwood, Randy Weaver of Ruby Ridge, and hundreds of other "little people." His penultimate chapter, "The Rise of the Fourth Reich," opens with the following sentence: "If we have not already fully arrived, the road we travel is one inevitably leading to a corporate-government oligarchy we may politely call electoral fascism."

Principled conservatives have also jumped into the ring. Bush called himself a "compassionate conservative" but the title of John Dean's book, *Conservatives without Conscience*, sardonically discredits him. It contends that recent decades have witnessed the takeover of the Republican Party by far-right legions composed of authoritarian personalities. Relying on studies by notable psychologists (e.g., Stanley Milgram and Robert Altemeyer) of how ordinary people can become closed-minded and brutalized, Dean says our government has been run by people who seek to dominate others, who have contempt for egalitarian principles, and who are vengeful, pitiless, exploitative, manipulative, mean-spirited, narrow-minded, intolerant, and dishonest. Bush and his cabal, Dean insists, are *not* true conservatives. They are exceptions that prove the rule because conservatives, in his opinion, respect the rule of law and have consciences.[366]

Dean rightfully fears that millions of extreme right-wing Americans would support a dictatorial government. Accordingly, he projects a bleak future for America if the "authoritarians" that dominate the Republican Party are not opposed. After reviewing Bush's assaults on the Constitution, he asks,

> Are we on the road to fascism? Clearly, we are not on that road yet. But it would not take much more misguided authoritarian leadership, or thoughtless following of such leaders, to find ourselves there. I am not sure which is more frightening: another major terrorist attack or the response of authoritarian conservatives to that attack. Both are alarming prospects.[367]

Paul Craig Roberts, a former *Wall Street Journal* editor and an Assistant Secretary of the Treasury under Reagan,[368] offered similar opinions. After Homeland Security Secretary Chertoff and Sen. Santorum prophesized a terrorist attack during the summer or fall of 2007,[369] Roberts wrote irritably,

---

366 Dean, op. cit. pp.183-84.

367 Ibid. p.180.

368 In addition, Roberts was an Associate Editor of the *Wall Street Journal* editorial page and Contributing Editor of *National Review*.

369 After opposition to the Iraq War soared in early 2007, Chertoff told the public that his "gut" told him that the risk of a terrorist attack would increase during the summer. Within days, Sen. Santorum also predicted that an attack might happen around the

Hitler, who never achieved majority support in a German election, used the Reichstag Fire to fan hysteria and push through the Enabling Act, which made him dictator. Determined tyrants never require majority support in order to overthrow constitutional orders.

The American system is near to being overthrown. Are coming "terrorist" events of which Chertoff warns and Santorum promises the means for overthrowing our constitutional democracy?

As Bush the King (not Oedipus Rex) devoured the Bill of Rights for dinner, bestselling political journalist, Joe Conason, joined the Greek chorus divining the nation's fate. Ironically echoing Sinclair Lewis' 1935 novel, *It Can't Happen Here*, Conason titled his prophetic book, *It Can Happen Here: Authoritarian Peril in the Age of Bush.* [370]

Justice William O. Douglas once said, "When a legislature undertakes to proscribe the exercise of a citizen's constitutional rights it acts lawlessly and the citizen can take matters into his own hands and proceed on the basis that such a law is no law at all." Douglas, of course, is not the only notable American credited with this stand. In 1849, Henry David Thoreau, in *On the Duty of Civil Disobedience*,

---

same time and get people to change their minds and support the war.

370 As Chapter 5 indicated, Lewis' novel depicted a racist, anti-Semitic, flag-waving demagogue who, backed by the army, won the 1936 presidential election and created an Americanized version of Nazi Germany. The Church Committee also documented the history of customary repression dating back to World War I, the 1920s, Thirties, and throughout the post Second World War period.

wrote: "If...the machine of government...is of such a nature that it requires you to be the agent of injustice to another, then, I say, break the law." Thoreau, no armchair activist, was opposed to slavery and the war with Mexico and was imprisoned for refusing to pay poll taxes.

During the Vietnam War, Daniel Ellsberg and Anthony Russo also took matters into their own hands. They stole and distributed classified documents, known as *The Pentagon Papers*. In addition, radicals calling themselves the Citizen's Commission to Investigate the FBI broke into a Philadelphia FBI office and stole secret documents that exposed COINTELPRO. These kinds of "lawless" actions had profound effects. The publication of the FBI documents, for instance, forced Hoover to cancel COINTELPRO. It justified the Senate Church Committee Hearings, whose final report declared,

> Many of the techniques used would be intolerable in a democratic society even if all of the targets had been involved in violent activity, but COINTELPRO went far beyond that . . . the Bureau conducted a sophisticated vigilante operation aimed squarely at preventing the exercise of First Amendment rights of speech and association, on the theory that preventing the growth of dangerous groups and the propagation of dangerous ideas would protect the national security and deter violence.

But, obviously, Douglas should have added a cautionary note to his statement and warned dissidents about the use of clubs, tear gas, rubber bullets, and tasers by law enforcement agents who insist that *they* (not the dissidents) are upholding the law. The progressive movement's response to these tactics has openly defied the *Fasces* by blocking main streets during demonstrations, linking arms, and forming virtually impassible human chains, or sitting-down, going limp, and turning their backs to police clubs. Fellow protesters were cheered when they defied laws of gravity, got on top of tall buildings and dropped billboard-sized banners with slogans. *Stop the War! Impeach Bush!*

In 1995, two renowned environmentalists, Mike Roselle and Howard Cannon, founded the Ruckus Society. Its members offer environmental, social justice, and peace (weeklong and weekend) "training camps" that instruct demonstrators in the use of direct action and civil disobedience. By February 2007, nonviolent civil disobedience was an integral part of progressive campaigns. Voices for Creative Nonviolence, for instance, launched the Occupation Project, a campaign of sustained nonviolent disobedience aimed at ending the funding for the war and occupation of Iraq. A number of anti-war organizations joined the campaign and, in three months, over 320 arrests occurred in the offices of 39 Representatives and Senators. The campaign also targeted officials in key cities in 25 states.

After Bush got Congress to fund the war, the Project promised to launch new acts of civil disobedience and office occupations during the summer of 2007. On July 6, for instance, police arrested 20 protesters ranging in ages from 20 to 72 who refused to leave Senators Grassley and Harkin's Cedar Rapids offices.

IMPEACH NOW!

www.ImpeachBush.org

The illegal war of aggression Bush launched against Iraq has killed hundreds of thousands of Iraqis, and killed or wounded tens of thousands of US soldiers.

(For Iraqi deaths see Johns Hopkins study published in the British medical journal The Lancet 10.6.2006.)

He set up a worldwide network of secret prisons, where torture has become the norm.

He gave himself the power to wiretap, open the mail of, search, and indefinitely detain any American.

Each second this president spends in office is harmful to the interests and values of the American people and the Constitution. It is time to take a stand and let the world know that he is not acting with our consent.

Articles of impeachment drafted by former Attorney General Ramsey Clark, available at www.impeachbush.org.

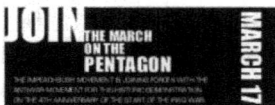

JOIN THE MARCH ON THE PENTAGON

MARCH 17

THE IMPEACH-BUSH MOVEMENT IS JOINING FORCES WITH THE ANTIWAR MOVEMENT FOR THIS HISTORIC DEMONSTRATION ON THE 4TH ANNIVERSARY OF THE START OF THE IRAQ WAR.

Demand Congress Impeach Bush.
Over 810,000 people have already voted to impeach — have you?

Take action today by going to
www.ImpeachBush.org

YES! — Congress should impeach George W. Bush and other high officials. I want to help.
Your contribution will be used to support this ad campaign and other organizing efforts of ImpeachBush.org through more advertising and other means.

NAME _____ E-MAIL _____

ADDRESS _____

CITY _____ STATE _____ ZIP _____

Make checks payable to Vote To Impeach. Mail to: Vote To Impeach 5505 Connecticut Avenue NW, #208, Washington DC, 20015-2601. Please include this coupon with your check. Contributions to Vote To Impeach.org and ImpeachBush.org are not tax deductible. You can make a credit card donation online through our secure server at www.ImpeachBush.org.

22 | Impeachment & Prosecution

"Our enemies are innovative and resourceful, and so are we. They never stop thinking about new ways to harm our country and our people, and neither do we."

—President G. W. Bush, Aug. 5, 2004

IMPEACHMENT

Another example of civil disobedience occurred in July 2007 when Capital Police cuffed and arrested Cindy Sheehan, Rev. Lennox Yearwood, Jr., Ray McGovern, and other prominent activists and put them on a police bus because they refused to leave Sen. Conyer's office and the adjoining hallway. The activists had asked Conyers to take action on impeachment and support a bill submitted a few months earlier by Rep. Kucinich calling for Vice President Cheney's impeachment. As they were led away to face a charge of disorderly conduct, the activists were followed by several hundred other protesters who had also filled the hallway outside the Senator's office. All of them chanted: *What do we want? Impeachment! When do we want it? Now!*

Sen. Conyers had been the least likely target for civil disobedience because of his indisputable progressive credentials. When Republicans controlled Congress, he had advocated impeachment; held a mock hearing on this issue, and even submitted a bill with 30 co-sponsors, calling for an investigation of possible impeachable crimes perpetrated by the administration. In July 2007, however, he refused to go along with the delegation occupying his office even though the delegation handed him a petition signed by almost a million people. After talking with Conyers, Sheehan emerged together with Yearwood and McGovern and angrily told the people waiting in the hall that Conyers had said "impeachment isn't going to happen because we don't have the votes." Conyers knew that a House majority would not back impeachment. As a result, the Speaker of the House, Nancy Pelosi, had explicitly refused to put the issue "on the table" and chairman of the House Democratic caucus, Rahm Emanuel, had said "Dennis [Kucinich] can do what he wants, I'm not going to support it."

Sheehan also informed the people in the hall that Conyers insisted the best thing for Democrats was to focus on "winning big in 2008." Progressives, however, were determined to buck Pelosi's stand on impeachment regardless. Prior to the sit-in at Conyer's office, in March 2007, more than 50,000 people braved snow and freezing rain to get to Washington. Led by Iraq war veterans, active-duty service-members, Gold Star families, and veterans from other wars, these progressives marched on the Pentagon to protest the beginning of the fifth year of the Iraq war. The Pentagon and Virginia State Police, many clad in riot gear, wearing gas masks, and wielding batons, blocked people coming from busses and subways who wanted to attend the demonstration.[371] Despite 20-mile an hour winds and a wind-chill factor in the teens, the protesters listened to speeches by Ramsey Clark, Cindy Sheehan, Cynthia McKinney, and other progressives.[372] Clark, who had served as the Attorney General during the Carter administration, authoritatively reviewed the "high crimes and misdemeanors" perpetrated by the Bush administration.

Remarkably, the March on the Pentagon was but one of more than 1,000 demonstrations that took place at that time. The Los Angeles demonstration drew 50,000 and the San Francisco demonstration, 40,000. A number of books calling for impeachment also appeared.[373] Ironically, Conyers and his staff

---

371 Breaking agreements allowed by the permit for the march, they also blocked buses from parking near the Pentagon. As a result, protesters had to walk nearly two miles to get to their buses after the rally.

372 Speakers also included constitutional rights attorney Mara Verheyden-Hilliard, Jonathan Hutto and Liam Madden (co-founders of Appeal for Redress; Iraq Veterans Against the War), Salt Lake City Mayor Rocky Anderson, and still others. You can view the rally by going to *cspan.org* and clicking on the March 17 anti-war rally under the video section. Ramsey Clark's speech is available on YouTube.

373 See, for instance, David Lindorf and Barbara Olshansky, 2006,

wrote one of them and it is entitled *The Constitution in Crisis: The High Crimes of the Bush Administration and a Blueprint for Impeachment*.[374]

After the July sit-in at Conyer's office, United for Peace and Justice, a coalition composed of 46 organizations, asked its members to conduct local events during the summer that would culminate in eight massive regional anti-war demonstrations in October. What's more, MoveOn began still another campaign, Operational Democracy, to pressure key members of Congress to reverse their stand on Iraq.

Then, on August 7, 2007, the AFL-CIO hosted a forum for the Democratic Party presidential candidates, held in a Chicago sports stadium filled with 17,000 union workers and their families. The candidates fielded questions from Olbermann, who had become the sharpest TV news commentator in the US. Union members who had lost their employment, pensions, and health benefits also posed questions. They wanted to know what the candidates would do about the outsourcing of jobs and industries, health care, and the deterioration of working class living standards.

The responses provided by most of the candidates seemed to promise the audience everything it wanted. But Kucinich was the only candidate not re-

cited above. Also, John Nichols. 2007. *The Genius of Impeachment: The Founder's The Case for Impeachment, Cure for Royalism and Why it Should be Applied to George W. Bush.* New York: The New Press.

374 John C. Conyers, Jr. and Staff. 2007. *The Constitution in Crisis: The High Crimes of the Bush Administration and a Blueprint for Impeachment* New York: Skyhorse Publishing.

sponding in generalities because he had, in contrast to the others, actually sponsored legislation that would accomplish these ends. For instance, he identified legislative initiatives that would provide for a universal single-payer health care system; and he reported that he would get rid of NAFTA altogether rather than "fixing it" as the other candidates preferred.

Kucinich courageously favored an immediate unqualified withdrawal from Iraq but the other candidates affirmed their support for the Democratic Party's open-ended stand on withdrawal. Furthermore, in addition to merely proposing a partial withdrawal, Obama opportunistically suggested that the US should consider expanding the "war against terrorism." He justified invading Pakistan unilaterally if "actionable intelligence" sources indicated that Pakistan has harbored Osama bin Laden. Senators Clinton and Dodd scolded Obama. They slyly implied that a candidate with greater foreign policy experience would realize that no president should let people know in advance that an invasion is being planned. But at no point did these two indicate that the American public should have anything to say about wars of aggression planned by warmongers who control the government.

In addition to the million Iraqis slaughtered since the US invaded Iraq and the 3684 (officially acknowledged) deaths of US military personnel, the cost of the war to US taxpayers by August 2007 was almost $500 billion and climbing. How many generations will it take to pay off the debt accumulated while Bush had been in office, and where will the candidates who favor a partial withdrawal find funds for rebuilding highways, bridges, mass transit systems, universal health care, and public education? Can these candidates actually make good on their promises while they continue to fund the armed forces, mercenaries, other private contractors, and military bases remaining after a partial withdrawal? What about the 750 plus military bases encircling the globe or the continued support for traditional, experimental and nuclear weapons? Who will really pay for these costs? The corporate rich? Like hell!

Americans during that August were experiencing the collapse of the housing market and tens of thousands of foreclosures. The Federal Reserve injected 38 billion dollars to stabilize volatile financial markets after a 387-point plunge in the Dow Jones index. Nevertheless, financial experts were accurately predicting a full-blown recession by 2008.

Democrats at that time escaped blame for the economic crisis or the inability of the government to cope with it even though they collaborated with Bush in waging a war of aggression no matter the cost. What else would one expect? In 2008, for instance, almost all the righteous Democratic Party candidates for President quit the race. Kucinich was the most consistently progressive candidate. And even though Edwards had moved toward a populist position, denouncing corporate domination of America, he withdrew his candidacy when he became involved in a scandalous extramarital relationship. Eventually, Obama and Clinton were left because they had acquired the tens of millions necessary for buying the election.

During Spring 2008, Clinton threw the kitchen sink at Obama. One of her slurs found him guilty of continuing to attend the Chicago Trinity United Church of Christ where an African American, Rev. Jeremiah Wright, had served as pastor. His membership in a church attended primarily by African Americans and European Americans was understandable. Obama was born in Honolulu and his parents were students at the University of Hawaii. His father had been at the university on a foreign student scholarship from Kenya and his mother was a European American student from Wichita, Kansas. Wright made national headlines when recordings of his sermons were scrutinized and journalists discovered that he had condemned the US government for war crimes and crimes against humanity. Discrediting Wright—and, by implication, Obama—relied on "sound-bites" that took Wright's politically provocative remarks out of context. Fortunately, *The Chicago Tribune*, on March 29, 2008, published the contexts in which the most notorious sound-bites had been excerpted.[375] Shortly after 9/11, for instance, Wright sermonized:

> We've bombed Hiroshima, we've bombed Nagasaki, we've nuked far more than the thousands in New York and the Pentagon and we never batted an eye. . . . We have supported state terrorism against the Palestinians and black South Africans, and now we are indignant. Because the stuff we have done overseas is now brought right back into our own front

375 The texts can be found online in "Rev. Jeremiah Wright's words: Sound bite vs. sermon excerpt." *Tribune* staff report. March 29 2008. *chicagotribune.com*.

yards. America's chickens are coming home to roost.

Wright's rhetoric was influenced by the Hebraic prophetic tradition. His sermon, in addition, was filled with biblical references to the slaughtering of innocent people. Referring to thoughts of "paybacks" in Psalm 137, he said,

> Look at the verse, Verse 9: 'Happy shall they be who take your little ones and dash them against the rocks.' The people of faith, by the rivers of Babylon, how should we sing the Lord's song if I forget thee? The people of faith have moved from the hatred of armed enemies, these soldiers who captured the King, those soldiers who slaughtered his sons and put his eyes out, the soldiers who sacked the city, burned their towns, burned the temple, burned their towers. They moved from the hatred of armed enemies to the hatred of unarmed innocents. The babies. The babies. Blessed are they who dash your babies' brains against a rock. And that, my beloved, is a dangerous place to be.

Yet that is where the people of faith are in 551 B.C. and that is where far too many people of faith are in 2001 A.D. We have moved from the hatred of armed enemies to the hatred of unarmed innocents. We want revenge. We want paybacks and we don't care who gets hurt in the process.

In another sermon filled with biblical quotations, Wright had informed his congregation that the US government had killed Native Americans and put them on reservations. It had enslaved Africans and interned citizens of Japanese descent in prison camps. After the civil war, African Americans were put in inferior schools, substandard housing, the lowest paying jobs, refused equal protection of the law, and kept out of the racist bastions of higher education. Regarding African Americans, Wright had declared:

> The government gives them the drugs, builds bigger prisons, passes a three-strike law and then wants us to sing 'God Bless America'?

> No, no, no, not "God Bless America," "God Damn America!" That's in the Bible, for killing innocent people. God damn America for treating its citizens as less than human, God damn America as long as she tries to act like she is God and she is supreme. The United States government has failed the vast majority of her citizens of African descent.

Immediately, after listening to the sermons, journalists and right-wing pundits circulated Wright's most provocative sound-bites (e.g., "God Damn America!") nationwide. They informed millions that Obama was guilty by association; therefore, Obama, despite his repudiation, agreed with Wright's condemnation. In the *Seattle Times*, David Sirota indicated that right-wing insinuations exploited the Wright incident in order to incite racist opposition to Obama's candidacy.[376] Sean Hannity accused Wright of supporting a black-separatist agenda while

---

376 David Sirota is a fellow at the Campaign for America's Future and a board member of the Progressive States Network. His blog is at *credoaction.com/sirota*. The *Seattle Times* article cited above appeared on March 31 2008.

Charles Krauthammer labeled [Wright's] pronouncement "vitriolic divisiveness." Pat Buchanan condemned Wright for saying "God damn America" even though Buchanan had avoided the draft while Wright, a former Marine, had demonstrated his loyalty to the country.

Hillary Clinton jumped into the ring. She exploited the Wright incident in televised interviews and campaign speeches. She declared that she would have left her church decades ago if her pastor had condemned America. "He would not have been my pastor!" Clinton cried out. "You don't choose your family, but you choose what church you want to attend!" Sirota wrote:

> [Clinton's aides] have been calling the states they believe Obama will lose their political "firewall." That's campaign-speak for "race wall"—one built with bricks like Pennsylvania and Indiana. These aren't the near-purely white states where racial politics is often muted (and Obama won). They are the slightly diverse states where racial politics simmers and where the black vote is too small to offset a motivated racist vote. This race wall is now being fortified.

Sirota justifiably believed that Clinton's tactic was designed to motivate racist support. Yet, her tactic also relied on myths about "American Exceptionalism" that reinforced the opposition to Wright's sermons. It brought an American *Deus ex machina—the God from the machine*—onstage to defame and silence any defense of Wright's condemnation of war crimes and crimes against humanity. When the fifth anniversary of the Iraq invasion rolled around on March 19, 2008, neither Clinton nor Obama promised to hold the heads of our government accountable for wars of aggression or crimes against humanity.

FALSE PROMISES

After the primary votes were counted, John McCain became the Republican candidate. To ensure support from the far-right, he chose Sarah Palin as vice president and both of them appealed for votes by offering stereotypes, myths, and demagogic proposals. But the electorate rejected them because of the disastrous performance of the Bush administration and the economic crisis.

Despite centuries of slavery, segregation, and discrimination against Africans and African Americans, Obama became the 44th President in 2008. His inauguration was attended by more than a million supporters and capped by his speech, "A New Birth of Freedom," that paid homage to Abraham Lincoln. In addition to concerts and an inaugural ball, inauguration events featured an astounding home-style parade composed of civic groups, union members, police, firefighters, cheerleaders, and high-school marching bands.

Subsequently, however, Obama, a seeming master at *realpolitik,* loaded his cabinet and department offices with a mere handful of genuine progressives. He drew most of his appointments from conservatives and moderates who had guided the government during Clinton and Bush administrations. As a result, the possibility of holding Bush and Cheney accountable for war crimes and crimes against humanity appeared remote, even though the House of Representatives had previously voted for impeaching President Clinton (because he lied about engaging in oral sex with an intern, Monica Lewinsky). In the context of an opportunistic right-wing political climate, Clinton's lie was considered more harmful than war crimes and crimes against humanity.

Given the notorious lack of bipartisanship since Obama was elected, few truly informed Americans believed that the Republicans would hold the Bush administration accountable. In fact, it finally became apparent that Obama was implicitly insisting on "bipartisanship" to justify conservative outcomes and discredit "biased" and "unrealistic" criticism from progressives. Instead of defining universal health care as a "human right," for instance, and directing his request for "health care reform" to Tom Harkin (the Chair of the Senate committee on Health, Education, Labor, and Pensions), he framed the health care issue as a crisis in federal expenditures and directed his call to Max Baucus (the Chair of the Senate Finance Committee) who was subservient to the private health care insurance corporations. Predictably, by December 2009, when the initial Senate deliberations over health-care reforms were completed, Obama's strategy had encouraged legislative deals that gutted any attempt to adopt a universal *public* health-care option. Instead, the Senate universal health-care legislation mandated that millions of middle-class and working-class Americans would be fined unless they bought insurance from *private* corporations.

Toward the end of 2009, the liberals who said that Obama should be given more slack (because he was being denounced for reneging on his campaign promises) were being contradicted by policies aimed at the destruction of independence movements in South America. Obama had appointed Hillary Clinton to Secretary of State and both of them tacitly supported a military coup in Honduras. In addition, his administration began to establish new military bases in Colombia—one of the most corrupt and repressive governments in South America. His administration also exported new shipments of arms to willing South American nations in order to encircle Venezuela and the Bolivarian Alliance, composed of South American social democratic governments.

Even the possibility of holding CIA agents accountable for torture was being trashed. Despite admitting during his confirmation hearing that "waterboarding" was torture, Obama's new Attorney General, Eric Holder Jr., suggested that the CIA agents who used waterboarding were not responsible because they believed the Department of Justice permitted it. But Holder's excuse for not prosecuting the agents was disingenuous. The Nuremberg and Tokyo war crimes tribunals long ago ruled out allowable conduct or "obeying orders" as a justification for torture. The Geneva conventions further stipulated, "No exceptional circumstances whatsoever, whether a state of war or threat of war, internal political instability or any other public emergency, may be invoked

A baton-wielding U.S. soldier forces an Iraqi prisoner, covered in feces, to try to walk in a straight line while his ankles are bound

as a justification of torture."

However, Holder's Justice Department had also reaffirmed one of Bush's flagrant positions on "extraordinary rendition." Bush had used false national security claims to quash judicial reviews of tortured victims. He also threatened to sever intelligence sharing with the British if it's courts allowed documents confirming that the CIA had flown Binyam Mohamed (an Ethiopian born British subject who was a prisoner in Guantánamo) to Morocco where he was repeatedly beaten and suffered broken bones. Reportedly, his clothes were cut off with a scalpel and the same scalpel was then used to make incisions on his body, including his penis. A hot stinging liquid was then poured into open wounds on his penis where he had been cut. He was frequently threatened with rape, electrocution, and death. [377]

377 John Schwartz. Feb. 9, 2009. "Obama Backs Off a Reversal on

The British court complied with the US threat to sever intelligence sharing. It refused to release the documents that would confirm Mohamed's "extraordinary rendition" and torture. Subsequently, Mohamed was flown back to Guantánamo and his charges were dropped. But he was not released! After joining a hunger strike conducted by 242 desperate detainees at Guantánamo, his physical and mental health deteriorated so drastically that his military defense counsel, Lieutenant Colonel Yvonne Bradley, told the *Guardian*, a British newspaper: "If this [Mohamed's case] keeps getting dragged out, he will leave Guantanamo Bay insane or in a coffin."

Shortly after Obama's election, the British High Court reviewed Mohamed's previous attempt at judicial redress. The majority of the High Court ruled that evidence of his rendition and torture at Guantánamo Bay must continue to remain secret because of threats made by the Bush administration to halt intelligence sharing. Yet two members of the court objected to this highhanded suppression. They declared, "We did not consider that a democracy governed by the rule of law would expect a court in another democracy to suppress a summary of the evidence contained in reports by its own officials." They added that it was "difficult to conceive" why the U.S. government still objected to the release of the documents, which would result in "no disclosure of sensitive intelligence matters."

Obama refused to challenge the British High Court's judgment, even though, as Blumner pointed out, federal judges in the US "are perfectly capable of

Secrets." *New York Times*.

reviewing classified evidence, and there are long-standing procedures to guard the nation's secrets in lawsuits. To suggest otherwise means that the executive branch can act with impunity whenever foreign intelligence matters are at issue."[378] In addition, during his campaign, Obama had condemned torture at Guantánamo and promised transparency in government. Regardless, responding to the British High Court ruling, his spokespersons hypocritically told the BBC: "The United States thanks the UK government for its continued commitment to protect sensitive national security information and preserve the long-standing intelligence sharing relationship that enables both countries to protect their citizens."

As a result, Blumner asked, "How is it that Obama, who made a dramatic public showing of reversing Bush administration's terror suspect treatment policies in his first days in office, would continue to use faux claims of national security to keep the public in the dark about the abuses inflicted on prisoners?" She felt that Obama was reading from the bloody Bush script. "After all, Obama had been a professor who taught constitutional law. He knows that upholding the rule of law requires more than rhetoric." The Executive Director of the ACLU, Anthony D. Romero, was also appalled. He declared:

> Hope is flickering. The Obama administration's position is not change. It is more of the same. This represents a complete turn-around and undermining of the restoration of the rule of law. The new American administration

---

378 Robyn E. Blumner. Feb. 6 2009. "Move-on, but Please don't Cover Up." *St. Petersburg Times.*

shouldn't be complicit in hiding the abuses of its predecessors.[379]

Early in April 2009, a leaked confidential report by the International Committee of the Red Cross (ICRC) sent to the US government was published in the *New York Review of Books*. The ICRC had investigated 14 prisoners in CIA custody who had been tortured and the report reminded the U.S. that torture and "cruel, inhuman and degrading treatment" are declared illegal under the Third Geneva Convention, the Convention Against Torture of 1984, and the War Crimes Act of 1996.

During 2010, a steady stream of disclosures continued to expose the fascist drift occurring during the Bush administration. Calling Obama "Bush-Lite" during that year was charitable because it emphasized token welfare state reforms while ignoring the imperial crimes, warrantless surveillance, assaults on anti-war and civil-rights activists, and fascist developments in the military. Trumpeting Obama's token accomplishments (e.g. health care and jobless stimulus acts) distracted attention from his continued support for the oppressive infrastructure that could be activated when a crisis occurs.

Previously, in 2009, *The New York Review of Books* published an article, "The Red Cross Torture Report: What It Means," written by Mark Danner, an award winning journalist.[380] Danner recalled that the

---

379 Anthony D. Romero. Feb 4 2009. "Obama Endorses Bush Secrecy on Torture and Rendition." *ACLU Press Release.*

380 Mark Danner's article and the ICRC Report on the Treatment of Fourteen "High Value Detainees" in CIA Custody (sent to the US government on February 2007) can be found in the. *New York*

Republicans had exploited the "politics of fear" successfully. (Many voters switched to Republican candidates because they felt they could do a better job in protecting America.) Cheney—in a televised interview—unabashedly admitted to authorizing torture and he justified his decision by referring to a secret intelligence report that "itemizes the specific attacks" stopped by information obtained from torture victims. Although Cheney claimed that he couldn't reveal the details of the report because it was classified, he assured Americans the report made reference to a large number of foiled attacks. Danner believed that if a terrorist attack does occur in the future, millions of Americans will remember Cheney's justification. He writes,

> Cheney's politics of fear—and the vice-president is unique only in his willingness to enunciate the matter so aggressively—is drawn from the past but built for the future, a possibly post-apocalyptic future, when Americans, gazing at the ruins left by another attack on their country, will wonder what could have been done but wasn't. It relies on a carefully constructed narrative of what was done during the last half-dozen years, of all the disasters that could have happened but did not, and why they did not, and it makes unflinching political use of the powers of secrecy. Barack Obama may well assert that "the facts don't bear him out," but as long as the "details of it" cannot be revealed "without violating classification," as long as secrecy can be wielded as the dark and potent weapon it remains, Cheney's politics of torture will remain a powerful if half-sub-

merged counter-story, waiting for the next attack to spark it into vibrant life.

In April, 2009, Obama refused to declassify photos of torture occurring at Gitmo and Abu Ghraib
when Bush and Cheney were in office. Despite his
pre-election promises, Obama's refusal shouldn't
have been surprising. He had voted for the FISA bill
before his election even though it prevented the telecom corporations from being sued for violating privacy rights. His administration invoked "sovereign
immunity" in April 2009 and expanded its *own* authority to withhold information. It decreed that the
government could not be sued by civil liberties agencies or individuals interested in obtaining classified
information found through unlawful surveillance.
Subsequent events provided further evidence of his
demagogic refusal to keep his promises about transparency. (More on this later.)

WHISTLEBLOWERS & DEMAGOGUES

The earliest American naval vessels were commissioned during the Revolutionary War to intercept
British supply ships and commercial shipping. Reportedly, Congress was divided over patronage and
merit when selecting naval commanders. Politics appears to have influenced the selection of Commodore
Esek Hopkins whose brother, a former Rhode Island
governor, had signed the Declaration of Impen-
dence. On the other hand, selection of the legendary
Captain John Paul Jones, commander of the *Bon-
homme Richard* and a Franco-American squadron

fighting in British waters, was based on maritime military experience.

After the thirteen colonies defied the British Empire, ten revolutionary sailors and Marines on the American warship *Warren* during the winter of 1777 accused their commander, Commodore Esek Hopkins, of participating in the torture of captured British sailors. The sailors' and Marines' petition to the Continental Congress claimed Hopkins had "treated prisoners in the most inhuman and barbarous manner." On March, 1777, Congress agreed and suspended Hopkins from his post.[381]

Outraged, Hopkins filed a criminal libel suit against two crewmen, a midshipman and a third lieutenant. It turned out that these officers happened to be in Rhode Island and were jailed. But they appealed to Congress on July 23, 1778 and claimed they had been arrested for doing their duty. Congress unanimously backed their claim. It enacted America's first whistleblower-protection law: It decreed that individuals who served the U.S. had the duty "to give the earliest information to Congress or any other proper authority of any misconduct, frauds or misdemeanors committed by any officers or persons in the service of these states, which may come to their knowledge." (To ensure that whistleblowers had the right to legal counsel, it authorized payment for their legal fees.) Furthermore, Congress mandated the release of all records related to Hopkins's suspension. The two crewmen at that time didn't need the ACLU or the Freedom of Information Act to

---

381 Stephen M. Kohn. 6/12/2011. "The Whistle-Blowers of 1777." *New York Times*.

vindicate themselves. Furthermore, Supreme Court justice William O. Douglas, almost two centuries later, praised the founders' commitment to freedom of speech. He wrote: "The dominant purpose of the First Amendment was to prohibit the widespread practice of government suppression of embarrassing information."

In 1989, Congress passed a law protecting from retaliation federal employees who exposed fraud and misconduct. But this protection has been discarded by current laws that give the government the right to strip security clearances and fire these employees without judicial review. Whistleblowers employed by the NSA, CIA, and national security programs are specifically exempted from government protection.[382] Yet, whistleblowers who are not exempt are silenced even though they are appalled at the waste, fraud, and abuse in national security programs. They risk their reputations, employment, and liberty whenever they expose malfeasance, negligence, and violations of international conventions.

On June 14, 2011, over twenty famous whistleblowers demanded that a "Transparency Award" Obama had received be rescinded. These whistleblowers included: Daniel Ellsberg, who leaked the Pentagon Papers; former CIA analyst Raymond McGovern; former Pentagon analyst Lt. Colonel Karen Kwiatkowski; and former National Security Agency analyst Russ Tice. These whistleblowers signed a pe-

---

382 Stephen M. Kohn is executive director of the National Whistleblowers Center and the author of *The Whistleblower's Handbook: A Step-by-Step Guide to Doing What's Right and Protecting Yourself*. Guilford, CT: Lyons Press, published in 2011.

tition written by Sibel Edmonds, a former FBI official and whistleblower and Coleen Rowley, a former FBI Special Agent and Division Counsel who was named one of *Time Magazine's* "Persons of the Year" in 2002 and whose May 2002 memo described some of the FBI's pre-9/11 failures. The petition crafted by Edmonds and Rowley declared:

> President Obama has not decreased but has dramatically increased governmental secrecy! According to a new report to the president by the Information Security Oversight Office — the federal agency that provides oversight of the government's security classification system — the cost of classification for 2010 has reached over $10.17 billion. That's a 15 percent jump from the previous year, and the first time ever that secrecy costs have surpassed $10 billion. Last month, ISOO reported that the number of original classification decisions generated by the Obama administration in 2010 was 224,734 — a 22.6 percent jump from the previous year. See 'The Price of Secrecy, Obama Edition.'[383]

Demagogues abhor whistleblowers who expose false promises. Edmonds and Rowley point out that Obama—in spite of his campaign promise to protect whistleblowers—had logged the "*worst* record in U.S. history for persecuting, prosecuting and jailing

---

383 The petition is available on *takeawardback.org*–It is also reprinted by the IPA Institute for Public Accuracy at *accuracy.org/release/whistleblowers-rescind-obama*. The petition also points out that the responses to Freedom of Information Act requests made to the thirty five largest federal agencies have decreased considerably compared to previous years even though the number of requests have increased.

government whistleblowers and truth-tellers." His DoJ is conducting more such prosecutions than have occurred in previous Administrations by spinning the 1917 Espionage Act to criminalize five alleged instances of national-security leaks.

Chelsea Manning's arrest and torturous imprisonment represented one of these instances. Manning was reported to have leaked classified information about incidents revealing, among other things, air-to-ground attacks on civilians conducted by a U.S. Army helicopter in Baghdad. These attacks violated laws originating in the Nuremberg trials and beyond. As a result, W. I. Pitt declared:

> It is widely considered facile and weak to make Nazi comparisons in any argument, but unfortunately for every citizen of this country, the comparison here is all too apt. During the Nuremberg trials in the aftermath of World War II, accused war criminals were often heard to claim, "I was only following orders," as a means of justifying their savage and barbaric activities. The excuse was rejected out of hand, further enshrining the idea that soldiers and officers are more than mere automatons who are expected only to do as they are told. Criminal acts, even in a military situation, are not to be condoned, coddled or tolerated. Men were hanged by the judges at Nuremberg to emphasize the point.[384]

Pitt contended that Manning acted in "the spirit of Nuremberg." He observed that Manning swore an oath to be faithful to the American Constitution.

384 William Rivers Pitt. June 26 2011. "Free Bradley Manning." *Truthout.*

"That same oath requires the oath-taker to follow the orders of the president and superior officers, but if those hanged men at Nuremberg prove anything, it is that unlawful orders are by definition void, and should not be followed if the oath sworn to the Constitution is to mean anything at all," according to Pitt. Pitt backed his opinions by noting U.S. classified files have revealed that inmates who could not have been terrorists were tortured including an 89-year-old Afghan villager, suffering from senile dementia, and a 14-year-old boy who had been an innocent kidnap victim.

Ironically, Manning was subjected to some of the tactics employed at Gitmo. She was deprived of sleep, humiliated, and berated by her captors, isolated, exposed to cold, and made to stand naked for extended periods of time. Illegal tactics against prisoners that Manning allegedly exposed were used against her, one more crime in a disgusting array of crimes. Public outrage finally forced the Obama administration to transfer Manning to Leavenworth.

PART EIGHT

THE STRUGGLE CONTINUES

— ◇ —

23 | Doing the Hokey-Pokey

You put your right foot in,
You put your right foot out;
You put your right foot in,
And you shake it all about.
You do the hokey pokey,
And you turn yourself around.
That's what it's all about!

—Dancing the *Hokey-Pokey*

PUT YOUR RIGHT FOOT IN

A prior section reported that Obama had refused to declassify photos of torture. Nevertheless, after expending considerable time and expense, the ACLU in April 2009 obtained four memos that had been classified even though they were not created lawfully. The memos were written by Bush's Office of Legal Counsel (OLC) between 2002 and 2005 and they attempted to conceal criminal violations of international law by granting torturers immunity from prosecution if they were "only following orders."

The descriptions of torture legitimized by the memos demonstrated that the Bush administration had deliberately attempted to dump the Nuremberg (and Tokyo tribunal) definitions of war crimes. The memos claimed that waterboarding conducted by Americans was justifiable if their victim did not actually suffer "extreme harm" (e.g., physical mutilation or death). They also justified the use of stress positions, slamming detainees against a wall, and sleep deprivation day after day for 11 days. They advised torturers to enclose a prisoner in a box with insects if that person experienced a severe anxiety attack when insects crawl on his skin. Television commentators and online bloggers horrified by the memos recalled the scene in a Hollywood film about George Orwell's novel *1984* where Richard Burton exploited his victim's intense fear of rats by placing his face against a cage filled with ravenous rats and informing him that they would devour his eyes and cheeks.

A *New York Times* editorial (April 19 2009) proposed that any investigation of these criminal violations should begin with "the lawyers who wrote these sickening memos. Jay Bybee was one of these lawyers. "Mr. Bybee," the editorial noted, "holds the lifetime seat on the federal appeals court that Mr. Bush rewarded him with." The editorial called for Bybee's impeachment and cited a "nauseating passage" where he admired a waterboarding tilt table that would lurch a victim upright if he stopped breathing. Bybee's memo also praised the CIA because it had doctors standing by and ready to perform an emergency tracheotomy if necessary. Waterboarding was implicitly legitimized by calling it "simulated drowning." But the drowning was not simulated. The victims being waterboarded were actually drowning and unless their breathing was revived, they died!

Unfortunately, in spite of shocking photographs, first-hand accounts, and condemnation surfacing during the Bush administration, Obama refused to discredit the memos and call for prosecution. He said that he would not prosecute those "who carried out their duties relying in good faith upon legal advice from the Department of Justice." To justify his refusal, Obama danced the *Hockey-Pokey*. Putting his right foot in, he declared that he was "moving forward" and not engaging in "retribution." He implied that a prosecution would be motivated by thoughtless rage and angry mobs rather than retributive laws where heinous crimes cry out for punishment. And even though he had taught constitutional law and promised to reinstate "transparency" in government, he claimed that the individuals responsible for the crimes should be given a "free pass" because their prosecution disclosed information that would undermine national security. His performance in this context signified that one of the most offensive crimes known to humankind would not be punished.

Truly, Obama's performance could not be legally justified. In fact, the U.N. Special Rapporteur on Torture, Professor Manfred Nowak, declared that Obama's refusal to prosecute CIA officials was a criminal act. Obama was not only obligated to investigate and prosecute torturers. *His grant of immunity made him complicit.* "The United States has, like all other Contracting Parties to the U.N. Convention Against Torture, committed itself to investigate instances of torture and to prosecute all cases in which credible evidence of torture is found," Nowak added.[385]

Obama's complicity was immediately confronted by human rights organizations, online bloggers, and thousands of phone calls. A coalition headed by Code Pink, gave Attorney General Eric Holder 250,000 signatures demanding the appointment of a Special Prosecutor for torture, warrantless wiretapping, and other Bush administration crimes.

This outcry forced Obama to leap in the air and turn around. He suddenly informed the public that he would not oppose a Congressional inquiry into "a dark and painful chapter" in the nation's history.[386] He reiterated his opposition to prosecuting CIA operatives yet he felt that a Congressional attempt to hold others accountable would be all right if it was conducted "in a bi-partisan fashion" even though he already knew that two leading Republican senators, McCain and Graham, had joined Lieberman and urged him not to prosecute the OLC lawyers. In addition, Republican legislators had overwhelmingly backed Cheney's claim that torture, legal or not, was

---

385 See the description of the interview (conducted on April 19, 2009 at 2:00 PM by the Austrian newspaper, *Der Standard*) written by Ryan Powers in "UN Rapporteur on Torture: Obama's Pledge Not to Pursue Torture Prosecutions of CIA Agents is not Legal." *Think Progress.* (*thinkprogress.org/2009/04/19/obama-violated-int-law*)

386 Sheryl Gay Stolberg. April 22, 2009. "Obama Won't Bar Inquiry, or Penalty, on Interrogations." *New York Times.*

justified—because it provided information enabling the US to thwart terrorists. Consequently, an American "bi-partisan" inquiry might be possible on another planet but it would have never taken place on Earth.

Obama's performance produced another fiction. He claimed that an investigation of the OLC lawyers would be up to Holder. Nevertheless, after he said Holder could deal with individuals who violated laws prohibiting torture, Holder jumped onstage and refused to prosecute anyone. Indeed, Holder actually claimed that John Yoo was entitled to absolute immunity. In addition, he used the self-styled "state secrets privilege" to have a lawsuit brought by a victim of torture thrown out of federal court.[387]

An avalanche of damaging documents, testimonies, and other forms of evidence discredited Obama's attempts to curb the rule of law. The Senate Armed Services Committee after an 18 month investigation had issued a 236 page report that claimed Bush's rejection of the Geneva conventions in 2002 had "opened the door" to torture. It also asserted that the CIA and Pentagon had made preparations for the use of torture before they had captured a single high-level Al Qaeda operative. Two alleged top Al Qaeda detainees were waterboarded an astonishing number of times because the Bush administration wanted anything that could justify the invasion of Iraq. In addition, Abu Zubaydah in August 2002 was waterboarded at least 83 times and Khalid Sheik

---

387 The lawsuit targeted a Boeing subsidiary that was used to transport the victim under the Bush administration's unlawful "extraordinary rendition" program.

Mohammed in March 2003 was waterboarded 183 times![388]

Congressional committees and legislators who were calling for a war crimes investigation also discredited Obama's refusal to hold Bush officials accountable. The former chairman of the Senate Intelligence Committee, Senator Jay Rockefeller (Dem-W.Va), indicated that the OLC lawyers operated under direction from Cheney and other top officials such as Condoleezza Rice (when she served as National Security Adviser).

Finally, damaging information had been scheduled for release in May 13 2009 because the Pentagon, in response to an ACLU lawsuit, had to declassify "a substantial number of photos" showing the widespread use of torture by US operatives in Iraq and Afghanistan prisons. Yet, despite the court ruling, the ACLU apparently did not get access to the photos because they might have demonstrated that torture at Abu Ghraib was systematic and widespread and not an aberration. As indicated, Obama eventually suppressed the release of Bush era photos of prisoner abuse in Iraq and Afghanistan. He declared: "The publication of these photos would not add any additional benefit to our understanding of what was carried out in the past by a small number of individuals." To validate his stand, he said: "In fact, the most direct consequence of releasing them, I believe, would be to further inflame anti-American

---

388 Liliana Segura. April 24 2009. "Thousands of Pages of Evidence and a Quarter Million Signatures: What Will It Take For Attorney General to Prosecute Torture Crimes?" *Alternet.org* (*alternet.org/story/138188*).

opinion and to put our troops in danger."[389]

The ACLU responded by issuing a press release entitled: "[Obama's] Decision Betrayed Commitment to Transparency and the Rule of Law."[390] Glenn Greenwald, a journalist and film-maker, also denounced Obama's rationale. He said that it implied that we should conceal or outright lie about all the criminal acts we do that might reflect poorly on us. Such acts included bombing and slaughtering civilians in Afghanistan which began during Bush's administration and continued under Obama's.[391]

The American Academy of Motion Picture Arts and Sciences never gave Obama an Oscar for dancing the *Hockey-Pokey*. But he was awarded the 2009 Nobel Peace Prize "for his extraordinary efforts to strengthen international diplomacy and cooperation between peoples." Although his administration had turned a blind eye to Pakistan's and Israel's clandestine development of nuclear weapons, the Nobel Committee claimed he deserved the prize because of his promotion of nuclear nonproliferation. It also said Obama deserved the prize because he was establishing a "new climate" in international relations—especially in reaching out to the Muslim world. Apparently, the Committee forgot that "reaching out" involved NATO combat units, mercenaries, and missiles fired from drones guided hundreds of miles

---

389 Scott Wilson. May 14, 2009. "Obama Shifts on Abuse Photos." *The Washington Post*.

390 ACLU Press Release. May 13 2009. "Obama Administration Reverses Promise to Release Torture Photos."

391 Glenn Greenwald. June 6 2009. "Defeat of the Graham-Lieberman and the Ongoing War on Transparency." *Salon.com*.

away by CIA operatives. Aside from rhetoric, Obama hadn't done anything that would justify the prize. In fact, his acceptance speech before the Nobel Committee echoed the Orwellian slogan, *War is Peace*. It reiterated every major point expressed by Bush when he justified the occupation of Afghanistan. It declared that the US "has helped underwrite global security for more than six decades."

After noting the striking similarities between the Bush and Obama administrations, David Swanson contended that Americans were living during "Bush's Third Term."[392] Swanson's assertion was warranted even though Obama could claim new ground. Darwin Bond-Graham, a sociologist, pointed out that his supporters were impressed by campaign promises to scale back the military-industrial complex and its nuclear weapons. By 2011, however, Obama had scored record budgets in spending on the military industrial complex. And his "administration," according to Bond-Graham, "has worked vigorously to commit the nation to a multi-hundred-billion-dollar reinvestment in nuclear weapons, mapped out over the next three-plus decades."[393]

OBAMA & WALL STREET

In 2011, James K. Galbraith, an economist, summed up Obama's place in American politics. He

392 David Swanson. Sept. 1 2009. "The More Things Change." *Tomgram. Tomdispatch.com.*

393 Darwin Bond-Graham. Sept 16-30 2011. "Succeeding Where Bush Failed: The Obama Administration's Nuclear Weapon Surge." *CounterPunch* Vol. 18 No 16.

said Obama represented the Wall-Street branch of the Democratic Party.[394] The revitalization of corporate profits being attributed to Obama's stimulus packages hardly affected the unemployment rate. The number of unemployed persons, at 14.0 million, was essentially unchanged in August 2011, and the unemployment rate held at 9.1 percent. In addition, by September 2011, 46.2 million Americans were living below the poverty line—the highest number since a government bureau estimated this figure 52 years ago. Millions of families were experiencing food insecurity and were eating less than they should be. African-American and Hispanic households in particular were undergoing conditions that had not been experienced since the Great Depression.

Obama's advocates trumpeted the fact that his "stimulus" proposals had reduced the number of jobless Americans, but they made no attempt to go below the surface. Like the great majority of Americans, they hadn't a clue about the complex changes affecting joblessness. The production of Chrysler's *Jeep Grand Cherokee* sports utility, for instance, was purported to show that Obama's proposals had increased jobs and prevented Chrysler from bankruptcy even though that production was based on Two-Tier wages and an exhausting "speed-up." The newest workers were earning half the wages ($14 an hour) of the wages earned by long-term workers and they were assembling a *Jeep* at an assembly plant in Detroit every 48 minutes. But what

---

394 James K. Galbraith. July 21 2011. "Obama and the Gang of Six." *The Real news.com.*

the hell. They were employed.[395]

On September 8, 2011, Obama asked a joint-session of Congress to pass a "Jobs Act" that would attempt to deal with poverty, unemployment, and economic stagnation. The Act proposed to provide funds for upgrading highways, bridges, and other parts of America's infrastructure. It also proposed to fund jobs for teachers, school construction, and unemployment benefits. To get support, Obama also proposed cutting payroll taxes and giving tax breaks that would encourage small businesses to employ more workers.

Yet the Act despite its scope provided further evidence of Obama's ability to give lip service to welfare state policies and organized labor while encouraging policies that fall short of these aims. Obama's plan, Robert Reich said, "isn't nearly large enough or bold enough to make a major dent in unemployment, or to restart the economy." Although Reich granted that Obama "explained why jobs and growth must be the nation's first priority now—not the federal deficit," he did not give the plan unqualified approval. He sarcastically expressed ambivalence by entitling his blog: "Two Cheers and One Jeer for the American Jobs Act."[396]

Many Americans also believed that Obama's stands on environmental pollution issues were inadequate. Indeed, public opinion polls during that September found 63 percent of Americans urging the

395 Bill Vlasic. Sept. 13 2011. "Detroit Sets Its Future on a Foundation of Two-Tier Wages." *New York Times*.

396 Robert Reich. Sept. 9 2011. "Two Cheers and One Jeer for the American Jobs Act." *Huffington Post.com*.

Environmental Protection Agency (EPA) to do more to prevent pollution and hold polluters accountable. Environmentalists called the 1,700 mile pipeline from the Alberta tar sands to refineries on the Gulf of Mexico the biggest "carbon bomb" on the continent. Tar sands extraction had wreaked havoc on Canadian indigenous communities and the tar sands pipeline, once ruptured, would pollute the largest source of fresh drinking water in the country. When Washington, DC demonstrations against the pipeline ended on September 6, 1,252 protesters had been arrested. Nevertheless, Obama had continued to do nothing to prevent the EPA from giving a Canadian company a permit to build the pipeline even though he did not need "bipartisan cooperation" to decide if that pipeline should be built.

Fortunately, the demonstrations had an effect. A month later, on November 10, Obama stalled the approval of the pipeline by sending it back to the State Department for a review that should take climate change into consideration. Bill Gibson of Tar Sands Action called the stall a "partial victory" and vowed to fight on until the project is killed.[397] While Obama has since declined support for the project and the drop in world oil prices have left investors less pushy at the moment, the pipeline project remains a possibility for a future government and its corporate sponsors, depending on prices and pushback.

---

397 Bill McKibben. November 10 2011. "Big News: We Won. You Won." *Tar Sands Action* (tarsandsaction.org). The Conservative government in Canada, a major tar sands promoter, was defeated in 2015 elections and the newly elected Liberal government favors a pipeline from the tar sands to the Atlantic.

What about Obama's policies toward Afghanistan, Iraq, Pakistan, and Libya? From the beginning of his administration, he had added to the trillions expended on these wars. Did his promise to withdraw troops really mean that he will end these wars? His administration, during the second week of that same September, was soliciting bids for the construction of a massive new prison in Bagram, Afghanistan?[398] This prison could cost American taxpayers as much as 100 million dollars.

Most of all, Obama had not stopped the deterioration of democracy in America. He had maintained and extended the incipient fascist infrastructure installed by the Bush administration. Nor did he attack the energetic efforts being made by one governor after another to suppress voting rights in their states.

In 2011, millions of Americans began to have serious doubts about Obama's competence as well as his sincerity. A Bloomberg National Poll, published on September 14, showed that 62% of the respondents felt Obama had failed to deal with economic stagnation and unemployment. Furthermore, 46% of the independent voters who responded said that they would not vote to reelect the President in the 2012 election.[399] Ominously, disappointment and anger with Obama's leadership was also being expressed by his core constituency. Almost 20% of the respondents who had previously supported him said that they would not support his reelection. Thirty-seven

---

398 Glenn Greenwald. Sept 19 2011. "US to Build New Massive Prison in Bagram." *Salon.com.*

399 Julianna Goldman. Sept. 14 2011. "Obama Approval Plummets Among Americans Skeptical of Jobs Plan." *Bloomberg.*

percent said their support was fading, and nearly a third of the respondents who were Democrats (or usually favored Democrats) said they would like to see Obama challenged in the Democratic primaries. Additional polls conducted during September suggested Obama's chances of being re-elected in 2012 were plummeting.

A few days after the polls were published Obama, in a September 19 Rose Garden ceremony, jumped onstage. He put his left foot out and shook it all about. He proposed raising new taxes on people with higher incomes, closing loopholes in the tax code, ending the Bush tax cut for wealthy Americans, and saving more than a trillion dollars in the federal budget by withdrawing troops from Afghanistan and Iraq. He vowed to veto any Republican measure that would "shave future Medicare benefits without raising taxes on the wealthiest taxpayers and corporations."[400] (In July, he had said that he would consider reducing cost-of-living adjustments for social security recipients but protests from members of his own party forced him to reverse his position in September.)

Of course, Obama's proposals did not target the underlying causes of the Great Recession. Nor did they reassure progressives that he would really fulfill yet another promise to withdraw troops from Afghanistan and Iraq. (His proposals even provided wriggle room to make cuts to Medicare if taxes on the wealthy were actually raised.)

Obama's proposals despite their limitations were

---

400 Jackie Calms, Sept 19 2001. "Obama Draws New Hard Line on Long-Term Debt Reduction." *New York Times*.

badly needed because they prioritized job creation, higher taxes on wealthy Americans, and preserving living conditions for children, the disabled, and the elderly. Nevertheless, his left-turn did not occur soon enough for leading progressives. On the same day Obama spoke at the Rose Garden, Ralph Nader and Cornell West published a letter that urged voters to challenge his candidacy in the 2012 Democratic Primaries. The letter had been circulated and endorsed by over 45 Americans who were distinguished by their role in leading progressive organizations. The letter suggested that progressives propose six candidates who would run against Obama, "each representing a field in which Obama has never clearly staked a progressive claim or where he has drifted toward the corporatist right." In the letter, Cornel West declared: "We need to put strong democratic pressure on President Obama in the name of poor and working people. His administration has tilted too much toward Wall Street; we need policies that empower Main Street."

The letter insisted that unless Obama is challenged he would not have to seriously articulate and defend his beliefs to his own party. Consequently, he should be forced to explain why he escalated the wars in Afghanistan and broadened America's covert war in Pakistan, and why he had supported the Bush Administration's national security apparatus in spite of its abuse of constitutionally protected civil liberties and Congressional prerogatives. The letter also asserted that a challenge would encourage debate about his silence and failed strategies to defend labor organizations.[401] It observed that Obama had decided to "bail out Wall Street's most profitable firms while failing to push for effective prosecution of the criminal behavior that triggered the recession." Obama's gutless extension of the Bush era tax cuts and acquiescence to Republicans in debt ceiling negotiations were also condemned. Finally, the letter asked progressives to suggest people who could serve as Democratic primary candidates in the fields of labor, poverty, military and foreign policy, health insurance and care, the environment, financial regulation, the empowerment of civil and political rights and consumer protection.[402]

---

401 "It's time for the White House to get into the trench with organized labor and lend a hand. We know what we need, and we don't need another campaign speech," said Chris Townsend, the Political Action Director, United Electrical, Radio and Machine Workers of America. Townsend was one of the progressives endorsing the letter.

402 Ralph Nader and Cornel West. Sept. 19 2011. "Ralph Nader and Cornel West Unveil Proposal to Challenge Obama in Primaries." *Single Payer Action.org.*

Occupy Wall Street

Occupy Wall Street: October 3 2011
[Photo: Leni Schwendinger.[407]]

During the winter and spring of 2010, a series of demonstrations exploded throughout the Middle East and North Africa. Known as the Arab Spring, the demonstrations often took place in capital cities where tens of thousands of protesters camped in central squares and engaged in strikes, marches, rallies, and civil disobedience, demanding an end to tyrannical rule.

In the winter of 2010, Wisconsin teachers, street cleaners, park rangers, clerks, librarians, fire fighters, and other workers surrounded the Capitol building in Madison. They protested their new governor's attempt to destroy a public worker's right to bargain collectively by hoisting signs, banging drums, playing bagpipes, and shouting defiantly. Then, entering the building, they boldly camped in the rotunda and upper floors and refused to leave! And notables such as Michael Moore, Susan Sarandon and Cornel West were actively supporting it even though the corporate media ignored or belittled it.

Toward the end of the following summer, demonstrations erupted across the nation. By September 28, Occupy Wall Street (OWS) had been taking place in and around Zuccotti Park in lower Manhattan for 11 straight days. At the beginning, the demonstration could be seen online. Despite police crack-downs and arrests, thousands of OWS demonstrators shouted slogans, held signs aloft, played drums, and blew trumpets while condemning Wall Street and capitalism near the New York Stock Exchange.[403] Astonishingly, by September 30, 5,000 they were cheering the arrival of the NYC Transit Workers, United Steelworkers, Postal Workers, Pilots Union, and Teamsters Union. The union members joined the occupation and episodic marches from Wall Street to nearby parks and squares where speakers condemned the frauds perpetrated by corporate CEOs and Wall Street financiers. "It's not a recession," they shouted, "it's a robbery!"

Then, the OWS protests began to spring up across the nation—in Boston, Chicago, Des Moines, Los Angeles, Seattle, and San Francisco. Additional protests, by the middle of October, had occurred in hundreds of cities and towns. Again, unlike the 1960s antiwar protests, columns of construction workers ("hard hats"), electrical workers, firefighters, pilots and teachers occupied public spaces and

---

403 This photograph of OWS onlookers and drummers in New York's Washington Square Park was taken by our daughter, Leni.

marched alongside university students.[404] Also the leaders of the Congressional Progressive Caucus and the Black Caucus joined Senator Bernie Sanders in endorsing the protests.

On the 5th, the New York demonstrators issued a declaration of grievances that urged people everywhere to occupy public spaces, assert their power and generate solutions to the problems they faced. The declaration stated that

> a democratic government derives its just power from the people, but corporations do not seek consent to extract wealth from the people and the Earth; and that no true democracy is attainable when the process is determined by economic power.

It insisted that corporations ran the government even though they placed "profit over people, self-interest over justice and oppression over equality." With regard to their effect on government policies, the declaration listed the following grievances:

> They have taken our houses through an illegal foreclosure process, despite not having the original mortgage.

> They have taken bailouts from taxpayers with impunity, and continue to give executives exorbitant bonuses.

> They have perpetuated inequality and discrimination in the workplace based on age, the color of one's skin, sex, gender

---

404 The OWS demonstrations in the U.S. even sparked similar demonstrations throughout the world—in Spain, England, France and elsewhere.

identity and sexual orientation.

They have poisoned the food supply through negligence, and undermined the farming system through monopolization.

They have profited off of the torture, confinement, and cruel treatment of countless animals, and actively hide these practices.

They have continuously sought to strip employees of the right to negotiate for better pay and safer working conditions.

They have held students hostage with tens of thousands of dollars of debt on education, which is itself a human right.

They have consistently outsourced labor and used that outsourcing as leverage to cut workers' healthcare and pay.

They have influenced the courts to achieve the same rights as people, with none of the culpability or responsibility.

They have spent millions of dollars on legal teams that look for ways to get them out of contracts in regards to health insurance.

They have sold our privacy as a commodity.

They have used the military and police force to prevent freedom of the press.

They have deliberately declined to recall faulty products endangering lives in pursuit of profit.

They determine economic policy, despite

the catastrophic failures their policies have produced and continue to produce.

They have donated large sums of money to politicians, who are responsible for regulating them.

They continue to block alternate forms of energy to keep us dependent on oil.

They continue to block generic forms of medicine that could save people's lives or provide relief in order to protect investments that have already turned a substantial profit.

They have purposely covered up oil spills, accidents, faulty bookkeeping, and inactive ingredients in pursuit of profit.

They purposefully keep people misinformed and fearful through their control of the media.

They have accepted private contracts to murder prisoners even when presented with serious doubts about their guilt.

They have perpetuated colonialism at home and abroad. They have participated in the torture and murder of innocent civilians overseas.

They continue to create weapons of mass destruction in order to receive government contracts.[405]

During the onset of the OWS protest, the corporate media branded the protesters as irresponsible

---

405 Rebecca Buel. Oct. 5 2011. "The First Official, Collective Statement of the Protesters in Zuccotti Park." *nationofchange.org.*

students, hippies, lunatics, communists, anarchists, and terrorists who were engaging in "class war." Ironically, the media was correct in one respect. A class war did exist but it had been started by Wall Street.

By occupying a specific "location," the protesters provided unique social spaces within which they could probe the powerful forces instigating their grievances.[406] To facilitate open debate, they adopted counter-cultural ideas and innovations. Although 'working groups' prepared the way, the leaders of the movement refused to institute bureaucratically organized relations that embraced everyone. Instead, they formed a "General Assembly" to express grievances collectively. The leaders and cliques shaping the OWS movement decided on public anonymity— perhaps because their tactics would be considered unlawful by the authorities. Still, whatever their motives, the tactic represented premeditated attempts to embolden public debate and to create interactions that increased their grasp of the conditions oppressing them. Consequently, Zuccotti Park Square did not fit the depiction of an utterly spontaneous and unorganized collection of hippies, lunatics, and losers provided by the mass media.

Jim Hightower visited the Zuccotti encampment after it had stabilized and describes what he found. "From a distance," Hightower writes, "the camps can

---

406 And their understanding was being expressed publically by the creation of a splendid website: Nation of Change *(nationofchange.org)* and *The Occupied Wall Street Journal*, four page, four color broadsheets, hawked on NY streets.

appear to be a disorderly motley collection of political vagrants. Come closer, however, and you'll find a remarkably well-organized democratic space, functioning on an Aristotelian model." He explains what this means by adding:

> Zuccotti Park in New York, for example, has a designated "front door" entry point, a welcome desk for visitors and supporters, a general assembly space, a media center, a legal desk, a library, and an arts area, as well as such necessities as a medical clinic (with health professionals volunteering their services), kitchen, sleeping area, and comfort desk (where protesters get such basics as toothpastes and sign up for showers and laundry facilities provided by area residents). Tasks are divided up into more than a dozen working groups, ranging from a direct action committee to a sanitation committee (yes, they regularly clean up after themselves).

> Food is regularly donated by New Yorkers and people anywhere on the globe can order pizza, tacos, paninis and other carry-out foods online from the several area eateries that deliver to the protesters.

> There is no "leader" or governing committee. Rather, the decisions are made by the General Assembly, which gathers twice daily and is open to all occupiers (a system akin to the one used this spring by Egyptian occupiers of Tahrir Square). All voices and ideas are welcome, and proposals are adopted by "modified consensus" (approval of nine out of 10 participants). This can be painfully slow and frustrating, but it engages and empowers everyone for the benefit of the whole group—which is

what democracy is supposed to do. If only Congress could make such a claim."[407]

Predictably, law enforcement began to forcibly repress the OWS movement. On October 27, the Oakland police, without warning, started lobbing flash bang grenades that were followed by tear gas and suddenly one of the demonstrators, Scott Olsen, was cut down. Olsen was a Marine who served two tours in Iraq. After returning to the U.S., he joined the Iraq Veterans against the War and participated in the demonstration. A tear gas canister fired by the police fractured his skull. Another veteran, Kayvan Sabehgi, was severely injured. He was clubbed mercilessly by a police officer and his spleen was ruptured. He writhed in agony for 18 hours on a cell floor in prison before he was sent to a hospital. He—like Olsen—had done nothing that would justify his brutal treatment. Still other demonstrators were injured. The Internet was full of photos of protesters with bruised backs, stomachs and legs and some with bloodied faces.

The Oakland police were supported by police detachments from the surrounding cities; moreover, the mayor of Oakland, Jean Quan, received advice on how to handle the demonstrators in a conference call from mayors in 18 cities across the nation. Reporters suspected that the suppression of the OWS movement was being coordinated nationally by the Dept. of Homeland Security. A new stage in customary repression had begun in the U.S. even though

---

407 Jim Hightower and Phillip Frazer (eds.) Nov. 2011. "From Occupy Wall Street to Occupy Nation in just Two Months." *The Hightower Lowdown.* Vol. 13, Number 11 pp. 3-4. (The Italian word, "Paninis" refer to sandwiches made from bread rolls.)

police brutality had not yet reached the level inflicted during the Vietnam period when gas grenades, pepper spray, rubber bullets, clubbing, and imprisonment were also used to terrorize demonstrators. (In addition, four Kent State University students were shot and killed and nine wounded by the Ohio National Guard and two students killed and twelve injured when shot by city and state police at Jackson State College in Mississippi.)

The OWS movement was becoming so widespread and its composition was so representative of middle and working-class Americans that government officials were being forced to calculatingly adjust their responses in light of political realities. These officials were finding that their justifications for attacking nonviolent protesters lacked credibility. Demonstrators were using cell phones, cameras, and transmitters to stream online photographs and videos of unprovoked attacks within minutes after they occurred.

Customarily, the police used "time and place" restrictions to violate constitutional rights to free speech and assembly. They exploited the notion that authorities alone should determine, in the interests of public safety, where, when and at what times, public protests can take place.[408] As the OWS demonstrations unfolded in New York City, health codes were also employed.

On November 15, Michael Bloomberg—the NYC

---

408 As indicated, the corporate media reinforced popular acceptance of this law enforcement prerogative by concentrating on vandalism committed by lone individuals or small numbers of demonstrators, with covered faces and black clothing, labeled as "anarchists."

Mayor and one of the richest men in America—commanded the NYPD to evict the protesters from Zuccotti square.[409] (We have mentioned Bloomberg in Chapter 6 which describes the cruel and unconstitutional treatment of people who protested the 2004 Republican National Convention.) The eviction of the OWS encampment took place in the dead of night as police invaded the encampment with klieg lights, clubs, pepper spray, riot gear, and sonic cannon booms. The police arrested more than two hundred protesters, including a city council member who was approaching the park to observe the invasion two blocks away. Police bulldozers stripped the square bare, throwing the protesters' belongings, their tarps, kitchen tent, medical tent, and other shelters into dumpsters.[410] The OWS library of 5,000 donated books was also thrown into dumpsters. "What's next," a protester jeered, "Book burning?"

The eviction wasn't the only violation of the First Amendment—the right to freedom of speech and assembly—committed by law enforcement. The NYPD tried to keep media personnel from filming and observing the arrests and destruction of the encampment. It even assigned a police helicopter the task of preventing media helicopters from filming what was happening in the square.

After the eviction, Bloomberg held a press conference. He announced that the protesters could return to the park after the area was cleared but they would

---

409 Gene Grabiner created the diagram depicting a Swastika inserted in Bloomberg's name.

410 The medical tent was torn down and slashed even though people were being treated inside of it.

not be allowed to camp out because it endangered public safety, posed the threat of fire, created unbearable noise, and undermined a law allowing the public to use the park for "passive recreation" 24 hours a day. He also said that the encampment had prevented police and "first responders" from protecting the protesters who occupied the encampment.

Bloomberg's justifications were rejected by thousands of New Yorkers who condemned his press conference and initiated mass protests. More than 30,000 people protested the eviction by marching throughout downtown Manhattan and along the Brooklyn Bridge even though local law enforcement and Homeland Security vans were parked ominously at the foot of the bridge. Protesters in other cities also staged demonstrations.

Of course, contagious diseases could spread rapidly within the encampment and in October its occupants were being threatened by the oncoming winter. Earlier, the protesters who were employed had to leave on weekdays if their jobs were at stake but many more supporters now had their health as well as their jobs and families to consider. They were exhausted and their numbers decreased.

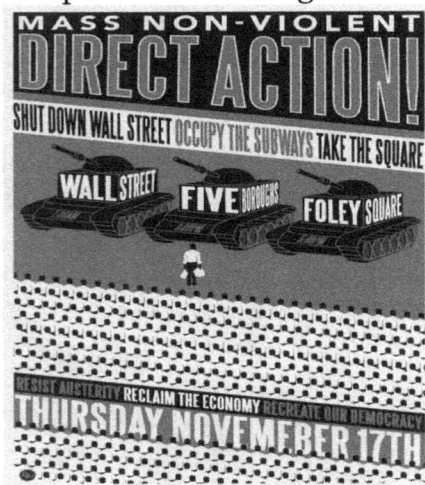

After the eviction, Bloomberg declared that the authorities had everything under control. But the reactions to his commands had sharply contradicted his statement. As a result, Olbermann, during a broadcast on *Current TV*, sarcastically recommended Bloomberg for an award because the public's angry reaction had reinvigorated the OWS movement.

Bloomberg should also be awarded for his political illiteracy. His raid on the encampment mistakenly assumed that the success of the OWS movement had depended on occupying a specific location. But other places would have been appropriate. After all, the OWS' primary objectives had to do with raising political awareness and changing public discourse on what was happening to the 99% of the population. These objectives empowered individuals and organizations to fight harder for changes that would alleviate the injustices created by Wall Street billionaires and their prostitutes in the government.[411]

On Thursday, November 17th, demonstrators throughout the U.S. celebrated the two month anniversary of the OWS occupation in New York City.[412] Although it had been in existence for an unbelievably short time, the movement was proving to be a spectacular example of how fighting for economic justice and democracy was blocking the highway to fascism.

---

411 The OWS movement was criticized because it had refrained from listing demands for reforming government policies, but its list would merely add another list to lists provided for decades by progressives.

412 A photo of this poster was provided online by Alexander Higgins. November 16, 2011 at 1:15 pm (*blog.alexanderhiggins.com*)

Still, whether or not the OWS protests will be electorally significant cannot be answered because time is running out. To increase their chances of winning the 2012 election, Republicans are passing legislation that suppresses votes by poor people, minorities and students. In Florida, for example, new bills will produce long lines and outrageous wait times for voters in populous counties, because it reduces early voting from 13 days to just 5. Also, women and students who have changed their residences will be confronted with requirements that did not exist previously (e.g., providing birth certificates or proof of residence). Grassroots ballot initiation campaigns are becoming almost impossible for anyone but wealthy special interests. [413]

The OWS movement will not save democracy unless it collaborates with organizations attempting to reverse policies gutting the Bill of Rights. The same can be said about achieving economic justice. Decreasing military spending and taxing the richest families are by no means all that must be done in this context. At the current rate of job growth, 14 million Americans will remain permanently unemployed and their plight will buttress wage stagnation, homelessness, and starvation. To top it off, answers to the cry for economic justice require a New Deal that massively funds public-works projects, reinstitutes the Glass-Steagall Act and the regulatory commissions that effectively control banks and financial speculation.

Robert Reich contends that rectifying America's

---

413 Republicans claim that these and other restrictions will prevent voter fraud even though this type of fraud is virtually nonexistent.

economic crisis will take a decade or more but it can be done. He points out:

> Rather than ushering in an era of political paralysis, the Great Depression of the 1930s changed American politics altogether — realigning the major parties, creating new coalitions, and yielding new solutions. Prolonged economic distress of a decade or more could have the same effect this time around.

The legislative gridlocks imposed during the present crisis by Republicans will hopefully not encourage a sharp shift in voting patterns toward the right—as it did in Germany during the early Thirties.

Saving democracy and achieving justice requires political know-how, dogged work, and the willingness to dissent despite the threat of illicit surveillance, no-fly lists, traitor-baiting, police brutality, detention without charge, and blacklists. Fortunately, many Americans, despite these threats, still heed Tom Paine whose words during a retreat were read to Washington's exhausted and discouraged soldiers: "These are times that try men's souls. The summer soldier and the sunshine patriot will, in this crisis, shrink from the service of their country, but he that stands by it now, deserves the love and thanks of man and woman." [414]

---

414 Thomas Paine. 1773. "The Crisis, no. 1." (In *The Writings of Thomas Paine*, ed. Moncure D. Conway, vol. 1, p. 170) Paine's work was written in the middle of winter during Washington's retreat across the Delaware.

"Pyramid of Capitalist System"
1911 IWW Poster

24 | For *Bread* And *Roses*

O ne hundred and forty-six garment workers employed on March 25, 1911 by the Triangle Shirtwaist Factory were either engulfed by flames or jumped to their death from the 8th, 9th, or 10th floors because their managers had locked the doors to stairwells and exits. On these floors, women's blouses, known as "shirtwaists," were produced primarily by young immigrant women who worked nine hours a day on weekdays and one hour less on Saturdays.

The factory owners claimed that the doors were locked to prevent stealing or taking unauthorized breaks. During the previous year, however, the International Ladies' Garment Workers' Union had won an agreement with other factories that improved working conditions for sweatshop workers.

The Triangle Shirtwaist Factory refused to sign the agreement.

The 1912 Lawrence Massachusetts textile strike was also composed chiefly of women. Upton Sinclair in 1916 called it the "Bread and Roses strike" because women on the picket line carried signs calling for *Bread* and *Roses*. The word *Bread* symbolized their fight for better wages and *Roses,* their right to be treated with respect and dignity. The slogan "Bread and Roses" itself originated in a poem whose opening paragraphs read:

> As we come marching, marching in the beauty of the day,
>
> A million darkened kitchens, a thousand mill lofts gray,
>
> Are touched with all the radiance that a sudden sun discloses,
>
> For the people hear us singing: "Bread and roses! Bread and roses!"
>
> As we come marching, marching, we battle too for men,
>
> For they are women's children, and we mother them again.
>
> Our lives shall not be sweated from birth until life closes;
>
> Hearts starve as well as bodies; give us bread, but give us roses!

International Working Women's Day (photo: public domain)

The Industrial Workers of the World (IWW) led the ten-week strike of 25,000 textile workers. Working conditions in the mills were intolerable. Also, more than half of the workers in the American Woolen Company's Lawrence mills were girls between 14 and 18 years of age. Dr. Elizabeth Shapleigh, a Lawrence physician, reported: "A considerable number of the boys and girls die within the first two or three years after beginning work . . . thirty-six out of every 100 of all the men and women who work in the mill die before or by the time they are twenty-five years of age." Malnutrition, occupational diseases, and speedup shortened an average mill worker's life by 22 years compared to a mill owner's life, Dr. Shapleigh observed.[415] In spite of the

---

415 Joyce Kornbluh. 1988. "Bread and Roses: The 1912 Lawrence

"Fighting the Triangle Shirtwaist Factory Fire"
March 25, 1911 PHOTO: Wikipedia Commons. First
published: *The New York World* 1911-03-26
[Public Domain].

textile Strike." In Joyce Kornbluh (Ed.) *Rebel Voices: An IWW Anthology*. Chicago: Charles H. Kerr Publishing.

state and local militia, police brutality, vigilantes, frame-ups, and stiff prison sentences, the workers fought successfully for "Bread and Roses," winning their strike in 1912.

But the mill owners struck back. They introduced labor spies, enabling the bosses to identify and dismiss union activists. They began to undercut wages and working conditions. A depression in 1913 increased the speedups, layoffs, and wage cuts that eventually canceled most of the gains made during the previous year.

Nevertheless, eventually, despite the setbacks, labor unions and their allies in the progressive movement fought successfully for worker's rights, anti-trust laws, the regulation of corporations, minimum wages for women, direct election of Senators, the right to recall elected officials, secret ballots, child labor laws, public education, an eight-hour workday, worker compensation laws, the right *to* unionize, and the creation of National Parks and Wildlife Refuges.

Extraordinary!

THE SECOND GILDED AGE

The anti-labor policies associated with the second Gilded Age surged a century later when Robber Barons popped champagne bottles and celebrated drastic declines in union membership. More than 33% of the private-sector labor force in 1946 belonged to unions. By 2010, this proportion had dropped catastrophically to 6.9 percent!

Public-sector unions had increased despite Reagan's anti-labor policies. However, newly elected Republican governors in 2010 blamed budgetary deficits produced by the 2008-2010 recession on public workers' earnings and pensions. They made public workers scapegoats even though the deficits were actually committed by Wall Street speculators, the abandonment of progressive taxation, and the greatest amount of fraud committed by CEOs since the 1980s and 1990s Savings and Loan scandals.

In Wisconsin, a new governor, Scott Walker, after giving tax-breaks to corporate interests, hypocritically asserted that Wisconsin could not solve its budgetary crisis without drastic cuts in public service wages and jobs. He also proposed to solve the crisis by eliminating collective bargaining altogether. When Walker's proposals were leaked, Wisconsin public workers went ballistic. They mounted the largest public protests seen in decades. Despite Walker's threat to use the National Guard if public workers caused "unrest," striking teachers, street cleaners, park rangers, clerks, librarians, fire fighters, and other workers surrounded the Capitol building in Madison. They hoisted signs, banged drums, played bagpipes, and shouted defiantly. Then, entering the building, they boldly camped in the rotunda and upper floors and refused to leave!

Meanwhile, Wisconsin Senate Democrats adopted the strategy used previously by Texas Democrats who tried to prevent Republicans from obtaining a quorum when enacting biased redistricting legislation. Fourteen Wisconsin Senators packed their bags and fled to Illinois—avoiding Wisconsin police who were by law compelled to ensure their presence when Walker forced a vote on his union-busting proposals. They refused to return until Walker abandoned his attempt to destroy the public unions. The Senators were viciously slandered by Murdock's Fox News and Glenn Beck, Limbaugh, and other far-right commentators. Fortunately, the Senators found opportunities on CNN and MSNBC cable-news programs to explain why they refused to return to Wisconsin.

As indicated, Walker had claimed that his drastic measures were compelled by a severe budgetary crisis. But, Paul Krugman said Walker's claims were fraudulent. Addressing Walker in a *New York Times* article, he added: "if you're serious about the deficit, you should be willing to consider closing at least part of this gap with higher taxes." Krugman's observations were ironic because Wisconsin was the first state to introduce a progressive income tax. It was enacted in 1911 and a Republican governor, Robert La Follette, proposed it.

Walker repeatedly reiterated the myth that a public worker's pension had nothing to do with wages. They were a "gift" from taxpayers. But public workers had *deferred* wage increases to obtain the pensions. They *earned* their pensions—it was not a "gift."

Walker also claimed corporate tax relief and tax cuts for the rich would create jobs; however, these policies had been enacted by the Bush administration and they failed to create jobs. Billionaires did not use the money to expand job markets. They spent it on the consolidation of financial corporations and on overseas investments regardless of the negative effects on jobs at home. They also used the tax cuts for conspicuous consumption—on bigger yachts, jewels, and mansions.

Faced with Walker's uncompromising stance, the Wisconsin unions agreed to accept wage cuts and make personal contributions to their pensions. Nevertheless, Walter adamantly refused their offers unless their right to collective bargaining was abolished. He threatened to decrease the deficit by firing thousands of public workers unless the fourteen Senators returned to Wisconsin.

Jobs for teachers were not the only jobs threatened by Walker's proposals. His "budget repair" bills would eventually produce massive layoffs among public safety workers, correctional officers, fire fighters and snow plow operators. Wisconsin's Republican Party legislators informed cable-news hosts that the firefighters supported Walker because he had excluded them from his threats to cut jobs. But these legislators lied. In point of fact, the firefighters were furious—they joined demonstrations in support of the public unions and their association withdrew savings (accumulated for their pensions) from a bank headed by some of the billionaires who had financed Walker's electoral campaign.

Then, suddenly, the Wisconsin standoff took a bizarre turn. Website hosts and MSNBC circulated a 20 minute recorded prank call made by a Buffalo reporter, Ian Murphy of the *Daily Beast*, who posed as the right-wing billionaire, David Koch. (Koch and his brother had during the 2010 election campaign contributed more than a million to Walker and organizations attacking his democratic rival.) The recording exposed Walker's servile relation with Koch.

While the recording was disseminated, Ed Schultz, the host of the MSNBC Ed Show, interviewed Rep. Kucinich who pointed out that Walker represented officials who wanted to convert the government into a cash cow for the wealthy. Kucinich added that the refusal to deal with the deficits by cutting military expenditures and taxing the rich represented a dangerous moment in American history.

Walker's indebtedness to corporate power was also confirmed by another proposal aimed at privatizing public utilities (i.e. state-owned heating, cooling, or power plants) without requiring competitive bids. After the crank call was publicized, people believed that this no-bid proposal was drafted with the Koch brothers and their billionaire associates in mind.

During the third week of the protests, Michael Moore traveled to Madison to deliver a speech. He took the high road and denounced the class war conducted by the rich for the past 30 years. Moore found that "the whole town" backed the protesters.[416] He observed,

> Yard signs and signs in store windows are everywhere supporting public workers. There are thousands of people out just randomly lining the streets for the six blocks leading to the

416 Goodman, Amy. "Michael Moore Joins Wisconsin Labor Protests: 'America Is Not Broke.'" *Democracy Now*. Mar. 7, 2011. http://www.democracynow.org/2011/3/7/michael_moore_joins_wisconsin_labor_protests

Capitol building carrying signs, shouting and cheering and cajoling. Then there are stages and friendly competing demos on all sides of the building (yesterday's total estimate of people was 50,000-70,000, the smallest one yet)!

The scene inside the Rotunda brought tears to Moore's eyes. He said,

It's like a shrine to working people — to what America is and should be about — packed with families and kids and so many senior citizens that it made me happy for science and its impact on life expectancy over the past century. There were grandmas and great-grandpas who remember FDR and Wisconsin's La Follette and the long view of this struggle. Standing in that Rotunda was like a religious experience. There had been nothing like it, for me, in decades.

Significantly, by the third week of protests, polls showed that the majority of Wisconsin's electorate did not support Walker. Moreover national polls found Americans opposed to stripping away public workers' right to bargain collectively by about a 2 to 1 margin.

Then, suddenly, a political bomb dropped! Someone in Walker's organization leaked a document proving that he was planning to wipe the public unions "off the map" altogether. His plan would affect 170,000 workers who had already taken pay cuts. It would also affect their pensions because Walker wanted to plunder their wages to fund 100% of their pensions.

Unions as Launch Pads

Progressive commentators justifiably felt Walker's attempt to destroy public unions involved more than money. He was attempting to destroy the unions because they overwhelmingly supported democratic candidates. Obviously, any reduction in union membership would create a significant reduction in Democratic Party support.

But there was another significant function being fulfilled by Wisconsin unions. They were helping to fill a void created by the customary suppression of left-wing organizations. Unlike grass-roots movements that normally respond to oppressive government policies, they can mobilize mass protests more rapidly.

Andy Kroll, a reporter for *Mother Jones,* investigated "How big labor and progressive pulled the biggest protests in forty years." He found that the secretary treasurer of the AFL-CIO in Wisconsin began to prepare for a "right-to-work battle" after hearing about the outcome of the November 2010 election. The AFL-CIO official contacted other union officials and started to plan a campaign opposing Republican "right-to-work proposals" in the Wisconsin legislature.

Robert Craig, the CEO of Citizen Action of Wisconsin, was being besieged with phone calls. He kept union officials up-to-date on the governor's hijinks. As news of Walker's plans circulated, Bruce Coburn, a Service Employees International Union (SEIU) official, joined other unions who were being activated to stop Walker. Makeshift "war rooms" were immediately set up a block from the capital building.

Volunteers poured into the headquarters of the Wisconsin Education Association Council (WEAC) and Wisconsin's teacher's union. *Within two days, these volunteers called 98,000 WEAC members!* Over the weekend, SEIU used the phone and Facebook to organize a rally that drew 10,000 people on Tuesday when the State Finance Committee was scheduled to hold a hearing on Walker's bill.

The Madison branch of the state teacher's union held a mass meeting in Madison Labor Temple to inform its members of the $5,100 a year in wages they would lose if Walker prevailed. The next day more than a thousand teachers joined the protests, forcing the Madison School District to close schools for the remainder of the week.

The protest rallies mounted in front of the capital building by public workers and their allies increased from 10,000 people on Wednesday, February 16, to 70,000 on Saturday. This huge increase was produced by a public-private coalition of unions created almost overnight by union organizers.

The Teaching Assistants' Association (TAA), the University of Wisconsin, Madison union, composed of teachers and graduate student project assistants, also contributed. They initiated the occupation of the Capitol building and converted the third floor into a command center, sent emails, ordered food, and constructed a website, *DefendWisconsin.org* that provided talking points, videos and press releases.

To highlight the critical role that well organized unions can play, we do not have to add to Kroll's report. Obviously, compared to reactions from loose networks formed by grass roots movements, labor unions possess the ability to move quickly when democratic rights are attacked. The Wisconsin unions and their supporters swiftly mobilized the largest progressive movement in decades.

The fight for democracy in Wisconsin at this writing is far from over. In the dead of the night on March 9, 2011, Walker's flunkeys in the senate without debate rammed through a bill that abolished public workers collective bargaining rights. To sidestep the Democrats who had fled to Illinois, Walker stripped the bill of all references to spending cuts that required ratification by a Senate quorum. The vote abolishing collective bargaining unmistakably confirmed that the budget shortfall had nothing to do with Walker's plan to destroy public unions.

Richard Trumka, the AFL-CIO president, on March 10, 2011, emailed millions of Americans. He declared, "This assault on worker's freedom will not stand." He denounced the Senate Republicans who wanted to destroy collective bargaining rights that the parents and grandparents of workers had "bargained for, marched for, went on strike for and sometimes even died for." On March 14, police estimated up to 100,000 people conducted a demonstration that was bigger than any protests the city had witnessed.

Wisconsin Capitol Building. February 26, 2011. Photo: Justin Ormont, {Wikipedia, CC-BY-SA}

WALKER'S COUP & AMERICA'S *SOZIALPOLITIK*

To a degree, the parallels between the conflicts over the Germany welfare state were being played out in Wisconsin. Robert Reich noted that the Wisconsin Senate had passed a bill stripped of all references to spending cuts. He wrote, "Governor Walker and his Senate Republicans have laid bare the motives for their coup d'état." Their goal had nothing to do with the deficit: "It's been to bust the unions." The bill prohibited almost all public workers from collectively bargaining for wage increases beyond the rate of inflation unless approved by referendum. It required these workers to submit to an 8% pay cut by paying more toward their pensions and health insurance. The bill also required unions to hold annual votes to allow workers to decide if they wanted to be members and their union dues would no longer be deductible from paychecks.

The bill also gave Walker dictatorial power to reduce health care for poor Wisconsites because he planned to cut Medicaid regardless of how many people would be put at risk. Also, the bill made almost 40 civil service jobs political appointments. Walker had proposed other measures incorporated by America's welfare state for solving the deficit. He favored increasing university tuitions and thereby keeping millions of hopeful students from enrolling because they do not have family resources. Furthermore, every public school was endangered. He threatened to virtually destroy public education by cutting 900 million dollars in public school expenditures!

Reich was not the only notable expert that called Walker's tyrannical move by its right name (coup d'état). William Rivers Pitt implored online readers to remember the words of Martin Niemoller who had been imprisoned in a concentration camp. Niemoller had said,

> First they came for the communists and I didn't speak out because I wasn't a communist. Then they came for the trade unionists, and I didn't speak out because I wasn't a trade unionist. Then they came for the Jews, and I didn't speak out because I wasn't a Jew. Then they came for me and there was no one left to speak out for me.

As a trade unionist, Pitt wrote that Walker and the

Koch brothers "moved in the darkness and with shameless deceit gutted the ability of labor to bargain for the right to earn a living wage and health care." He also noted that Walker's bill enabled him to fire anyone who engages in a strike. He added,

> The story of the 20th century was written by workers who dared to face the truncheon in order to fight for their basic rights, and the strike was integral to that struggle. Any Wisconsin worker who dares to stand in defiance of The Bosses now faces personal annihilation, not just for themselves, but for their family. America was made in the struggle of union workers standing shoulder to shoulder in defiance of the idea that being rich means being right. That struggle is now in mortal peril, and the outcome affects all of us.

Public workers called Walker a "tyrant" because he was trying to turn Wisconsin into a "police state." Their responses triggered protests against budding fascists across the nation.

On Saturday, February 11, thousands of Chicago demonstrators shouted "Welcome" to the Wisconsin Senators who were hiding out in Illinois. Over 100,000 people rallied in Madison itself and at least 50,000 in other state capitals and major cities. Protests appeared in Indiana, Ohio, New Jersey, New York, Pennsylvania, and other states where too many Democrats were collaborating with Republicans who were attempting to transform public workers into a species of cheap labor.

Representatives on the federal level were also singing a funeral dirge for organized labor. HR 1135, sponsored by Reps. Jordan (Ohio), Scott (South Carolina), Garrett (New Jersey), Burton (Indiana), and Gohmert (Texas) would deny food stamps to federal workers who require the stamps because they refuse to work unless they get Bread and Roses. Entire households, including children, are counted in this proposal. Also, If these workers are already receiving food stamps, their allotment could not be increased regardless of whether members of their household are starving. In regard to HR 1135, Olbermann caustically remarked, "In short, you want to go on strike, whether over unsafe conditions or subsistence wages or forced unpaid overtime? Prepare to *starve* too. That is where we are today, in the greatest nation on earth, at the time of the greatest wealth in its history, at a time that would make the Robber Barons of the 19th Century think about turning themselves in to the police."

While the Wall-Street CEOs are committing their colossal frauds with impunity, their sociopathic puppets are attempting to destroy support for unemployed workers, public education, teachers, and individuals suffering from autism, Down syndrome, cerebral palsy, and other developmental disabilities. They are trying to destroy abortion rights, the regulation of health and safety on the job, drug rehabilitation programs, laws preventing environmental degradation, etc. In Florida, they are even attempting to deregulate laws that try to safeguard lives by licensing trained technicians, semi-professionals, and professionals who provide myriad services that can be harmful if they are conducted by incompetent or inexperienced individuals. In addition, utilities and other parts of the public infrastructure that sustains "life, liberty and the pursuit of happiness" for middle- and working-class people are being gutted and privatized by political prostitutes.

Alarmingly, Wisconsin's class warfare is being reproduced on all levels of government—in federal policies and in states, cities and towns where right-wing and "moderate" democrats are influencing America's *sozialpolitick*. Meanwhile, these political puppets are using every possible means to buy off their middle-class supporters and provide billions to the "masters of the universe."

Incredibly, after pro-union demonstrators protested an 86 percent cut in corporate taxes and cuts to school budgets, Michigan's Senate passed a "financial martial law" that grants emergency powers to "managers" who can take control of cities and towns, dismiss elected officials, void union contracts, and supervise financially strapped cities and schools. Can budding fascists in the *democratically* elected Senate actually impose *dictatorial* control of Michigan communities? Yes, they can!

Almost every Michigan city and town is financially strapped; but Benton Harbor, which is largely composed of African Americans (hit hard by job losses at its Whirlpool plant) was the first community placed under 'martial law'. The Governor's 'manager,' Joseph Harris, stripped Benton Harbor's city council of its powers and decreed that the council cannot spend money, raise or lower taxes, issue bonds, or impose regulations without his approval. Benton Harbor's Klock Park contains a beautiful sandy beach bordering Lake Michigan that was donated by the Klock family in 1917 in memory of their daughter. As a result, Benton Harbor families have enjoyed the park for almost a century. Nevertheless, Harris is attempting to privatize this public park, by turning it into a golf resort with a 350 room hotel, two marinas, a 60,000-foot water park (for members only), and a fancy golf course open to all who can afford a $5,000 entry fee and be approved by the club. Understandably, Benton Harbor families have initiated a lawsuit to stop Harris even though he is backed by powerful right-wing interests.[417]

Unfortunately, despite the fact that many people are opposing the attacks on human rights, they are actually accomplishing little to block the economic forces behind the current recession. Indeed, the failure to control these forces ensures continued stagnation or worse.

As Kucinich has observed, Americans are entering a long twilight while they battle for worker's rights. This battle is a struggle for human rights as well as a fight for the soul of American democracy.

---

417 Eartha Jane Melzer. Oct. 26 2011. "Jesse Jackson calls for an uprising in Benton Harbor." *The Michigan Messenger.*

25 | Inequality and Neo-Fascism

Over the past generation . . . the country has returned to the Gilded Age levels of inequality.

—Paul Krugman

Progressives during the first Gilded Age fought the rise of monopoly capital. Today, this fight includes organizations spanning the globe. The largest demonstrations occurring since the turn of this century have protested the IMF, World Bank, and worldwide trade agreements (NAFTA, CAFTA, GAT, etc.). The demonstrators in every case encountered police brutality. In 2010 alone, the people who protested the G20 meeting in Toronto, Canada, experienced threats, beatings, arrests, and even sexual assaults perpetrated by thousands of police officers backed by a 1 billion dollar expense budget![418] When the meeting concluded, Obama congratulated the Toronto Chief of Police, Bill Blair, for enabling the conference to take place without interruption. In investigation of the assaults conducted by the Ontario Ombudsman, Andre Marin, predicted that the suppression of the G20 protests will live in infamy as the "most massive compromise of civil liberties in Canadian history."[419]

Protesters have targeted the IMF and World Bank because they have forced third world countries to assume and pay off unbearable debts by imposing the privatization of public assets and destruction of working conditions and social programs. The inequalities and exploitative conditions produced by these agencies have been paralleled by a surging financial sector. With deregulation, the banks, investment firms, and accounting agencies concealed their sleazy transactions and fraudulent operations. Along with new forms of speculative investments, financial agencies have repeatedly produced speculative bubbles and their collapse.

Deregulation, however, has not been the underlying force driving these developments. The growing dependence on financialization reflects the decline of investment in the "real economy" (e.g., industrial firms and farms) and a slowdown in the global econ-

---

418 For the G20 protests in Pittsburgh, see Bill Quigley. Sept 27 2009. "Street Report from the G20." *Common Dreams.org.* Episodes providing interviews and onsite photos of the Toronto G20 brutality on June 26–27, 2010 were available online beginning in July 1, 2010 at *The Real News Network.* (*therealnews.com/t2/index.php.*)

419 Andre Marin. December, Dec. 2010. "Ombudsman Report, Caught in the Act." [G20 Summit]. *YouTube.com*

omy. An overcapacity of productive enterprises has created surplus capital that has been diverted into financial speculation because it cannot be reinvested as profitably in industrial firms and farms.[420] This diversion has been hardened by millions of Americans who, experiencing stagnant incomes in the face of inflation, compensated by accumulating enormous debts to maintain their living standards.

Obama's charismatic performance in March and April 2009 at the G20 meetings received glowing coverage by the corporate media. But his attempt to obtain European collaboration merely produced a promise to contribute a trillion dollars to bail out the IMF and World Bank. This money reinvigorated the old world order but it hardly affected the living standards of the poor in third-world countries. And it made little difference to negative economic trends and their impact on democratic institutions in the US.

Nor would this money abolish the effects of neoliberal "free market" policies toward South American, African, Middle Eastern, and Southeast Asian nations. At the behest of American financial interests, the IMF and World Bank have for decades triggered economic catastrophes in one nation after another. They imposed "austerity" measures that have made millions penniless and supported client fascist governments.[421]

---

420 John Bellamy Foster provides a superb analysis of these developments in April 2007. The Financialization of Capitalism. *Monthly Review* Vol. 58 No 11 pp. 1–12.

421 Naomi Klein. 2007. *The Shock Doctrine: The Rise of Disaster Capitalism*. New York: Henry Holt & Co.

INEQUALITY & COUPS

Chapter 14 on the right-wing culture wars contained a graph demonstrating the rise and fall of inequalities based on incomes enjoyed by the wealthiest families in America. However, two economists, James K. Galbraith and George Purcell, ask whether there exist systematic relationships between state violence and economic inequality in countries around the world. The question, they grant, is understandable.

> Entire lexicons exist that describe economic relationships in terms that evoke violence; such words and phrases as exploitation, dependency, unequal exchange and class struggle are but prominent examples. And the case histories of war, revolution, state terrorism and coups d'état are certainly loaded with analyses of what seem transparently to be efforts either to rectify gross inequalities, or else to impose them.

Galbraith and Purcell analyzed changes in inequality in 27 nations five years before a violent coup d'état and after. They found, strikingly, "Coups typically follow the emergence of a government or policies that result in a sharp reduction in inequality. [But] in the five years following the coup, inequality rises. This is the mechanism of violent repression." In Chile, for instance, Galbraith and Purcell observe that inequality had declined sharply through the Sixties and up to 1973, when it was a democracy. However, after the military slaughtered the people who defended the Allende government and suppressed democracy for 17 years, inequality "rose promptly and continuously, accelerating sharply with the financial crisis of 1979."

If inequality provides an index of the forces that encourage fascism, would an upward trend foretell its rise in America? When would we expect to see changes that step-up customary repression and resume a formative phase in the development of neo-fascism? A genuine or fabricated crisis certainly could offer an opportunity to actualize this possibility. But, there are other—less transparent—conditions inviting this outcome.

Figure 2

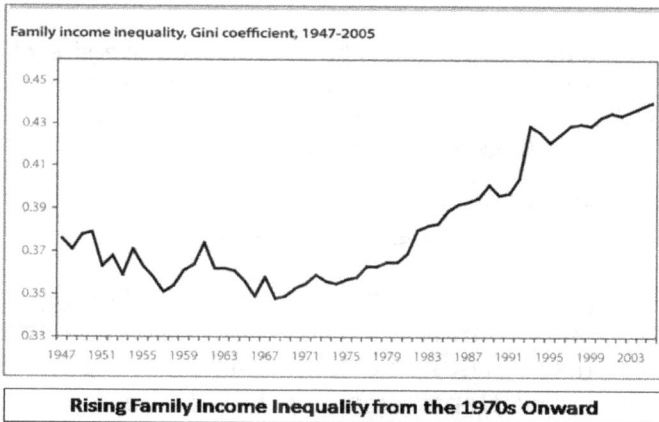

Family income inequality, Gini coefficient, 1947-2005

Rising Family Income Inequality from the 1970s Onward

Recall our description in Chapter 14 of the rise and fall of income enjoyed by the wealthiest families in America. However, Figure 2, above—from Lawrence Mishel, Jared Bernstein, and Sylvia Allegretto's article, The State of Working America 2006/2007—employs a measure of income inequality among all American families from 1947 to 2005.

It is not limited to the wealthiest families. (The graph signifies the degree to which annual family income is distributed *unequally*.)[422] After a gradual downward trend bottoming in the early Eighties, inequality in family incomes took a sharp turn upward and was still climbing. The rich were getting richer and the poor—poorer.

Furthermore, wealth is more important than annual income for determining inequality. When 2006 rolled around, a mere 10 per cent of the families in America had more wealth than all other American families combined. Chuck Collins, the Director of the Program on Inequality and the Common Good at the Institute for Policy Studies, declared:

> The income gaps show us the relative size of the skyscrapers and row houses; wealth is about the mountains and the valleys where the buildings stand. The income story is annual. Wealth is generational—and more revealing of the deep fissures that have opened in our society over the past three decades.

The political leverage exercised by wealthy networks today reminds us that even though their plot to overthrow FDR and establish a fascist regime during the Great Depression had failed, they continued to use other means to enrich themselves despite the

---

422 Mishel, Bernstein, and Allegretto's work is *An Economic Policy Institute Book*, Ithaca, N.Y.: ILR Press, an imprint of Cornell University Press, 2007. Source of data: US Census Bureau. The graph employs Gini coefficients to measure inequality of a distribution of income. It is defined as a ratio with values between 0 and 1: The numerator is the area between the Lorenz curve of the distribution and the uniform (perfect) distribution line; the denominator is the area under the uniform distribution line.

costs to the rest of society. Nor have these networks calmly accepted the successful outcomes of the civil rights, women's rights, free speech, and anti-war movements during the 1960s and 1970s. Toward the end of the 1970s, they quietly introduced a long-term strategy for suppressing organized labor, political antagonists, corporate taxes, government regulation, welfare state policies, etc. That strategy has largely been successful.

CORPORATE DOMINATION & NEO-FASCISM

But did this strategy also jump-start neofascist developments? Before reiterating our answer to this question we must recall that the debates about the causes of fascism have preoccupied journalists, politicians, novelists, and social scientists for three quarters of a century.

Intellectuals in these debates have used a remarkable number of benchmarks to identify fascism and its causal determinants. Fascism, they say, can be spotted by the patriotic fervor of its political movements, its nationalism, racism, anti-Semitism, male supremacy, militarism, and imperialism. Fascism idealizes "strong leaders" and despises liberalism, socialism, anarchism, communism, feminism, and "modernism." Bewilderingly, proto-fascist or fascist regimes have been called *Garrison* States, *National Security* States, *Police* States, and *Authoritarian* or *Totalitarian* states. Fascism has even been depicted as a duel at high noon between an evil Sheriff defending the capitalistic system and a revolutionary Communist representing the people.

Nevertheless, a desperate attempt to preserve the

capitalist system was not really at stake in Germany, Italy, or Chile. Granted, Hitler's electoral support may have declined sharply if he hadn't consolidated his power forcibly. And even though electoral support for communist candidates might have increased (had the Nazis not crushed their opposition by force and the Republic remained free to conduct future elections) most of the long-term support for socialist candidates would have probably been offered to the Social Democratic Party, which had repressed a communist uprising and sustained the Grand Coalition with industrialists. The Social Democrats had enabled capitalism to survive. They did not shoot it down. Also, Mussolini suppressed organized labor and left-wing parties but he did not actually face a revolutionary attempt to overthrow the capitalist system.

Still, aren't some of the characteristics associated with classical fascism applicable to American conditions? Gross provides an answer when he insists that "friendly fascism" is generated by big government in league with corporate capital. Furthermore, his insistence makes sense when we considered the forces behind the Bush and Obama administrations. An explanation of fascism closer to empirical reality (and more useful in the American context) should therefore start with the owners and managers of great corporations and financial institutions providing key structural agents deliberately backing the creation of 'friendly fascism'. As far as right-wing movements and ideological causes are concerned, the readers can fill the gaps between the dots. A militant right-wing movement is certainly indispensable for the growth of neo-fascism but readers should also consider the causal impact of distinct corporate networks.

For example, our description of the rise of fascism in Germany emphasized the role played by its military industrial complex. Years before Hitler acquired significant electoral support, the German Officer Corps secretly flouted the terms of surrender imposed by the Versailles treaty. It created a "shadow army" and supported irregular military units (e.g. the Freikorps and its assassination squads). Meanwhile, Krupp enterprises, the largest in Europe, initiated a covert rearmaments program. By the end of the 1920s, the Officer Corps began to make plans for the next imperial war. These and other members of the military industrial complex promoted ultra-right nationalist movements that eventually converged on the Nazi Party and the thinly veiled overthrow of the Weimar Republic.

The corporate networks that underpin right-wing nationalist movements in America certainly include its Military-Industrial Complex (MIC). Since Dwight D. Eisenhower warned the public about its capacity to determine government policies, this complex has become even more powerful. By the early 1980s, the fifty largest defense contractors have combined and recombined and become today's top five contractors whose dependence on the government is astonishing. For example, one contractor, Lockheed Martin, is a private corporate entity but it has been wryly dubbed a "quasi public entity" because its income and profits are almost totally dependent on government funding. Nick Turse's 2008 book on how the

MIC affects the everyday life of ordinary Americans describes the vast—and partially concealed—government links that ensure corporate profits.[423] As a result, the government expenditures and deficits racked-up during the Weimar Republic by Krupp and other industrialists are miniscule compared to their contemporary American counterparts.

During the last month of 2009, the government under the Obama administration was poised to allocate more for "defense," in dollars adjusted for inflation, than any other allocation made during a presidential term since World War II. Yet, despite its devastating costs, the MIC symbolizes a 20,000 pound Pliocene Mammoth munching jelly beans in Congress while Republicans and their Democratic collaborators act as if they have played no role in the creation of trillion dollar deficits and loudly insist that the government cannot afford a universal health care system.

Of course, pharmaceutical corporations, health insurance companies, and other Big Business networks are important in estimating the quality of democracy and the corporate opposition to welfare state policies. But all of these networks are like streams drifting downward and merging into a raging river. Each stream has causal significance because of its incremental *systemic* effect. (When impacted by precipitating causes—such as economic or political crises—they can coalesce.)

If we do not know where an individual network is heading, its drift at any given instance provides few

---

423 Nick Turse. 2008. *The Complex: How The Military Invades Our Everyday Lives*. New York: Henry Holt & Co.

clues for gauging its individual contribution to the formation of a raging river. Furthermore, some networks have become mainstreamed because they are fed by underground springs created by government agencies decades ago. These networks include global drug traffickers and their bankers who have provided the CIA's lawless operations with money and services that it could not obtain through normal channels.[424]

Possibilities for transforming the government into a neofascist regime can be compared to systemic drifts. Some of these drifts, for instance, are composed of corporate networks that have the potential to activate policies that can be used to repress political dissent. (A fascist regime unmistakably demonstrates its existence by its ruthless activation of weapons of mass repression.)

Consequently, our final chapters listed the *Fasces* that Democratic and Republican administrations assembled with the aid of Congress. The axe of these *Fasces* has been honed by the abrasive impacts of the Patriot Acts, the Detainee Treatment Act, the Military Commissions Act, the suppression of the Posse Comitatus Act, and the 2007 executive order entitled "Blocking Property of Certain Persons Who Threaten Stabilization Efforts in Iraq." These measures compose but a fraction of the measures intended to nullify the Bill of Rights, especially the First, Second, Fourth, and Sixth Amendments. In addition, during the Obama administration, a fright-

---

424 Peter Dale Scott. 2010. *American War Machine: Deep Politics, the CIA Global Drug Connection, and the Road to Afghanistan.* New York: Rowman & Littlefield.

ening number of previously undisclosed Presidential decrees that tear down the Bill of Rights have surfaced. As indicated, Obama has refused to change these policies.

He has even extended these policies. In June 2013, a whistleblower, Edward Snowden, revealed the existence of a government surveillance program devoted to collecting billions of Apple and Microsoft quests, Google chats, digital photos, commercial transactions, Facebook profiles, social networks, political affiliations, phone calls, and emails made by American citizens. This vast program was being assisted by corporations funded by the government and additional billions were being expended to store the data acquired and analyzed by the program in the 1.5 million square foot "Utah Data Center"—whose insipid name belies its unconstitutional aims and harmful potential.

Snowden's leak encouraged critical reporters to replace the phrase, "National Security State," with "National Surveillance State." It also encouraged the use of "Military Industrial-Surveillance State' because the corporate base for the industrial complex had been significantly expanded by world-wide surveillance programs. Meanwhile the pursuit of Snowden reinforced pressure being placed on the media to refrain from criticizing the government. Journalists, in addition, were being intimidated because they realized that the NSA can identify their networks and sources.

Snowden was accused of being a traitor. He fled to Hong Kong to avoid capture and a possible death penalty. After a short time, he flew to Moscow where he was interviewed by a *Guardian* correspondent. He observed that Obama had ordered Biden "to pressure the leaders of nations from which I have requested protection to deny my asylum petitions." Snowden added:

> For decades the United States of America has been one of the strongest defenders of the human right to seek asylum. Sadly, this right, laid out and voted for by the U.S. in Article 14 of the Universal Declaration of Human Rights, is now being rejected by the current government of my country. The Obama administration has now adopted the strategy of using citizenship as a weapon. Although I am convicted of nothing, it has unilaterally revoked my passport, leaving me a stateless person. Without any judicial order, the administration now seeks to stop me exercising a basic right. A right that belongs to everybody. The right to seek asylum.[425]

Snowden concluded that the Obama administration was afraid of "an informed, angry public demanding the constitutional government it was promised—and it should be." It was not afraid of whistleblowers like Chelsea Manning and himself.

It should be recalled that some of the most repressive measures initiated during the Bush administration had never been implemented. Yet they were being kept in reserve because they would give him the authority to turn Americans dissidents into "enemy combatants," imprison them without trials and

---

425 Edward Snowden. July 1, 2013. "Statement from Edward Snowden in Moscow."
[http://www.commondreams.org/view/2013/07/01-13].

confiscate their assets. Obama at this date has not dared to activate most of these measures. But his reluctance has not eliminated them. The selection of these options—with or without other possibilities—has merely been postponed until an economic or political crisis occurs and a credible pretext for mass repression becomes available.

Refusing to destroy the fasces created by Bush has cleared the way for the resurgence of incipient fascist developments symbolized by Tea Party networks, armed "patriotic groups," and politicians like Sarah Palin who advised them to "Water the tree of liberty with the blood of tyrants!" and "Reload rather than Retreat!" To this we might add the openly racist and xenophobic, ad apparently wildly popular, campaign of Donald Trump for Republican presidential nominee with its calls for border walls and the suspension of entry into the US for Muslims.

During President Barack Obama's first year in office, Tea Party demonstrators called him *Foreigner! Socialist! Thief!* They accused him of bailing-out sleazy financiers, threatening civil liberties, imposing unjust taxes, destroying free markets and American dreams. Alarmingly, these demonstrators posed the threat of violent retribution. Fights had broken out at Town hall meetings. Men with side arms and rifles were spotted at the rallies, where posters depicted fanged venomous snakes poised to strike back and coiled under boots symbolizing Obama's "tyrannical" government.

Additional threats surfaced. Recall that The Southern Poverty Law Center had found that responses to immigration, recession, and election of an

African American president increased the number of hate groups operating in the United States. Also, the Department of Homeland Security had warned that "right-wing extremist groups" were recruiting returning veterans from Iraq and Afghanistan.[426]

Justine Sharrock's article (in *Mother Jones*) verified this threat. She investigated the Oath Keepers, a fast growing "patriot group" that was recruiting soldiers, veterans, police officers, and other uniformed men and women to resist Obama's administration. "At regular ceremonies in every state," Sharrock reported, "members reaffirm their official oaths of service, pledging to protect the Constitution—but then they go a step further, vowing to disobey 'unconstitutional' orders from what they view as an increasingly tyrannical government."[427]

David Barstow, a *New York Times* reporter, found Tea Partiers justifying their rage with this narrative of impending tyranny.[428] Although corporate support and conservative media had rejuvenated them, their ideas (when coherent) were drawn from neoliberal and religious dogma. Tea Party candidates for public office proposed to privatize social security, abandon unemployment insurance, and deny abortion even to a teenage girl who had been raped by her own father. They opposed economic and job stimulus bills, tax

---

426 Mark Potok. March 3 2010. "Right-Wing Rage: Hate Groups, Vigilantes and Conspiracists on the Verge of Violence." Southern Poverty Law Center.

427 Justine Sharrock. March/April 2010. "Age of Treason." *Mother Jones*, p. 28.

428 David Barstow. Feb. 16 2010. "Tea Party Movement Lights Fuse for Rebellion on Right." *New York Times*.

increases for extremely wealthy Americans and an affordable public health option for the rest of the population.

Populists are often associated with the left but Tea Party supporters are right-wing populists. They demand an "end to big government" by disassembling the welfare state. Their aims include abolishing the policies attempting to recover the economy from the Great Depression, instituted during the Roosevelt administration. But, as Keith Olbermann reported in the closing days of the 2010 election, Tea Party representatives were proposing "nothing short of an attempted use of democracy to end this democracy, to buy America wholesale and pave over the freedoms and the care we take of one another, which have combined to keep us the envy of the world." Electing individuals who will follow orders in exchange for money and power will goose-step our nation as far backward as they can get—"backward to Jim Crow or backward to the bread lines of the '30s, or backward to hanging union organizers, or backward to the trusts and the robber barons."[429]

Krugman agrees. He stated, "[F]uture historians will probably look back at the 2010 election as a catastrophe for America, one that condemned the nation to years of political chaos and economic weakness."[430] In his opinion, the economy was in dire straits and we need massive federal intervention to get us out of current economic trap. However, this

---

429 Keith Olbermann. Oct. 27 2010. "If the Tea Party Wins, America Loses." msnbc.com.

430 Paul Krugman. Oct. 28 2010. "Divided We Fail." *New York Times*.

intervention would not take place if Tea Party candidates ensured that Republican policies moved further to the right.

The 2010 electoral changes were reminiscent of the 1932 surge in voters favoring Hitler and the "National Opposition." One third of the German voters had shifted right and Hitler was appointed Reichschancellor. Since the German parliament was gridlocked and social democratic leaders refused to activate their paramilitary forces, he was given the space to stage a national emergency and the power to suppress everyone who stood in his way. Ironically, most of Hitler's supporters eventually traded their votes for graves. If members of incipient American fascist movements were transported by mystical powers back in time-and-place, they would—like these Germans—shout with joy even though the boot brought into existence by their rage could be slammed in their own faces.

In the U.S., decades ago, well-heeled Americans had kept the public from identifying the enemies of democracy. In the middle of the Second World War, for instance, a famous investigative journalist, George Seldes, claimed that the key fascist sympathizers in America were not composed of those few persons imprisoned at the beginning of the war or indicted for sedition. (This handful, he insisted, were unimportant figureheads "just as Hitler was before the Big Money in Germany decided to set him up in business.") Seldes said the mass media refused to identify the "fascist Empires" led by DuPont, Ford, Mellon, and Rockefeller who had worked against democracy. A growing democracy, he said, would have created a nation free of discrimination based on race, color, and creed. It would not have allowed millions of people to be unemployed during the Great Depression or forced to work at semi-starvation wages without adequate food, clothing, and shelter. Although he recognized that many would not approve his use of the phrase *fascist Empires*, he declared,

> You may substitute Tories, Economic Royalists or Vested Interests or whatever you like for the flag-waving anti-Americans whose efforts and objectives parallel those of the Liga Industriale which brought out Mussolini in 1920, and the Thyssen-Krupp-Voegeler-Flick Rhineland industry and banking system which subsidized Hitler when Nazism was about to collapse. Their main object was to end the civil liberties of the nation, destroy the labor unions, end the free press, and make more money at the expense of a slave nation.

Today, a half century later, neo-fascism, after all, symbolizes capitalism in the raw. Corporations have no souls. (Nor did they acquire souls when the Supreme Court backed the legal fiction that their "personhood" also gave them the right to create the best democracy money can buy.) Corporations are amoral entities and they will accommodate themselves to welfare-state policies and organized labor but, as a rule, they only do it when they are forced to make this accommodation or when it avoids substantial risks and sustains their bottom lines. Because democracy provides millions of people with political leverage to lower exploitation, protect their health and safety, enables them to bargain collectively and improve working conditions, corporate networks habitually oppose political movements that defend democracy or try to bring it into being.[431]

Consequently, if we also keep William L. Shirer's observations about the primacy of corporate domination in mind, there is much more than the overt use of naked force and surveillance to consider when identifying a formative phase. By ensuring US hegemony, the transnational consolidation of capital has tightened the bands around the *Fasces* while its blade has been sharpened by wars of aggression, neocolonial armies, the CIA, and "economic hit-men" sent by international monetary agencies to keep client states in line.[432]

These larger forces are ignored when critics personify neofascist developments by merely attributing them to the Bush or Cheney. These officials were products of these forces and their appointments included Negroponte, Abrams, Poindexter, and Gates, because preexisting developments had generated a pool of professionals who worked with assassins in client fascist states or led projects expressly prohibited by Congress. This pool also included people like Rove who have no moral qualms about anything they do to serve corporate interests.

In contrast, some people are exposing the danger-

---

431 For superior coverage of the development and impact of global economic networks, see Jeff Faux. 2006. *The Global Class War: How American's Bipartisan Elite Lost Our Future—and What It Will Take to Win It Back.* Hoboken, NJ: John Wiley & Sons

432 John Perkins. 2007. *The Secret History of the American Empire: Economic Hit Men, Jackals, and the Truth about Global Corruption.* New York: Dutton

ous paths being taken by these interests. Take Robert Kennedy Jr. as an example. He is a leading environmentalist and the author of *Crimes against Nature: How George W. Bush and his Corporate Pals Are Plundering the Country and Hijacking Our Democracy*. He contends that the Bush administration had learned the lessons taught by the Nazis. Kennedy declares: "While communism is the control of business by government, fascism is the control of government by business." He adds, "My American Heritage Dictionary defines fascism as 'a system of government that exercises a dictatorship of the extreme right, typically through the merging of state and business leadership together with belligerent nationalism'." He quotes Herman Goering, who said,

> It is always simply a matter to drag the people along, whether it is a democracy, or a fascist dictatorship, or a parliament, or a communist dictatorship. The people can always be brought to the bidding of the leaders. That is easy. All you have to do is tell them they are being attacked, and denounce the peacemakers for lack of patriotism and exposing the country to danger. It works the same in any country.

In Kennedy's opinion, the biggest threat to American democracy is corporate power. His opinion is echoed by other authors who have also become alarmed at the concentration of this power in the executive branch of government and changes in the other branches that have made this possible.

The war in Afghanistan and Iraq has been the longest wars the US has ever conducted and a new one will either occur or take their place. Furthermore, the officials who have replaced Bush and keep the Empire going are keenly aware that millions will eventually defy their imperial policies. Coping with the defiance may exceed their reliance on customary repression and fully activate the *Fasces*.

After all, the *Fasces* never evolved merely because Bush & Co. believed it would deal with the threat of terrorism. The decades old shift to the right has made Americans (and the corporate media) more receptive to fascist solutions when dealing with political crises. Republican Party leaders who spearheaded this shift had no qualms about conducting a disguised coup by stealing the Presidency in the 2000 election and then exploiting 9/11 by normalizing a state of emergency to realize their dystopian visions of a "free America."

Motivated by ideological and opportunistic reasons, the Democrats who backed the Republican play have been equally culpable in war crimes and crimes against humanity. At this writing, it is increasingly unlikely that a decisive majority of the leading Democrats will sincerely attempt to try to turn things around by ending the carnage.

Still, movements for peace and justice, despite their limited ability to stir the nation, are trying to stop the wars. Big Brother is watching them because political dissidents helped end the "*American* War" against Vietnam.[433] Unless Americans despite the odds continue to fight back, the "endless war against terrorism" will outlast Hitler's short-circuited "thousand year Reich."

---

433 Vietnamese today call it the "American War" not the "Vietnam War."

Bibliography

Abraham, David. 1986. *The Collapse of the Weimar Republic: Political Economy and Crisis.* (Second Edition) New York: Holmes & Mercer.

ACLU April 14, 2004. "Tell the Airlines to Protect your Data."

ACLU May 30, 2003. "ACLU Criticizes CAPPS II."

ACLU Press Release. May 13, 2009. "Obama Administration Reverses Promise to Release Torture Photos."

ACLU Report. 2003 May. *Freddom Under Fire: Dissent in Post-9/11 America.*

ACLU, September 30, 2003. "As Congress Puts Controversial CAPPS II Program on Hold, ACLU Urges TSA to Abandon Super Snoop Profiling System."

Altemeyer, Bob. (1988, March/April) "Marching in Step: A Psychological Explanation of State Terror." *The Sciences,* pp. 30–38.

Alvarado, Francisco. December 4, 2003. "Press Pass and Gas Mask." *Miami New Times.*

Aslam, Abid. March 21, 2005. "US Rallies Mark Iraq Anniversary, Reflect Anti-War Groups' Growth, Challenges." *OneWorld*.net.

Bader, Shawna. 2002 Oct. 4. "Disgrace at Freedom Plaza." *DC-IMC*.

Bageant, Joe. 2008. *Deer Hunting with Jesus: Dispatches from America's Class War*. New York: Crown.

Barstow, David. February 16, 2010. "Tea Party Movement Lights Fuse for Rebellion on Right." *New York Times*.

Bass, Carol and Greg Burns. 2002. "Photos of US Military Sightseeing at Anti-IMF Demo." *Atlanta IMC* (8:45am Sun Sep 29.)

Berrigan. Philip. 1996. *Fighting the Lamb's War: Skirmishes with the American Empire*. New York: Common Courage Press.

Bill Berkowitz, Oct. 18, 2006. "The Mouth that Roars." *Media Transparency*. (http://old.mediatransparency.org)

Bird, Keith W. 1977 *Weimar, The German Naval Officer Corps and the Rise of National Socialism*. Amsterdam: B.R. Gruner Publishing Co.

Black, Edwin. 2001. *IBM and the Holocaust: The Strategic Alliance between Nazi Germany and America's Most Powerful Corporation*. New York: Crown Publishers.

Black, Edwin. 2003. *The War against the Weak*. New York: Four Walls Eight Windows.

Blumenthal, Max. September 8, 2006. "Discover the Secret Right-Wing Network behind ABC's Deception." *The Huffington Post*.

Blumner, Robin E. January 18, 2004. "Making the Right to Counsel Vanish." *St. Petersburg Times*.

Blumner, Robyn E. December 7, 2003. "From Tommy Franks, a Doomsday Scenario." *St. Petersburg Times*.

Blumner, Robyn E. November 30, 2003. "Miami Crowd Control would do Tyrant Proud." *St. Petersburg Times.*

Blumner, Robyn E. February 6, 2009. "Move-on, but Please don't Cover Up." *St. Petersburg Times.*

Bond-Graham, Darwin. September 16-30 2011. "Succeeding Where Bush Failed: The Obama Administration's Nuclear Weapon Surge." *CounterPunch* Vol. 18 No 16.

Brustein, William. "The 'Red Menace' and the Rise of Italian Fascism." *American Sociological Review*, Vol. 56, No. 5 (Oct., 1991) pp. 652–664.

Buel, Rebecca. Oct. 5, 2011. "The First Official, Collective Statement of the Protesters in Zucotti Park." *nationofchange.org.*

Bugliosi, Vincent. 2008. *The Prosecution of George W. Bush for Murder.* Cambridge, MA: Vanguard Press

Bush, President George. July 17, 2007. "Message to the Congress of the United States Regarding International Emergency Economic Powers Act: Executive Order: Blocking Property of Certain Persons who Threaten Stabilization Efforts in Iraq." (Office of the Press Secretary).

Butterfield, Fox. 2002, Sept 22, "Some Experts Fear Political Influence on Crime Data Agencies." *New York Times,* p. 23.

Calms, Jackie, September 19, 2001. "Obama Draws New Hard Line on Long-Term Debt Reduction." *New York Times.*

Carsten, F. L. 1980. *The Rise of Fascism* (2nd Edition). Berkeley: The University of California Press.

Chernus, Ira. Monday, January 27, 2003. "Shock & Awe:

Is Baghdad the Next Hiroshima?"
CommonDreams.org.

Chomsky, Noam and Edward S. Herman. 1979. *The Washington Connection and Third World Fascism*. Boston: South End Press.

Chomsky, Noam. 1976. *COINTELPRO: The FBI's Secret War on Political Freedom*. New York: Monad Press

Churchill, Ward. 2003. *On the Justice of Roosting Chickens—Reflections on the Consequences of U.S. Imperial Arrogance and Criminality*. Oakland, CA: AK Press.

Cockburn, Alexander and Jeffrey St. Clair and Allan Sekula. 2000. *5 Days that Shook the World: Seattle and Beyond*. New York: Verso.

Cockburn, Alexander and Jeffrey St. Clair. 2004. Torture: as American as Apple Pie. *CounterPunch* 11(April 16-31) 1–2.

Cockburn, Alexander. March 3/4, 2007. "A Federal Witchhunt: The Persecution of Sami Al-Arian." *CounterPunch* (Weekend Edition).

Coggins, Paul. 2002, Sept 27. "The Year of the Rats." (Law.com)

Cole, Jonathan R.. Spring 2005. "Academic Freedom under Fire." *Daedalus*.

Corn, David. 2003, September 22. "Homeland Insecurity." *The Nation*.

D'Adamo, Chuck. 2002 Sept 28 "Denied the Right To Dance! Day One of the Protests against the IMF/World Bank." *Baltimore IMC*. Maryland.

Danner, Mark. April 30, 2009. "The Red Cross Torture Report: What It Means." *The New York Review of Books*. Vol. 56, Number 7.

Dershowitz, Alan M. 2001. *Supreme Injustice: How the High Court Hijacked Election 2000.* Oxford University Press: New York.

Dinges, John. 2004. *The Condor Years: How Pinochet and His Allies Brought Terrorism to Three Continents. New York:* The New Press.

Dobkowski, Michael N. & Isidor Wallimann. 1989. *Radical Perspectives on the Rise of Fascism in Germany, 1919–1945.* New York: Monthly Review Press.

Donner, Frank J. 1981. *The Age of Surveillance: The Aims and Methods of America's Political Intelligence System.* New York: Vintage Books Edition.

Donner, Frank. 1990. *Protectors of Privilege: Red Squads and Political Repression in Urban America.* Berkeley: University of California.

Douthett, Trent. April 6, 2005. "Horowitz Funding Sources." [Memo to Senator Fedor.] AAUP.

Dreifus, Claudia. July 6, 2004. "The Chilling of American Science: A Conversation with Robert C. Richardson." *The New York Times.*

Dulles, Allen Welsh. 2000 (orig. 1947). *Germany's Underground: The Anti-Nazi Resistance.* (Intro. Peter Hoffman) New York: DaCapo Press Edition.

Dwyer, Jim. March 25, 2007. "City Police Spied Broadly Before G.O.P. Convention." *New York Times.*

Edgar, Timothy Feb 14 2003. "Interested Persons Memo: Section-by-Section Analysis of Justice Dept. Draft 2003 Domestic Security Enhancement Act, Patriot Act II. ACLU Legislative Counsel." (http://www.aclu.org/SafeandFree/SafeandFree.cfm?ID=11835&c=206}

Editorial. 2002 Nov. 18. "A Snooper's Dream." *New York Times*.

Engelhardt, Tom. May 30, 2006. "Thirty Flew into the Cuckoo's Nest. The Tangled Web of American 'Intelligence.'" (http://www.tomdispatch.com/)

Faux, Jeff. 2006. *The Global Class War: How American's Bipartisan Elite Lost Our Future—And What It Will Take to Win It Back*. Hoboken, NJ: John Wiley & Sons.

Foster, John Bellamy. April 2007. "The Financialization of Capitalism." *Monthly Review* Vol. 58 No 11.

Frank, Joshua. 2005. *Left Out! How Liberals Helped Reelect George Bush*. Monroe, Main: Common Courage Press.

Frank, Thomas. 2008. *The Wrecking Crew: How Conservatives Rule*. New York: Henry Holt & Co.

Franklin, Mitchell. 2000 *Dialectics Of The US Constitution: Selected Writings Of Mitchell Franklin*. Edited by James M. Lawler. Minneapolis, Minnesota. MEP Press.

Free Sami Al-Arian. "Political Prisoner since Feb. 20, 2003." freesamialarian.com.

Fuentes, Annette. October 5, 1998. "Trustees of the Right's Agenda." *The Nation*.

Galbraith, James K.. July 21, 2011. "Obama and the Gang of Six." *The Real News.com*.

Glick, Brian. 1989. *War at Home*. Boston: South End Press.

Goldman, Julianna. September 14 2011. "Obama Approval Plummets among Americans Skeptical of Jobs Plan." *Bloomberg*.

Gossweiler, Kurt. 1989. "Economy and Politics in the Destruction of the Weimar Republic." In *Radical Perspectives on the Rise of Fascism in Germany, 1919–1945*, Michael N. Dobkowski and Isidor Wallimann, eds. New York: Monthly Review Press, pp.150–171.

Graham, Adams Jr. 1966. *The Age of Industrial Violence: 1910–1915*. New York: Columbia University Press.

Graham, Bob and Jeff Nussbaum. 2004. *Intelligence Matters: The CIA, the FBI, Saudi Arabia, and the failure of America's War on Terror*. New York: Random House.

Greenhouse, Steven. Dec 14, 2004. "How do you Drive Out a Union? South Caroline Factory Provides a Textbook Case." *American Rights at Work.org*.

Greenwald, Glenn. June 6, 2009. "Defeat of the Graham-Lieberman and the Ongoing War on Transparency." *Salon.com*.

Greg Palast. 2002. *The Best Democracy Money Can Buy: An Investigative Reporter Exposes the Truth About Globalization, Corporate Cons and High Finance Fraudsters*. Pluto Press: London.

Gross, Bertram. 1980. *Friendly Fascism: The New Face of Power in America*. New York: Boston.

Gumbel, E. J. 1958. "Disarmament and Clandestine Rearmament under the Weimar Republic." In *Inspection for Disarmament*, Seymour Melman, ed. New York: Columbia University Press.

Hamilton, Richard F. 1982. *New Light on Hitler Voters: Who Voted for Hitler?* Princeton: Princeton University Press.

Havemann, Joel. March 19, 2007. "Scientist Accuses White of 'Nazi' Tactics." *Los Angeles Times*.

Heberle, Rudolf. 1944. "The Ecology of Political Parties: A Study of Elections in Rural Communities in Schleswig-Holstein, 1918–1932." *American Sociological Review*, Aug. 401–414.

Hedges, Chris. 2006. *American Fascists: The Christian Right and the War on America.* New York: Free Press.

Hentoff, Nat. 2007. "The Gestapo Inheritance: 'We do not Torture': Groans from the CIA's Black Sites Beg to Differ." *Village Voice.* October 23.

Hentoff, Nat. January 28th 2005. "Condi Rice: Misrule of Law: The New Secretary of State, the President's Confidante, Plays by His Code of Justice." *Village Voice.*

Higham, Charles. 1983.*Trading with the Enemy.* New York: Barnes & Noble.

Hitchens, Christopher. 2002. "The Latest Kissinger Outrage: Why is a Proven Liar and Wanted Man in Charge of the 9/11 Investigation?" *Slate.* (http://www.slate.com/?id=2074678)

Hitler, Adolph. 1939. *Mein Kampf.* New York: Hurst and Blackett Ltd.

Horowitz, David. 2006. *The Professors: The 101 Most Dangerous Academics in America,* Washington DC: Regnery Publishing, Inc.

Ivins, Molly and Lou Dubose. 2007. *Bill of Wrongs: The Executive Branch's Assault on America's Fundamental Rights.* New York: Random House.

Ivins, Molly. May 20, 2004. "How Fascism Starts." (Creators Syndicate) Information Clearing House: News You Won't Find on CNN.

Jacoby, Mary. September 12, 2003. "Homeland Security Sputters into Reality." *St. Petersburg Times.*

Jaschik, Scott. 2006. "Frays on Academic Freedom."
Inside Higher Education, Sept 11. (See file, "Academic
Freedom Cases" Mon 11 Sep 2006).

Jaschik, Scott. Aug 15. 2007. "Pessimistic Views on
Academic Freedom." *Inside Higher Ed.*

Jerome, Fred. 2002. *The Einstein File: J. Edgar Hoover's
Secret War against the World's Most Famous
Scientist.* New York: St. Martin's Press.

John Hopkins University Bloomberg School of Public
Health. 2004. "Mortality Before and After the 2003
Invasion of Iraq: Cluster Sample Survey." *The Lancet*,
Volume 364, Number 9445, October 30.

Jones, Alan. June 16, 2006. "Connecting the Dots."
Inside Higher Education.

Jones, Nigel. 2004. *A History of the Birth of the Nazis:
How the Freikorps Blazed a Trail for Hitler.* Revised
Paperback Edition. New York: Carol and Graf
Publishers.

Kennedy, Robert Jr. 2004. *Crimes against Nature: How
George W. Bush and his Corporate Pals are
Plundering the Country and Hijacking Our
Democracy.* New York: HarperCollins.

Kerans, Pat. May 13, 2004. "Don't be Surprised by US
Torture." CBC Radio Commentary.

Klare, Michael T. October 1 2002. "Oiling the Wheels of
War." AlterNet.org.

Klein, Naomi. 2007. *The Shock Doctrine: The Rise of
Disaster Capitalism.* New York: Henry Holt & Co.

Klemperer, Victor. 1999. *I Will Bear Witness 1933–1941.*
New York: Random House.

Kohn, Stephen M. 2011. *The Whistleblower's Handbook:
A Step-by-Step Guide to Doing What's Right and*

Protecting Yourself. Guilford, CT: Lyons Press.

Kohn, Stephen M. June12, 2011. "The Whistle-Blowers of 1777." *New York Times*.

Kornbluh, Joyce. 1988. "Bread and Roses: The 1912 Lawrence textile Strike." In *Rebel Voices: An IWW Anthology*, Joyce Kornbluh, ed. Chicago: Charles H. Kerr Publishing.

Korten, Tristam. December 4, 2003. "Pick Your Reality: Either FTAA Protesters Viciously Assaulted Police, or Police Viciously Assaulted Protesters." *Miami New Times*.

Kristof, Nicholas 2003 July 19. "Going Home, to Red Ink and Blues." *New York Times*.

Kroeber, Theodora. 1969. *Ishi in Two Worlds: A Biography of the Last Wild Indian in North America*. Berkeley: University of California Press.

Krugman, Paul. October 28, 2010. "Divided We Fail." *New York Times*

Krugman, Paul. October 29, 2007, "Fearing Fear Itself." *New York Times*.

Lane, Diane. 2002. "Repression Goes Local: Joint Terrorism Task Forces Could Easily Become the New 'Red Squads.'" *Toward Freedom Online Magazine*.

Langguth, A. J. 1978. *Hidden Terrors*. New York: Pantheon

Larkin, Graham. April 25, 2005. "David Horowitz's War on Rational Discourse." *Inside Higher Ed*.

Lembcke, Jerry.1998. *Spitting Image: Myth, Memory, and the Legacy of Vietnam*. New York: New York University Press.

Leonard Levitt. 2002, September 30. "No Connection to

Intelligence." *Newsday.*

Lichtblau, Eric. January 14, 2009. "Criticism of Ex-Official in Hiring at Justice Dept." *New York Times.*

Lindorff, Dave and Barbara Olshansky. 2007. *The Case for Impeachment: The Legal Argument for Removing President George W. Bush from Office.* New York: Thomas Dunne Books, St. Martin's Press.

Lopez, Linette. Oct 25, 2011. "The Congressional Budget Office Just Jumped Into The Debate About Inequality, And It Definitely Picks A Side." *Business Insider.* (businessinsider.com/the-congressional-budget-releases-a-report-on-inequality).

Ludendorff, Eric. 1919. *My War Memories, 1914–1918.* London: Hutchinson.

Mamdani, Mahmood. 2004. *Good Muslim, Bad Muslim: America, the Cold War, and the Roots of Terror.* New York: Pantheon Books.

Manchester, William. 1968. *The Arms of Krupp: 1587–1968.* New York: Little Brown and Co.

Marin, Andre. December, Dec. 2010. *Ombudsman Report, Caught in the Act.* [G20 Summit]. *YouTube.com*

Markovits, Andrei S.. 1984. "Review of *Who Voted for Hitler?* by Richard Hamilton." *Contemporary Sociology*, January: 19–21.

Mathiesen, Thomas. 2002. "Expanding the Concept of Terrorism." In *Beyond September 11: An Anthology of Dissent*, Phil Scraton, ed. London: Pluto Press.

McKibben, Bill. November 10, 2011. "Big News: We Won. You Won." Tar Sands Action (tarsandsaction.org).

McGowan, David. 2001. *Understanding the F-Word: American Fascism and the Politics of Illusion.*

Lincoln, NE: Writers Club Press.

McSherry, J. Patrice. *2005. Predatory States: Operation Condor and Covert War in Latin America.* Boulder: Rowman & Littlefield Publishers.

McSherry, J. Patrice. 2005. "The Undead Ghost of Operation Condor." *Logos* (http://www.logosjournal.com/issue_4.2/mcsherry.htm)

Meeropol, Mike. July-August, 2006. "Dangerous Academics." *Dollars and Sense.*

Melzer, Eartha Jane. Oct. 26, 2011. "Jesse Jackson Calls for an Uprising in Benton Harbor." *The Michigan Messenger.*

Milbank, Dana and Claudia Deane, Saturday, September 6, 2003; "Hussein Link to 9/11 Lingers in Many Minds," *Washington Post*, A1.

Mishel Lawrence, Jared Bernstein, and Sylvia Allegretto. 2007. *The State of Working America 2006/2007.* Ithaca, N.Y.: ILR Press

Moore, Michael. 2001. *Stupid White Men...And Other Sorry Excuses for the State of the Nation!* New York: Regan Books.

Morales, Frank. 2002. "U.S. Military Civil Disturbance Planning: The War at Home." In *Police State America*, Tom Burghardt ed. San Francisco: Arm the Spirit/Solidarity Publishing.

Nader, Ralph and Cornel West. September 19, 2011. "Ralph Nader, Cornel West Unveil Proposal to Challenge Obama in Primaries." *Single Payer Action.org.*

Nason, David. October 9, 2007. "Secret Trial for Terrorists, Says US Judge." *The Australian.*

Nearly, Dylan M. 2002. "Police Aggression is Costing You Money." *Earth Times News Service*. (Posted on *justdissent.org*, Feb. 5, 2002.).

Nichols, John. 2007. *The Genius of Impeachment: The Founders' Cure for Royalism and Why It Should be Applied to George W. Bush*. New York: The New Press.

Nichols, John. March 2, 2003. "Donahue's Demise." The Nation.com.

Nuremberg Trial Proceedings. 1945. Volume 4. "Twenty-third Day—Morning Session Wednesday, 19 December 1945." *The Avalon Project* at Yale Law School.

O'balance, Edgar. 1989. *Terrorism in the 1980s*. London: Arms and Armour.

Olbermann, Keith. Oct 27 2010. "If the Tea Party Wins, America Loses." msnbc.com (updated 9:33:43 PM ET).

Orwell, George. 1960. *1984*. With an "Afterword" by Erich Fromm. New York: Harcourt Brace & Co.

Pagosa, Dorothy. 2002 July 13. "School of the Americas Protesters Lock Gate to Fort Benning After 37 Activists Sentenced." *School of the Americas Watch*. commondreams.org

Paine, Thomas. 1773. "The Crisis, No. 1." In *The Writings of Thomas Paine*, Moncure D. Conway, ed. New York: G.P. Putnam's Sons.

Palmer, A. Mitchell. 1920. "The Case against the 'Reds.'" *Forum*. 63: 173–185.

Pape, Robert 2005. *Dying to Win: The Strategic Logic of Suicide Terrorism*. New York: Random House.

Partridge, Ernest. April 20, 2011. "Shameless GOP Lies: Is There Any Limit to What Republicans Will Say—And What People Will Believe?" Alternet.org.

Patzold, Kurt. 1989. "Terror and Demagoguery in the Consolidation of the Fascist Dictatorship in Germany, 1933–34." In *Radical Perspectives on the Rise of Fascism in Germany, 1919–1945*, Michael N. Dobkowski and Isidor Wallimann, eds. New York: Monthly Review Press.

Paxton, Robert O. 2004. *The Anatomy of Fascism*. New York: Alfred A. Knopf

Perkins, John. 2007. *The Secret History of the American Empire: Economic Hit Men, Jackals, and the Truth about Global Corruption*. New York: Dutton

Pincus, Walter and Dan Eggen, Wednesday, February 15, 2006. "325,000 Names on Terrorism List: Rights Groups Say Database May Include Innocent People." *Washington Post*.

Pitt, William Rivers with Scott Ritter. 2002. *War on Iraq: What Team Bush Doesn't Want You to Know*. New York: Context Books.

Pitt, William Rivers. Tuesday 26, April 2011. "Free Bradley Manning." *Truthout*.

Pizzigati, Sam. 2004. *Greed and Good: Understanding and Overcoming the Inequality that Limits Our Lives*. New York: The Apex Press.

Potok, Mark. March 3, 2010. *Right-Wing Rage: Hate Groups, Vigilantes and Conspiracists on the Verge of Violence*. Southern Poverty Law Center.

Powers, Ryan, 2009. "UN Rapporteur on Torture: Obama's Pledge Not to Pursue Torture Prosecutions of CIA Agents is Not Legal." *Think Progress*.org.

Purdy, Jedediah S. January–February 1998. "The Chicago Acid Bath: The Impoverished Logic of Law and Economics." *TAP*.

Quigley, Bill. Thursday June 29, 2006. "Ten Months after Katrina: Gutting New Orleans." CommonDreams.org.

Rampton, Sheldon and John Stauber. 2004. *Banana Republicans: How the Right Wing is Turning America into a One-Party State*. New York: Jeremy P. Starcher/Penguin.

Rangwala, Dr. Glen. February 2003. "Claims and Evaluations of Iraq's Proscribed Weapons." Posted on Traprock Peace Center (http://traprockpeace.org/weapons).

Redondi, Pietro. 1987. *Galileo Heretic*. (trans. Raymond Rosenthal) New Jersey: Princeton University Press.

Reich, Robert. Sept 9, 2011. "Two Cheers and One Jeer for the American Jobs Act." *Huffington Post.com*.

Report No. 06-22. March 2006. "The Office of Program Policy Analysis and Government Accountability."

Rich, Frank. August 14, 2005. "Someone Tell the President the War Is Over." *New York Times*.

Riley, Kevin Jack and Bruce Hoffman. 1995. *Domestic Terrorism: A National Assessment of State and Local Preparedness*. Rand (USA).

Roberts, Michael. 2004. "I Fathered a Terror Suspect: Losing the Name Game at our Country's Airports." *New Times, Inc.*

Robinson, Randall. 2007. *An Unbroken Agony: Haiti, From Revolution to the Kidnapping of a President*. New York: Basic Civitas Books.

Romero, Anthony D. February 4, 2009. "Obama Endorses Bush Secrecy on Torture and Rendition." ACLU Press Release.

Rothschild, Matthew. 2002. March 14. "Red Squad Hits Denver." *The Progressive*.

Sanders, Richard. 2004. "John Spivak." March (#53). *Press for Conversion!*

Scahill, Jeremy. 2007. *Blackwater: The Rise of the World's Most Powerful Mercenary Army*. New York: Nation Books.

Scahill, Jeremy. Nov 4, 2003. "The Miami Model: Paramilitaries Embedded Journalists and Illegal Protests. Think. This is Iraq? It's Your Country." *CounterPunch.*

Scheer, Robert. 2010. *The Great American Stickup: How Reagan Republicans and Clinton*

Democrats Enriched Wall Street While Mugging Main Street. New York: Nation Books.

Schneider, Nathan. Oct. 31, 2012. "From Occupy Wall Street to Occupy Everywhere." *The Nation.*

Schwartz, John. February 9, 2009. "Obama Backs Off a Reversal on Secrets." *New York Times.*

Schwendinger, Herman and Julia Schwendinger. 1974. *Sociologists of the Chair, A Radical Analysis of the Formative Years of American Sociology, 1883–1922*. New York: Basic Books.

Schwenninger, Sherle R. July 18, 2005. "Reconnecting to the World." *The Nation.*

Scott, Peter Dale. 2010. *American War Machine: Deep Politics, the CIA Global Drug Connection, and the Road to Afghanistan*. New York: Rowman & Littlefield.

Segura, Liliana. April 24, 2009. "Thousands of Pages of Evidence and a Quarter Million Signatures: What Will It Take For Attorney General to Prosecute Torture Crimes?" *Alternet.org* (http://alternet.org/story/138188/).

Seldes, George. 1947. *1000 Americans*. New York: Boni & Gaer.

Sharrock, Justine. March/April 2010. "Age of Treason." *Mother Jones*.

Solomon, Norman. 2006. *War Made Easy: How Presidents and Pundits Keep Spinning Us to Death*. Hoboken, New Jersey: John Wiley & Sons.

Spivak, John. Feb 5 1935. "Wall Street's Fascist Conspiracy: Morgan Pulls the Strings." *New Masses*.

Spivak, John. Jan 29 1935. "Wall Street's Fascist Conspiracy: Testimony that the Dickstein McCormick Committee Suppressed." *New Masses*. (Reproduced in http://coat.ncf.ca/our_magazine/links/53/spivak-NewMasses.pdf)

Stolberg, Sheryl Gay. April 22, 2009. "Obama Won't Bar Inquiry, or Penalty, On Interrogations." *New York Times*.

Strachey, John. 1933. *The Menace of Fascism*. New York: Covici Friede.

Stuber, Doug. 2002. October 1–15. "Green and Grounded." *CounterPunch*.

Swanson, David. Sept. 1, 2009. "The More Things Change." *Tomgram*. (Tomdispatch.com.)

Swanson, David. February 19, 2007. "Impeachment Politically Smart or Dangerous?" *AfterDowningStreet.org*.

Taylor, General Telford. 1970. *Nuremberg and Vietnam: An American Tragedy*. New York: Times Books.

Thyssen, Fritz. 1941. *I Paid Hitler*. New York: Farrar & Reinhardt.

Tigar, Michael E. and John Mage. 2009. "The Reichstag

Fire Trial 1933–2008." *Monthly Review*. Vol. 60. No. 10, March.

Tucker, Cynthia. Monday, February 7, 2005. "The Administration that Cried Wolf: Campaign against Social Security is Full of Falsehoods." *Universal Press Syndicate*.

Turse, Nick. 2008. *The Complex: How the Military Invades Our Everyday Lives*. New York: Henry Holt & Co.

Veblen, Thorstein. 1973. *The Theory of the Leisure Class*. "Introduction" by John Kenneth Galbraith. Boston: Houghton Mifflin.

Vidal, Gore. 2002 July 18. "The New War on Freedom." Reproduced online at AlterNet.org.

Vietnam Veterans against The War. 1972. *The Winter Soldier Investigation: An Inquiry into American War Crimes*. Boston: Beacon Press.

Vlasic, Bill. September 13, 2011. "Detroit Sets Its Future on a Foundation of Two-Tier Wages." *New York Times*.

Wagenen, William Van. July 6, 2005. "Shock and Awe: Aerial Bombardment, American Style." *Electronic Iraq* (electroniciraq.net).

Waltz, Mitzi. 1997. Summer. "Policing Activists: Think Global Spy Local," *Covert Quarterly Times*.

Warren, Patricia Nell. 2001. June. 14. "Dollars." *A&U Magazine*.

Weil, Frederick D. 1989. "The Sources and Structure of Legitimation in Western Democracies: A Consolidated Model Tested with Time-Series Data in Six Countries Since World War II." *American Sociological Review*, Vol. 54, No. 5 (October): 682–706.

About the Authors

Julia and Herman Schwendinger were among the main participants in the Berkeley School of Criminology. Their innovative works have made crucial contributions to the development of radical criminology, particularly in areas of the exploitation of women and women's resistance, adolescent subcultures, surveillance, class analysis, and sociological theory. Among their books are *The Sociologists of the Chair, Adolescent Subcultures and Democracy*, and *Rape and Inequality*. Their significant innovations in criminology are recognized with their inclusion in the text Fifty Key Thinkers in Criminology (Routledge, 2013). Activists as well as academics, Julia helped found the first rape resistance crisis center in the US. Both were actively involved in anti-racist, anti-war, feminist, labor, and community struggles over the course of decades (some of which are described in *Who Killed the Berkeley School* ◄). Both taught for years at SUNY New Paltz, as well as numerous visiting professorships. Julia and Herman were married for almost 68 years, true life partners and intellectual collaborators. Julia passed away in 2013 but her profound legacy continues. Their book *Who Killed the Berkeley School?: Struggles over Radical Criminology* was published as the first Thought | Crimes title. ◄

Thought | Crimes

The twenty-first century is an age of crime—state crime, corporate crime, crimes against humanity, crimes against nature. Elite crime. It is becoming increasingly clear that capitalism itself is a criminal system and the liberal democratic state a racket. In the current period of political repression, economic austerity, ecological destruction, criminalization of dissent, and mass resistance to these, the need for radical criminology is pressing. Radical criminology offers important insights into the composition of contemporary social struggles—and state maneuvers within those struggles. Radical criminology challenges openly practices of surveillance, detention, punishment and situates these within relations of exploitation and oppression that are foundational to capitalist society.

Notably, radical ("to the roots") criminological analysis is emerging from the movements as much as, even more than, from the academy. Indeed much of the most incisive thinking and writing in criminology is coming from movement organizers rather than academics.

Fully open access, and an imprint of **punctum books**, the press is a project of the **Critical Criminology Working Group** at Kwantlen Polytechnic University. **Thought | Crimes** aims to bring together the most exciting and insightful new radical writings in criminology.

* submissions * catalog *
free downloads / print orders:
www.thoughtcrimespress.org

Who Killed the Berkeley School? Struggles Over Radical Criminology

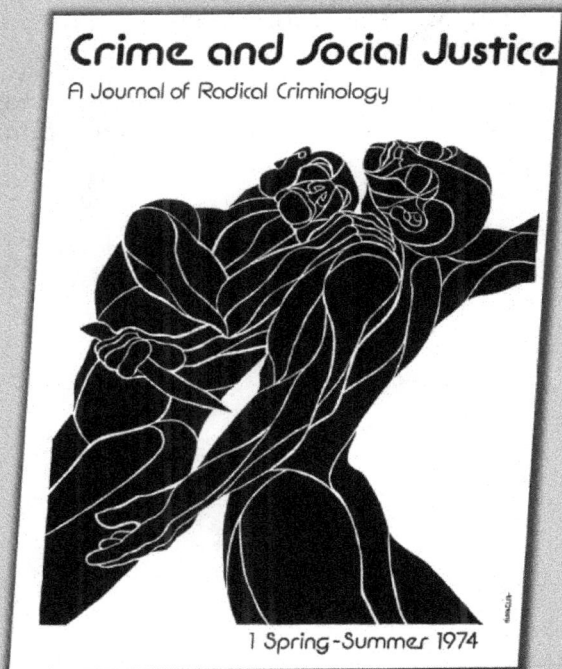

Crime and Social Justice

A Journal of Radical Criminology

1 Spring-Summer 1974

by Herman & Julia Schwendinger

with a foreword from Jeff Shantz

Weiner, Bernard. June 9, 2003. "Germany In 1933: The Easy Slide Into Fascism." *The Crisis Papers.* (http://www.crisispapers.org/Editorials/germany-1933.htm).

Whitney, Mike. July 16, 2005. "Genesis of an American Gestapo." *dissidentvoice.org.*

Willan, Philip. 2005. April 7. "G8 Summit Officers on Trial." *Guardian*/UK.

Wilson, Scott. May 14, 2009. "Obama Shifts on Abuse Photos." *The Washington Post.*

Zinn, Howard. March 23, 2007. "Howard Zinn Replies to MoveOn's support for the Supplemental." *Information Clearing House.*